Local Glories

Local Glories

OPERA HOUSES ON
MAIN STREET
WHERE ART
AND COMMUNITY MEET

Ann Satterthwaite

OXFORD
UNIVERSITY PRESS

OXFORD
UNIVERSITY PRESS

Oxford University Press is a department of the University of Oxford. It furthers
the University's objective of excellence in research, scholarship, and education
by publishing worldwide. Oxford is a registered trademark of Oxford University
Press in the UK and certain other countries.

Published in the United States of America by Oxford University Press
198 Madison Avenue, New York, NY 10016, United States of America.

Library of Congress Cataloging-in-Publication Data
Satterthwaite, Ann
Local glories : opera houses on main street, where art
and community meet / Ann Satterthwaite.
pages cm
Summary: "This book explores the creative, social, and communal roles of thousands of
'opera houses' that appeared in towns in the late 1800s and flourished with an astounding
array of cultural performances and public activities until the advent of movies. Now, these
entertainment halls are coming back to life as theaters and art centers, as people
become increasingly aware of their potential for 'historic preservation,' 'cultural
activities,' and 'community vitality.' "— Provided by publisher.
Includes bibliographical references.
ISBN 978–0–19–939254–4 (hardback)
1. Theater—United States—History.   2. Centers for the performing arts—
United States—History.   3. Theater and society—United States.
I. Title.
PN2226.S28 2016
792.0973—dc23

1 3 5 7 9 8 6 4 2
Printed by Edwards Brothers, USA

*To all those who made opera houses happen then
and now—and to Sheafe.*

Contents

Introduction

Dowagers in mink coats and men in tuxedos gracing New York's opulent Metropolitan Opera House spring to mind at the mention of "opera house." So it is not surprising that I was curious about the opera houses I kept finding in small American towns such as Stonington, Maine, and Minden, Nebraska, and even in off-the-beaten-path Death Valley, California.

A fascinating tale unfolded. In the fifty years after the Civil War thousands of opera houses stood proudly in small towns, with innumerable traveling performers appearing on their stages. They brought live entertainment to more towns than at any other time in US history, making this a golden age of live entertainment and also the heyday of the small-town opera house.

By 1900, opera houses were everywhere: on second floors over hardware stores, in grand independent buildings, in the back rooms of New England town halls, and even inside a Mississippi department store. Midwestern states were dotted with them. Almost every town in newly settled states like Nebraska and Iowa had an opera house, in places as small as David City, Nebraska (population 1,845) and Pella, Iowa (population 2,623).[1] By the late nineteenth century opera houses were being incorporated in public town halls—even in New England, despite its puritanical antipathy toward theater. Tough mining towns in the Colorado Rockies displayed a newfound urbanity with their handsome opera houses, and Appalachian coal-mining companies followed suit. Even public assembly buildings and music halls joined the bandwagon and were renamed "opera houses."

Thousands of actors, hundreds of theater troupes, dozens of opera companies, and 500 troupes solely performing *Uncle Tom's Cabin,* played in these houses. Circuses, magicians, lecturers, minstrel shows, hypnotists, pugilists, medicine shows, and other varied performers also rode the newly extended rail lines to appear in opera houses across the country. While Edwin Booth, Sarah Bernhardt, Mark Twain, and John Philip Sousa were among the popular stars in these halls, most performers were not so well known. "Half a dozen times during each winter . . . a traveling stock company . . . thrilled and entertained us for a week," reminisced Willa Cather about her hometown opera house in Red Cloud, Nebraska, which ignited her lifelong interest in theater.[2] For eager youngsters like Cather, as well as for isolated farm families, homesick immigrants, lonely workers, and culture-seeking townspeople, the opera house offered entertainment, community sociability, and a lifeline to civilization beyond their hometowns.

Without school gyms or auditoriums, flat-floored opera houses became the stage for student plays, recitations, graduations, and sports like basketball along with bicycle racing, boxing, and roller-skating. Usually the largest hall in town, as well as neutral turf, the opera house was also where political events and town meetings took place. Before radio, movies, and cars, townspeople socialized at the many opera-house programs that punctuated the long winters. In fact, one of the most enduring features of these halls is their role in community life. The bank, stores, and courthouse were the economic and civic underpinnings of a town, but it was the opera house that often pulled the town as a community.

The opera house also signaled to the world that a town was civilized, even au courant, a place with a sense of permanence and respectability. Not surprisingly, these halls became a source of enormous pride and delight. "It seems almost incredible that so fine a building with such a splendid Hall can stand today on ground so lately part of [Jesse C.] Bickle's cornfield," the *Saline County Union* commented in 1877 on the recently built Band's Opera House in newly settled Crete, Nebraska.[3] On main streets, the opera house stood out as an important building due to its prominent location, its distinctive architecture, or just being a bit taller than its neighbors. Although these symbols of prevailing optimism were often propelled by local businessmen's pride in their towns, many opera houses were built as a result of pressure from women, who nudged husbands and fathers to provide a local venue for culture.

After the Civil War, ubiquitous rail lines, increasing populations, burgeoning cities and towns, and new inventions and industries transformed how people lived and worked. Old ways and values were being challenged in this fast-paced world by powerful monopolies, robber barons, a widening gulf between rich and poor, and urban and rural populations. Rural places felt the might of the remote monopolies, whose freight rates and crop prices determined their economic welfare. Yet, ironically, small-town opera house patrons wanted entertainment from the very world of power and monopolies they had fled for a fresh start in a new place. Eastern culture remained their standard of civilization.

This quest for entertainment and culture flourished as lingering puritanical fears of theater were fading and new immigrants, including many Germans and Czechs with a love of music and opera, were introducing their own cultures in places where they settled. Serious theater professionals looked with some disdain on opera house fare, which they viewed as entertainment rather than legitimate theater. However, the vernacular and distinctly American nature of minstrel shows, melodramas, band concerts, and family troupes provided a rich medley of entertainment. For an isolated, hardworking farm family buffeted by big-city decision makers, a thrilling melodrama provided both diversion and a validation of their moral values threatened by changing times. For the urbane theater critic, Emma Abbott's operas, in which she inserted hymns like "Nearer, My God, to Thee," might seem simplistic, but for those living in a rural town, they were like grand Metropolitan Opera performances.

Now these entertainment halls are coming back to life, after being dormant for many decades when alternative entertainment like movies and television made them obsolete. Many were demolished, while surviving structures were used as warehouses or abandoned to bats and pigeons. Today as these derelict buildings are being resuscitated, there are fewer road shows, so opera house managers now rely more on homegrown talent in plays, musicals, children's theatre, dance recitals, and concerts—even grand opera.

In little more than an hour's drive from Rutland, Vermont in summer 2013, for example, one could attend performances of operas by resident companies in four opera houses: Donizetti's *Lucia di Lammermoor* by Opera North at the Lebanon Opera House in Lebanon, New Hampshire; Tchaikovsky's *Eugene Onegin* by the Opera Company of Middlebury in the Town Hall Theater in Middlebury, Vermont; Rossini's *Barber of Seville* by the Hubbard Hall Opera Theater at Hubbard Hall in Cambridge,

New York; and Donizetti's *Lucia di Lammermoor* by the Green Mountain Opera Festival at the Barre Opera House in Barre, Vermont. Who would have thought that these small places, ranging in size from fewer than 2,000 to about 13,000 inhabitants, would have established local companies performing grand opera? Discovering these revived opera houses has provided an unexpectedly happy ending for my research.

The ingredients that can help make places lively and satisfying for living and working have long interested me as a city planner and historian. Planning demonstrates how the layout of neighborhoods, public facilities such as schools and parks, transportation networks, as well as the provision of public services can make communities function. However, these physical elements do not necessarily infuse the dynamics that provide vitality or a sense of community. This is where culture can play a role.

Today's plethora of electronic entertainment and communication devices, creating a global village with endless opportunities for instant connections, might seem to lessen the importance of live performances and local participation for both individuals and communities. Yet, ironically, these new devices have also isolated us from one another as we lose live, face-to-face encounters. Kansas newspaper editor William Allen White once observed that electricity made the country a neighborhood. Now our sophisticated electronic gadgetry is making our communities a figment of electronic circuitry. Our public places and the real communities where we live and work have been diminished as we rely on machines to connect with one another. That remoteness, combined with a sense of powerlessness in today's increasingly anonymous global village, concerns me.

Earlier I studied shopping and how its traditional social and public role has shrunk as we hunt for branded products online or at vast discount warehouses on outlying highways. When everyday connections with friends and neighbors at familiar stores in civic cores dwindle, so does the sense of community, as I wrote in *Going Shopping: Consumer Choices and Community Consequences* in 2001.

Perhaps more important is the role of cultural activities for community vitality and individual uplift. The satisfactions of participating with others in live plays, dances, orchestras, and choral groups—whether on stage, behind the scenes, or in the audience—nourish the soul and help bind people into a community. And people of all ages, backgrounds, and incomes can participate, providing a healthy antidote to the jolting gap between rich and poor and old and young today. These personal and community benefits help explain the renaissance of opera houses today; in fact, with their often locally generated programs, they may produce more communal creative energy than the earlier halls with their many traveling entertainers.

This new life for opera houses emerged in the 1970s, 1980s, and 1990s when people became increasingly aware of the potential of historic preservation and cultural activities in revitalizing towns and cities. Reviving these halls has sparked a new pride in towns as people see how they can make a difference. "Incite art, create community," the motto of Stonington, Maine's Opera House Arts, aptly expresses the goal of most revived opera houses.

The history of small-town opera houses is an American story. The surge of interest in them today, as well as in their earlier heyday, has drawn on some basic elements in the American character: an energetic "can do" attitude, buoyed by a confidence in the future and the belief that individuals or groups of individuals can create or change institutions and places for the better. Thus, most of these halls have relied not on governments but on local civic and cultural entrepreneurs. And unlike single-purpose opera houses in most countries and music halls in England, American small-town opera houses have been multipurpose community halls for culture, entertainment, and civic activities.

As the Union healed after the Civil War, massive changes were transforming the nation into an urbanized country with powerful industries and monopolies, new and swifter communications, and ever-expanding rail lines connecting cities and towns from coast to coast. These forces also changed attitudes toward culture as cities were beautified, museums and universities were founded, women gained a voice, and philanthropists eagerly improved their images. These same forces were felt even in rural towns where local entrepreneurs and sometimes the towns themselves joined this civilizing bandwagon and built opera houses.

In these new times, centuries-old opposition to theater and entertainment faded, resulting in a burst of pent-up demand for cultural diversions. This welcoming of theater and entertainment, together with the emergence of thousands of eager performers and newly minted opera houses, produced one of the most exuberant periods of American theater. The stars, troupes, and various entertainers who trod the boards of these halls also helped introduce the country to mass entertainment.

These opera houses played a unique public role in communities. In these venues, civic and public events in a town's community life took place. Their distinctive architecture has made them stand out on main streets as important local landmarks. They have functioned through cooperative local public and private efforts, sometimes even operated by local governments in town halls.

The surprising comeback of so many of these neglected opera houses since the 1970s provides a happy ending. Like the phoenix, these revived halls are providing new cultural and economic stimuli to their towns and creative and social benefits to individuals. These revivals result from the struggles and commitment of stalwart resuscitators, supporters, and, most important, of managers or directors.

Since there are so many earlier opera houses, along with ongoing renovations taking place, I decided to focus my research initially on four states with distinctly different histories, thus offering a picture of the diversity of opera houses, programs, audiences, buildings, promoters, and supporters, along with their hopes, dreams, and ambitions. These four states are Nebraska, a Plains state with excellent National Register of Historic Places data, also home to theater enthusiast and critic Willa Cather; Kentucky, a southern state with an early, strong, and persistent interest in theater and entertainment; Vermont, a rural New England state with many opera houses in town halls where theater has been treated almost like a public service; and Colorado, featuring early mining-town opera houses, which provided entertainment to remote gulches in the nineteenth century and now play to local residents and many tourists. As my research progressed, I discovered considerable material from many other places, including Oregon, Oklahoma, Maine, New York, and Texas, some of which I have included in this book; but there is a rich lode of opera house data awaiting further study.[4]

Today, with times so changed from the early opera house days, many of those given-up-for-dead structures are once again connecting people within towns, sparking communal creative energy, and enriching towns all over the country. These "local glories" are where art and community meet.[5] They are indeed stirring souls, forging connections, and making communities, as they did in the nineteenth century.

PART ONE

A Heady Time

Thousands of Opera Houses

CHAPTER 1

Signs of Civilization

It was front-page news when the public poured into the prestigious and usually staid Metropolitan Opera House on September 22, 2006, to enjoy an open house organized by its new manager, Peter Gelb. The curious could wander all over this famous New York City building, backstage and on stage. They could even eat a brown-bag lunch and sit in any seat in the house while enjoying a free rehearsal of *Madama Butterfly*. Certainly the Metropolitan Opera (the "Met"), like many other cities' preeminent opera companies, appealed to the elite, so Gelb launched programs to widen interest in the Met and in opera. The Met's initiatives of open houses, innovative staging, $25 tickets, and live telecasts of performances reaching millions of people in movie theaters here and around the world were probably overdue. However, there was a time when going to the opera house was not just for a community's upper crust.

More than a century earlier, in December 1888, twelve-year-old Willa Cather watched the Andrews Family Opera Company's production of *The Chimes of Normandy* at the Red Cloud Opera House in her 796-person hometown of Red Cloud, Nebraska. Tens of thousands of Americans in towns of all sizes across the country then enjoyed similar performances at their local opera houses. By 1900, there were thousands of these small opera houses; Iowa alone had more than 1,200 opera houses. Some towns had several operating simultaneously, while others had a succession of opera houses when fire or other catastrophes destroyed them. Many places morphed their town halls, Odd Fellows Halls, and even churches into opera houses to keep pace with the growing popularity of theater, music, and entertainment after the Civil War. Here townspeople—men and women, young and old, rich and poor, newcomers and old-timers—would gather to meet with friends and strangers to enjoy Joseph Jefferson as Rip Van Winkle, the Christy's Minstrels' shows, Houdini's magic, Mark Twain's lectures, John Philip Sousa's band music, lyceum lectures, and lesser-known regional troupes and performers.

Not all the activities at these opera houses were offered by out-of-towners. Often the only large assembly hall in a town, the local opera house was host to a myriad of local events. Here townspeople attended everything from homegrown plays, basketball games, and band concerts to public occasions such as high school graduations and political rallies, including those headlined by the ubiquitous spellbinder, William Jennings Bryan. Even church services were held in some of them, as at Leadville, Colorado's Tabor Opera House and Brattleboro, Vermont's Town Hall Opera House. With all these local and out-of-town entertainments and activities, the opera house became a significant institution in towns throughout the country in the latter half of the nineteenth century—before being eclipsed by radio, movies, cars, and later new school auditoriums. Most towns had halls in a variety of churches and fraternal organizations (Red Cloud, Nebraska, had eight fraternal organizations in 1886), but they were exclusive or seemed exclusive. In contrast, the opera house provided neutral turf devoid of social, economic, or religious associations. That neutral turf and its equality of opportunity enhanced the public nature of these halls making them places where all townspeople could connect with each other, their community, and, most important, worlds far beyond their daily lives.

"A building devoted solely to stage entertainments," according to early-nineteenth-century actor Noah Ludlow, indicated "that a town had achieved some tone and social capacities."[1] That is what newly settled towns were seeking when, after establishing a bank, hotel, and stores, they built their first opera houses. In both newly settled places and older towns, these opera houses were seen as symbols of advancement and civilization. Naming these buildings "opera houses" provided an élan to both humble and haughty towns and cities. It evoked images of fancy Venetian and Viennese opera houses and helped erase long-held negative impressions of theater. In fact, an opera house became a barometer of the economic and social life of a town; it meant the town had advanced beyond the survival stage of development.

The sense of civilization that these new opera houses brought was made possible by the ambitions of local town leaders and entrepreneurs and the expanding rail lines in the second half of the nineteenth century. As Willa Cather noted, "the railroad is the one real fact in this country."[2] By 1869 East and West were connected with transcontinental rail service, and by the early 1880s major rail lines such as the Union Pacific, Northern Pacific, Southern Pacific, and Santa Fe were steaming through the new territories. They not only raced across the country but also laced the entire United States with a network of rail lines, making it possible for people, goods, and resources, as well as entertainers and theater companies, to move around as never before. Important as these long-distance rail routes were, it was the branch lines to remote towns that made it possible for small towns to have opera houses with sought-after traveling performers. As soon as the railroad came to town, or even before its routes were finalized, town fathers, newspaper editors, culture-hungry women, and ordinary citizens campaigned for an opera house on Main Street. In Nebraska, opera houses sprouted along the branch lines that served smaller places such as Red Cloud and David City, while the main line of the Union Pacific served larger cities like Fremont and Kearney. In 1896 half of Nebraska's opera house towns had fewer than 2,000 residents (some with only 600 people), and the other half had fewer than 20,000 residents, except for Omaha and Lincoln. These halls in Nebraska clearly depended on the railroad, especially its branch lines.[3]

During the eighteenth and early nineteenth centuries, a rigid divide between the North and the South, based primarily on religious beliefs, determined the fate of much theater and entertainment in the United States. The hardened opposition to thespian activities by the Puritans, Quakers, and other strict religions in the North and the Middle Atlantic states contrasted with the early acceptance and flourishing of theater in the South and early West in this period. Only the most intrepid actors headed north, often ending up in confrontations with the law. Today it is difficult to appreciate how these underlying and radically different cultural attitudes toward thespian performances and entertainment in the North and South influenced the development of theater, entertainment, and opera houses until the twentieth century. The tens of thousands of opera houses built in the late nineteenth century resulted from a tsunami of life-altering changes, from railroads to electric lights, which helped create an urbanized country where entertainment and theater became accepted as indispensable for civilized living. Amid the turmoil of these changes, older religious restrictions gradually were ignored or considered irrelevant.

The South, with its Anglican proclivities, did not have to cope with Puritanical hostility to thespian activities and consequently enjoyed theater in its early days of settlement. Londoner Lewis Hallam and his troupe of English actors performed *The Merchant of Venice* and *The Anatomist* in Williamsburg, Virginia in 1752. In 1790, Transylvania Seminary students performed a tragedy and a farce in Lexington, Kentucky; in 1791 an amateur group, the Theatrical Society, produced plays at the Washington County, Kentucky courthouse; and in 1808 Luke Usher established the first building in the state devoted solely to theater in Lexington. Between 1817 and 1827, Samuel Drake's company of actors played throughout the South and burgeoning West. From 1835 to 1851, Sol Smith and Noah Ludlow joined forces to perform up and down the Mississippi, with Smith building the first major theater in St. Louis, Missouri. These Southern and Western states continued to enjoy theater for more than a century, participating in the post–Civil War boom of opera house construction in many county seats and smaller towns; some, like Lexington's, continued to function into the 1930s.

In Colorado, in the far West during the six decades after 1860, 132 opera houses were built in sixty-eight towns and cities. By the 1880s, theater entrepreneur Peter McCourt operated a theater circuit in the Rockies, the Silver Circuit, which included Aspen, Colorado Springs, Greeley, Grand Junction, Leadville, and Trinidad and later added towns in Wyoming and Utah.

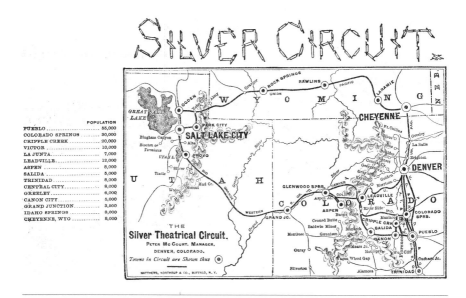

Silver Circuit: bringing culture and entertainment to many places in the Rockies. 1903. *History Colorado*

Colorado's opera houses came in many sizes and were in many places, including remote gulches and small mining towns in the Rockies. Unlike many small-town opera houses, where the auditorium occupied the upper floors of business buildings, several in Colorado, such as the Odd Fellows Hall in Paonia, had the performance space on the ground floor with upper-story meeting rooms for the organization. It was common for towns in Colorado, as elsewhere in the country, to have a succession of opera houses, as calamities destroyed the buildings or, in some cases, towns just wanted to build grander edifices as public entertainments became more popular. Pueblo, an important trading city on the Front Range, had four successive opera houses between 1879 and 1890 due to fires and inadequate facilities. The last of these, the 1890 Grand Opera House, was considered one of Colorado's grandest and largest theaters.

Established cities, such as Omaha, Philadelphia, and Milwaukee, either built new, large opera houses or expanded old ones (often renamed the "Grand Opera House"). These stood out as elaborate and visible symbols of the city's wealth, culture, and ambition. Denver's $850,000 Tabor Grand Opera House was built and financed in 1881 by silver magnate Horace Tabor, after his success in Leadville and before his downfall in the silver boom collapse. It was one of the most extravagant to date and considered to be the best-equipped theater between the Midwest and San Francisco.

Not to be outdone by larger cities, Kearney, Nebraska, a smaller city but a railroad junction with a population of ten thousand in 1896, built a grand and massive 1,200-seat opera house in 1891, described by the local newspaper as showing "Kearney's wealth and Kearney's work; Kearney's beauty and Kearney's manhood."[4] Such substantial halls differentiated their cities from rural towns with over-the-store opera houses. However, some small places, often those endowed with lucrative resources such as mining or lumber, benefited from local philanthropy, as in Menomonie, Wisconsin where lumber magnate Andrew Tainter built and endowed a grandiose opera house and library.

Because of larger populations and access to rail lines, bigger cities attracted leading performers such as Maude Adams and James O'Neill (Eugene O'Neill's father). When Willa Cather was living in Lincoln, Nebraska, the state capital and a university town, she enjoyed both the Funke Opera House and the Lansing Theatre, where she reviewed concerts and plays featuring actors such as Joseph Jefferson and Madame Helena Modjeska, who would never have appeared at a small-town opera house like her hometown Red Cloud Opera House. For small town or even small city residents everywhere, going to the "Grand" was a big occasion, as noted in the diary of Kansan Martha Farnsworth, who reported in 1894 going to the "Grand" in Topeka "to hear the new star., Miss Ellen Beach Yaw—who is proving a rival to Patti in Grand Opera. . . . It was just splendid."[5]

For theatergoers in the North, it was a different story. Not until the late nineteenth century did the North start to ignore its forebears' opposition to theater, but then mostly in the western sections settled by those often escaping the dogmatism of established eastern churches.

Vermont, distant from the rigid mainstream churches and with a historical legacy of experimental religions like that of New York's upstate "burnt over" district, had, by 1910, more than fifty opera houses in major towns like Burlington and Rutland and also in many smaller places like Londonderry and Hyde Park, despite some lingering Puritanical restrictions. The twenty-two theatrical organizations formed in Vermont towns in the 1870s clearly ignored the state's 1836 antitheater law, which declared theatrical exhibitions, along with circus riding, juggling, and magic arts, "public offenses."[6] Elsewhere in northern New England, interest in theater and opera houses appeared in cities and towns such as Camden, Rockport, and Stonington in Maine and Claremont, Lancaster, and Rochester in New Hampshire. Even in Connecticut, where legislation opposing theater was enforced for a longer period than in other New England states, William Goodspeed, an important regional entrepreneur, ignored obstructive regulations when he built the majestic Goodspeed Opera House in East Haddam in 1877. By the early 1900s, rural Washington County, New York, abutting Vermont northeast of Albany, had seven opera houses in towns with populations ranging from slightly more than two thousand to just under five thousand, even though its considerable Scotch-Irish Presbyterian population otherwise was influenced by that denomination's rigid behavioral code.

By 1900, all parts of the country were aboard the opera-house bandwagon. As the *Fremont Weekly Herald* noted in its report on opening night of the Love Opera House in 1888, "theatricals have become almost an indispensable adjunct to civilization today."[7]

This popularity of theater was matched by the numbers of opera houses established in the fifty years after the Civil War and the exploding number of performers, theater troupes, opera companies, circuses, and lecturers traversing the country. The new opera houses lining the nation's rail lines and mellowing attitudes toward theater created boundless opportunities for performers.

However, local theater was not an entirely new phenomenon. Ever since the seventeenth century, actors and entertainers had performed in taverns, halls, courthouses, and military garrisons at makeshift theaters despite moral objections to theater and actors. In 1777, bored British prisoners of war staged performances, including Shakespeare, at Henry Dering's converted brewhouse in Lancaster, Pennsylvania. In 1800, prosperous Lancaster with a population of 4,200 had sixty-one taverns, which hosted acrobats, jugglers, magicians, traveling wax museums, performing elephants, and plays. The quality of the plays might have slipped from those performed by the educated British prisoners of war: a tavern advertised plays such as *The Learned Pig and His Critic*s. Humor clearly was an essential ingredient in such entertainments.

In addition to popular entertainment and humor, Americans could find some serious theater. By 1800 150 actors, all of British descent, were roaming the country performing wherever they could in halls, taverns, or parlors. Even in New England, where bans on theatrical performances were rigidly enforced, actors found their way onto makeshift stages. Harvard students put on plays in the 1760s. By 1792, under the guise of "moral dialogues," plays were being furtively produced and enthusiastically received in lecture halls such as Boston's first theater, New Exhibition Hall. In city after city, local producers, including P. T. Barnum, conducted thespian activities in museums with "lecture halls" at the end of a corridor lined with cabinets of curiosities. The immensely popular *Uncle Tom's Cabin* was first performed in 1852 in the Troy Museum in Troy, New York. The well-known Boston Museum and Gallery of Fine Arts' concert hall/saloon/theater was respected for its long run of morality plays and its stock company, which operated from 1841 to 1894.

Before the Civil War, small theatrical troupes such as Samuel Drake's and well-appreciated stars such as Joseph Jefferson Sr. endured rough travel by horse, boat, and stagecoach in the South and West to perform in improvised halls in distant places. In Pekin, Illinois, Jefferson's son recalled, the actors and audiences at the theater, formerly a "pork house," could hear distant squeals from the banished pigs.[8] Such troupes were completely self-sufficient, traveling with their own scenery and costumes. Drake's traveling kit consisted of six drops featuring a street, forest, parlor, kitchen, palace, and garden; three sets of wings with aprons; a painted expandable proscenium; an act curtain; and a green carpet, all of which could be erected or taken down in two to three hours. After setting up their theaters, these early actors then took on multiple roles in a variety of plays performed back-to-back in weeklong stands. Noah Ludlow reported playing in 425 "different pieces during five seasons" between 1840 and 1844.[9] An evening at these theaters would involve plays, lectures, and variety shows; in fact, theatergoers felt cheated if they did not get a tragedy, a farce, and a comedy all in the same night. While audiences did not always enjoy such a variety of plays in a single evening in later years, actors continued to perform multiple parts in different plays. Minnie Maddern Fiske, considered one of the greatest American actresses, recalled that during her childhood in the Midwest in the 1870s she was drafted for children's roles when traveling troupes "thought nothing of giving a different play every night."[10]

In cities and larger towns, resident companies were often reinforced by traveling groups and stars. By 1825, twenty theaters across the country supported permanent stock companies with a large repertoire of plays; by 1860, stock companies numbered fifty, but by 1878 that number had shrunk to seven or eight as the "combination system" took hold. This combination system was organized to send on the road a one-play tour complete with scenery, costumes, properties, and sometimes a star. With this system the need for a resident company was eliminated. Managers at local opera houses, who previously had some creative responsibilities, were reduced to booking agents. The number of these combinations on the road grew from one hundred in 1875 to four hundred in 1904. Theater on the road was popular. In an 1887–1888 tour, Edwin Booth and Lawrence Barrett gave 258 performances in 72 towns and cities.

Road shows also proved to be lucrative, as managers Charles Frohmann, Abraham Erlanger, and Alf Haym, upstate New Yorkers transplanted to New York City, discovered. Their creation of the Syndicate in the late 1890s was the next step in the monopolizing of road tours. The Syndicate signed up actors, assured them a steady income, and organized circuit tours for them. The circuits included as many as seven hundred theaters, which the Syndicate either owned, leased, or operated. By the early 1900s, this New York–based theatrical trust had a firm grip on mainstream theater. Small-town opera houses like Red Cloud's lost out in the era of the Syndicate, as they could not afford the Syndicate's touring shows and were not located on major rail lines. That meant the Syndicate mainly served larger and more affluent places such as Omaha. While there were holdouts, such as Sarah Bernhardt and Minnie Maddern Fiske, who refused to join the Syndicate, and groups trying to stop the Frohmann/Erlanger juggernaut, the Syndicate prospered as New York became the theater capital.

In the late nineteenth and early twentieth centuries, theater on the road was dominant, and by 1905 touring and theater became almost synonymous. More than five hundred traveling theater troupes were road companies, some with nationally known stars such as Ethel Barrymore and James Herne, but there were also many regional troupes such as the Chicago Comedy Company. At the turn of the century, 500 "Tommers," troupes only playing the popular *Uncle Tom's Cabin*, roamed the country. Many lesser-known troupes like Holman's Opera Company never played in the first-class theaters that the Syndicate operated, so they functioned as they always had. John Drew, James O'Neill, Madame Helena Modjeska, Otis Skinner, Maurice Barrymore, Minnie Maddern Fiske, Lillian Russell, and Maude Adams appeared everywhere. For live theater, popular entertainment, and opera houses, this was certainly a heyday.

But the heyday did not last. By the 1920s, movies from Hollywood were replacing live performances. Automobiles enabled people to travel to bigger places where well-known stars appeared on the silver screen at new, lavish movie theaters. And then radio brought entertainment right into the living room. This plethora of new entertainment opportunities spelled the end of a long history of live, often high-quality theater and entertainment in opera houses, especially in small towns. Mass entertainment was entering a new chapter.

CHAPTER 2

A Time of Change

Tectonic changes were occurring in the second half of the nineteenth century as the United States healed from the fractures and frictions of the Civil War and matured into an urbanized and industrial powerhouse. At the same time as vast expanses of the West were being settled with encouragement of the Homestead Act, the country was rapidly urbanizing. From 1865 to 1900, the country's population more than doubled, the number of urban places experienced a fivefold increase, and larger cities with more than 100,000 increased almost sevenfold. Industry was overtaking agriculture as the economic driver and manufacturing income was expanding tenfold compared to agriculture's fourfold growth in the last half of the nineteenth century. The infusion of immigrants, helped by the 1864 immigration legislation, was changing the character of cities, as well as of rural areas, as the number of foreign-born newcomers swelled by 12 million from 1870 to 1900. Revolutionizing how people worked and lived were inventions such as the telegraph, the Bessemer process, the telephone, and electricity.[1] In the short period from 1864 to 1869, more cotton spindles revolved, iron furnaces were lit, steel was produced, copper and coal were mined, lumber was sawed, houses and stores were built, and types of manufacturing were established than in any equal time in earlier history.[2]

Some of these changes and inventions had direct benefits for opera houses and the entertainment industry. Electricity improved the lighting in theaters and reduced the incidence of fire from gaslights, a bane of older opera houses. For opera house managers, theater companies, and performers, the telegraph and telephone immensely improved communications and logistics. But the railroad remained a prime agent for the development and functioning of opera houses as well as for opera house towns. Its importance to opera houses is evident in Julius Cahn's *Theatrical Directories*, the essential handbook for information on opera houses and theaters from 1896 to 1910, which listed its entries by rail lines, the towns they served, and each town's theater and hotel facilities.

The railroads, like many other large corporations born in this period, assumed monopolistic powers as they acquired wide swaths of land in the West through federal grants, established their own rates, often determined where towns would be located along their routes, and even set up standard time zones for the whole country without any court, congressional, or presidential action. Sinclair Lewis, a son of the Midwest, understood the walloping power of the railroads. "The railroad was more than a means of transportation to Gopher Prairie," wrote Lewis in *Main Street*. "It was a new god. The towns had been staked out on barren prairie as convenient points for future train-halts. To Gopher Prairie, the tracks were eternal verities, and the boards of railroad directors an omnipotence."[3]

Along with the railroads, other powerful corporations and their tycoons were transforming the country into an industrial powerhouse, which in turn was transforming the lives of everyday workers and their families. Work and home were being separated in the new industrial system. This meant set hours of work and new leisure time. Factory work, which could be tedious and repetitive, was assigned and supervised by others. Thus, while gaining new spare time, workers were losing some of the independence they had when working independently on the farm or in small trades like harness or carriage making. Now they were insignificant parts of a powerful industrial system, captives of distant economic forces. The loss of independence and tedium of the work, combined with new free time, created a fundamental change in attitudes toward leisure pursuits: entertainment became a diversion and an escape from the alienation of the workplace.

A host of insecurities surfaced as long-held values and customs were unsettled in the new laissez-faire world. Cracks began to appear in the modus operandi of all-powerful corporations, perhaps most apparent in major labor upheavals like the Pullman Strike (1894) and corrective federal legislation like the Interstate Commerce Act (1887) and the Sherman Anti-Trust Act (1890). Even the settlement of the West, often pictured as the outcome of pioneer yeomen occupying 160-acre homesteads, was skewed, as only one-tenth of new farms were acquired through the Homestead Act (1862),

INDIANA.—Continued.

25 ft. Footlights to back wall, 36 ft. Curtain line to footlights, 3½ ft. Dist. bet. fly girders, 42 ft. 8 grooves. Depth under stage, 8 ft. Dist. bet. side walls, 60 ft. Height of grooves, 18 ft. Height to rigging loft, 38 ft. 3 traps, center and back. Grooves can be taken up flush with fly gallery. Scene room. Theatre on second floor. White, prop. man. Bryan, stage carp. 6 in orches. Donnell, leader. Printing required, 5 stands, 25 3-sheets, 75 1-sheets, 90 ½-sheets. Dates read, New Opera House, Franklin, Ind. Transfer Co., Hill & Baldwin. Express offices, Adams and American. L. L. Whitesides, physician. Miller & Barnett, lawyers. W. H. Woodsmall, typewriter.

Newspapers—Daily, "Star." Weekly, "Republican," "Democrat."

Hotels—Clarendon, $2 single, $1.50 double. Merchants', $1.50, $1. Hays, $1. Mrs. Wilson, $1.

Railroads—Penn., Sam McClellan, agt. Big 4, Mr. Brown.

Publisher of programme—Gus Byfield.

* * *

GARRETT—Pop., 3,500. Wagner's Opera House. J. Wm. Wagner, mgr. and bus. mgr. S. c., 600. Illum., gas. Width prosc. opening, 20 ft. Height, 13 ft. Depth footlights to back wall, 21 ft. Dist. curtain line to footlights, 3 ft. Dist. bet. side walls, 40 ft. Theatre second floor.

Newspapers—"Clipper," weekly, Thurs. "Herald," weekly, Fri.

Hotels—Ross House, City Hotel.

Railroad—B. & O., J. H. Kooken, agt.

* * *

GOSHEN—Pop., 10,000. The Irwin. Frank Irwin, mgr. S. c., 1,000. Prices 35c to $1. Illum., gas and elec. Width prosc. opening, 28 ft. Height, 20 ft. Footlights to back wall, 25 ft. Curtain line to footlights, 5 ft. Dist. bet. side walls, 65 ft. Dist. bet. fly girders, 48 ft. Grooves from stage, 20 ft. Stage to rigging loft, 32 ft. 4 grooves. Depth under stage, 5 ft. 3 traps, located center, R. and L. 5 bridges. Grooves can be taken up flush

with fly gallery. Theatre on second floor. 5 in orchestra. Printing required, 7 stands, 30 3-sheets, 100 1-sheets, 100 ½-sheets. Dates read, The Irwin.

Newspapers — Daily, "News," Mr. Starr. "Times," Mr. Harrison. Weekly, "Democrat."

Hotels—Hascall, $2. Neufer, $1.50. Hattle, $1.

Railroads—L. S. & M. S., Geo. Slate, agt. C., C., C. & St. L., J. M. Ober. Transfer Co., Al. Keith.

* * *

GREENFIELD—Pop., 7,000. Greenfield Opera House. Wm. A. Hough, mgr., bus. mgr. and press agt. S. c., 500. Prices 35c. and 50c. Illum., elec. Enos Gerry, elec. and stage carp. Width prosc. opening, 24 ft. Height, 12 ft. Depth footlights to back wall, 20 ft. Dist. curtain line to footlights, 4 ft. Dist. bet. side walls, 40 ft. Theatre on 2d floor. Isaac Doris, leader of orches. 9 in orches. Enos Gery, prop. man.

Newspapers—"Tribune," daily. "Republican," daily and weekly. "Democrat," "Herald," "Republican," weekly, Thurs.

Hotels—W. C. Dudding, E. S. Bragg, $1.50. M. K. Cummins, $1.

Railroad—Burlington Route.

* * *

GREENFIELD, HANCOCK CO.— Pop., 6,500. Gant's new Opera House. W. S. Gant, mgr. S. c., 600. Stage, 31x 50. Prices 25c. to 50c. Stephens & Branham, bill posters.

Hotels—Columbia, Guymon House.

Newspapers — " Evening Tribune " (daily), "Evening Republican." Weekly, "Hancock Democrat," "Greenfield Republican," "Greenfield Herald."

Elmer J. Buford, attorney.

* * *

GREENSBURG—Pop., 5,000. Grand Opera House and Rink Opera House. George H. Dunn, Jr., mgr. S. c., Grand, 500; Rink, 700. Illum., gas and elec. Printing required, 3 stands, 10 3-sheets,

All the information a traveling entertainer needs to know about each town on a railroad's line. "Julius Cahn's Official Theatrical Guide 1897."
Theatre Division, Library of the Performing Arts, New York Public Library

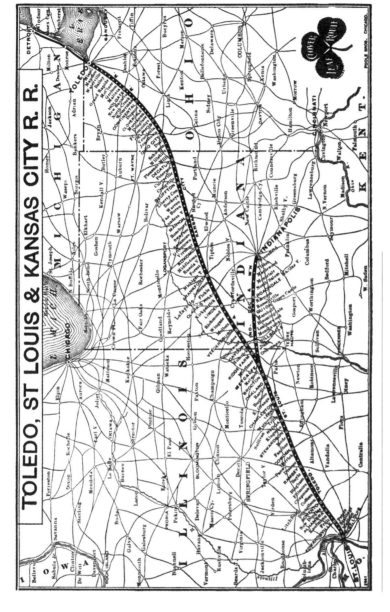

There were many towns on a rail line awaiting actors and performers.

the rest bought from railroads, land companies, or states. These increasingly monopolistic practices affected how opera houses functioned, as once-independent traveling theater troupes were drawn into syndicates.

Despite the overarching powers of corporations along with new and alarming corruption, gaps between the rich and poor and the rural and urban, and the crushing of small operators, the newly empowered laissez-faire world also generated remarkable changes. Railroads, telephones, radios, and electric lights, to name a few, enormously benefited people's everyday living—and also opera houses and many other cultural and recreational institutions. That people could enjoy cultural and entertaining diversions meant there was leisure time and disposable income for such nonproductive pursuits as well as societal recognition of the value of secular activities for individuals and the country.

Faith in the future, which buttressed the risk taking of entrepreneurs, whether captains of industry or small-town bankers, made many opera houses become realities. For the lone entrepreneur to think that constructing an opera house over the drugstore might make his town seem cultivated and metropolitan took a leap of faith. Behind this faith in the future and the "can do" mentality lurked a remarkable confidence in the individual and the country. It might be considered an expression of exceptionalism that the United States enjoyed a superiority derived from its early egalitarian principles empowering its citizens and differentiating it from other countries. While that confidence and energy disrupted the old ways, it generated new outlooks, values, and ideas, many influencing the future of culture, theater, and entertainment—and the life of opera houses. Especially important to the development of opera houses were the new interests that emerged in this period in philanthropy, the arts, and the empowerment of women.

This post–Civil War era produced remarkable cultural enterprises, as the newly rich became patrons of the arts and launched cultural institutions of every sort. This new refinement was in the air not only in the large cities but also in small, remote towns. Appreciating this new refinement, many successful local businessmen built and endowed major cultural institutions, which continue today as outstanding civic monuments in city after city. As self-serving as these gifts were in refining the rough-edged images of many of these often hard-nosed entrepreneurs, they added a welcome respectability to many towns. And the new cultural and art institutions established in this era also provided visible evidence of both the young country's artistic ambitions and the gravitas of its commitment to cultural affairs. In the

1870s, major art museums were founded in New York, Boston, Philadelphia, and Chicago. Universities bearing the names of such donors as Johns Hopkins, Stanford, and Vanderbilt appeared from 1860 to 1890. Although best known for the almost three thousand libraries he helped to establish and New York City's Carnegie Hall, steel tycoon Andrew Carnegie also founded the Carnegie Institute of Technology in Pittsburgh as a "first-class technical school" for local steelworkers' children.

Carnegie perhaps articulated better than other industrialists of this period his strong commitment to philanthropy as a payback to society—in contrast to those, including John D. Rockefeller, who saw it as a religious duty. The millionaire "labors to acquire that he may wisely administer for others' good," Carnegie declared in his *Gospel of Wealth*.[4] For him, the millionaire is a trustee of wealth who can benefit society twice, first by making a fortune, which provides employment and offers goods for consumers, and second by wisely distributing the fortune he earns. Despite his Scottish background, Carnegie believed in play as well as work, so much of his early generosity went to recreational facilities. He particularly identified with the places that were important in his life—his hometown in Dunfermline, Scotland, and his early Pennsylvania mill, the Edgar Thomson works in Braddock. Thus, his first philanthropic "payback" gifts went to Dunfermline in 1877 for a recreation hall, swimming pool, and later a library, and then in 1881 he donated a library to his Braddock steel plant. For Carnegie, philanthropy was a shared experience. His library gifts, for example, depended on the commitment of local jurisdictions to pay for most of their maintenance, which Carnegie hoped would prevent excessive dependence on private donations.

Such philanthropy by local benefactors could be found in cities and towns of all sizes. St. Johnsbury in northern Vermont boasts an array of educational and cultural institutions, including an Athenaeum founded in 1871 that houses a library, gallery, and lecture hall, and a science museum founded two years later, both benefiting from the philanthropy of the local philanthropists Horace and Franklin Fairbanks. Their fortune from the manufacture of the country's first platform scale provided St. Johnsbury (population 4,665 in 1870) with cultural and educational institutions that are still thriving today. The art gallery in the Athenaeum is known for its large collection of Hudson River School paintings and the famous *Domes of Yosemite* by Albert Bierstadt.

Certainly, opera houses were direct beneficiaries of local leaders' generosity, whether in Denver with the silver king Horace Tabor's Tabor Opera

House; or in small towns like Fort Edward, New York, where local lumber magnate George Bradley built the Bradley Opera House, or Aspen, Colorado, where Jerome Wheeler, R. H. Macy's chairman and Aspen Mining and Smelting Company shareholder, built the Wheeler Opera House. Local stockholders or towns built many opera houses, but the majority resulted from the munificence of local entrepreneurs-cum-benefactors. The motives for such largess were mixed. Certainly many of these local benefactors had a sincere interest in culture and theater. In Fremont, Nebraska, James Wheeler Love, an educator who became a local real estate magnate and his wife, Thirza, were local benefactors genuinely involved with the arts. They participated in the local Shakespeare Club, made theater jaunts to Lincoln and Omaha, and took an inspiring trip to Europe. An energetic man, Love even tried to establish an opera house circuit in San Salvador when he was a US consul there in 1891. Henry Putnam, who developed Bennington, Vermont's opera house, ran a successful fruit jar and bottle stopper business and was a devotee of Shakespeare.

These local businessmen's interest in the arts was, however, often tinged with boosterism and, in some cases, even a vain hope of financial return. Certainly art and culture displayed conspicuously the status of the benefactors and, most important, provided them, as well as their towns, with a patina of respectability. Whatever the motives, towns and cities appreciated the generosity of their philanthropists. "Bennington owes Mr. H. W. Putnam a debt of gratitude," the *Bennington* (VT) *Banner* stated after the opening of the Opera House on December 10, 1892, "for not only relieving us from the discomforts of Library Hall, but for giving to a country town a metropolitan Opera House."[5]

Like philanthropy, growing interest in the arts and even a new cultural sophistication countered the dominant materialism of the late nineteenth century. "Truth and morality ... the touchstones of American art" before the Civil War, writes art historian Michael J. Lewis, were being jolted now by a new pragmatism and experimentalism.[6] Artists such as Richard Morris Hunt were studying in the classical tradition at the prestigious École des Beaux-Arts in Paris, while the Impressionists were revolutionizing how painters expressed themselves. The number and talents of artists in this period are remarkable. The list of American artists reads like an honor roll of the famous and still-revered.[7] Painters such as John Singer Sargent and William Chase Merritt pictured the lives of the fashionable and famous, while at the same time Eastman Johnson, Winslow Homer, and Hiram Bingham were painting ordinary people at their everyday pursuits. Such realism could be seen as the forerunner of the Ashcan School painters, including John Sloan, Edward Bellows, and Robert Henri, who portrayed the lives not only of ordinary people but also of those left behind in fast-paced industrializing cities.

Among writers, the materialism of this robber baron era produced a variety of reactions. Henry James expatriated, although never completely severing his ties to his homeland. Hamlin Garland remained in the United States writing about his Midwestern upbringing and the perennial problems facing farmers in that region. Edith Wharton wrote of the lives of sophisticated Gilded Age Easterners and their moral conflicts with capitalistic values. For playwrights, their melodramas provided popular thrills to opera house audiences for decades and also reinforced traditional moral values threatened in these new times. Not surprisingly, this period also produced a surge of social commentators. There were the defenders of the new laissez-faire such as intellectuals like William Graham Sumner or the popular orator Russell Cronwell, whose "Acres of Diamonds" speech extolled the new cult of success. Matching these defenders were a bevy of vocal critics of the new era and its corrosive values: Edward Bellamy, Theodore Dreiser, Henry George, and Jacob Riis. The number of newspapers and readers soared from 2.5 million to over 15 million from 1870 to 1900, and the number of monthly magazines increased from 280 to 1,800 between 1860 and 1900. Americans were being exposed not only to current news but also to the latest thoughts of contemporary thinkers.[8] Even the academic field of philosophy enjoyed a period of vibrant, intellectual experimentation in this period. The noted triumvirate of philosophers at Harvard, William James, George Santayana, and Josiah Royce, represented a range of theories from Royce's quest for a binding community to James's easing into a new pragmatism.

For architects, artists, and socially conscious civic leaders, this was a time of enormous energy and notable results: buildings, parks, professional associations, and a new recognition of responsibilities for the development of cities. Architects such as Dankmar Adler and Louis Sullivan were designing new and powerful buildings, while Daniel Burnham and McKim, Mead, and White were carrying the Beaux Arts tradition to popular heights in the emerging City Beautiful movement. Landscape architecture became a recognized profession as Frederick Law Olmsted designed parks in almost every major city. New York's Central Park, designed by Olmsted and Calvert Vaux, set a new standard for transforming landforms and vegetation to provide beauty and respite for the many urbanites living in increasingly crowded cities. Playgrounds were promoted by advocates like Boston's Joseph Lee for healthful exercise to counter the hardships of urban living. Settlement houses like Chicago's Hull House and social welfare organizations like Charles Brace's Children's Aid Society in New York were established to meet the needs of underserved city dwellers. Proliferating municipal societies such as the American Civic Association focused on improving both the appearance and the functions of cities.

This groundswell of interest in cities certainly was spurred by the City Beautiful movement. Although associated with monumental buildings like New York's Pennsylvania Station and Washington's Union Station, the City Beautiful advocates awakened concerns for broad civic improvement. In displaying the "progress" of the country, the spectacular 1893 World's Columbian Exposition in Chicago, primarily designed by Daniel Burnham and Frederick Law Olmsted, showed that it was possible to start from scratch and build a grand and beautiful city. While ostensibly celebrating the 400th anniversary of Columbus's arrival in the New World, the exposition proved to the world and to its twenty-seven million visitors that Chicago had risen from the ashes of the fire and was an important city. One visitor, banker J. C. Rogers from Wamego, Kansas, was so inspired by the exposition that he bought exposition paintings, artifacts, and even an eagle, which adorn the opera house he built and named, appropriately, the Columbian Theatre. The message of the exposition as expressed in Burnham's pronouncement, "Make no little plans," was heard throughout the country.

The drive and physical accomplishments of the City Beautiful movement, along with social critics' concerns about the housing and health problems of the urban poor, provided groundwork for the future field of city planning. There was a contagious confidence that design and planning could improve the appearance and life of cities and towns—and that confidence was empowering.

The opera house, whether in Fremont, Nebraska, Paris, Kentucky, or Denver, Colorado, displays this pervasive confidence. The commitment of a local leader to build an impressive public building like an opera house represents the same mixture of motives that stirred most City Beautiful designers: to provide a handsome building, improve the appearance of a town, and make it a better place to live by attracting attention to the town as a prosperous place. Although the rural hamlets where most small opera houses were located were not necessarily part of the intellectual ferment in the world of the arts, they nevertheless felt reverberations from the City Beautiful movement and benefited from it.[9]

The Rogers Opera House, now known as the Columbian Theatre (Opera House), Wamego, Kansas. Built in 1895 by J. C. Rogers, who adorned it with an eagle from the 1893 Columbian Exposition. *The Columbian Theatre Foundation, Dave Mathias, photographer*

Women played critical roles in shaping culture and the moral values of the nation and, in turn, the arts and theater. Indeed, women were the "sivilizers," as Aunt Sally said to Huck Finn. This urge to uplift society was especially evident in the newly settled West and later in states like Nebraska and Iowa, which had an extraordinarily high number of opera houses. Here recent arrivals, both refugees from the East and Midwest and immigrants from older European towns and cities, found a startlingly new and barren environment in endless miles of undulating plains and prairies. Willa Cather recalled the countryside around Red Cloud shortly after her family arrived there in 1884: "The roads were mostly faint trails over the bunch grass in those days. The land was open range and there was no fencing. As we drove further and further out into the country, I felt a good deal as if we had come to the end of everything—it was a kind of erasure of personality."[10]

Women faced traumatic changes when they left their extended families and familiar communities, endured a difficult trip, and then started a home and sometimes a family. These pioneers were often ill prepared for the ruggedness and devastating loneliness of frontier life. For Isabella Diehl, a settler with her husband Martin on a farm in the Dakotas in the early 1880s, "the vast prairie was a strange and lonely place, so far from home and loved ones."[11] While the men were busy sod busting and trying to eke out a living, women were trying to make homes in tough conditions with the few provisions brought from their former abodes. Many felt cooped up in their houses. "While their husbands and brothers enjoyed the country in hunting and fishing," Margaret Fuller noted of Wisconsin and Illinois in the 1840s, the women "found themselves confined to the comfortless and laborious indoor life."[12] They also missed their distant families, and especially their female friends. And for many, their new life was often nomadic as restlessness and disappointments stirred these pioneer families to move to yet-newer frontiers in the hope that they might be more promising.

Wherever pioneers settled, the women tried to "sivilize" the home and community. The reed organ, prominently displayed in Solomon Butcher's photograph of the David Hilton family at its Nebraska homestead, indicates the importance of that symbol of civilization for these pioneers. The hardships of frontier life allowed little time for leisure. Many pioneer women were educated and interested in enriching their cultural lives, but many were not, as former Geneva, New York teacher Caroline Kirkland discovered in Michigan. There she found little interest in education and "few and feeble" intellectual activities.[13] In later years, however, as the plains and prairies filled up with neighbors and new communities, they established schools, started newspapers, and launched cultural activities. Pioneer women found themselves with more leisure and with more like-minded neighbors to form literary societies, singing evenings, dances, and amateur theatrical groups performing everything from Shakespeare to informal skits. In 1888, the Nebraska novelist Frank H. Spearman was surprised to find not only organs in out-of-the-way sod houses but also impressive literary club meetings. "Literary clubs, which members ride all the way from five to twenty miles

The David Hilton family with their organ near Weissert, Nebraska in 1887. Mrs. Hilton and her eldest daughter did not want to pose in front of their sod house because friends and relatives would see that they were still living in a dirt house. Posing with the organ lent an air of civilization to their homestead. Solomon DeVore Butcher, photographer. *Nebraska State Historical Society*

to attend, and where they discuss with great earnestness everything from the latest political problem to the most abstruse point in metaphysics, are quite the regular thing with our homesteaders," he reported.[14]

Immigrants, free of religious strictures and probably accustomed to different social and cultural events in their home country, were quick to organize dances and social gatherings in their new American settlements. Whether they came from Europe, the eastern part of the United States, or nearby Western settlements, there was a tendency to look over their shoulders and rely on the ways of their former homes or homelands. Even in the early twentieth century in small settled towns, a yearning to connect to the larger world persisted. When Sinclair Lewis's Carol Kennicott in *Main Street* was at the lake house, she felt sadly removed from the world because she could not hear the train whistles: "She realized that in town she had depended upon them for assurance that there remained a world beyond."[15] And she was not alone. "Even in this new era of motors," Lewis wrote, "the citizens went down to station to see the trains go through. It was their romance . . . and from the trains came lords of the outer world."[16]

Women's yearning for culture and sociability led to the development of many opera houses in newly minted towns in the West and long-settled towns in the East. In town after town, women encouraged the men in their lives to establish opera houses, so that they could experience the culture and entertainment that faraway places enjoyed as well as their homegrown cultural activities.

When women arrived in mining towns in the Colorado Rockies after the men discovered lodes of silver and gold, they found themselves out-numbered two to one by men. With their deep commitment to place, women started turning these "bivouacs into settlements."[17] As one of the few public places in town, the saloon was where most local entertainment occurred. Even such worthy actors as John Langrishe and his company performed in saloons in Colorado, Montana, Wyoming, South Dakota, and Idaho on his Gold Circuit in the 1860s. But in later decades, whether under pressure from the newly arrived women or from the more socially conscious men, the saloon was considered an inappropriate place for enter-tainments for women and for the more refined people in those mining towns. In Leadville, Colorado, in the days after the discovery of silver in California Gulch and shortly before its lavish Tabor Opera House opened in 1879, "ladies" leased a tent theater and called it the Vivian Opera House. The Vivian Opera House was an alternative: "a clean, first-class place of amusement," where "you need not be afraid to take your wife, your daughter, your aunt, nor even your mother-in-law." Its productions were considered "pre-eminently first class," but its tenure was short because Leadville residents did not want to patronize performances given in a tent. Fortunately, they did not have to wait long to see performances in one of the grandest opera houses of its day, the Tabor Opera House.[18]

Many small towns lacked a respectable hall for plays, entertainments, public meetings, or local school plays and graduations, so their more affluent residents traveled to larger cities to enjoy cultural events. In David City, Nebraska in the mid-1880s, Martin Novotny ran the local saloon, which, as in the Rockies, was where early theater took place. Novotney's saloon, with a raised platform at one end, could seat four hun-dred people. For more cultivated residents such as William Brownsfield Thorpe, a prominent David City citizen, founder of the Butler County Bank, and real estate investor, Novotny's saloon was not a suitable place for his music-loving wife and daughter to take in culture. In order for the

Margaret and William B. Thorpe and their daughter Estelle, who directed the December 22, 1894 benefit for the poor at the 1889 Thorpe Opera House, David City, Nebraska. *Thorpe Opera House Foundation and Beth Klosterman*

women in his life to be able to attend musical and cultural events right in their hometown instead of having to travel to Omaha or Lincoln, in 1889 Thorpe built the thousand-seat Thorpe Opera House, modeled on the Booth Theatre in New York. Not only did Mr. Thorpe provide a venue for the musical events his family enjoyed, but he decorated the interior of the opera house not in the usual red and gold but in blue, the favorite color of his musical daughter, Estelle. Fittingly, after graduating from school in Omaha, Estelle returned to David City, where she performed in and directed shows at her father's opera house.

In the upstate New York village of Fort Edward, a prosperous lumber town in the mid to late nineteenth century, Margaret Bradley, the wife of local lumber magnate George Bradley, was a strong-minded woman who happened to be musical. She aspired to be more than a passive member of an audience; she wanted to participate in productions of musical events and even conduct them. In 1872 her husband built the Bradley Opera House, which his wife managed and where she produced, participated in, and enjoyed musical activities for decades. Both Bradley daughters took part in these shows and, in particular, daughter Mary, who as a piano teacher and singer, enjoyed an active role in opera house musical productions for most of her life. Unlike many opera houses, which featured out-of-town troupes and productions, the Bradley Opera House concentrated on musical events that were produced and performed by local people, including an 1897 May Carnival with a cast of a hundred children. Mrs. Bradley trained all the singers for the 1889 Olde Folkes' Concert, but because a woman could not wield a baton in public at that time, she had to yield it to a local musician, Fred Bratt, who conducted for her. The Bradley Opera House was also the venue for nonmusical events, including lectures by suffragettes such as Carrie Chapman Catt because of Mrs. Bradley's ardent support of the women's rights movement.

In nearby Granville, known as the nation's roofing-slate capital, the Pember Opera House was yet another venue that a cultivated woman persuaded her husband to build, so that she and her fellow townspeople could enjoy good theater. Ellen Pember, a businesswoman with considerable real estate holdings in Iowa, enjoyed theater in New York City, where she owned a house so she could go to the theater every night. Her scrapbook of playbills included performances by Edwin Booth, Joseph Jefferson, and Neil Burgess, and even French opera at the Park Theatre. In contrast to Mrs. Bradley of Fort Edward, Mrs. Pember's interest was to bring quality theatrical groups to Granville rather than to organize local productions. Thus, while Granville had had an earlier opera house, her husband, Franklin Pember, saw the need for a real theater, so Pember Opera House opened in 1901.

Hiring Thomas A. Boyle as the opera house manager turned out to be an important decision for the Pember. Aside from managing the opera house, Boyle, like many opera house managers, took on the management of two other nearby opera houses, one in Rutland and the other in Poultney, Vermont, creating a small theater circuit. This gave him a

The Blue Belles ready to perform at the 1872 Bradley Opera House in Fort Edward, New York. *Fort Edward Historical Society*

better chance of attracting good troupes than if he were booking for just the single opera house in Granville. The opening night of the popular *Way Down East* was reported to resemble an opening night at New York's Metropolitan Opera House on a smaller scale, as many attendees were in evening dress at the standing-room-only performance.[19] Special trains on the Delaware and Hudson Railroad were organized from nearby towns to Granville for productions of hit plays like *Coming thro' the Rye* and operettas like Gilbert and Sullivan's *Pirates of Penzance*. Granville did not want to be left out of mainstream theater. Some of its productions, such as *The Traveling Salesman,* were advertised as having been performed in New York, Chicago, and Boston. Since the Pember Opera House opened later than many, its life span was relatively short, with live entertainment displaced by movies that began to be shown by 1910.

Mrs. Pember, Mrs. Bradley, and the Thorpes were but a few of the cultivated women in the United States who persuaded the men in their lives to build opera houses for public enjoyment of shows and cultural events not previously available in those areas. Some women's cultural influence extended even beyond their lives, when their husbands, fathers, or families would construct halls in their memory—among them the Diller (Nebraska) Opera House built by local magnate William Diller to honor his late wife.

In the second half of the nineteenth century, women were able to participate in public life and assert themselves, as they never had before. In all parts of the country, middle-class women organized voluntary associations, promoted the arts, and worked on improving the living and educational conditions of other women. The surging industrialism and increased urbanization in this period brought not only opportunities but also many challenges to women and the traditional family. Major organizations started and run by women were established to help their sisters cope with problems arising from new working and living situations, especially for the many who left farmsteads for city jobs. The Young Women's Christian Association (YWCA; popularly known as the "Y"), founded in 1858 as the Ladies Christian Association with a moral agenda to protect working women, provided educational and vocational programs and boarding-house-like dormitories. The Y's influence expanded nationally and internationally, and by 1894 there were YWCAs in 175 countries.

A more strident organization, the Woman's Christian Temperance Union (WCTU), started in 1874, grappled with the problem of alcoholism, a growing concern in this industrial era. Recognizing alcoholism as a societal problem, the WCTU dealt with a host of problems facing women, including suffrage, but concentrated on its all-important battle for prohibition of alcohol. The organization's membership, which jumped from 23,000 in 1881 to 158,000 in 1901, indicates the popularity of the issue and the WCTU. Its focus on the moral values of the home and family clearly reflected the Victorian era's conservative tone, which pervaded many popular melodramas like *The Drunkard*, performed over many decades in opera houses nationwide. More direct messages on the evils of alcohol were made by temperance speakers, who appeared on opera house programs for decades.

The awakening of women in this post–Civil War period was seen by the feminist reformer Charlotte Perkins Gilman as "the most important sociological phenomenon of the century." New opportunities were being created to educate women in more than the traditional feminine subjects such as etiquette, sewing, and penmanship.[20] Secondary schools like Emma Willard's Troy Female Seminary (1821) and Baltimore's Bryn Mawr School (1885), founded by women including M. Carey Thomas (later president of Bryn Mawr College), offered girls the same education as boys. From 1865 to 1889, all Seven Sisters colleges had been founded except for Mt. Holyoke, which dates back to 1837. More women were not only receiving rigorous higher education but also being empowered as independent thinkers and emerging leaders.

American women everywhere were enjoying new freedoms—even in the spheres of theater and shopping, the consumption of material and cultural goods. The department store gave women new freedoms as these handsome cathedrals of commerce multiplied after the Civil War in city after city, making shopping a respectable and pleasurable experience. Lavishly decorated stores such as Marshall Field lured women to spend the day, enjoy its restaurants, read in its libraries, and, of course, shop at counters manned by knowledgeable clerks selling a wide array of clearly marked and priced items. Significantly, theaters and opera houses arose near these inviting stores, often clustered in a shopping district such as New York's Miracle Mile, so that a whole section of a city became imbued with middle-class decorum, providing women with opportunities for consumption and entertainment not previously possible.

Theater managers had long recognized the market possibilities of attracting women to theaters to add needed respectability and also to gain new patrons. The days of aristocratic Anglican traditions, when George and Martha Washington enjoyed plays at the sedate New Theater in Philadelphia, were overtaken by more plebeian audiences. Theatergoing had become a rowdy activity where "ladies" dared not venture. As early as 1817, Samuel Drake's adventurous theater company tried to lure women to its performances in the South by setting up coffee rooms with confections and other refreshments for the women, while the men retired to the bar. Most plays until the mid-nineteenth century were interactive, with the audience sometimes even sitting on the stage itself until David Garrick banned the custom in London's Drury Lane Theatre. Audiences in the pit and balconies hissed, screamed, corrected actors, and flirted with one another as prostitutes and dandies mingled in the upper balconies. Such rowdy participatory theater was generally deemed unsuitable for "ladies." To combat this behavior, as late as 1896 in Lexington, Kentucky, a city ordinance declared it "unlawful for any person in any public place of amusement to stamp their feet, make cat calls, whistle, hiss, halloo, or make any other noisy demonstrations except clapping of the hands."[21] Likewise, to counter the image of unruly audiences and also to lure more women to theaters, waiting rooms for them, matinees, and Ladies' Nights appeared. Now with a new respectability, theater lost some of its former participatory vitality, as audiences' public responses were limited to clapping. A new refinement was in the air in this Gilded Age.

Despite new opportunities and freedoms for women, as well as new voices for women's rights, their overall influence had a conservative tone in this Victorian time. Respectability was a paramount concern as the harsh

Calvinism of Jonathan Edwards and intellectualism of authors such as
Hawthorne gave way to a softer sentimentality and anti-intellectualism.
The family was considered of prime importance, and the home was a har-
bor in this changing world as the new industrial corporations, infusion

An advertisement for a performance of *East Lynne,* the heart wrenching and popular
melodrama, by the Georgetown Players at McClellan Hall, Georgetown, Colorado,
1882. *History Colorado*

of immigrants, and emerging class conflicts presented problems beyond the control of most people. The churches too were changing. Old-line Protestants were losing their influence as Catholics, Methodists, and Baptists outnumbered them, and by 1855 the Roman Catholic Church was the most important religious denomination. Instead of Protestant virtue righting the wrongs of overwhelming capitalism, Protestants seemed to retreat to the paradise of the middle-class family. The passive, peaceful nature of the home and of the women tending it became a counterforce to the corrupting influences of the outside world. Andrew Carnegie realized the important role of women in culture and the arts when he noted on one of his trips that a lack of music seemed to be due to the absence of women, the "very soul of European civilization."[22]

Culture could be an antidote to the unruly outside world—a world that was being increasingly influenced by new machines, materialistic values, and immigrants. As an element of social control, culture might be a means of calming troubled waters and warding off the threats of class warfare, labor unrest, and even potential revolutions. For the theater, the turn from intellectualism to sentimentality and the quest for an escape from the corrupting influences of the outside world were reflected in the surge of melodramas. The troupes performing *Uncle Tom's Cabin* became more absorbed in portraying the drama of the personal crises of Eva and Topsy than in focusing on the social ills of slavery that provoked Harriet Beecher Stowe. As entertainment, the melodramas popular in this era provided excitement as villains were vanquished and heroines were rewarded. But they provided few cerebral challenges. When people poured into the local opera house in Salida, Colorado to see the popular melodrama *East Lynne*, they were hoping to be entertained and diverted.

That interest of so many women in their local opera houses has continued in the twentieth and twenty-first centuries as women have spearheaded efforts to prevent the destruction of these halls and then to encourage their revivals. In Newberry, South Carolina (where women barricaded the opera house to ward off the wrecking ball), East Haddam, Connecticut, and David City, Nebraska women have led local campaigns to resuscitate their opera houses. It is clear that women's "sivilizing" influence continues.

CHAPTER 3

Culture and the Public

During the Gilded Age in the last decades of the nineteenth century, the popularity of opera was partly due to its respectability. In contrast to theater with its reputation of dissolute actors and raunchy audiences, opera evoked a "high-class exclusiveness," as sociologist Richard Butsch states in *The Making of American Audiences*.[1] That exclusiveness was evident in New York City where an interest in music merged with a powerful desire to be in the social whirl. When the Astors, Morgans, Vanderbilts, and other social leaders could not get boxes in New York's popular and over-booked Academy of Music, they banded together to provide themselves a new and grand opera house, the Metropolitan Opera House. When the building committee chairman for the new opera house announced before it was designed that "no Theater or Opera House in this country . . . can be taken as a model for what we intend to have," he was correct.[2] It was grand. Ever since the 1840s elaborate opera houses and music halls had been built in major American cities, but it was New York's 1883 Metropolitan Opera House that captured the headlines and became the envy of operagoers throughout the country.

Thousands of smaller towns and cities were not to be outdone. Soon they, too, boasted elegant opera houses in handsome buildings with cherubs dancing around the walls, velvet-covered "opera chairs," gilded designs, frescoes, elaborate chandeliers, many curtains, balconies, boxes (fancily called "loges"), as well as large stages with ornately decorated proscenia and many dressing rooms. This grandeur and extravagant decoration in theaters, not previously known in such places, was a

Interiors of opera houses like Burlington, Vermont's 1879 Howard Opera House could be as elegant as a New York theater. *Special Collections, University of Vermont Bailey/Howe Library*

Victorian way of displaying status. As Victorian parlors were busy with velvet curtains, Tiffany-style lamps, Persian rugs, gilded chairs, and many paintings, so too were the interiors of Victorian theaters fancily decorated.

The high-style theaters of the Gilded Age appeared not only in the large, fashionable cities but also in cities and towns of all sizes. In the boomtown of Leadville, Colorado in the Rockies in 1879, local silver magnate Horace Tabor built the three-story Tabor Opera House, touted as "the largest and best west of the Mississippi."[3] It was an impressive building with an exterior of imported stone and brick and stores on the ground floor separated by the opera house entrance of double doors, which led to a spacious lobby and stairs wide enough for a regiment of soldiers. The second-floor opera house, with carpeted, mirrored boxes flanking each side and a large balcony, was luxury itself. There were parquet floors, a frescoed ceiling, Andrews patented orchestra seats just like those in New York theaters, seventy-two gas jets, "furnace warmed" air, good ventilation, fire-extinguishing arrangements, and curtains with romantic and distant scenes. But unlike many opera houses, its dressing rooms were large and well appointed. And all this was built in one hundred days at the height of Leadville's boom and even before the railroad had arrived there.

Likewise, the Brown Grand Opera House in Concordia, Kansas, constructed by Colonel Napoleon Bonaparte Brown to replace an earlier opera house that had burned down, was hailed as the most elegant between Kansas City and Denver. The *Boston Herald* reported the new

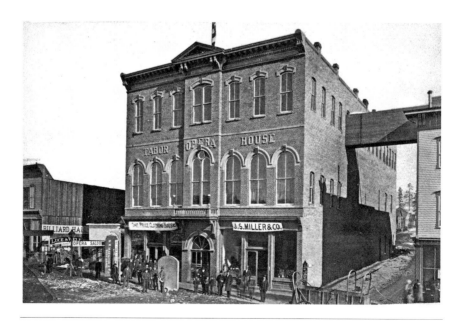

Leadville, Colorado's handsome Tabor Opera House was built in 1879 by silver magnate Horace Tabor before the railroad reached Leadville. A second-floor walkway connected the opera house to the hotel. *History Colorado*

Bennington Opera House in Bennington, Vermont, dedicated by the governor in 1892, to be "by far the best of Vermont, and one of the best in New England outside of Boston," amid the hundreds of opera houses in New England.[4] On December 31, 1890, opening night of the Bourbon Opera House in Paris, Kentucky, the *Kentuckian-Citizen* reporter described the opera house's auditorium as "the handsomest room in the State" and the opera house itself as "the pride of our people—'a thing of beauty, a joy forever.'"[5]

Superlatives abounded when town fathers described their new opera houses. These buildings became local landmarks, not just because they were grand with fancy interiors but also because these towns could now have culture like New York and Boston or even Paris and Vienna. Shakespeare and Wagner now came to Leadville, Colorado. Understandably, the halls evoked enormous pride as well as a confidence that their towns now had a new respectability and permanence. They had arrived.

Most opera houses were private ventures of ambitious local entrepreneurs, although sometimes others took the initiative, like local workmen in New Britain, Connecticut and two women in Lisbon, North Dakota. Often part of a row of attached commercial buildings on Main Street, opera houses could be identified by large windows on the second floor often coursing upward through a third story, a parapet, or a sign or incised letters indicating that the building was an "opera house" and its dates of construction. Willa Cather's Red Cloud Opera House was typical of many small-town opera houses. Embedded in a commercial block on Webster Street, the town's main thoroughfare, the building's triangular peak with the words "Opera House 1885" differentiated it from the other brick buildings on either side. Two local businessmen built it and their commercial establishments, the Morhart & Fulton hardware store and Mizer's grocery store, occupied space on the ground floor. Between the two stores was a double door opening onto a wide staircase, which led to a second-floor hall with the ticket booth and entrance to the performance hall directly ahead. This was a flat-floored hall with little ornamentation; it had a stage at one end and 500 wooden chairs, which could be moved around to accommodate different events ranging from basketball to theater to political rallies. Simple as it sounds, the building was considered an important landmark in Red Cloud. The local newspaper, the *Chief*, which spurred interest in constructing the opera house, found it and the Red Cloud Bank to be among "the handsomest buildings in town."[6]

The 1885 Red Cloud (Nebraska) Opera House, in Willa Cather's hometown, prepared for the 1903 high school graduation ceremony. *Willa Cather Foundation*

   While the second-floor opera house was a common design solution, simple one-story and more elaborate upper-story structures could be found everywhere. Many upper-story opera houses followed the same pattern of the second-floor halls by renting ground-floor spaces to retail establishments, which were essential to support the usually unprofitable theater and entertainment activities. The halls with three or more stories could be very grand, indicating the town had achieved a level of prosperity warranting a lavish hall. Architects were often hired, and no expense was spared. A front curtain in Fremont, Nebraska's Love Opera House cost $900. With handsome exteriors and fancily decorated interiors with parquet and dress circles, balconies, boxes, frescoed walls, and sometimes large domes, many of these larger opera houses benefited from the philanthropy of a single local entrepreneur. In Leadville, Colorado, it was Mr. Tabor; in Aspen, Colorado, Mr. Wheeler; in Bennington, Vermont, Mr. Putnam; and in Fremont, Nebraska, Mr. Love. Today, having withstood the vicissitudes of changing tastes and calamities, especially fire, a considerable number of these larger opera houses, especially those in stone buildings, still stand proudly. These elaborate buildings were symbols of local pride when they were built and again today as many are enjoying a renaissance.

Some opera houses, like the thousand-seat Love Opera House, which were attached to other buildings in then-thriving commercial areas, stand alone now, as their neighboring commercial structures have disappeared through demolition, neglect, or urban renewal. However, other handsome opera houses such as the well-known Goodspeed Opera House in East Haddam, Connecticut were built as "loners," that is, as single, unattached buildings—and persist as significant local landmarks.

Hotels, however humble, appeared early in the development of towns, as they were essential for a thriving town and opera house. This is demonstrated in Julius Cahn's *Theatrical Directories*, whose entries included essential details of their local hostelries. Poor lodging had been one of the curses of touring troupes, so it is not surprising that Fremont's handsome Love Opera House advertised itself not only as the "Finest and Most Complete in the State" but also as "well located as to hotel and street cars." An example of the symbiosis of theaters and lodging, John A. Stevens built both the opera house (1886) and an adjoining hotel (1889) in Garden City, Kansas. In Colorado, the opera houses in Leadville and Central City benefited from adjacent hotels, which provided not only lodging for traveling performers but also a gathering place before and after shows. Aside from serving continuously as lodging for both actors and tourists, the Teller Hotel, still functioning as a hotel next door to Central City's opera house, had provided an early venue for plays and concerts. In Leadville, the Clarendon Hotel was attached to the opera house by a third-floor walkway. Such hotels enabled actors to enjoy comfort and convenience in remote places. Horace Tabor himself had an elaborate suite in his opera house where he entertained dignitaries such as General Ulysses S. Grant, who visited when the railroad came to Leadville in July 22, 1880, and stayed in the adjacent Clarendon Hotel. Hotels became more than a convenience; they were a lure to attract top performers, especially in off-the-beaten-path towns like Leadville and Central City.

Confirming the importance of opera houses in the life of towns, opera houses literally came to be part of city halls. This happened in places as scattered as Bozeman, Montana; Dothan, Alabama; Stoughton, Wisconsin; and Claremont, New Hampshire. Sometimes a town hall even evolved into an opera house. Hudson, New York's 1855 City Hall, which housed the local bank and the Franklin Library as well as the municipal offices, became known as the Hudson Opera House around 1880. On its first floor were the city offices (the post office, police station, and Common Council), while its second-floor auditorium became the "opera house" where plays, lectures, musicals, dances, and many public meetings and expositions took place. In the hamlet of South Londonderry, Vermont, tucked into the Green Mountains, the 1859 town hall, which had its rear extended to make room for a larger stage and its front altered to accommodate a ticket booth and access to the balcony, is now primarily an opera house.

It is ironic that New England, the area of the United States most antagonistic to theater in the eighteenth and early nineteenth centuries, embedded opera houses in or added them to many town halls in the late 1800s. As the moral absolutes against fun-loving activities frayed and the rest of the country was enjoying theater, opera, and entertainments, New England did not want to be left behind. For many New England towns, theater and entertainment came to be seen almost as a public service in publicly built and maintained buildings.

The burst of opera house construction in New England occurred in the second half of the nineteenth century, especially in the 1870s, 1880s, and 1890s. Many existing town halls and meetinghouses then were considered inadequate or in bad repair, so the vogue of opera houses was well timed to meet the needs of a growing number of more sophisticated townspeople and new or expanded town halls. For decades, Brattleboro, Vermont's 1855 Town House had served as the venue for town meetings and public events, such as concerts by choral groups and local bands or lectures by out-of-towners such as Mark Twain and Henry Ward Beecher. There were rooms to spare in the Town House, which housed the post office, stores, and private offices, including a studio for Beaux Arts architect William Morris Hunt. However, by the 1890s, it was clear that this once-adequate town hall no longer met community needs. The town wanted a "festival hall" for expositions, including popular poultry shows, and an "opera house" for local and out-of-town performances. Thus, at the annual town meeting in 1895, Brattleboro approved $25,000 for major renovations to meet these needs without any mention of the immorality of theatergoing or the building's public costs in the minutes of the meeting. The "Opera House," a fifty-foot addition to the rear of the building, modeled on New York's Abbey Theater, was dedicated in 1896.[7] Its double balconies, ornate boxes, good acoustics, and "well-appointed" stage made the town an appealing stop for traveling companies on trains traveling between New York and Montreal.

Barre, Vermont, nationally known as the leading source for granite tombstones, is a small New England city that persevered through catastrophes of snow and fire to maintain a combined city hall and opera house, which is still thriving today. In 1860 the citizens of Barre voted at its town meeting to build a town hall, which was expanded in 1882 to include a stage in the second-floor town space, referred to as the "opera house" and used for public meetings as well as for entertainment, lectures, and plays.[8] The life of this new, expanded town hall was cut short when three years later its roof caved in under the weight of snow and rain. The next year another town hall was built at a new site, but it succumbed in 1898 to the most common catastrophe for public buildings, fire. Once again, a new town hall and opera house arose the next year.

That new—and handsome—four-story granite and brick town hall/city hall and opera house, facing the town square, was considered the finest theater in Vermont when it was built in 1899. By this time, the city's requirements had grown, with a water department, city engineer, assessor, various courtrooms, aldermen's rooms, police headquarters, city lockup, and even a room for the fire alarm system all requiring space in the new building. However, there was still room for the Opera House seating more than 1,200, with 850 on the floor, 350 in the horseshoe gallery, and four boxes with wood-veneered chairs to blend with the hall's interior finish. Elaborate curtains depicted "a splendid scene on the Grand Canal in Venice" on the main curtain, and a street scene, autumn landscapes, and other varied settings on the drop and wing scenes. Unlike most opera houses in communities the size of Barre (population of approximately 8,500 in 1900), the floor was raked, so only plays, meetings, and lectures could occur there, not basketball games or roller skating. Its entrance was distinctly separate from the Town Hall's entrance. Ten days after the building was dedicated on August 5, 1899, the first city meeting was held there, and its first theatrical event, Mildred Holland in *Two Little Vagrants*, on August 23.

With its large Italian population of masons and granite workers, Barre had a ready-made audience for opera, so aside from the usual lectures and plays by traveling troupes and local groups, there was serious opera. Local Italians organized an opera company, which performed for years at the opera house. Today the building still functions as it did in 1900 with both a city hall with municipal offices and an opera house. Much of its original interior is still intact, including ornamented boxes, glass fanlights, and a pressed-metal ceiling, following an extensive renovation during the 1980s that improved access and provided a new main entrance in the rear adjacent to the parking area.

Barre, Vermont's third and current city hall-opera house, built in 1899. Its opera house continues to flourish and now has a new rear entrance. *Author photograph for front* (top photo), *Holly Simpson for rear* (bottom photo).

Across the Connecticut River, two New Hampshire towns with flourishing mills in the late nineteenth century, Claremont and Lebanon, have impressive town halls with large opera houses, both designed by Dartmouth graduates, Claremont's by Charles A. Rich in 1897 and Lebanon's by the Hanover, New Hampshire firm Larson & Wells in 1923. Both halls are prominently located in the center of their communities facing their town squares with the buildings' main entrances used for the opera houses. In Lebanon, while the engraved sign over the main entrance says "City Hall," the municipal offices are now located on the side of the building with the opera house using the main front entrance. In Claremont the first-floor city offices and the opera house are approached by the same front door, but two broad staircases lead to the gilded, frescoed second-floor opera house. Claremont's 1897 opera house, which cost $62,000, was built much earlier than Lebanon's 1924 opera house, but Lebanon's is slightly larger than Claremont's. However, Claremont's earlier start meant that it enjoyed the entertainment of road companies' plays, musicals, minstrel shows, and vaudeville in the heyday of opera house activities as well as local musical, theatrical, and political events. Today both opera houses are active again, with Lebanon's known for its outstanding Opera North performances and programs.

In many small towns, the opera house has been in the town hall, which is often the only large public space in a town. Vergennes, Vermont is a good example. This small city with an 1890 population of 1,773 has juggled municipal and entertainment activities in the same hall for more than a century. The town clerk, all the town offices (except for the police, who now have a separate building), and the opera house share the same building. However, it is in the second-floor opera house where the town council and public meetings are held. In Hudson and Salem, New York, all of the town's municipal offices and cultural facilities, such as the opera house and library, were located in one public building. In Mineral Point, Wisconsin, its hundred-year-old multipurpose city hall, library, and opera house building continues to function as the city's municipal and cultural center.

At the end of the nineteenth century at a time of new enthusiasm for public libraries spurred by Carnegie's gifts, multipurpose cultural buildings were built by important local entrepreneurs or wealthy families to commemorate family members. And they are often exceedingly handsome and almost lavish.

The imposing Richardsonian Romanesque Mabel Tainter Memorial Theater in the small lumber town of Menomonie, Wisconsin is such an example, with a gilded interior, Tiffany windows, Turkish rugs, and a handsome arched entry. Today considered one of the top-ten American historic theaters by the League of Historic American Theatres, this cultural center was built in 1890 by lumber magnate Andrew Tainter in memory of his daughter. He established a nonprofit corporation to own and carry on the building's purposes: theater space for lectures, instructions, musical concerts, "dramatic representations," and provision of a "free library and reading room"—all to "promote general interest in any lawful games and modes of amusement," a progressive proposal for that time. The Tainter survived with lectures, school functions, and plays, never as many as in larger cities; the Crago Players, a surviving Midwestern stock company, were still performing there regularly in the 1930s. By the 1950s the theater was empty, but the library and other rooms were still being used. Until its more recent renovation, the Tainter suffered like most opera houses from a period of poor maintenance and makeshift uses. Its library is now the Laura Ingalls Wilder Information Highway, as the author of the *Little House* series was born in nearby Pepin County in 1867.

Salem, New York, a rural town abutting the Vermont border with an 1890 population of just over 3,000, enjoyed a combined library and opera house, thanks to public support and local philanthropy. The first step in this venture was an election when the town's library supporters defeated those promoting a village water system. In 1886, a $13,000 town bond issue augmented Benjamin Bancroft's $12,000 gift for a town library, and then in 1889 the children of prominent local resident A. M. Proudfit added $5,000 to enlarge the hall. Thus in 1890 Salem's Main Street was graced with a new building housing Bancroft Library and Proudfit Hall, the opera house and venue for entertainments. There was also space in this building, designed by Boston architects Sturgis and Cabot, for the village offices, police department, local hook-and-ladder company, post office, and commercial tenants.

Despite the town's Presbyterian heritage, Salem was well endowed with entertainment halls. Proudfit Hall was by far the largest, seating 700 people, but there was also a hundred-seat assembly room on the fourth floor in the town's public school, Washington Academy, and three were "opera houses" and halls of different sizes in four other buildings. These included the Odd Fellows Hall; one on the second floor of the Maxwell

Hardware building; and another, popular with roller skaters, on the third floor of the Fairchild Block. But it was in Proudfit Hall where most of the plays, especially by out-of-town groups, took place as well as lectures, balls, minstrel shows, musicals, and local events like high school graduations and basketball games. A new central school with a gymnasium and stage, opening in 1939, usurped some of the activities previously held in Proudfit Hall, but the death knell for the hall was a devastating fire in 1976.

Everyone knows of Andrew Carnegie's libraries, but what is not widely known is that many of his libraries also had music halls. These music halls, which Carnegie considered important to the cultural well-being of a city, remain significant in the musical and theatrical life of cities where they are located. After Carnegie's early library projects, he then built libraries with music halls in the 1890s in Pittsburgh, Munhall, and Allegheny City, just across the Allegheny River from Pittsburgh. Allegheny City's music hall, equipped with one of the largest pipe organs in the world and a city-paid organist, held free standing-room-only concerts three days a week, organ concerts at lunch, and plays at other times.[9] The writer Theodore Dreiser when a reporter in 1894 in Allegheny City was said to have enjoyed these lunch-hour concerts so much that his antipathy toward Carnegie's robber-baron treatment of his employees somewhat abated.

This multipurpose nature of opera houses—with town halls, libraries, or churches—reflects the importance of these halls in the civic, social, and cultural life of towns of all sizes. Whether publicly or privately built, incorporating these halls into public buildings indicated culture was considered a civic responsibility.

The mushrooming of opera houses resulted from a phenomenal surge of interest in entertainment and culture, increased leisure, changed attitudes toward recreation and entertainment, and the railroad. In older towns and cities, as well as newer settlements, people wanted to be abreast of current cultural and entertainment activities—and have some fun.

Yet as modern America with all its sweeping changes was emerging, it also retreated into a safer haven of domestic and often sentimental values, leaving behind some of the more vigorous intellectualism of earlier times. Melodramas like *East Lynne* were overtaking *Richard III*. The swelling numbers of performers, opera houses, and patrons, however, compensated for the loss of cerebral challenges. Ironically, most patrons, who were establishing new lives in the burgeoning new territories or in the western parts of settled states, wanted mainstream entertainment from the very places from which they fled. They could not escape the fact that the urban East or the homelands of immigrants set the standards of culture and civilization for them and their opera houses.

PART TWO

On Stage

Performances, Performers, and Patrons

CHAPTER 4

Early Struggles

George Washington, along with ten friends and family members in the winter of 1787, was enjoying the Old American Company's performance of one of Washington's favorite plays, *The School for Scandal*. They sat on cushioned seats in a stage box adorned with red draperies and the United States' coat of arms at the South Street Theater in Philadelphia, at a time when ardent Philadelphia Quakers strongly objected to theater. In fact, the South Street Theater, also known as the Southwark Theater, was located just outside the city to avoid the Quakers' antitheatrical codes. Like the Puritans of New England, the Quakers along with Presbyterians and other concerned religious sects tried to squelch theater in Philadelphia and Pennsylvania with bans and legislation. But, they did not succeed for long. As early as 1723, comedians were performing beyond the city limits of Philadelphia to escape these Quaker restrictions. In 1759 Governor William Denny overrode the vocal Quaker opposition to theater and allowed actor David Douglass to build the South Street Theater. However, the next year the Pennsylvania Assembly passed a law banning all plays, which city officials tried to enforce, only to have the law repealed in 1761 by King George III of England. By the time the Washingtons attended *The School for Scandal*, the Old American Company's performance was "by authority" because prominent Philadelphians had succeeded in persuading the Assembly to repeal the antitheater law.[1]

Some years later, in 1792, actors in Boston raised money through subscriptions to build a theater, carefully named the "New Exhibition Hall" to avoid problems with the local Puritans. The popularity of their lectures, dialogues, and various other entertainments emboldened them to put on plays openly. However, that initiative came to a halt on December 5, when the sheriff interrupted a performance of *The School for Scandal* on the grounds that it violated the antitheater law. The audience argued that the performance should continue, but the Boston authorities, tougher than their brothers in Philadelphia, closed the theater and arrested the co-manager of the hall. The incident, however, did spur Bostonian theater lovers to get the antitheater law repealed in 1793 and then launch another subscription drive for a permanent theater, opened in 1794 and boldly called the "Boston Theatre."

Within the next century, the entire country, including the laggards in Boston and New England, enjoyed a flowering of theater and entertainments. Theater survived and even flourished despite protestations through the ages, from Plato in the fourth century B.C.; the Puritans, Quakers, and European Catholics in the seventeenth and eighteenth centuries; and from the Methodist Church, which finally in 1939 removed its ban on theatergoing from its Doctrines and Discipline. As late as 1920, the Methodists looked "with deep concern ... on the general prevalence of harmful amusements, and lift up a solemn note of warning and entreaty, particularly against theater-going."[2] Even some Episcopalians, usually considered sophisticated, held on to antitheater sentiment until the late nineteenth century. When the actor Joseph Jefferson tried in 1870 to arrange a funeral service at his local Episcopal church in New York City for his friend, the well-known actor George Holland, the Reverend Lorenzo Sabine refused to perform the service because the deceased was an actor. However, the minister suggested the "little church around the corner," the Church of the Transfiguration, where the Reverend George Hamilton did conduct the funeral service for Holland. The Reverend Sabine's denial aroused a vigorous outcry, which was offset by the enthusiastic response of the theater world to the Church of the Transfiguration, known ever since as "The Little Church Around the Corner" and favored by actors and artists.

For theater to survive over the years and overcome such deep-seated hostility, true passion was needed by all those associated with it. This passion, bolstered by determination, spurred actors, managers, and opera house owners faced with fines, jail, and debt to continue offering public entertainments under adverse conditions. Warding off naysayers' hostility to theater bound thespians into a tight community as they closed ranks. Despite intermittent hostility to theater over the centuries, audiences of all stripes welcomed theater's dramatization of everyday life with its mysteries, glamour, and fears. The sociability of theatergoing, including companionship and shared reactions, added to the pleasures of attending theater.

It was in small-town opera houses where most Americans enjoyed theater during the last half of the nineteenth century. Through their opera house experiences, they could connect with the plays' ideas and situations involving moral dilemmas as well as with the culture and memories of the old country or their former homes in the East. There also were connections with neighbors and townspeople as well as between audiences and performers and among performers themselves. Willa Cather recalled how thrilling it was to be transported from the Red Cloud Opera House to Madame Danglars's salon in Paris when Frank Lindon performed in *The Count of Monte Cristo* in December 1888. At a time of great societal disruption when new, powerful, yet remote industries and monopolies were changing the way of life and values of ordinary people, these connections provided essential uplift, escape, and enrichment.

The vernacular heritage of theater, with performances in streets, marketplaces, and cathedral districts, created a lively, infectious, and sometimes rowdy atmosphere. Jesters in street dramas, fools in morality plays, and performers in the medieval fair midways were part of this long history of vernacular drama, which produced for some an uneasy feeling. Although the scholar of homo ludens, Dutch historian Johan Huizinga considered "genuine, pure play … one of the main bases of civilization," critics of theater have felt differently. In fact, attitudes toward fun and play have been at the root of much criticism of theater over the years.[3] Such critics feared what Huizinga saw as the heart of the play: the freedom of losing oneself to other worlds, "a stepping out of 'real' life into a temporary sphere of activity with a disposition all of its own."[4] Undoubtedly, that spell worried opponents of theater, who saw playgoing as engaging people too deeply. Instead of refreshing, plays dissipated playgoers, impeded work by weakening the will to be industrious, and would "kindle a very hell of lusts within your soules," according to William Prynne, who lost his ears in 1634 when the king interpreted his antitheater book as a reflection on royal entertainments.[5] The Puritans' rigid Calvinist objections were partly a reaction to the degenerate lifestyle of the upper classes and the newly minted rich in England. They believed that dancing and theater, like most amusements, would lead people to the wanton idleness of the English upper classes and monarchy, who danced, watched performers, enjoyed cockfights, played cards, and bowled. These severe decrees on amusements, and particularly theater, can be seen as a strong surge of republicanism. Yet ironically, later democratization undermined the strictures regarding theater and amusements.

As the Puritans clamped down on public amusements in England in the sixteenth and seventeenth centuries, across the Channel in Flanders medieval morality plays and street drama became popular. Every town had its own theatrical troupe and *rederijkerskamer*, or literary society, which sponsored public and private drama as well as poetry performances. Performed on a temporary stage, often in a public square, the drama of these *rederijkers* consisted of humorous plays, farces, and serious allegorical plays. The audience of craftsmen, artisans, and shopkeepers in towns and cities reveled in the performances, as portrayed in Bruegel's paintings. Large cities like Brussels had major *rederijkers*, including processions with

A theater in a bustling marketplace in the Lowlands in the sixteenth century. This line engraving by H. Cook was made from a drawing by Peter Bruegel the Elder. *Richard Southern Collection, University of Bristol Theatre Collection/ArenaPal*

many floats and hundreds of *rederijkers* on horseback, which were enjoyed by both upper and lower classes.

Although these allegorical plays balanced entertainment and moral instruction, comedy was a major component.[6] Audiences having fun and laughing—throwing away the cares of the world—at the raucous behavior of these *rederijkers* confirms the observation of Johan Huizinga that "the spirit of an age is better revealed in its mode of regarding and expressing trivial and commonplace things than in the high manifestations of philosophy and science."[7]

Flemish enjoyment of its *rederijkers* contrasted with a pervasive hostility to theater. The grounds for opposition to theater were many: social factors such as unruly audiences, unreliable troupes, dissolute actors, vulgar performances, and obscene language, as well as moral objections such as imitation, competition with the church, threats to diligence and work, and promotion of sexuality. Visions of Roman orgies, drunken dandies cavorting with prostitutes, riotous theater crowds spilling onto city streets, and untrustworthy actors fleeing towns without paying their bills swirled in people's minds when theater was mentioned—and with some reason. Not only Puritans, but Catholic Europe also objected to theater. Molière's popular *Don Juan* was censored after its first production in 1665; its full text was not printed until ten years after his death and then not in France, but in Amsterdam, far removed from the French censors. For Molière the final blow was the denial of last rites after he died in 1673, as he refused to renounce the world of theater, which was required of actors for burial in consecrated ground. However, after friends successfully petitioned the archbishop of Paris and the king, Molière was buried in a churchyard.

Objections to theater appeared in bursts, especially when theater was prospering, whether in ancient Greece, Renaissance England, or seventeenth-century France. In American colonies and the newly independent nation, hostility to theater peaked in the eighteenth and early nineteenth centuries when Congregationalists, Quakers, and Presbyterians all feared the evils of thespian activities. Such fears still haunt the entertainment world as movies are graded for their probity and recordings are threatened with censure. Two different but interwoven lines of opposition to theater, one philosophical and the other pragmatic, keep reappearing throughout history in outcroppings of antitheater venom.[8]

Imitation and its effects have been at the core of this philosophical opposition. Acting does not produce original creations but counterfeit copies, and such imitation can be formative as an actor may become whom he imitates in words and spirit. Plato expressed this line of opposition, but he has been joined by such diverse supporters as Hobbes, Wordsworth, Nietzsche, and many church spokespersons through the ages. For the prominent Presbyterian and sixth president of Princeton University, John Witherspoon, the concern was simply "the loss of sense of sincerity and truth in those who assume characters other than themselves."[9] For later critics of theater and its imitative qualities, there were other objections. Hobbes disliked the feigned or artificial person; Nietzsche thought such imitation erased men's identities; and the church's suspicions ranged from concern about parodying the sacraments to theater's vilifying effects on viewers. Although "old hatred has ebbed," as the scholar of theatrical prejudice Jonas Barish notes, the queasiness about theater has never totally disappeared.[10]

While Christianity was rife with concerns about theater's licentious spectacles, its enervation of the soul, and its competition with the pulpit, the hostility to theater in the United States was directly rooted in Puritanism in England. The English Puritans' concerns about theater reflected not only their joy-killing asceticism but also their criticism of royal pleasure-seeking, and later their uneasiness with changes that industrialism's new wealth was creating. Accepted moral and social codes and older rank and status were being challenged, the division between town and country was widening (London's population tripled from 1650 to 1750), and the gap between rich and poor was growing. Theater was both popular and democratic at this time. In a ten-year period at the end of the sixteenth century, London's famed Rose, Swan, and Globe theaters were built, all on the south bank of the Thames, outside the city limits, because various city laws curtailed such entertainment. Going to the theater was cheaper than drinking a quart of ale at the pub, so workmen joined men of all ranks in the audience. In fact, not until the introduction of movies was there such broad patronage of theater.

Yet a buildup of timeworn grievances, including the fear that theater was encouraging idleness, threatening social order, and even causing the spread of infectious diseases, led the recently empowered Puritans to get Parliament to close down the theaters in 1642. Theater's degenerative influence, Sunday performances, men in the roles of women, sumptuous playhouses, and effete aristocratic patrons just whetted the Puritans' fears. Adam Smith worried that theater attendees were spectators, not the rational and productive citizens needed to stoke the economy's fires.

With liquor flowing freely in theaters, the audiences were often unruly, only bolstering public concern for social control.

With this hefty inheritance of prejudices against theater, it is not surprising that the Puritans settling on the shores of New England in the seventeenth century disdained thespian activities. Establishing communities and churches, preparing land for farming and homesteads, and organizing town governments left little time for recreational pursuits even if they were approved. But as their society matured, frontiers moved westward, and New England grew, the economy diversified and the tough theocracy evolved into a political and more secular state. Gradually, there was more spare time and interest in education and pleasure—including plays.

A divide in attitudes toward theater arose between the North and the South in the eighteenth century, with theater flourishing in the South, both in cities and in the countryside, with traveling troupes performing on courthouse steps and in parlors of private houses. Accompanying this divide was a rift in the attitudes toward theater between educated English settlers and commoner Americans. In the North "the playhouse was still considered the highway to hell."[11] Minister Increase Mather, not known for his playfulness, supported the Puritan ethic, and New England states translated that ethic into stiff antitheater legislation.

Massachusetts led the way. Its 1750 Act to Prevent Stage-Plays and Other Theatrical Amusements declared that such activities "not only occasion great and unnecessary expenses, and discourage industry and frugality, but likewise tend generally to increase immorality, impiety, and a contempt of religion."[12] Other New England states passed similar laws, which they tried to enforce with jail terms and fines. A troupe in 1761 was not allowed to perform in Portsmouth, New Hampshire, because its House of Representatives thought plays had "a peculiar influence on the minds of young people and greatly endanger their morals by giving them a taste for intriguing, amusement and pleasure."[13] That did not daunt brave thespians, who performed plays surreptitiously in private homes, taverns, "lecture halls," and "museums" throughout New England. Harvard and Yale students produced plays in 1760; this was more dangerous for the Yale students, considering the rigidity of Connecticut's blue laws, reflected in their college President Timothy Dwight's pronouncement as late as 1824 that "to indulge a taste for playgoing means nothing more or less than the loss of the most valuable treasure, the immortal soul."[14] In Massachusetts, Nathaniel Ames, who participated in plays at Harvard, later played in performances in Dedham and Boston in the 1760s and 1770s with no interference from the gendarmes since these performances seemed to be private and orderly occasions. Other New Englanders, such as the prominent Bostonian Josiah Quincy, enjoyed theater in New York: in fact, he would have gone to every performance if he had been there for a month. "But as a citizen and friend of the morals and happiness of society I should strive hard against the admission and much more the establishment of a playhouse in any state of which I was a member," Quincy reported when he returned to a theaterless Boston in 1773.[15]

In 1761 Hallam's American Company, popular with George Washington and armed with a letter of support from Virginia's lieutenant governor William Dinwiddie, tried to bring its thespian fare to Newport, Rhode Island. But even that city, considered sophisticated, voted to ban theater. Not daunted by the town's action, prominent Newport citizens urged the troupe to continue, which it did, attracting large audiences. Returning to Newport the next year, the troupe was so well received that it decided to move on to Providence, where once again its plays were enthusiastically received by large crowds from as far away as Massachusetts and Connecticut. However, antitheater mobs attacked the school where the American Company was playing, and the militia was called in to quell the disturbance.

In spite of many hurdles, New Englanders were being exposed more and more to plays and other entertainments by the mid-nineteenth century, as Nathaniel Hawthorne describes in his 1852 *Blithedale Romance* about the Brook Farm–like community near Boston.

> The scene was one of those Lyceum halls, of which almost every village has now its own, dedicated to that sober and pallid . . . mode of winter-evening entertainment, the Lecture. . . . [T]here is a rich and varied series of other exhibitions. Hither comes the ventriloquist, with all his mysterious tongues; the thaumaturgist [magician], too, with his miraculous transformations. . . . Here, also, the itinerant professor instructs separate classes of ladies and gentlemen in physiology. . . . Here is to be heard the choir of Ethiopian melodists, and to be seen, the diorama of Moscow or Bunker Hill, or the moving panorama of the Chinese wall. . . . Here is displayed the museum of wax figures, illustrating the wide catholicism of earthly renown. . . . And here, in this many-purposed hall, (unless the selectmen of the

village chance to have more than their share of the puritanism) . . .
the company of strolling players sets up its little stage, and claims
patronage for the legitimate drama.[16]

Whether in a museum or "lyceum hall," more than lectures were taking
place in these New England halls—and not so surreptitiously, thanks to
the remarkable passion of actors, entertainers, and eager audiences.

CHAPTER 5

Theater Thrives

It was a different story in the South where the cultivated colonists brought many aristocratic English tastes and customs, including theater. Williamsburg, the capital in 1699, became an early theatrical hub: William and Mary students performed plays for the governor in 1702, plays were staged in a theater in 1716, and later Hallam's troupe performed there in 1752. Attending plays, mostly by traveling English troupes, was a socially accepted and popular activity. When the Cherokee emperor and empress and their family were in Williamsburg for the governor's inauguration, they were taken to Hallam's production of *Othello*, which was so realistic that the empress almost sent one of her guards to the stage to prevent a killing in a sword fight.[1]

Charleston quickly challenged Williamsburg as the seat for theater and won it. In fact, it remained a theatrical center for a century. Charleston's first dramatic season in the city's courtroom in 1735 featured *The Orphan* by Thomas Otway, whose prologue ridiculed New England's censorship of theater. Another first in that courtroom was the country's first musical production, *Flora*, also performed in 1735. The next year the Dock Street Theater was founded and continued at various sites and buildings, including a theater built in 1937 inside an old hotel with Works Progress Administration (WPA) staff and funds. In the 1773–1774 season, David Douglass's troupe produced fifty-eight plays, including twenty musicals. Charleston's receptivity to theater attracted productions and resident companies, the first in 1793, and playwrights such as William Ioor and John Blake, both of whom commented on social and political situations.

The patrons of Charleston's theater so enjoyed the productions that an 1820 letter to the editor of the *Charleston Courier* listed the benefits of theater: "imparts information . . . quickens thought . . . corrects taste . . . tends to introduce proper pronunciation . . . inculcates politeness, ease and grace and teaches society how to mingle together without jarring and collision."[2]

The colonial South was often exposed to the best of English drama by professional troupes, which toured in smaller cities and country towns. As taverns, courthouses, and newly organized theaters offered stages and eager audiences to traveling thespians and local amateur actors, a theatrical synergy developed. Word of this Southern interest in theater got out, so Northern actors such as Samuel Drake, Sol Smith, and Noah Ludlow formed companies that traveled by boat and stagecoach to perform all over the South.

In Kentucky, referred to as a Western state in the late eighteenth and early nineteenth centuries, eight plays had been performed by 1800. Within ten years of becoming a permanent settlement in 1779, Lexington called itself the "Athens of the West." It could boast of the first Western newspaper and the first university west of the Alleghenies (Transylvania Seminary). With a population of two thousand and lively trade, politics, and culture, Lexington became a major stop for those traveling west through central Kentucky. Along with concerts, dances, debates, and a variety of homegrown amusements, the city enjoyed the first amateur theater in the new West, as an unnamed tragedy and farce was performed by Transylvania students "in the presence of a very respectable audience" on April 26, 1790, according to the *Kentucky Gazette.* Seven years later a "Theatrical Society" in Mason County, an early settlement on the Ohio River, produced the second stage performance in Kentucky, consisting of three plays presented in the courthouse.[3]

Entertainment blossomed in Lexington with the opening of a new exhibition hall in 1797 featuring tumblers and other acrobats, then in vogue, and later Transylvania students performing plays, including the popular *Love a la Mode.* By 1799, two amateur groups were producing popular plays in the Lexington courthouse. Courthouses were sites for performances in many cities such as Pittsburgh, Cincinnati, and St. Louis before they had real theaters. By 1801 plays were advertised at a theater and then in 1802 Edward Moore's *The Tragedy of the Gamester* and John O'Keefe's *The Dead Alive; or, the Double Funeral* were performed at the Theatre in Lexington. The opening of the New Theatre by Lexington

businessman Luke Usher in October 1808 heralded a new era for thespians in Kentucky. "The audiences were gratified," according to the *Kentucky
Gazette*, "on their entrance of the Theatre, with a species of accommoda-
tion not heretofore known in this country—convenient and safe seats . . .
as in theatres in the Atlantic cities." Expressing the South's appreciation
of drama at a time when New Englanders were disguising plays as "moral
dialogues" and halls for plays as "museums," the *Gazette* in October 1808
discussed the respectable performance and the audience's pleasure in the
new dramatic opportunities.

> We cannot quit this subject, without congratulating the lovers of
> drama, and the friends of morality, upon the success of the first
> attempt which has been made to introduce a Theatre in the west-
> ern country. The fastidious and cynical may regret it—but the lib-
> eral minded and enlightened portion of society must be pleased. An
> entertainment, innocent and instructive, which makes us moralize
> whilst we enjoy pleasure, which brings home to the bosoms of men
> the works of genius, of learning and poetry, of such men as Addison
> and a Johnson, of a Dryden and Shakespeare, can have no other effect
> than to refine and polish, and amend the morals of society. Such have
> the impressions of every enlightened people, and such are ours.[4]

That enthusiasm for drama may well have accounted for the almost
six hundred productions of plays in Kentucky between 1790 and 1820
and may have spurred Kentucky's first professional theater manager,
Luke Usher, to organize a touring troupe and to control theaters in
Louisville, Frankfort, and Lexington. By the end of the century, when
Paris, Kentucky, just north of Lexington, opened its opera house, there
was another burst of journalistic enthusiasm in the *Kentuckian Citizen* on
December 31, 1890:

> With more than ordinary pleasure we congratulate our people on
> the completion and possession of this gem of the builders art, our
> Opera House. . . . As we stand on the stage commanding a general
> view of the hall, noting the perfection of its symmetrical and har-
> monious proportions, it makes one feel that he breathes the very
> atmosphere of music, and that he drinks in the spirit of the immor-
> tal dramas produced by Goethe, Wagner and other illustrious com-
> posers of the divine art.[5]

Actors and newly organized troupes were lured from the North to ply their trade in the new West and the South. Tales of the experiences of these early actors and their troupes illustrate the passion and commitment of the actors. Sarah Bernhardt gave solo performances in forsaken places like Waco, Texas during her 1905–1906 tour, after her gangrene-infected leg had been amputated in France; the Grand English Opera Company performed in weeklong stands in small towns with limited facilities; Joseph Jefferson endlessly portrayed Rip Van Winkle; and Blind Boone pounded away on the piano week after week. These early troupes' struggles and successes, especially in the new West and South, provide poignant pictures of the passion of the profession. While these itinerant troupes were often considered at the low end of professional theater, they displayed the outstanding qualities of the acting profession as it prospered in the nineteenth century: industry, passion, celebrity, and versatility.

From 1750, when English troupes like Hallam's introduced theater to Williamsburg and then struggled to do the same in New York, Philadelphia, and Rhode Island until 1900, there were remarkable changes in the world of acting. Once seen as spreading immoral and salacious messages, by the second half of the nineteenth century actors became admired as celebrities for their talents, although they were never fully respected as individuals. When theaters proliferated, so did the numbers of entertainers. In 1800, 150 professional actors were estimated to be performing in the country; by 1850 that number had risen to 722 and, according to the census, the number of actors and actresses kept doubling until 1890, when almost 10,000 actors were listed in the census.

Even though the number of actors increased radically from 1800 to 1850, theater was a precarious activity until midcentury. In the early nineteenth century, intrepid actors, really actor-managers, and their troupes, such as Hallam's American Company and David Douglass's, toured up and down the East Coast performing Shakespeare, Restoration plays, and contemporary dramas such as Oliver Goldsmith's *She Stoops to Conquer.* They produced many plays and performed many roles in often inadequate conditions, with sometimes inhospitable receptions and meager remuneration. City theaters such as the Boston Museum and Philadelphia's Walnut Street Theatre might have stock companies, which were like acting schools, run by managers who owned or leased a theater and hired actors. They often produced hundreds of plays in a season, sometimes a play a night, with Shakespeare a favorite. Although stock companies usually offered the benefit of a settled life, many actors from these companies joined touring groups.

The early theater was offered primarily by troupes, many from England and often family endeavors, performing mostly English plays since there were few American playwrights then. In the early 1800s, troupes like Drake's and Sol Smith's mobilized actors and family members to set off for the frontier, where theatrical prospects were brighter than in the North. Acting was still viewed as a disgraceful profession by many respectable Northerners. When Noah Ludlow decided to be an actor in 1813 and later joined Drake's troupe, his family went into mourning: "My mother's grief was very great, my sister drooped and became melancholy, my brother Joseph said little, and seemed to be unwilling to talk about me."[6] In 1928, Katharine Hepburn faced similar family reprobation from her father, who was "disgusted and heartsick over the fact that I wanted to act. Thought it a silly profession closely allied to street-walking."[7] Even in the 1950s, Cicely Tyson's religious mother threw her out of the house when she learned that Cicely wanted to be an actor and then did not speak to her daughter for two years.[8]

To appreciate the endurance and passion of the early traveling troupes, the tales of groups like Drake's and Sol Smith's are informative. Samuel Drake was a pioneer of drama in the West. Born in England, where he did some acting and theater management, he came to Boston in 1810. There he performed at the Federal Theater before becoming manager of John Bernard's theater in Albany, New York. After his wife died in 1814, Drake set off trouping from Albany to Kentucky with his family and actors enlisted from Bernard's theater, such as Noah Ludlow and Noble Luke Usher. Drake lined up theaters for his troupe in Lexington, Frankfort, and Louisville with the help of Usher's nephew. However, the troupe made many stops in upstate New York towns, where it performed after young Noah Ludlow had scouted out a place that could serve as a theater: first in Cherry Valley; then in Cooperstown, where James Fenimore Cooper attended one of his performances and, Ludlow recalled, "encouraged our pioneer efforts in the cause of Drama"; and then in Skaneateles, Herkimer, Onandago Hollow, Marlius, Utica, Auburn, Geneva, and Canandaiqua. Often their performances were the first ever seen in these towns. At Olean, Drake traded his wagons and horse for a flat-bottomed boat on which they floated for ten days down the Allegheny River to Pittsburgh, hitting sandbars, missing turns, and luckily finding lodging at farms along the way. In Pittsburgh Drake organized an orchestra for the "well-received" English comic opera *No Song, No Supper* and other comedies for the fall months.[9]

In November they were back on the ark, floating down the Ohio River to Kentucky, disembarkimg at Limestone, now Maysville, where they traded their boat for a horse and a small wagon. Fortunately, they found Kentuckians "kind and hospitable." They stayed in farmers' houses, since they discovered no inns on their slow trip to Lexington, Frankfort, and Louisville. Frankfort was their first stop, where they played from December 1815 to March 1816 to "the best-educated and most respectable people of the town and country," who appreciated their professionalism. Previously, Frankfort had been exposed only to strolling parties of two or three performers. A professional troupe like Drake's was "somewhat singular in the history of the stage" there, noted Noah Ludlow. The next stop was Louisville, where the troupe arrived in March, before the theater was ready for them. After painting the theater and readying it for their performances, for which Louisvillians were on "tip-toe expectation," their run lasted eleven weeks, with a filled house every night. Three thousand attended the last night's benefit for the company, a common practice for many traveling troupes. Ludlow described Lexington, the next stop, as "the seat of learning and aristocracy of wealth," where their run began in June and lasted through September, with an interruption for the "extreme heat." Returning to Frankfort when the legislature met, they performed *Othello* and *Macbeth*, Richard Brinsley Sheridan's *The Rivals*, and Thomas Morton's *Speed the Plough*, among other plays.[10]

For more than thirty years, from 1817 to 1851, Drake, Ludlow, and Sol Smith performed, often as the first professional troupe ever to perform places in the new West and South. They went first to Cincinnati by horse, then to Nashville, and then took another boat trip, this time on an old keel boat called "Noah's Ark," to Natchez to fill the 500-seat theater every night, and then to New Orleans, where they gave the first professional performance in English for 700 people in the French theater. Then back they went to Natchez, where people were "in high glee" when the troupe returned. In St. Louis, reached by Noah's Ark, they started a theater with subscriptions from an amateur theater group. Although their performances were well attended, they were forced to close down in the winter as the stoves provided inadequate heat. They then wandered around the South, performing in parlors, hotel ballrooms, and even in a room over a confectionery store in Huntsville, Alabama. Their audiences learned of the performances by word of mouth. In many of these thinly populated locales, Noah Ludlow reported, not surprisingly, the "wealthiest and best informed class" was the troupe's principal support, as these patrons "began to consider theatrical amusement necessary to their pleasure."[11] These actors loved their work, as Sol Smith wrote in his *Theatrical Management in the West and South for Thirty Years*. For Smith, one of the few early native-born actors from a rural background, a half-price ticket to *Highland Reel* at Mr. Bernard's Albany theater in New York convinced him that he was destined for the stage, not storekeeping as his family intended. With his "head full of acting from that time forward," Smith was able to become an apprentice at the Albany theater, where he met the Drakes.[12] For the next thirty years, with a break to study law, which he took up in his last years, his life was devoted to theater. Along with Drake and Ludlow, Smith played in Southern and Western towns and cities, forming his own company in 1823 and playing anywhere he could find money to pay his actors: small places such as Wellington, Virginia and Steubenville, Ohio, as well as in larger cities such as Pittsburgh and Cincinnati. Like the Drakes and Ludlow, he was ever on the move, on a circuit in upstate New York with stops in Schenectady, Utica, Saratoga, Rochester, Niagara, and even Toronto, Canada.

At Warren, Pennsylvania, his troupe embarked on two skiffs down the Allegheny River, where he met up with Drake and disembarked at Maysville, proceeded to many towns in Kentucky (Lexington, Paris, Harrodsburg, Versailles, Nicolesville), and then moved on to Natchez and New Orleans. His troupe wandered around Tennessee and Georgia, playing in many theaters built in a matter of days for their performances. Time and time again Drake, Ludlow, and Smith reported eager audiences, well-received performances, and educated, cultured patrons, even though their work was rarely remunerative. They were sustained by "more applause than wealth," noted Smith.[13]

As the lives of Smith and Drake suggest, over the years troupes split and reassembled, formed new troupes, and added recruits like the well-known stars Junius Brutus Booth, Edwin Forrest, Ellen Tree, and Tyrone Power, along with the talented wives and offspring of the principals, such as Julia Dean, daughter of Julia Drake and Edwin Dean. The theaters in which they performed became more substantial, their audiences more supportive, their repertoire more varied, and the travel logistics improved over the early flat-bottomed boats and horses. The commitment of these actors was certainly tested by all the physical and professional challenges of travel at this time. Their entire set, drops, wings, proscenium, curtain, and carpet, which could be put up or taken down in a few hours, were carried with them in a small wagon from town to town in Kentucky and then on the ark down the Ohio River to points south. In 1820, in another example of the commitment to the profession, Junius Brutus Booth, when playing the popular *Richard III* in a Richmond-Petersburg-Norfolk circuit, missed the carriage to Petersburg and had to walk twenty-five miles to get to the theater on time.

While these early and even later troupes have often been disparaged as almost vernacular theater, it is notable that a large number of well-known and accomplished actors and actresses joined these tours. Edwin Thomas Booth, Junius Brutus Booth, Edwin Forrest, and Charlotte Cushman were some of the stars touring the South. Many performers in city stock companies, enjoying the increased acceptance of theater, relished their popularity on the road and the increased income from such tours. For a small city or town, the out-of-town star added considerable glitter to performances.

By the 1880s, as theater became popular and rail lines reached more and more places, touring companies were being transformed into large-scale sophisticated businesses. The theater entrepreneur Dion Boucicault launched the star system, recognizing the financial potential of combining well-known celebrities such as Edwin Booth with theater companies. The next leap was the Syndicate system, in which highly centralized organizations like Klaw and Erlanger in New York would rent or control theaters and organize the bookings of leading actors and theatrical productions. The savvily engineered Syndicate withstood assaults from stubborn actors alarmed by the heavy hand of New York entrepreneurs, but the eventual downfall of the Syndicate in the early 1900s came from moving pictures, which carried a bevy of stars to innumerable cities simultaneously by screen. In all these changes in the nineteenth century, peaking around 1900, acting and stars were firmly implanted in the social landscape of the United States. However, for the small-city theater or small-town opera house, the changes in the New York booking operations culminating in the Syndicate meant that the live stars they had enjoyed in the past no longer came to them.

This post–Civil War boom time for live entertainment and theater saw the number of professional actors increase from 1,490 in 1860 to 9,728 in 1890, the number of touring combinations jump from 138 in 1881 to 420

in 1904, and 4,000 theaters built from 1865 to 1900. The arrival of the
railroad ushered in the era of the opera house: two-thirds of Nebraska's
opera houses were built between 1870, the year after the Union Pacific's
intercontinental rail line was completed, and 1890, when three east-west
rail lines and many spurs brought the railroad to a multitude of Nebraska
towns. In Iowa alone, 80 percent of its opera houses were built between
1870 and 1910, and in Colorado, where the rail lines did not reach the
mountain towns until 1880, four-fifths of its opera houses were built
between 1880 and 1910. Aside from thousands of performers, many others like curtain artists, musicians, managers, playbill printers, and builders benefited during this exuberant era.[14]

In this period, old taboos about theater were vanishing. In cities,
theaters attracted more and more patrons as the sheer number of city
dwellers increased along with their leisure time. The dreary repetition
in much industrialized work begged for diversions and personal fulfillment. In rural areas, populations were growing with newcomers from
the East or overseas, machinery was reducing some work hours, and the
urge to keep up with the modernizing world was ever-present. The divide
between cities and rural areas was deepening, however. As recreation was
becoming more specialized in the cities with sports such as baseball, billiards, skating, and bicycle riding, so were cities' theatrical performances,
which included ethnic, vaudeville, burlesque, opera, legitimate, and
popular shows.

Small towns in rural areas had fewer and usually less sophisticated
options. While audiences at small rural opera houses could enjoy many
types of entertainment, as well as some indoor sports and community
activities, their options were limited compared to the offerings in a large
city. Therefore, the performers who did reach small towns attracted considerable excitement, as indicated by the attention of Willa Cather and
her Red Cloud friends to the arrival and performances of theater troupes.
For people in isolated rural areas, these performers opened windows to
other worlds of culture and excitement, and for recently arrived immigrants they opened windows to American culture, which helped them
adapt to the new world.

As the frontiers of the country stretched and railroad lines reached
more towns, itinerant troupes, both national and regional, became an
increasingly dominant part of the theatrical world in the nineteenth
century. They were the essential providers of entertainment to small
and large towns everywhere. Traveling conditions improved with

stagecoaches and trains, so troupes did not have to travel five hours by horse to meet a commitment, as Sol Smith did in the 1830s and 1840s. The expansion of rail lines from 3,000 miles of track in 1840 to 30,000 in 1860, and to 129,000 in 1885, paralleled the growth of traveling troupes.

As the West and Rocky Mountains were being settled in the last half of the nineteenth century, actors and managers established circuits through new mining camps and emerging towns similar to the travels of the Drakes and Sol Smith in the early West and South. Two well-known circuits were Jack Langrishe's Gold Circuit and Peter McCourt's Silver Circuit, both in the Rocky Mountain States, with Colorado as their initial base. Like many early theatrical entrepreneurs, Langrishe had numerous roles as actor, manager, and impresario, but he was probably best known as a comedian. He was aided by Mrs. Langrishe, who starred often as the leading lady in her husband's productions. With his partner, the jovial Mike Dougherty, Langrishe formed a popular comedy team starting in Cherry Creek, Colorado. In January 1861, they performed George Washington's and many others' favorite play, Sheridan's *The School for Scandal*, at Denver's Apollo Hall. Langrishe ran a well-regulated, orderly theater, presenting many of the melodramatic hits of the time, such as William H. Smith's *The Drunkard; or, The Fallen Saved* and Edward Bulwer-Lytton's *Lady of Lyons*, and employing an expanding troupe of actors. Like many theater troupes, which operated on a shoestring, Langrishe held benefits usually for the actors but also one for Mike Dougherty and another for the town's poor. In the spring, the pair played in Golden City, Central City, and Nevada City, which must have spurred Langrishe to consider touring the rough-and-tumble mining camps because he sent Dougherty off to explore the possibilities.

Dougherty's search successfully located camps for their performances, and in June 1861 Langrishe and Dougherty were able to launch the Gold Circuit, with stops in such places as Georgia Gulch, South Park, Central City, and later Laurette and Montgomery City. Central City had the People's Theatre, but most of the mining camps had only rudimentary stages, hastily constructed by eager miners. In Georgia Gulch, with little level land, the theater consisted of two shelves dug into the hillside, one for the auditorium and the other for the stage, with a narrow entrance uphill between a saloon and a restaurant. Reportedly, one thousand people jammed into the small space for the opening show, which was said to have been enthusiastically received, with many encores. Through the summer the troupe constantly added new players, often amateurs, and kept on performing to equally enthusiastic audiences in gulches and camps in the southern mountains. By September, camps were erecting more substantial theaters for the troupe, as reported in *Miner's Record:*

> At Parkville is located Langrishe and Dougherty's theatre, which they have recently completed, and which is the largest and best building of the kind in the mountains. It is well seated, with a roomy and well arranged stage, thirty by forty feet. This mammoth building is capable of accommodating all the theatre-going population of Georgia and the surrounding gulches, and is a great ornament to the town of Parkville, and reflects the great credit of its enterprising proprietors.[15]

Langrishe, like so many actors at that time who led a peripatetic and tiring life, eventually closed down his Gold Circuit operation. Nevertheless, his reputation remained so high that Horace Tabor chose Langrishe as the star for the opening performance on November 20, 1879 at his new, majestic opera house in Leadville. Tabor also had a hand in creating a new theater circuit in the Rockies, known as the Silver Circuit, reflecting the change in mining from gold to silver. With the arrival of rail service in the Rockies in 1880s, Peter McCourt, the savvy manager of Horace Tabor's 1881 Grand Opera House in Denver and brother of Baby Doe, Tabor's second wife, saw the possibilities for a new circuit, which he first called the Tabor Circuit and later the Silver Circuit.

This new circuit, established twenty years after the Gold Circuit, was a far more sophisticated and extensive operation than Langrishe's. McCourt was not an actor-manager like many earlier circuit managers, but rather a manager and booking agent for traveling theater and opera groups. All his Silver Circuit towns and cities were located on new rail lines, which allowed this enterprise to include many mountain towns that had grown up since the 1860s, such as Salida, Trinidad, and Glenwood Springs, Colorado, as well as Salt Lake City, Utah and Cheyenne, Wyoming. McCourt hitched up with the sharp New York booking agency run by Al Hayman, later an organizer of the Syndicate. With McCourt's keen business sense, he was constantly expanding his circuit with new theaters, replacing ones that had burned down or failed.

When he saw the handwriting on the wall with the advent of movies, he introduced the first films to Denver in 1897, and later talking movies. Movies were the death knell of many of the opera houses and theaters in his Silver Circuit and eventually of the Silver Circuit itself, which ceased functioning around 1915.

Theater circuits proliferated as the rail lines coursed through the country in the late nineteenth century. States such as Texas had the Lone Star Circuit, but most were smaller circuits such as the Saginaw Valley in Michigan; the eastern New York/Vermont circuit of Granville, New York and nearby Vermont towns of Rutland and Poultney; and in Nebraska, where Robert McReynolds, manager of Fremont's Love Opera House, controlled a circuit of Grand Island, York, and Beatrice.[16] Railroads catered to these circuits and actively promoted them. The rail lines advertised the theaters on their routes and arranged reservations and the transportation of troupes' luggage and equipment. Trains approaching Kearney, Nebraska, a convenient stop on the Union Pacific between Omaha and Denver, would slow down so that the show people finishing plays at 11:00 p.m. could get on the train by midnight instead of the scheduled 11:45 p.m. departure time. "Obliging railroads catered to the touring companies which booked passage across the continent," the Kearney newspaper noted in a history of its 1891 opera house.[17] Not only did the obliging railroads not leave the traveling troupes behind, but they reduced their per mile cost of travel and provided free baggage space for their baggage and scenery.

Circuits like McCourt's Silver Circuit were advertised in *Julius Cahn's Official Theatrical Guide*, along with names of relevant railroad agents in towns on the circuit and information on local opera houses and hotels. Railroads continued to be important for both transportation and promotion of the traveling show companies, even as the circuits became more organized business operations with the packaged popular entertainments that New York promoters found so profitable.

By the end of the nineteenth century, a myriad of lecturers, actors, singers, musicians, dancers, circuses, magicians, and jugglers, sometimes in a company but often alone, were traveling the rails to opera houses sprouting up in new as well as settled towns. The quality of the performances of these "strollers" varied, strollers being a pejorative term used by high-culture critics, who regarded them as entertainers, not Broadway-level actors, and located them at the bottom of the theatrical

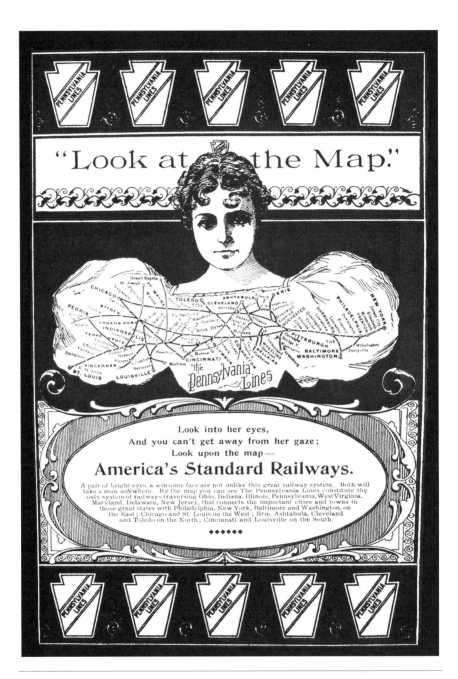

Pennsylvania Railroad advertised in "Julius Cahn's Official Theatrical Guide 1896" it could transport theater troupes and performers to the many towns and cities on its rail lines. *Theatre Division of the Library of the Performing Arts, New York Public Library*

ladder. As strollers proliferated along with the number of performing spaces like opera houses, city theaters were gaining respect. This created a boom in theater construction in New York, which boasted large new theaters like the 4,500-seat Broadway Theatre, and even in New England, where many new theaters were still called "museums."

Although museums might have passageways with relics and oddities, serious plays and lectures would take place in the hall or auditorium at the end of the passageway. The Boston Museum and Gallery of Fine Arts, opened by Moses Kimball in 1841 on Tremont Street, was one of the best-known museum/theaters with a collection of curiosities and a "concert saloon" that was transformed in 1843 into a theater with its own accomplished stock company and leading actors such as William Warren. The popular temperance play *The Drunkard* in 1844, followed by equally "moral" plays, established the Boston Museum as a respectable theater, earning it the nickname the "deacon's theatre." With its success, the Boston Museum moved to a new building in 1846 and thrived through the 1870s. In 1894 it fell prey to the Syndicate and was disbanded.

Uncle Tom's Cabin, the most popular play of the late nineteenth and early twentieth centuries, was first performed not in a theater but in the Troy (New York) Museum. Despite condescending comments by some highbrow critics, talented and serious actors among these itinerant actor-managers and actors often performed serious plays at museums like Troy's and in opera houses.[18]

Playgoers' interest in serious theater is evident in the frequent Shakespeare and other respectable plays performed in museums and opera houses. This interest in theater and serious plays was influenced by the important role that the oral tradition played in the lives of earlier generations. Schoolchildren recited long poems and sonnets and participated in "rhetoricals." An announcement of Bennington High School students reading essays and doing recitations on topics ranging from "How Sayings Originated" to "Dispensations of Providence" was front-page news for the *Bennington Banner* on December 16, 1892. With memorizing and recitations such a large part of their education, adults, like Mr. Putnam, the patron of the Bennington Opera House, could readily reel off lines of Shakespeare. Before radio and television, playing word games like charades, performing plays, and reading novels out loud were forms of entertainment for educated families.

Another indication of the influence of the oral tradition was the number of serious plays performed in military garrisons and by military officers in public halls. Such officers, usually educated and often bored and isolated in remote garrisons, enjoyed the early theater offerings. The oral tradition of reciting plays and sonnets, especially those of Shakespeare, was part of their education and heritage, so it is not surprising that they staged plays, often Shakespeare, in their free time. Instances of soldiers performing plays at garrisons, forts, and even taverns kept popping up in histories of both settled towns and frontier areas.

Imprisoned British soldiers in 1777 performed the earliest theatrical productions in Lancaster, Pennsylvania at Henry Dering's brewhouse. The next year, George Washington celebrated his forty-sixth birthday at camp with a military band serenade and a performance of Joseph Addison's *Cato* by the younger officers, for which Washington had been granted special permission since Congress forbade theatrical productions during the war. The first recorded theatrical performance in the Ohio River Valley was at Fort Pitt, where the garrison's officers and their wives staged plays in the mess hall using tables for the stage and benches for seating. When General Macomb was in command in Detroit from 1815 to 1821, his officers constructed a theater in an upper floor of a government storehouse. In the distant outpost of the Hudson's Bay Company at Fort Vancouver on the Columbia River in what is now Oregon, Captain Thomas Baillie, his officers, and the men of the H.B.M. sloop of war *Modeste* staged plays, dances, and other entertainments for the Americans in 1845. The Hudson's Bay Company hoped the entertainments might quell what seemed like growing tensions between the Americans and the British at Fort Vancouver. Canada's first theater, the New Grand Theatre was established in 1789 because Halifax residents had so enjoyed amateur military theatricals.[19]

The most dramatic performance by the military may well have been at Faneuil Hall in March 1776. Since the Puritans had no theater in Boston, British General William Howe converted Faneuil Hall, later known as a patriotic shrine of the early American democrats, into an elegant theater. Here British officers and their American Loyalist friends produced plays, such as *Maid of the Oaks*, written by Major John Burgoyne, also stationed in Boston, who was an accomplished playwright having had a play produced at London's Drury Lane Theatre. To fire up his bored British troops, Burgoyne staged his new farce, *Blockade of Boston*, ridiculing the Americans and transforming George Washington into a bumbling caricature, on the night that the Americans attacked nearby Charlestown. The audience mistook the distant roar of guns and a frantic cry by an actor, dressed as an American soldier in farmer's garb, that "the rebels—the rebels—they're attacking the Neck," for part of the comical play. Realizing that these signals of war were grim reality, not part of the farce, the actors quickly fled the stage, removed their costumes and makeup, and hastened to their posts, where their boredom was quickly relieved.[20]

Seventy years later, future US President Ulysses S. Grant, stationed with the army in Corpus Christi, Texas—and also thin and beardless—played the role of Desdemona in a traveling production of *Othello* until an actress was found for the role in New Orleans. These military thespians along with all the many early traveling troupes and showboats illustrate the timeless passion for theater of actors and their audiences, who together laid the foundation for the huge popularity of plays, operas, lectures, and entertainments in the post–Civil War heyday of opera houses.

CHAPTER 6

Celebrities and Stars

"Such yells and whoops" greeted the British actress Ellen Tree when she played in St. Louis in 1839, the *St. Louis Missouri Gazette* reported, as would "enliven the wigwams of the Pawnees and Pottawatamies."[1] The importance of star performers remains another constant in the story of opera houses. Stars made a production a special event, as strong personalities were what audiences wanted. Theater history is studded with stars like Swedish Nightingale Jenny Lind and British actress Lillie Langtry. Well-known players, whether the Barrymores, Edwin Booth, or Lawrence Barrett, would often overshadow the plays themselves and sometimes even the roles they played. People came to see performers, not drama.

As press attention focused on actors' lives, and managers ramped up publicity, a star's persona became increasingly significant. In the early part of the nineteenth century, a well-known actress like Charlotte Cushman was known for her acting, not her feminine beauty or her personal life; a male star like Edwin Booth was a dramatic hero, not a cult figure. There were many such theatrical celebrities: Edwin Forrest, Lotta Crabtree, James O'Neill, Maurice Barrymore, Fanny Janauschek, and Minnie Maddern Fiske. Some were known primarily for single roles, such as Edwin Booth's Hamlet and Joseph Jefferson's Rip Van Winkle. Others were known as comedians (John Drew and George Cohan) or as tragedians (E. H. Sothern and Charlotte Cushman). Many even played the same role for decades: Jefferson played Rip Van Winkle for thirty years, and Frank Mayo played Davy Crockett for twenty.

Sarah Bernhardt, considered by many as one of the world's most talented actresses, cleverly used her personality and style for publicity purposes in her tours from the 1880s to 1905. While attracting considerable attention, she, like most actors and actresses of that time, was tarnished with the reputation of engaging in an immoral profession and hence never accepted socially.[2] By the 1890s, beauty was becoming critical for the success of female stars. This new cult of personality was demonstrated when actresses like Lillian Russell were considered stage beauties. By 1900, as stage stars were being treated as celebrities and written up in women's magazines and national newspapers, they became objects of press exploitation, with movies soon capitalizing even further on this cult of personality.

Celebrities were lures for opera houses in cities and even in some small towns. In 2005, Vermonter Bruce Shields recalled his grandmother telling him of the excitement of hearing Caruso perform at the Tabor Opera House in Leadville. For the December 10, 1892 opening night performance of *Hamlet* at the Bennington Opera House, the "peerless queen of tragedy, Madame Janauschek" was featured in the local newspaper's publicity article a month prior to the event. Fremont's new Love Opera House opened in December 1888 with Minnie Maddern, who "heartily enlists the supreme sympathy of her audience," the local paper reported.[3] Although theater stars were highly featured attractions at opera houses, other celebrities lured large and enthusiastic audiences. Lecturers like Mark Twain, magicians like Harry Houdini, opera stars like Adelina Patti, circuses like the Ringling Brothers, and even athletes like boxers John Sullivan and James Corbett were a few of the celebrities touring the country in the heyday of opera houses.

The roster of peripatetic celebrities reveals a diversity of talents as well as remarkable passion and endurance. But equally important were the many lesser-known performers and troupes, such as the Earle Comedy Company and the Fay Templeton Opera Company that were mainstays of opera houses in small places. They did not achieve celebrity status and there is little record of them.[4] Although these performers were considered minor or vernacular, if they were considered at all by big-city critics, they enthralled audiences for years. Whether minor or major, all these performers provide a glimpse of the rich world of live entertainment available to opera house patrons.

The love of acting and life of the itinerant theater captivated Joseph Jefferson, known as Joseph Jefferson III.[5] Like many actors, he came from a theatrical family. Seven generations of Jeffersons, thirty-five family members, and seven of Joseph Jefferson III's nine children were involved with theater across two centuries. Joseph Jefferson III inherited his interest in the stage and his endurance for the rigors of traveling from his father who acted in upstate New York en route to his job as manager of a new theater in Chicago in 1838. While Jefferson lived in Chicago, his father's troupe, in order to make ends meet, took to the road in an open wagon over the prairie to Galena, Illinois, then Dubuque, Iowa, and to Burlington, Peoria, and Springfield, Illinois. They constantly coped with the many problems of traveling troupes, even competition with religion in Springfield, where exorbitant taxes on the "unholy" calling of acting were said to have been removed by local lawyer Abraham Lincoln, who represented Jefferson's troupe. Although scholars have questioned the specific nature of Lincoln's legal services, it is clear that Lincoln did help the Jefferson troupe.[6]

Joseph Jefferson, like many actors at that time, started out playing a variety of roles. At the age of thirty, however, after becoming engrossed with Washington Irving's writings, he found his lifetime career as Rip Van Winkle. "Attracted by the poetic nature of the legend" of Rip Van Winkle, Jefferson thought "an American story by an American was surely just the theme suited to an American actor."[7] Jefferson was also proud that Washington Irving had seen him act. The play, which Jefferson arranged into three acts, was not an immediate hit. He resisted making it more spectacular, but he did accept actor-impresario Dion Boucicault's human-interest additions to the script, which improved the play by strengthening Jefferson's role as the hero of the Catskills while keeping the "poetic nature of the legend" that Jefferson admired.[8] Soon Jefferson was playing Rip Van Winkle everywhere, even overseas in London and in Australia. His audiences were "largely made up of people who seldom go to the theatre and whose presence is the highest form of compliment that can be paid to an actor," Willa Cather wrote in 1896.[9]

> Many of them had seen the same actor in the same part time and time again and found in his work still the same delight, the same rare perfection of a gentle art. Joseph Jefferson's *Rip Van Winkle* has been before the public now for five-and-thirty years, yet it has lost none of its matchless charms. It never became hackneyed any more than Schubert's "Serenade" has.[10]

For Jefferson, his winning performance took place in a skating rink converted into a theater in Catskill, New York, attended by a large crowd of local farmers and their wives, who probably saw "for the first time on the stage the story which Washington Irving had laid almost at their very doors," according to Jefferson. There he felt he "had never seen an audience so struck with the play before."[11] Although Jefferson successfully played other roles such as Bob Acres in Sheridan's *The Rivals* and Salem Scudder in Boucicault's *The Octoroon*, he was best known for Rip Van Winkle. Jefferson's portrayal of Rip reminded Harriet Beecher Stowe of Lear.

Joseph Jefferson in his early days as Rip Van Winkle about 1887 in a gravure by
Gebbie & Husson, London. *Library of Congress, Prints and Photographs Division
LC-USZ62-63622*

Like many members of acting families, Jefferson enjoyed his travels and his audiences. "There is nothing a young actor enjoys more than itinerant theatricals. It is so grand to break loose from a big tyrant manager in the city and become a small tyrant manager in the country."[12] And that he did. In 1884 he traveled to Michigan, Illinois, Iowa, Indiana, Ohio, New York, New Jersey, Pennsylvania, Delaware, and the District of Columbia and later to the Southwest and New England. Not only did he cover the United States, but he took Rip overseas. While considered a comic actor who could blend pathos and silliness in a good-hearted manner, and often scorned by high-culture tragedians, Jefferson's Rip performances proved to be immensely popular and lucrative. He left an estate of $600,000, owned properties in Buzzards Bay, Massachusetts and New Iberia, Louisiana, enjoyed lengthy stays in Palm Beach, and counted Grover Cleveland and Standard Oil/Florida East Coast Railroad magnate Henry Flagler as his friends—all signs of the success of his acting skills, his love of America and its provincialism, and his single-minded hard work.

Another star and inveterate traveler was Sarah Bernhardt. Starting in 1880, this fabulously popular French star made nine tours in the United States, one in 1905–1906 during which she visited sixty-two cities. Her final tour, in 1917, ended with fourteen curtain calls in her last performance, *La Dame aux Camelias*, in New York City. She was "wild with delight" at the thought of travel, she claimed, as she had not traveled much before her 1880 tour.[13] One of her motivations was to earn money to erase her 100,000-franc debt to the Comédie-Française in Paris for breaking her contract—and she succeeded, as she made the equivalent of more than 20,000 francs per performance. Most important, she clearly loved her travels and celebrity status in the United States. Her interest in romantic theater and her almost anti-intellectual inclinations appealed to the simpler tastes of Americans and separated her from the progressives in theater like Shaw and Ibsen, who grappled with social problems. Of the American public, she said, "I can't call them anything but delightful. They adore me."[14]

There was often "a dizzy round of smaller towns, arriving at 3, 4, and sometimes 6 o'clock," she recalled, "and then leaving immediately after the play."[15] Bernhardt thrived, it seemed, on her travels, her discoveries, and the adulation she received. In Baltimore, she felt her "success . . . had been colossal in that charming city"; in Chicago, she was struck by the "vitality of the city" and "left that city fond of everything in it—its people, its lake as big as a small inland sea, its audiences, who were so enthusiastic, everything, everything, but its stockyards."[16] But Bostonians puzzled her; they seemed "the most mysterious of all American races.... All the reserves of heart are expended in intellectuality. They adore music, the theatre, literature, painting and poetry." They were different from the "Latin race," she observed, but "they are interesting, delightful—captivating."[17]

Her audiences were as enthusiastic about her as she was about them. Her first visit to Louisville in February 1881 illustrates the fervor that she loved to generate. Even before her performance, there was excitement. The minister of the First English Lutheran Church, J. S. Detweiler, provided the actress with a powerful advertisement as he preached a rousing sermon, "Going to See Sarah Bernhardt," on the horrors of theater and the "difference between the holy and the profane ... and the clean and the unclean." That stirred new interest in Bernhardt, upped the price of tickets, and caused unexpected speculation in ticket sales: the usual $1.00 seats went for $3.00 and the dress circle and parquet tickets went for $4.00 and $3.50. Even though her train did not arrive until 1:00 a.m., crowds of reporters and eager fans greeted her at the railroad station when she alighted in "a long tightly fitted ulster with hood and fur muffler." Her two performances, *Frou Frou* and *Camille*, were met with "rapt attention" of the audience, which was not daunted by her French, according to the local newspaper. But it was after her performance of *Camille* when Louisville and Bernhardt really bonded. She was presented with a large "floral tribute in the beautiful design of the flag of France" as the orchestra struck up the "Marseillaise." "The effect upon the audience was indescribable," the newspaper reported. "The greatest enthusiasm prevailed and the great actress was called before the final curtain again and again." That was the first of five visits to Louisville. Later she played there in an "unforgettable performance in *L'Aiglon*." Her final visit occurred after her leg was amputated following a poorly treated infection.[18]

But she was not welcomed everywhere. In Burlington, Vermont, the Howard Opera House opened in 1879 with a season of opera, which was enthusiastically received. Joseph Jefferson's *Rip Van Winkle* later in the season was so eagerly anticipated that a fracas occurred when people were hired to stand in line for the sought-after tickets. When it was announced that Sarah Bernhardt would appear the next year, the excitement causing people to wait in line all night for tickets was matched by outbursts about the alleged immorality of her private life. In the end, the moralizers won; Bernhardt's performance was canceled when her agent required a high guarantee, which would have boosted the ticket price beyond what Burlingtonians could pay.

Some critics, though not driven by moral concerns, found Bernhardt and her performances overrated. Ed Howe of the Atchison, Kansas *Globe* wrote a scathing review of her March 1881 performance in *Camille* in St. Joseph, Missouri, across the border from Atchison. Her persona and beauty escaped Howe, who found her "distressingly ugly . . . her smile painful" and "her arms as long and wiry as the tendrils of a devil fish." The embrace "for which she is said to be the champion of two countries" seemed to Howe "neither graceful nor natural, and only original in its awkwardness." However, Howe granted "the Bernhardt kiss is a little better, but there are millions of women who can kiss a man more naturally and acceptably than Sarah Bernhardt." He did admit "the only thing Bernhardt does well is put her arms around a man, and look into his eyes. If her face could be hidden at these moments, she could be sublime."[19] Clearly, the Divine Sarah did not fit Howe's, or probably many Americans', standard of pulchritude. Perhaps parochial defensiveness and rejection of the highfalutin Eastern and European culture drove Howe to express what many other Americans felt but were afraid to mention about an unusual artist such as Bernhardt.

Her independence and pluck did not endear her to everyone. She would not let the powers that be dictate to her. When the bishop of Montreal excommunicated her for performing in Ernest Legouvé and Eugène Scribe's *Adrienne Lecouvreur,* Bernhardt noted that, as the bishop and she were in the same profession, they ought to show more consideration to each other. Her observation that she shared her acting profession with the bishop repeated earlier reflections that puritanical ministers' dread of theater rose partly from their jealousy of actors' dramatic skills, often lacking in their long and dreary sermons.

Bernhardt's resistance to the Syndicate was an example of her independence. The Syndicate, organized by Klaw and Erlanger, allowed little room for independence. In the era of rampant laissez-faire, the Syndicate grew into a powerful operation controlling actors, theaters, and managers, but its almost monopolistic control was challenged by the new theatrical management group run by the Shubert brothers in New York and some outspoken actresses like Bernhardt and Minnie Maddern Fiske. Bernhardt signed on with the Shuberts for her final tour in 1905, which meant that she was blacklisted at the many Syndicate theaters, forcing her to appear at odd venues like the Peachtree Auditorium Skating Rink in Atlanta and a combined swimming pool and auditorium in Tampa, Florida.

The inadequacies of these facilities spurred her to tour with a tent specially designed for her, capable of seating six thousand, and requiring three railroad cars for the tent itself and another car for the twenty-eight men needed to erect it. Although the tent received much publicity, it had problems: heavy rain in Austin, Texas forced her to abandon the tent and head to the Syndicate-managed Hancock Opera House, where she recruited a stage crew and put on her production despite objections from the opera house's manager. She continued to tour some cities with the tent, but performed far more often in actual theaters. This last tour, aside from earning her more American fans, certainly helped establish the Shuberts as solid rivals to the Syndicate.

Along with the theater stars crisscrossing the country were many other star performers—magicians, lecturers, piano players like Blind Boone, acrobats like the Hanlon brothers, bandleaders like John Philip Sousa, and politicians and feminists. Many of the latter were serious, promoting temperance and woman suffrage. In Rushville, Illinois, Belva Lockwood, the first woman to run for president, gave a speech titled "The Women of Today" on February 6, 1885, several months before Susan B. Anthony spoke at the nearby Beardsville Opera House. Less serious were

Sarah Bernhardt in front of her 6,000 seat tent in Dallas, Texas on March 26, 1906. *Library of Congress, Prints and Photographs Division LC-USZ62–58556.*

magicians, who nevertheless created enormous excitement in small-town opera houses. In reminiscing about the heyday of Granville, New York's Pember Opera House, newspaper columnist Morris Rote-Rosen recalled the thrills produced by Kellar the Magician, second only to Herman the Great. The audience was baffled by Kellar's levitation act, in which a woman would float in midair through a hoop and then totally disappear from sight. And that was just one trick.[20] Like actors and their troupes, all these performers traveled to towns as obscure as Red Dog, California and to major cities like Chicago and New York, facing all sizes and types of audiences in tents, churches, saloons, theaters, and opera houses.

Featured in opera houses everywhere were lecturers, as audiences steeped in the oral tradition seemed eager to learn and be entertained. Lectures met with public approval as they implied education, in contrast to the negative image of theater. Opera house programs were filled with lectures on every conceivable topic from temperance, witchcraft, women's rights, phrenology, religion, public affairs, arts, and music. Some of these lectures were lengthy. A two-and-a-half-hour lecture on tariffs was not unusual. Many lectures were packaged by lyceum agencies, the more prominent of which was the Boston Redpath Agency, but many regional agencies like the Lyceum Bureaus from Lincoln and Omaha, Nebraska offered programs for small towns throughout the state. Travel was a popular topic, especially if it concerned exotic places that a Nebraskan, for example, might never visit. In David City, Nebraska, Captain S. Alberti lectured with a stereopticon on Russia and Siberia, Miss Ethel Dunn gave a combined recital and lecture on the Oberammergau passion play she attended in Germany, and Colonel Copeland entertained with his program "Seeing the Elephant." As public oratory was ingrained in the educational system in the nineteenth century, it was not surprising that lecturers and political speakers are often mentioned as attractions in histories of opera houses. William Jennings Bryan seemed to be everywhere. And what would a Fourth of July festivity have been without a band concert, a parade, and a speech by a prominent citizen or politician such as Senator Thomas Hart Benton, whom Mark Twain recalled having heard in Hannibal, Missouri.

One unlikely lecturer in some parts of the United States in the late 1800s was Oscar Wilde. With his silk breeches, velvet suit, fluffy handkerchief, and diamonds, Wilde attracted curious and often enthusiastic crowds. In rough mining country, people filled Leadville's Tabor Opera House in the 1880s to hear Wilde speak on the bizarre topic, "The

Practical Application of the Aesthetic Theory to Exterior and Interior House Decoration, with Observations on Dress and Personal Ornament." "I read them passages from the autobiography of Benvenuto Cellini and they seemed much delighted," he recalled. Confirming his finding that "the knowledge of Art, west of the Rockies" was "infinitesimal," the Leadville audience wondered why Wilde had not brought Cellini along. Wilde explained that Cellini "had been dead for some time," to which someone asked, "Who shot him?"[21] Part of Wilde's success in Leadville was due to his acceptance of an invitation to an evening with some miners at a saloon, where he surprised the locals by his ability to outdrink them. He even joined the miners at their place of work when he went down to the bottom of the famous Matchless silver mine where he proudly opened a new lode named "The Oscar." Wilde hoped he would be offered shares in the lode, but instead he was given the silver drill.[22]

In Fremont, Nebraska, where Wilde lectured at the Love Opera House in April 1895, the *Fremont Tri-Weekly Tribune* reported that, unlike in Leadville and other towns where Wilde was thought to have whiskey for breakfast, lunch, and dinner, he visited a Fremont creamery and "drank a deep libation of buttermilk with a gusto that nearly established it as a beverage fashion."[23] However, after he left town, Fremonters learned more about him and were horrified by his "degeneracy." In the larger Nebraska cities of Omaha and Lincoln, Willa Cather reported that Wilde "made a big hit."[24]

He attracted considerable attention when he arrived in Louisville, just as Sarah Bernhardt had. Newspaper reporters tracked him down at a hotel where he had signed in as "J. Smith," but they had trouble eliciting much information from him, as he posed in many different positions, drank many glasses of wine—"that wicked stuff," in his words—and, after a reporter complimented him, made some gracious comments about Louisville as the "only English town in America."[25] He ventured into the deeper South where he lectured at the Springer Opera House in Columbus, Georgia, reportedly enjoying "great popularity," although the editor of the local newspaper, *The Enquirer,* slept through his aesthetic decoration lecture. However, the "good ladies of Columbus," clearly interested in Wilde's welfare, tossed sunflowers in his path so his feet never had to touch "rude earth."[26] In fact, he found his American lectures extremely popular. "I have a sort of triumphal progress. . . . I am deluged with poems and flowers in every town."[27]

Another adventurous English writer touring the United States in the post–Civil War period when readings and lectures were so popular was

Charles Dickens. In contrast to Wilde, who seemed to relish his trips to off-the-beaten-path places like Leadville, Dickens's public readings in 1867–1868 were in East Coast cities, with a jog to Buffalo, Syracuse, and Rochester, New York. In a longer tour, twenty-five years earlier, when he was anxious to see the young republic, he gave more readings in more cities—and even in some small places like Lower Sandusky, Ohio and Lebanon Springs, New York. The second tour was less exploratory and more focused on potential financial return, so his readings were not in opera houses but rather in large auditoriums such as Providence's City Hall, New York's Steinway Hall, and Baltimore's Concordia Opera House. For Dickens, these public readings provided him with opportunities, which he cherished, to communicate and bond with his audiences. Unlike Wilde, who was often more of a spectacle and spectator on his lecture tours, Dickens kept the focus on his readings, not on himself as a celebrity.[28]

Although Dickens had an interest in acting and directing going back to his childhood, as well as a lifelong enjoyment of popular entertainments such as circuses, Punch and Judy shows, and even sensational melodramas, his readings were primarily impersonations. "He reads as well as an experienced actor would," the well-known nineteenth-century actor William Macready noted.[29] There were no costumes or sets, only a barren reading stand with a lamp, a glass of water, and a bag of raisins—and his voice and gestures. He wanted to appear a proper gentleman, so his initial impression was rather stiff and brisk, almost businesslike, not the outspoken and creative writer people imagined him to be. And so Mark Twain found him when he heard Dickens read in New York in December 1867:

> But that queer old head took on a sort of beauty, bye and bye, and a fascinating interest, as I thought of the wonderful mechanism within it, the complex but exquisitely adjusted machinery that could create men and women, and put breath of life into them and alter all their ways and actions, elevate them, degrade them, murder them, marry them, conduct them through good and evil, through joy and sorrow, on their long march from the cradle to the grave, and never lose its godship over them, never make a mistake! I almost imagined I could see the wheels and pulleys work. This was Dickens—Dickens. There was no question about that, and yet it was not right easy to realize it. Somehow this puissant god seemed to be only a man, after all. How the great do tumble from their high pedestals when we see them in common flesh, and know they eat pork and cabbage and act like other men.[30]

Charles Dickens at that little red table equipped with a bag of raisins and a glass of water, 1867. Charles A. Barry. *Library of Congress, Prints and Photographs Division LC-USZ62-132077*

As a lonely writer, Dickens found immense personal satisfaction in the two-way communication between reader and audience that occurred at his readings. At his first reading in Birmingham, England, he declared his purpose in reading was to meet his public face-to-face. "I have long held the opinion, and have long acted on the opinion, that in these times whatever brings a public man and his public face to face, on terms of mutual confidence and respect, is a good thing."[31] Like Joseph Jefferson, who enjoyed the give-and-take of earlier, more rambunctious theater audiences, in contrast to sedate Victorian listeners, Dickens encouraged the audience to participate as it lived with his characters in his readings.

The audience's laughter and tears lifted him out of himself, he often said. "So real are my fictions to myself, that, after hundreds of nights, I come with a feeling of perfect freshness to that little red table, and laugh and cry with my hearers, as if I never stood there before."[32] This interaction between Dickens and his audiences was, indeed, exhilarating for him, providing much-needed support at a time when he was burdened emotionally, financially, and physically. He died just two years later.

The pleasures of these readings seemed to be mutual. "The country was in a frenzy of enthusiasm about Dickens," Mark Twain noted.[33] People queued up the night before his first reading in New York, so that by 9:00 a.m., when the ticket office opened, the line was three-quarters of a mile long. New Yorkers braved freezing weather on December 17, bringing blankets and mattresses for sleeping, while others sang and danced. That sold-out reading brought in $16,000. In Baltimore several months later, all seats for the galleries and "floor" were sold, so "a large number of persons," according to the *Baltimore Sun*, "who expected to gain admission . . . were compelled to go away disappointed."[34] In Boston, Henry James was startled to find almost a thousand people in line by 9:00 a.m. on the first day of ticket sales for Dickens's reading. The success of his readings was heartening for Dickens in many ways because he, like Sarah Bernhardt, hoped his American readings would be profitable so he could erase some debts and build up his bank account. With ten children and an annual settlement to his wife from whom he was separated, he was burdened with many financial responsibilities, which spurred much of his productivity.

Although Dickens's readings were in large halls in major cities, his experiences at these readings and his long-held enthusiasm for popular entertainment encouraged many lesser-known lecturers and performers. In the days before the mass entertainment of movies and large-scale sports events, Dickens championed public entertainers such as traveling circuses, jugglers, and pantomime performers, often considered low-class and vulgar in the early Victorian era and eventually banned from fairs and fetes. So much did Dickens enjoy the simple and spontaneous nature of these entertainments, which could lift people from the grim realities of their daily lives, that he encouraged villagers to use a field at his Gad's Hill house for sports and play. He would no doubt have enjoyed much of the simple fare that local amateurs and lesser-known troupes and performers staged at opera houses around the United States. Such offerings at American opera houses and at English village fetes, considered "popular entertainment," met neither the educational standards of the Victorians nor the artistic standards of theater critics. The widespread amusement and diversion that such simple entertainers provided was killed not by Victorians' righteous snobbery but by new, far-reaching mass entertainment like movies and radio.[35]

As Kellar the Magician performed his tricks at the Pember Opera House, the energy he derived from his audience was as important to him as it was to Dickens. Dickens, however, articulated his honest need and satisfaction more movingly than many. Because Dickens was so famous, one might think that he would not require that companionship with audiences. But he did, and so do all performers; it creates the electricity of live performances.

An American usually associated with the Mississippi River and Missouri, but who actually got his start as a lecturer and raconteur at MacGuire's Opera House in San Francisco in October 1866, was Mark Twain. Three years earlier, he had begun working as a reporter under his given name, Samuel Clemens, on the *Territorial Enterprise* newspaper in Virginia City, Nevada, writing news and play reviews and later covering the state legislature. Twain had his first try at lecturing at a mock legislative session where he gave the Governor's Message, which he signed "Mark Twain." It was a great success. Around that time he also heard the popular storyteller Artemus Ward, who clearly influenced him to consider storytelling as an alternative to newspaper reporting.

After a trip to the Sandwich Islands (Hawaii) for the *Sacramento Union* a few years later, Twain, finding himself "without means and without employment," searched for "a saving scheme" and came upon the idea of a public lecture.[36] He negotiated with Tom MacGuire, proprietor of the new MacGuire Opera House in San Francisco, to rent him space at half price: fifty dollars on credit, plus half the receipts for the evening of October 2, 1866. After investing $150 on handbills for the lecture with the last line "Doors open at 7 1/2. The trouble will begin at 8," he began worrying whether he could recover his investment. Fortunately, the crowd poured into the MacGuire Opera House: all his worries vanished, his debts were erased, he made a $400 profit, and his career as a lecturer was off to a good start.

"I launched out as a lecturer, now, with great boldness. I had the field all to myself, for public lectures were almost an unknown commodity in the Pacific market," Twain remarked.[37] In the next six weeks, he hit eight cities from Sacramento to Grass City in California, and Carson City to Virginia City in Nevada, with his lecture about the Sandwich Islands. Not only was he attracting packed houses paying "full dollar" in most cities, but he clearly enjoyed lecturing. However, the wear and tear of traveling, especially in the West, took its toll. In 1869, Twain wrote his sister that he had "resolved not to lecture outside of the New England states next year. My western course would easily amount to $10,000, but I would rather make 2 or 3 thousand in New England than submit to so much wearing travel."[38] Getting on the lyceum circuit was an important step for any lecturer, especially James Redpath's well-respected Boston Lyceum Bureau. In 1869, Twain signed on to Redpath's New England lyceum tour with his "Curiosities of California" lecture, advertised thus: "Mark Twain is widely known as one of the most humorous writers in the country. He has made a very successful lecturing tour in the West, but has never, we believe, appeared before in a New England Lyceum."[39] Quoting from the *Cleveland Herald*, Redpath's flier stated that "the humor of the lecture is peculiar and irresistible, the descriptive portions brilliant and eloquent. And the whole tone humanitarian and elevating."[40]

Mark Twain, "America's Best Humorist," entertaining an audience in 1885. *Library of Congress, Prints and Photographs Division LC-DIG-ds-04498.*

Twain's lecture tour of 1869 took him all over the Northeast, and even there he had to contend with the many hazards of travel: lost baggage, missed mail, late-night train trips, and long stretches without meals. But the tour had its rewards: Twain's lectures were profitable. In Cambridge, New York, where he gave his Sandwich Islands talk, the local newspaper editor remarked that Twain "is the first man that ever made sandwiches profitable."[41] He seemed to enjoy lecturing, his audiences, and the places he visited. In Fredonia, New York, Twain liked the "warmth and intelligence" so much that he settled his mother, sister, and niece there.[42] And audiences must have found his lectures a refreshing contrast to those of more serious circuit lecturers such as Henry Ward Beecher and Elizabeth Cady Stanton.

The many stars and celebrities such as Mark Twain and Joseph Jefferson, who performed during the late nineteenth and early twentieth centuries in innumerable opera houses in small towns and large cities, exposed tens of thousands of Americans to top-flight live theater and entertainment as never before or since.

CHAPTER 7

Other Entertainments and Enlightenments

Not everyone in the late nineteenth century sought entertainment when diversions from operas to magicians' shows could be found in almost every town's opera house. Some townspeople wanted more serious fare. The answer for the many Americans seeking intellectual enrichment was lyceums and then Chautauquas.

Lyceums, begun in 1827, were an early effort at continuing education, offering lectures and classes in the arts, science, history, and public affairs in small towns and cities. Their public affairs lectures stirred interest in public issues as their programs featured well-known speakers such as suffragette Susan B. Anthony, abolitionist Lloyd Garrison, and young Abraham Lincoln, who spoke in 1838 on the perpetuation of political institutions at the Young Men's Lyceum in Springfield, Illinois. Such lectures and classes would be held in a lyceum building in prosperous towns but more often in public halls, tents, and opera houses. By the late nineteenth century, as the Lyceum movement waned, lyceum speakers appeared more frequently in opera houses at the same time that many lyceum programs were absorbed by the new and popular adult education programs of the Chautauqua movement, started in 1874.

Sinclair Lewis's Carol Kennicott hoped the weeklong Chautauqua that visited *Main Street*'s rural Gopher Prairie in 1917 would offer her the intellectual and creative stimulation she craved. "She pictured a condensed university," but she was sorely disappointed after listening to lady elocutionists, storytellers, band and musical entertainments, and nine lecturers, four of them ex-ministers, all delivering "inspirational addresses." She concluded that "it did not seem to be any kind of a university: it seemed to be a combination of vaudeville performance, Y.M.C.A. lecture, and the graduation exercises of an elocution class."[1] She did not know the history, goals, and limitations of Chautauqua, nor did her impressions jibe with those of many rural Americans.

For serious learning, clean entertainment, moral uplift, and self-help, the Chautauqua meetings, institutes, and programs proved immensely popular with middle-class white Protestant audiences in the late nineteenth and early twentieth centuries. Started in 1874 by Methodist layperson Lewis Miller and Methodist minister John Heyl Vincent as the Sunday School Teachers' Assembly at Fair Point on Lake Chautauqua in western New York State, this summer gathering mushroomed into a large and established educational and cultural operation, spawning many Chautauqua assemblies and programs throughout the country. Its theme of Mother, Home, and Heaven fit in with the safe haven of the epoch's Victorian parlors and also the widespread interest in lyceums. "The Chautauqua," according to an Alma, Nebraska program, "undertakes to bring to a community the refinement, the culture and the entertainment of the city with none of the attendant vices."[2]

Chautauquas and opera houses spread rapidly through the same states from the 1870s to the 1920s. Nebraska had 274 Chautauquas and 310 opera houses in the early 1900s. Some Chautauquas were independently run by local committees but many, like the lyceums and independent lecturers, were also part of opera house programs. The leaders of Chautauquas, well imbued with Methodism and hence wary of secular amusements, considered most opera house fare crass entertainment compared to the moral uplift and self-help guidance of their programs. However, with influence from the Social Gospel movement, particularly Congregational minister Washington Gladden, the Chautauqua Assembly eventually recognized and even validated the role of popular amusement: a sharp turn, indeed, for a Methodist-based organization. "Amusement is not an end, but a means—a means of refreshing the mind and replenishing the strength of the body," Gladden wrote in 1885. He realized the Puritans became "extravagant in their judgment," considering "every species of amusement . . . sinful." For Gladden, the reality emerged that "popular amusement is a great fact."[3]

The challenge, therefore, was to manage amusements so they met the needs of a higher nature, but that could not be done by the current entertainment managers, whom Gladden deemed handicapped by their low moral standards and strong pecuniary drive. He was also aware that opera houses, concert halls, and other places for amusement drew larger crowds than churches, reviving churchmen's perennial fear that popular amusements could threaten local preachers and the well-being of their churches. "In one inland city of 60,000," Gladden reported, "there are two opera houses. In each of these there is an average of five performances a week during the season," which produce more money "than is paid for the support of all the Protestant churches in the city." Since drama at the opera house was clearly popular, "it is conceivable," Gladden suggested, "that drama might be a great friend to morality," and it is "undeniable there are a few noble men and women now upon the stage ... they can lift up its standards." He also realized that was the exception, as drama "tends to the degradation rather than the elevation of the people."[4]

Gladden's recognition of the need for amusement was well timed. By the 1890s, more and more people were spending their leisure time at opera houses, amusement parks, and other entertainment venues. Even the Mother Assembly at Lake Chautauqua in upstate New York had competition from the nearby Celoron amusement park with its toboggan water slide, dancing pavilions, and electric fountain, which sent the assembly into debt. Other Chautauqua assemblies took Gladden's words to heart and included secular entertainment in their programs. The Connecticut Valley Chautauqua Assembly in Northampton, Massachusetts in 1894 had James S. Burdette, "the celebrated humorist and impersonator," and entertainers such as Rosani the "Juggler and Magician," on its program, along with the usual preachers and inspirational lecturers.[5]

Including such entertainers, long popular at opera houses, at Chautauqua assemblies caused concern at headquarters. The Methodists' 1920 Doctrines and Discipline confirms this anxiety:

"Some amusements in common use are positively demoralizing and furnish the first easy steps to the total loss of character.... We therefore look with deep concern on the great increase of amusements and on the general prevalence of harmful amusements, and lift up a solemn note of warning and entreaty, particularly against theater-going, dancing, and such games of chance ... all of which have been found to be antagonistic to the vital piety, promotive of worldliness, and especially pernicious to youth."[6]

Methodists officially continued to ban theatergoing until the Doctrines and Discipline was revised in 1939.[7] So it is no surprise that "drama was introduced on the Chautauqua platform gradually and in small palatable doses," according to Chautauqua scholar Andrew Reiser.[8]

Dramatic impersonators and pantomime were appearing by the end of the century at the Chautauqua (New York) Institute, but how much drama was on local programs depended on the number of Methodists in a town. Introducing theater in the programs coupled with the growing numbers of Chautauquas, and competition between them, caused schisms within the movement. "Competition will be the death of Chautauqua assemblies in Nebraska, unless the pressure is relieved," warned Lincoln resident W. E. Hardy, where there were four assemblies within a fifty-mile radius.[9]

An attempt at collectivizing helped ward off some of the competition and commercialization, but the mainstream interest in theater remained. Drama at Chautauquas in the early twentieth century continued the anti-urban bias that had permeated most of their programs. Plays like *Turn to the Right* pitted the perils of urban life against the innocence and worthiness of country living, a theme in Russell Conwell's popular lecture "Acres of Diamonds," which led thousands of Chautauquans to think they could find riches in their own backyards. As Chautauquas were seeking ways to use theater for moral uplift, they were also responding to the Progressives of that era by introducing civic responsibility into their lecture programs with charismatic public speakers like William Jennings Bryan and Robert LaFollette. Despite the strong rural and moral bent, Chautauquas were soon going down a path that led them into manipulative aspects of modern consumer capitalism: advertising. Through Conwell's lectures, Bruce Barton's book *The Man Nobody Knew: A Discovery of the Real Jesus Christ*, and the Dale Carnegie–like lectures of William Rainey Bennett, the power of personality became a part of the Chautauqua program. But then the power of personality had always been critical to the popularity of most charismatic preachers and lecturers.

Although the Chautauquas sought the high road in entertainment, they were more closely allied to opera house audiences and programs than they would have liked to admit. Both Chautauqua and opera house offerings appealed to a simple, usually rural or isolated audience, questing for answers to the challenges of moral disruptions of the rapidly urbanizing and industrial world around them—and often hoping to return to an older and more familiar world with stable values they understood. Including drama in Chautauqua programs reflected a recognition by these Methodists of societal changes wrought by greater religious and population diversity.

An important by-product of this Chautauqua decision was its help in making theatricals more palatable to some Midwestern audiences, who had lingering doubts about the morality of theater. However, even those closely involved in theater realized that drama does not necessarily provide direct educational benefits. As New York theater manager Daniel Frohman commented, drama appeals to the imagination and emotions, contains some ethical values, and may or may not have an educational quality.

Carol Kennicott's disappointment in the Gopher Prairie Chautauqua is not surprising; neither the lectures nor the "entertainment" and drama could provide her with the substantive, creative programs she wanted. No doubt she would have found less didactic and moralistic fare at the local opera house, and she might have had more fun. But for Carol Kennicott and many Americans, the options of Chautauquas and opera houses for entertainment or uplift vanished in the 1920s as these institutions faded with the advent of radios, movies, cars, and a more urban and pluralistic society.

In the heyday of opera houses, however, a remarkable number of star performers roamed the country, often performing in small places and exposing audiences to wonders formerly available only in large cities. The well-respected actress Minnie Maddern Fiske "traveled all the highways and byways of this country," her biographer Alexander Woollcott stated. "Indeed, there are no nooks or crannies she has not explored."[10]

Most opera house audiences, however, did not see the likes of Minnie Maddern Fiske, Charles Dickens, and Sarah Bernhardt. Instead, these halls had a parade of lesser-known performers and many community events. It might seem surprising that a small stage at a rural town's opera house could accommodate a circus or a production of *Ben Hur*, but amazingly clever stage effects could produce storms, train wrecks, and chariot races, and savvy managerial skills could transform a small stage into a distant parlor or a circus tent. The different-sized places in Nebraska like David City, Fremont, Red Cloud, and Lincoln, as well as for Lexington, Kentucky, Leadville, Colorado, and Oregon towns, illustrate the variety of performances, the types of troupes, and the interests of audiences, managers, and out-of-town booking agents.

For the 1895–1896 season at the Thorpe Opera House in David City, Nebraska, population about two thousand, the only dramatic play was J. T.

Viegard's *The Dutch Recruit; or, The Blue and Grey*. But the programs for the rest of that season, mostly by touring companies, included elocution drills and posings by the Tableau d'Art Company; *Jane* by the Osborne Comedy Company; hypnotism by Professor Deal; a St. Valentine Masquerade Ball given by the Social House Club; another Masquerade Ball given by the fire department; a lecture by the national secretary of the Woman's Christian Temperance Union (WCTU); a production by the Eclipse Comedy Company; a musical review by the Tennessean Jubilee Singers; the David City High School commencement; two productions by the Boston Comic Comedy Company and the Payton Comedy Company; a political debate society contest; and the Nineteenth Annual Ball given by the fire department on Christmas Eve.

In Fremont, a bigger Nebraska town with a thousand-seat opera house, a population of almost seven thousand, and important rail connections, the program for 1893–1894 season included more dramatic plays than in David City and a typical mix of local and out-of-town talent: *Cleopatra*, a burlesque with twenty girls; Shakespeare's *Julius Caesar* with Charles Hanford; the North Nebraska Oratorical Contest; a Memorial Day service; *Living Whist* by Fremont Rebekah Lodge; "athletic entertainment"; *Si Perkins* with Sam J. Burton, a twelve-piece orchestra, and a realistic threshing-machine scene and sawmill; *Richelieu* with Walter Whiteside, "the probable successor to Booth"; and *Damon and Pythias* by the local Knights of Pythias, for which one hundred seats were reserved in the first hour of sales. These events were publicized in photographs of lead actors displayed in store windows, as well as posters for many shows, including Professor Norris's dog show with twenty dogs; *Faust*; Victor Hugo's *Ruy Blas* with Alexander Salvini; and Oscar Wilde's *Lady Windermere's Fan* with the Frohman Company.[11]

At the Red Cloud Opera House, serving a small town with around eight hundred people and several thousand more in Webster County, the 1886 program began with Ann Eva Fay, a spiritualist whose spirits failed to materialize but who still provided good entertainment, according to the *Chief*, the local newspaper. Then in March, the opera house presented the Stewart Grand Concert Company and the Jay Simms Comedy Company, whose hit *Kerry Cow* was very popular; in April Jay Simms and his company returned with an adaptation of Alexandre Dumas's novel *The Count of Monte Cristo*, "one of the finest plays ever written," according to the county newspaper. The house, like most opera houses, was dark in the summer during the heavy farm-work season, but in the autumn the Georgia Minstrels were followed by Blind Boone, who played to a full house. The Georgia Hamlin comedy company returned to "delighted audiences," who would always put out their "dramatic latch string" for this popular troupe, as the county paper noted. *Uncle Tom's Cabin* was played for two nights in November by McFadden's Boston Troupe to repeated encores, and the final production for the year was Henry J. Byron's *Blow for Blow*, produced by "home artists ... with an able array of talent" and a "good" new orchestra, according to the *Webster County Argus*.[12]

In Lincoln, the state capital with a population of slightly more than 55,000 in 1890, more accomplished troupes would appear than in smaller towns, as recorded in the diary of Flavia Canfield, mother of Vermont novelist Dorothy Canfield Fisher and wife of the dean of the University of Nebraska. In 1892–1893, Mrs. Canfield attended *Monte Cristo*, a lantern show of a Paris salon, many concerts, *La Carceau* with Rhea, a Metropolitan Opera performance, a "splendid performance" by Helena Modjeska, and Joseph Jefferson's *Rip Van Winkle*, which Mrs. Fisher considered "very good indeed."[13]

In Lexington, Kentucky, the early interest in theater was reflected in the diverse and usually topflight programs of the Lexington Opera House through the 1920s. In the 1895–1896 season, Lexingtonians could attend a satirical comedy, *The Politician; Tennessee's Pardner*, based on Bret Harte's short story; the Kimball Opera Comique Organization's *Corinne; Trip to Chinatown; Spar of Life; Faust* with John Griffith in Henry Irving's "spectacular version of Goethe's Sublime Inspiration"; *Ben Hur* for three nights; *Si Perkins*; Shakespeare's *Twelfth Night* with Julia Marlowe Taber and Robert Taber; *Jane*, "Queen of Comedies" by Gustave Frohman's Company; John Philip Sousa's band; and James A. Herne's *Shore Acres*, advertised as a hit in New York City, where it ran for 306 nights.[14]

Leadville, Colorado was in its heyday in the early 1880s, when Horace Tabor was determined that this mining town would get the best of everything and attract leading actors and actresses along with the best shows from New York theaters. Lotta Crabtree, W. E. Sheridan, Mrs. Fiske, William Gillette, Maud Adams, and Madame Janauschek all appeared at the Tabor Opera House along with the Metropolitan Opera Company and nationally known performers such as John Philip Sousa and Houdini. Shakespeare, especially *Macbeth, Hamlet*, and *As You Like It*, was popular with the Leadville audiences, as were *Uncle Tom's Cabin* and Gilbert and Sullivan's *H.M.S. Pinafore*. A single evening would often include several entertainments. During the intermission of *H.M.S. Pinafore*, Leadvillites could listen to the Turkish Patrol Orchestra. Often a show would be advertised as having produced crowded houses at leading theaters in the East, an imprimatur that it was top-notch. Later, as a stop on the Silver Circuit, Leadville was assured that some of the better companies would perform at its opera house. Leadville caught opera fever in the mid-1880s and sponsored a season of Italian grand opera with the Milan Graw Italian Opera Company producing Verdi's *Il trovatore* and *Faust*, which Leadvillites could follow with librettos for sale locally. Soon Leadville was back into *East Lynne, A Parlor Match, Under the Gaslight*, and a never-ending stream of melodramas whose excitements overshadowed any particular actor.

In the far Northwest, troupers appeared shortly after settlers arrived in Oregon. By the 1850s, the French actress Mademoiselle Duret gave Shakespeare readings in Oregon City. Strolling troupers performed at inns and courthouses, just as in Kentucky. Well-known actors and actresses such as Charles Kean, Ellen Tree, the Chapmans of showboat fame, and Lotta Crabtree toured towns in this new territory, which was soon building opera houses in Salem, Albany, Eugene, and Astoria; the Ross Opera House in the latter seated two thousand. With the railroad's arrival, all the popular minstrel shows and opera groups, such as Emma Abbott's Grand English Opera Company with its twelve-piece orchestra, appeared. Hits from the East played as well, including Sheridan's *School for Scandal*, Shakespeare, and *East Lynne*, which edged out *Uncle Tom's Cabin* in box-office sales. Tent shows with the amusing Toby Wilson, Chautauquas, and lively wagon shows were entertainments available to people in towns and remote outposts. It was at the opera house, "a place of magic," that Oregonians enjoyed serious theater and entertainments as Americans did throughout the country in the late nineteenth century.[15]

Many of the popular plays of this period appeared over and over in a given city. *Uncle Tom's Cabin*, of course, outdid all other plays. At Burlington, Vermont's Howard Opera House, twenty-six plays or operettas performed more than five times. *Uncle Tom's Cabin* was the winner, with thirty performances. Gilbert and Sullivan's *H.M.S. Pinafore* and *The Mikado*, and the English opera *The Bohemian Girl* by Michael Balfe, were the runners-up with twelve performances each; but *Faust, Nights in a Bar Room, Chimes of Normandy, East Lynne*, and the Joseph Jefferson/Dion Boucicault production of *Rip Van Winkle* were also favorites.

In upstate New York, a small rural town like Salem filled its 1890 Proudfit Hall with many comedies and melodramas, such as *Old Soldiers, My Wife's Dentist, The School Ma'am*, and *The Sleeping Car*. These were complemented by temperance lectures, university extension classes, concerts, school performances, sports, and innumerable "socials" and dances, but no operas or New York stars.

Performers often honed their skills and established professional and personal friendships in opera houses. The careers of some performers, inspired by opera house performances, were even launched in these halls. The Mazomanie Opera House in Mazomanie, Wisconsin is an example. Here, not far from Madison, the Ringling brothers' first circus was performed. Al. Ringling, one of seven sons of the German immigrant August Rungeling, followed his father's trade as a harness maker in Baraboo, Wisconsin. However, after seeing a circus in an Iowa opera house, Al. soon forsook harness making for the world of entertainment. He realized that he and his brothers had enough talents as clowns, jugglers, acrobats, musicians, and even financial managers to form their own company, which they did with Al. as its leader.

The first public performance of the Ringling Brothers Classic and Comic Concert Company in the Mazomanie Opera House in 1882 was a success, netting the brothers $300. That first show launched their entrepreneurial venture. In two years they collaborated with another regional showman, Old Yankee Robinson. When Robinson died, they were on their own again, using Baraboo as their winter headquarters. Six years after their first performance, the Ringlings bought an elephant; soon they were traveling by train and acquiring interests in larger circus companies, eventually merging with the Barnum and Bailey Circus in 1907 to become "The Greatest Show on Earth." Al. Ringling never forgot his early days in Baraboo where, shortly before he died in 1916, he was able to enjoy the opening of the sumptuous Al. Ringling Theatre he had built for $100,000 as a gift to the city.

Flourishing in the nineteenth century, and appealing to the same ordinary folk who patronized circuses and other performances at opera houses, were the many "floating theaters" or showboats that plied the rivers primarily in the South. This unique and distinctly American type of popular entertainment depended on theatrical troupes performing on boats crafted as theaters. As touring opera house troupes moved from town to town on land, showboat troupes moved from riverfront town to riverfront town. Both shared many of the same pleasures and challenges

Al. Ringling's 1915 New York–style Theatre in his hometown of Baraboo, Wisconsin. *Author photograph*

of providing popular programs to small-town audiences. One early entertainment promoter/actor, Sol Smith, was even involved with both. Showboats, primarily a Southern institution, displayed the South's early and hearty enjoyment of theater as well as of the plucky passion of the operators, often family groups that manned these boats floating down the rivers of the South, mainly the Ohio and Mississippi.

The Chapman family was early into operating showboats on the Ohio and Mississippi Rivers. William Chapman Sr., an English-trained actor, had played in New York at the Bowery Theatre before he toured the West, where he came upon the idea of bringing theater to river towns by boat. In 1831 or 1832, Noah Ludlow recalled seeing tied up at a Cincinnati boat landing "a large flat-boat, with a rude kind of house built upon it, having a ridge-roof, above which projected a staff with a flag attached upon which was visible the word 'theatre.'" Ludlow learned "that it was used for a theatrical company, under the management of a Mr. Chapman," for floating down the Ohio River. When Ludlow went to visit it the next day, it had gone its "winding way to New Orleans."[16] Although Chapman's was the first in the 1830s, many others floated down the Ohio and Mississippi Rivers, entertaining river towns until the 1940s. Their heyday was from 1870 to 1910, just as it was for opera houses.

These "entertainment boats" came in all sizes and types, from the New Grand Floating Palace seating 1,000 to the Bryant's Princess, seating 140, and from simple flat-bottomed barges to extremely elaborate floating palaces, all with bright flags and calliope music. Some of the best-known showboats were Chapman's Floating Palace and Edmund Rice's Water Queen Riverboat. Townsfolk flocked to these "temples of amusement" for their varied entertainment of musicals, fiddlers' contests, museums, minstrel shows, concerts, movies, lectures, religious revivals, and, in their last days, even New York stage shows.

"When the showboat rounded the bend in the river, all the kids in town beat it to the river to watch the boat come into the wharf and tie up," reminisced Lucile Gerber about the showboats she knew from living in the Ohio River town of Cannelton, Indiana. Loud calliope music let everyone in town know the boat had landed. Later in the day, the boat's brass band, often of better quality than the subsequent theatrical performances, would parade up and down Main Street drumming up trade. The most thrilling part of the day's visit, according to Mrs. Gerber, came around seven o'clock in the evening when "the band came out on top of the brilliantly-colored boat and played a 'concert' just before the performance."[17] That practice of a parade preceding performances was taken up by some troupes before their appearances in opera houses.

These river showboats were often the only source of the latest popular plays and music for river towns in their early days. "They provided patrons with spectacles and glimpses of other worlds," commented Betty Bryant in reflecting on the benefits of her family's showboats on the Ohio River. As the early touring theater troupes were family-operated enterprises, so, too, were many of the showboats. In the early twentieth century, of the fourteen to eighteen showboats on the Mississippi, ten or more were family boats. Bryant stressed her family's moral tone of entertainment, which was "BY families and FOR families." They never played on Sundays but had performances every other night, with tickets costing twenty-five cents for general admission, fifty cents for the balcony, and seventy-five cents for reserved seats. The cast consisted of the Bryant family plus four or five actors who lived on the boat, with the crew sleeping on the main deck. The entire family was involved in the productions, usually featuring full-length plays such as the popular melodramas *East Lynne, Uncle*

Tom's Cabin, and *Ten Nights in a Bar-Room*. Sometimes farmers and their families would follow the Bryants up and down the river for two or three performances as they were "loath to have the magic slip away," as Betty Bryant recalled. Their shows, Bryant noted, provided "interruptions in the monotony of work."[18]

Like all touring troupes, showboating required endurance, versatility, and commitment—similar to land-touring troupes like Sol Smith's, which purchased Chapman's Floating Palace when Mrs. Chapman retired in 1847. Showboating was hard work. To avoid morning winds, the Chapmans would start off at three in the morning, then often go twenty miles in a day. They would dock, create onshore advertising, prepare for the evening performance, and then produce it—after which, late at night, they would head off to the next town. But the rewards were clearly worth all the tribulations. Their performances provided the only legitimate theater as well as an essential escape for hundreds of river towns.

The Bryants, Chapmans, and other showboat operators knew their performances could "magically transport" their patrons to worlds where love and truth prevailed and where they felt free to laugh and cry, just like opera house patrons.[19] Although showboats were primarily a Southern phenomenon, they could be found elsewhere. A showboat docked at Canal Street in New York City prior to the Civil War. In Oregon, which had been exposed to early maritime theater by the sailors aboard the H.B.M. Sloop *Modeste*, actors went up and down the Columbia and Willamette Rivers in sternwheelers performing for sawmill towns, salmon-packing hamlets, and small communities. Whether in outposts in Oregon or established river towns in Kentucky, these floating theaters provided magical escapes for local townspeople and even for famous performers like opera soprano Lily Pons, who in Cincinnati took in a performance from the balcony of the Bryants' showboat laughing and applauding, eating popcorn, and even joining the audience in the community sing.

As Betty Bryant emphasized the clean, family fun her family showboat offered, many of the lectures and "enlightenment" at opera houses were equally upright. The moral tone of the Chautauquas and of the many lecturers, including all the WCTU speakers, stifled the opportunities for intellectual stimulation that the Carol Kennicotts were seeking at their hometown opera houses. The high road had its limitations.

CHAPTER 8

Music and Opera

When the Reverend William Sweeney in 1958 thought back about all the music—*Carmen, Il trovatore*, and many comic operas, musical comedies, and light operas—he had heard at Paris, Kentucky's "Grand" (Grand Opera House), he found himself "humming or whistling 'The Message of the Violet' or the rollicking chorus 'The Stine Song,' or maybe 'O Promise Me.'"[1] Today, people hum "Oh, What a Beautiful Mornin'" from *Oklahoma!*, tap their feet to jazz favorites, or take the family to hear "Yankee Doodle" at a Fourth of July band concert. Music has always been a favored kind of entertainment in the United States, and it was important in opera house programming. Music came in many guises: local orchestras that accompanied opera house performances, choral groups, traveling musical groups, bands, soloists, operas, operettas, minstrel shows, and musical comedies. America's musical heritage, particularly jazz and musical comedies, may be the country's most important cultural export. The early acceptance of and interest in music in the nineteenth century stimulated American musical culture—and also helps explain why thousands of entertainment halls and theaters, built in the nineteenth century, were called "opera houses."

Music escaped the worst of the Puritanical prejudices that had plagued theatrical performances. It is said that the Pilgrims even sang hymns to bide their time on the long voyage to Plymouth. Only Connecticut, with its rigid blue laws, prohibited "play on any instrument of music, except the drum, trumpet and jews-harp," even though the Puritans in England cast a friendlier eye on music.[2] Acceptance of music in Puritan England is evident in the savvy actions of Sir William Davenant in the seventeenth century. In his complicated life, Davenant, a playwright, a supporter of theater, and possibly the son of Shakespeare by the wife of an Oxford innkeeper, conjured the idea of avoiding all the problems of theater by setting up "an *Italian Opera* to be performed by Declamations and Musick: And that they might be performed with all decency, seemliness and without rudeness and profaneness."[3] Dryden pronounced Davenant's efforts on behalf of Italian opera to be "examples of moral virtue. Writ in verse, and performed in recitative music."[4] Even though it was a thinly disguised play, Davenant did manage to have an "opera" performed during Puritan rule.

Early American music was not a disguise of plays, but it often had a moral veneer to avoid any possible reprobations. The upright music of New Hampshire's Hutchinson Family Singers illustrates the need of early traveling musicians to stay well within moral bounds. The Hutchinson group, consisting of father Jesse and his eleven children, entertained in the 1840s throughout New England, southward to Philadelphia and westward to the emerging frontier, with twelve thousand concerts of "respectable" music. Their music was so respectable that they often performed in churches, in contrast to the suspect plays heard at local taverns. The Hutchinsons' pro-temperance, patriotic, and New World music, praising the natural wonders and simple values of the expanding country, resonated well in both small towns and cities. Their performance in Philadelphia on a cold night in early January 1844 was attended "by a tasteful, musical, respectable and highly gratified auditory," as reported in the family's *Journals.* "The excitement pervaded the whole house . . . and when we told them of our being 'Yankies' the applause was deafening. The patriotic feeling of '76 pervaded every bosom."[5] This concert inspired a "Miss F.A.C." to write a ten-stanza poem, "The Granite State Minstrels":

> Not from the shores of England,
> Or the vine clad hills of France
> Have they come to us with gift of song;
> With the light and mazy dance.
> But they hail from the lofty granite hill,
> From a free and northern home:
> 'Tis a minstrel band of our own loved land
> Of the "land of Washington."[6]

The homespun Hutchinsons, who veered into spiritualism, along with other family singing groups such as the Barkers, the Peaks, and the Lucases, broke the ice for future musical groups like the Andrews Family Opera Company.

Opera house programs were filled with local chorales, operettas, band concerts, and recitals. Music would be part of a long evening at the opera house, interspersed between farces and tragedies. And music was a sociable activity. Diaries of women on the prairie, in the Rockies, and in sod houses on the Nebraska plains mention pleasant times at dances, band concerts, and singing evenings.

Various ethnic groups, whether Scandinavian, Cornish, Czech, Irish, Welsh, or German, brought a love of music with them to their new homes on the prairie or in the city. German beer gardens in Milwaukee would echo with strains of "Die Lorelei," groups of Germans would form music clubs and *Singvereins*, and Swedes would not miss a Christmas concert. Swedes could even enjoy American musicals with Swedish dialect in Fremont, Nebraska's opera house. Czechs were said to be born with a violin under the pillow. The Irish had community sings, and Welsh in the slate country on the border of Vermont and New York sang at their *eisteddfods*. Big cities attracted foreign stars such as Jenny Lind the Swedish Nightingale, promoted by P. T. Barnum, and the Norwegian violinist Ole Bull. Thousands clamored to attend their concerts; forty thousand greeted Lind on her arrival in New York City.

Band concerts were perennial favorites, whether performed by a small town's band or by the ever-popular John Philip Sousa. Sousa's Peerless Band concerts always drew crowds; his performances from 1910 to 1917 in Paris, Kentucky's Grand Opera House were reported to have "brought down the house."[7] The Bellows Falls, Vermont opera house was "jammed" for Sousa band concerts in 1910, 1912, and 1928, and local cornet and brass bands were extremely popular in the nineteenth century. In Gloucester, Massachusetts, with a population of 25,000 in 1891, citizens were not daunted that the town had no park or "place of public resort" to enjoy popular band concerts. They took to the street for their concerts. "The band takes the sidewalk, and the people stand in the street," according to the First Annual Report of the Trustees of Public Reservations in 1891.[8] In Boston, a whopper of a concert organized in 1872 by Patrick Gilmore, lyricist of "When Johnny Comes Marching Home," featuring the World Peace Jubilee orchestra and 1,000 performers, 40 soloists, and a 10,000-person chorus, indicates the enormous interest in popular music.

Two blind and unusually talented black musicians, Blind Tom and Blind Boone, drew enthusiastic crowds at opera houses in small towns, large cities, and even overseas.[9] Their backgrounds differed considerably. Blind Boone came from Missouri, where his mother, a runaway slave descended from Daniel Boone, was a cook for a federal army camp, and Blind Tom was the son of slaves owned by James Bethune of Columbus, Georgia. Boone's eyes had been surgically removed to save him from "brain fever," and Tom was born blind. However, both had rare musical ability in improvising and playing the piano. Blind Tom's considerable earnings went to his master, and Blind Boone's to black causes. Their travels were mind-boggling: at nine years of age, Tom was on a schedule of four shows a day, and Boone gave six concerts a week for almost thirty-nine years. Mark Twain, like thousands of others, marveled at Tom's skills: "It is said," Twain wrote, "that he could accurately play any piece of music, howsoever long and difficult, after hearing it once; and that six months later he could accurately play it again, without having touched it in the interval."[10] No doubt the novelty of their blindness added to the performers' popularity, especially in museum theaters with their corridors of scientific oddities and programs with "freak performers," but the sheer talent of these musicians was what endeared them to their many audiences.

Most music performed in opera houses, especially in rural areas and small cities, was popular music—band concerts and local chorales—but that did not mean that serious classical music was not welcome. The Boston Symphony Orchestra played at Fremont, Nebraska's Love Opera House in January 1889, soon after the Love had been rebuilt after a fire, and again in May 1894. Hubbard Hall in Cambridge, New York hosted the Boston Symphony with two solo artists and one harpist, considered "to be the greatest harpist of the present day," according to a local newspaper.[11] Theodore Thomas brought the Chicago Symphony, which he founded, to the Springer Opera House in Columbus, Georgia in 1872, soon after it was built, and several times thereafter. The Metropolitan Opera performed in Leadville, Colorado and Lincoln, Nebraska; Adelina Patti, the renowned soprano, appeared in Omaha, Cincinnati, and other cities in the new West; and Cincinnati's opera house was inaugurated in 1859 with a five-week opera festival including works by Verdi, Mozart, Rossini, and Bellini.

Vermont in the second half of the nineteenth century saw a blossoming of musical groups, minstrel shows, operettas, and singers, especially in its larger towns. Sometimes a touring company member would break away and stay in a town as a musical jack-of-all-trades, organizing choruses and musical conventions.[12] Choruses could be large affairs with 500 members, of whom 200 might assemble for a concert. Bands, especially cornet and brass bands numbering at least thirty by 1860, were exceedingly popular in the state. They played at rallies, hotel openings, school commencements, state competitions, and evening concerts. Vermonters' tastes seemed to lean toward comic rather than serious music, indicating a preference for entertainment rather than culture. Professor G. Goodwall was a hit because he could play nine instruments at once, as was Dandy Jim, "the Virginia Rattler, greatest banjoist ever," who combined his music with a lecture on phrenology.[13]

However, there was serious music in the state as well. In St. Johnsbury, the philanthropic Fairbanks brothers set up an Academy of Music in 1858 for the concentrated study of music and weekly concerts, culminating in a grand finale at the end of each quarter. Serious prodigies such as the Norwegian violinist and composer Ole Bull, who traveled throughout the country, made it to the small state of Vermont. Local professors gave lessons in piano, organ, and voice. A major Vermont contribution to music in the latter part of the nineteenth century was the Estey reed organ, which was manufactured in Brattleboro from 1846 to 1960 by four hundred employees in a phalanx of slate-walled buildings. The organ's small size and low cost made it both

Family time with the Estey organ. *Estey Organ Museum, Brattleboro, Vermont*

popular and portable. In fact, no parlor was complete in the Victorian era without an Estey organ, around which family members would sing.

"Opera is the rage," the *Spirit* reported in February 1853. Opera troupes, many foreign, were all over the country, as America had become known as a gold mine for foreign stars and troupes. New York even had an Italian Opera House. And opera, often called "grand" opera, did take place in small-town opera houses. Cities in the early nineteenth century became enamored with opera: in 1825 Manuel Garcia's Italian Opera Company was formed in New York; and in 1827 John Davis's French Opera Company was founded in New Orleans, where the *New Orleans Bee* reported that operas "amuse our citizens more than any other form of public entertainment—except balls."[14] For Westerners, a new era of opera began with an Italian opera company performing Rossini at the American Theatre in Louisville, Kentucky in 1836. Not to be outdone, another Louisville theater, the City Theatre, with no performers who could sing in Italian, offered an English version of *Cinderella*, which the American Theatre then produced in its original Italian version, upholding its position as the local theater capable of performing operas in Italian.

Early opera in the United States was considered appropriate for more than the musical and social elite. Like Shakespeare and early theater, opera was popular entertainment appealing to all Americans, as it often combined vernacular music with original scores. In contrast to today's image of opera as appealing to the upper crust, opera audiences in the mid-nineteenth century were heterogeneous and lively, until the latter part of the century when they were segregated into different sections of the performance hall. The pit, what today is called the "orchestra section," attracted many who liked its good view of the stage as well as the "unclassified miscellany," whom Walt Whitman described as "alert, well-dress'd, full blooded young and middle aged men, the best of American born mechanics."[15]

The seeds for transforming opera into a more exclusive cultural activity first emerged with Garcia's early New York Italian Opera Company, whose programs advertised opera hats and cloaks, clearly appealing to the wealthy. On the other hand, the crowds that swarmed into New York's Castle Garden and Niblo's Opera House (founded in 1828) were a mixed bunch. Competition among the Astor Place Opera House, the Castle Garden, and Niblo's peaked when Jenny Lind sold out performance after performance in the Castle Garden on her 1850–1852 tour. The Astor Opera House, founded by 150 wealthy New Yorkers in 1847, instituted a dress code of evening clothes, including kid gloves for men, which strengthened its image of opera as entertainment for the upper classes, as distinct from the hoi polloi at other opera houses.

This was a golden age of opera before the Civil War. "Of the making of opera troupes there is no end," writes opera scholar Katharine Preston of this period. Indeed many operatic stars and troupes were touring during the 1830s, 1840s, and 1850s. In 1843 nine opera companies toured mostly in the East, but with a few stops in Ohio and Michigan and many in Southern cities like Charleston, New Orleans, and Mobile. There were six Italian opera companies touring in 1853 and eight English opera companies in 1854.[16] The success of these varied opera companies indicates how much Americans in this antebellum period enjoyed musical entertainment, especially operas.

After the Civil War, with fresh audiences in the newly settled parts of the country as well as in older towns and cities, opera companies proliferated, reaching their acme during the 1890s. This period saw the popularity of Italian opera companies, such as the Milan Italian Opera Company and the Grand Italian Opera Company; English companies, such as Her Majesty's Opera Company and the Pyne and Harrison Company; and American companies, such as the Emma Abbott Grand English Opera Company. Even off-the-beaten-path locales like Calumet in the Upper Peninsula of Michigan were eager for opera during mining and logging boom times, when they built opera houses as proud symbols of their material achievements. A troupe's circuit in the mid-Michigan towns of St. Johns, Ithaca, St. Louis, Alma, and Mt. Pleasant might include performances of Faust, *Rigoletto*, Gilbert and Sullivan's light operas, and *The Bohemian Girl*—a pattern not uncommon in smaller towns.

However, throughout the country there were many holdouts for "Englished" operas, as foreign opera seemed pretentious to some music devotees in this republican country. Why should people who had fled from the Old World and established themselves in a new country want to listen to music written for other cultures in foreign languages? "We have long enough followed obedient and child-like in the track of the Old World," Walt Whitman observed in an article in the *Brooklyn Daily News* in 1847. "We have received her tenors and her buffos, her operatic troupes and her vocalists of all grades and complexions, listened to and applauded the songs made for a different state of society . . . and it is time that such listening and receiving should cease."[17]

Opera companies from England did tour the country. One of the most successful was the Pyne and Harrison Company, which traveled as far west as Madison, Wisconsin, giving five hundred opera performances and a hundred concerts in three years in the mid-1850s. Unlike many theater troupes, which would perform a play a night in different cities, Pyne and Harrison would stay several weeks in a city. In Cincinnati, they staged sixteen performances of eight operas in three weeks and were so well liked that their admirers hoped the group would linger. But their schedule took them next to Louisville, where they performed again to packed houses night after night, and then onto New Orleans, via a dangerous trip down the frozen Ohio River where they were marooned on ice floes for days. Later they toured Mobile, St. Louis, Richmond, and Washington, DC, a schedule that understandably caused them to tire of such constant traveling. The popularity of the Pyne and Harrison Company confirmed that not all Americans wanted Italian and German opera. Americans liked light opera; Germans, instead, "are built for heavy music," Willa Cather noted. "But Americans, like the French, prefer action to music.... This is not a depravity of taste; it is merely a temperamental difference."[18]

The many opera troupes traversing the country in the mid- to late nineteenth century did not seem to be daunted by the demands of traveling. There were eager audiences, money to be made, and artistic satisfactions to be garnered. On-the-road opera remained a democratic art. Evidence of the exclusivity of opera and the love of foreign opera could be found in large cities, but both rural townspeople and many urbanites liked English comic operas as well as some translations of Italian, German, and French operas. However, tensions between average, unpretentious Americans and denizens of the upscale world of the Metropolitan Opera were always lurking. Not wanting to be left out, audiences everywhere were anxious to see celebrities and attend performances by famous companies, especially the Metropolitan Opera Company. Leadville, Colorado boasted having the Metropolitan Opera on its stage at the Tabor Opera House, and Burlington, Vermont's Howard Opera House opened with the Strakosch Opera Company's presentations of Donizetti and Verdi operas. However, most of the arias and choruses wafting across the wooden floors and tin ceilings of opera houses were simple fare. "People, especially in pioneer areas, were eager for music and laughter," astutely remarked Cornelia Andrews DuBois of the well-known Andrews Opera Company, which toured the Midwest in the 1870s.[19] And that is what they got.

The Emma Abbott Grand English Opera Company might sound like another English company, but it was not. It was all-American, hailing from the Midwest and appealing to Midwestern audiences. Born in Chicago in 1849, Emma Abbott began her career playing the guitar and singing to an audience of coal miners in an Edwards, Illinois schoolhouse, and then as a teenager she gave parlor concerts in Midwestern hotels.

A talented soprano, she was soon studying in Milan and Paris, later appearing as Marie in Donizetti's *Daughter of the Regiment* in London's Covent Garden and making her American debut in 1877 in New York, where she was highly praised by the city's music critics.

With her husband's managerial assistance, she organized a small touring company with three singers, a pianist, and a cornetist, which expanded into

Emma Abbott, a popular soprano, was the first woman to organize an opera company, the Emma Abbott Grand English Opera Company. *Library of Congress, Prints and Photographs Division LC-DIG-cwpbh-05200*

the highly successful Emma Abbott Grand English Opera Company, touring the country singing opera and operettas. Emma herself performed at
the Metropolitan Opera. Her company was commissioned by the demanding Horace Tabor to open his new Grand Opera House in Denver, with
a two-week booking including *Lucia di Lammermoor, Fra Diavolo* (twice),
Il trovatore, Martha (twice), *Olivette, The Bohemian Girl* (twice), *Faust, The
Chimes of Normandy* (which Willa Cather saw in Red Cloud, Nebraska), and
Cecelia's Love. This broad range of performances was all in English. Emma
Abbott altered librettos and added freely what she liked to well-known
operas. She substituted a moral woman named Cecilia for the immoral
Violetta in *La traviata*, and she injected popular hymns into *Faust*, to the
consternation of critics and to the pleasure of her audiences.[20]

The company was in demand in the West, especially in Colorado, where
it was booked six times in Denver and twice in Leadville and Colorado
Springs. A highlight for Abbott was her dedication of the Grand Opera
House in Peoria, Illinois, where her family lived and her father directed the
choir of the First Baptist Church. Many other troupes of varying quality
were performing Gilbert and Sullivan, *The Chimes of Normandy*, and *Faust*,
but the Emma Abbott Grand English Opera Company was one of the best.

Appealing to the eagerness of small-town audiences for music and
laughter were many ubiquitous and popular musical and opera groups,
some with good talent, but others often missing the skills and breadth of
competent musicians like Emma Abbott and her company. A respected
but humbler troupe than the Abbotts' was the Andrews Family Opera
Company of Minnesota.[21]

This family's musical career truly bespoke of the heartland. The
Andrews Family Opera Company was so American that, it was reported,
it would not hire Enrico Caruso as a member of the company shortly
after he arrived in the United States because he could not sing in English.
Their family-centered musical activities began with the purchase of a reed
organ by Methodist minister John Andrews, which launched his family into morning and evening hymn sings at home and then providing
music in churches. Fortunately, the Reverend Andrews had a large family
with ten children (with different degrees of musical talent), similar to the
Hutchinsons. He was also fortunate, maybe as a result of his Virginia
heritage, to suppress the rigid Methodist church's antagonism to opera.
As long as the troupers "kept to high ideals of entertainment and as long
as they maintained family relationships, taking husband and wives and
children with them on the road," the Methodist hierarchy avoided con-
demnation, according to his great-niece.[22]

It was a Horatio Alger story. The troupe began with a red bandwagon with tiered seats led by six plumed horses, as a band of cornets, horns, and a bass drum played marches down small-town streets, similar to the preperformance publicity of circuses and showboats. Initially performing in Iowa, Kansas, and Nebraska, the troupe eventually went all over the country, performing both sacred and secular music, comic skits, dances, and light opera, and finally "grand" opera (in English, of course). The red wagon was replaced with a private Pullman car with staterooms for the group and another rail car for baggage. They were constantly learning and improving. Their repertoire included all the popular light operas of Gilbert and Sullivan, *The Chimes of Normandy*, *Fra Diavolo*, and *Erminie*, and eventually grand operas such as *Martha*, *Cavalleria rusticana*, *Faust*, *Il trovatore*, and *Carmen*. They boasted of performing thirty operas, but they would blend in nonoperatic music such as daughter Florence's rendition of "My Mother's Little Broken Ring." The troupe was well received in large cities like Minneapolis, where they had a six-week engagement in 1891, as well as in hundreds of small towns. In fact, the list of towns they visited "reads much like a railroad time table."[23]

For twenty-five years after 1875, the Andrews Family Opera Company, which was often referred to as "The Mikado Company," survived train wrecks, fires, financial problems, all the hazards of traveling, the problems of keeping a troupe intact, and even the failure of a hotel/resort with trotting races and abundant musical performances it established on Lake

The Andrews Family Opera Company's private railroad car was a grand achievement for a troupe that began its touring with a horse-drawn bandwagon. *Minnesota Historical Society*

Tetonka, Minnesota in 1896. In looking back at her family's musical heritage and its diverse engagements, they "were not above appearing in any town that would give them a two-hundred-dollar guarantee, and their seat prices never went above a dollar top," according to Cornelia Andrews DuBois, the family historian. For this family member, "the most significant contribution consisted of taking opera to the people—of producing grand opera in English for those whose opportunities to see and hear any form of entertainment, good or bad, were extremely meager." She summed up the significance and poignant story of these hardworking troupes: "To countless people living in new, rough country just emerging from its frontier beginnings they took entertainment and conveyed the sense of beauty and inspiration that comes from hearing great music."[24]

Although serious opera and theater critics tended to scorn the tastes of the heartland, Nebraska enjoyed a golden era of grand opera in the late nineteenth and early twentieth centuries. Grand opera came early to the state. Seven years after Nebraska achieved statehood, the first grand opera troupe, the Adelaide Phillips Company, performed *The Barber of Seville* and *Don Pasquale* in Italian. In the 1880s, twenty-four operatic performances were given by such opera companies as Emma Abbott's, the Boston Ideal Opera Company, Her Majesty's Opera Company, the Milan Italian Opera Company, and the National Opera Company. In 1887 Adelina Patti, one of the greatest sopranos of the time, sang in Omaha. The city's location on the first transcontinental rail line meant that many leading opera companies and stars would stop there as they headed to San Francisco.

The state's major cities, Omaha and Lincoln, enjoyed many operatic performances in their opera houses, the Boyd in Omaha and the Funke in Lincoln, and for larger crowds the Coliseum in Omaha. Operas were reviewed by the young theater critic for Lincoln's *Courier*, Willa Cather, with memorable comments such as those on a performance of *Carmen* in Lincoln: "[Mme. Dorre's Carmen was] frankly sensual, with eyes glowing with lubricity," making Carmen "the wickedest of my acquaintance" and the music "a happy compromise between the old Italian tuneful if unintellectual succession of airs and concerted pieces and the later Wagnerian 'leading motive' dramatic and emotional strains." Cather concluded that the "opera is so replete with human interest, and its music so genuinely good, that I believe it will hold the boards when modern music has grown musty."[25]

A five-day opera festival in Omaha in 1894 with performances of *Faust*, *Lucia*, and *Carmen*, in English, indicates the popularity of opera in this heartland city whose population had expanded by 1890 to 140,452. The city's massive Coliseum was converted into an opera house with lavish

Adelina Patti, a hugely successful soprano who toured the
United States and abroad in the late nineteenth century. *Library
of Congress, Prints and Photographs Division LC-USZ62–68664*

boxes and an elaborate stage and sets, matched only by the elite audience of Omaha, who saw Verdi's *Il trovatore* sung in Italian by Lillian Nordica, and later Adelina Patti in Rossini's *The Barber of Seville.* Patti's performance attracted the largest crowd in Omaha's theatrical history, an estimated 8,500, including children who had a holiday from school to attend the opera. She responded to this enthusiasm, finding Omaha one of the "grandest towns in America ... because the audiences here are always appreciative."[26] Opera, especially grand opera, continued in Nebraska despite a dip in the economy and threats from vaudeville in the 1890s. Comic opera flagged in the early 1900s, but Omaha and Lincoln had more opera performances from 1900 to 1910 than they had had in the previous decade, and then twice the number in the next decade. Not until the arrival of movies did the popularity of opera fade in Nebraska.

Melodramas and light musicals were the mainstay of many small-town opera houses, but it is clear that Wagner, Rossini, Verdi's *Il trovatore* (the Midwest's favorite opera), and many operas in both Italian and English were exceedingly popular in the new state of Nebraska in the late 1800s and early 1900s. Adelina Patti might be performing only in large cities like Omaha, but Emma Abbott's and other operatic troupes reached smaller Nebraska towns like Red Cloud. While New Yorkers attending performances at the new Metropolitan Opera House no doubt considered Nebraska a backwater of culture, this Plains state like many others enjoyed an unusual flowering of theater, music, and opera in this period. And like New Yorkers, Nebraskans' motivations may have been as much socially as culturally oriented. They may have sought the opera because it was fashionable, but they also attended because they enjoyed it.

Competing with melodramas and musicals for popularity with American audiences in the latter half of the nineteenth century were minstrel shows. It would be hard to find an opera house in the United States then that did not have at least one minstrel show on its program every season. Often several minstrel shows by different troupes would appear in a town in one season. The Leadville Minstrels and Sam Gardner's Minstrels both performed in Fremont, Nebraska's Shad Opera House in 1880, and the 1873–1874 season at Lincoln, Nebraska's Hallo's Opera House included shows by both Robinson's Minstrels and Sharpley's Minstrels. Instead of several troupes, the Tabor Opera House in Leadville, Colorado had a four-day engagement of the Callender Minstrels in 1883. Innumerable minstrel troupes traveled around the country from the 1840s to the 1910s. While the popularity of the fast-paced and unpretentious minstrel shows peaked at the end of the nineteenth century, especially in cities, minstrelsy continued in the early twentieth century. In February 1903 the Lexington Opera House had a *Big Minstrel Sensation*, and by the 1910s minstrel shows were reported to have drawn the largest crowds at the Paris (Kentucky) Grand Opera House. As late as the 1930s, the high school in the northern Vermont town of Enosburgh Falls produced an annual minstrel show.

Considered the only genuinely indigenous form of American drama, minstrel shows had spontaneity, with no set plot, speeches, music, or character development, but instead an engaging verve and humorous banter that appealed to audiences throughout the country. While musical troupes such as the Emma Abbott Grand English Opera Company and Andrews Family Opera Company and individual musicians such as Jenny Lind were trying to provide serious music with uplift and beauty, the minstrel show offered entertainment and escape.

The first full-evening performance of a minstrel show was given in 1842 by Dan Emmett's Virginia Minstrels show, with four singers and dancers in blackface with tambourines and bones, in New York, where the group then staged its first major performance in February 1843 at the Bowery Amphitheatre. Within a year, a group named the Ethiopian Serenaders was entertaining at the White House during the administration of John Tyler. The origins of these blackfaced whites' minstrel shows go back at least as far as 1769, when Lewis Hallam impersonated a drunken Negro in *The Rivals*. Later there were impersonations of Negroes in interludes at plays, as when Edwin Forrest's cook, Andrew Allen, performed between acts at a theater in Albany in 1815. In 1828 Thomas Dartmouth Rice, known as "Jim Crow" Rice, joined Samuel Drake's group at the Louisville Theatre, where he did his first "Jim Crow" dance in *The Rifle*. Rice, usually a solo dancer sometimes accompanied by a banjo, often performed between acts, as he did at performances of *The Hunchback* and *Catherine of Cleves* in New York in 1832. While he also introduced "Ethiopian operas," Rice was best known for his "Jim Crow" jump, a contorted dance, which he continued doing almost until his death in 1861.

Dan Emmett's group of four friends and other small groups of four to eight men were soon introducing minstrel shows around the country. E. P. Christy organized a larger show with ten to fifteen and later up to thirty men and, most important, created the two-part show for which minstrelsy was known for decades. In this format, the whole company would march onstage and arrange themselves in a semicircle with the master of ceremonies, the Interlocutor, in the center asking questions, joking, and setting up a comic dialogue with the two endmen, Mr. Tambo with a tambourine and Mr. Bones with bones. The entire group would sing various choruses, and then this first part would end with each person walking around inside the circle several times and then performing some special act in the center. The second part, called the olio, was more like vaudeville: freeform skits, often spoofing and ridiculing people, current events, and plantation life.

While minstrelsy was no doubt created as yet another way to try to make money in theatrical entertainment, it perpetuated the stereotypical image of a lazy, flashy, happy-go-lucky—and musical—plantation slave. Most of the early shows were staged by blackfaced whites, but before and during the Civil War Negro minstrel show performers such as the Luca Family entertained in the North. As minstrelsy evolved into elaborate, vaudeville-like shows in the latter part of the century, the moral messages about slavery and racism as well as the shows' spontaneous humor became obscured. Also lost in these grander and more complicated minstrel shows was the free and easy music and light banter of the early minstrel shows. These shows, as minstrelsy scholar Robert C. Toll noted, "provided common Americans with folk-based earthy songs, vital dances, and robust humor as well as with beautiful ballads and fine singing that they could enjoy at reasonable prices."[27]

Looking at minstrelsy today, it is hard to ignore our contemporary view of slavery and the racism of that era as we try to understand the popularity of these nineteenth-century shows. Minstrels "provided a non-threatening way for white Americans to cope with the questions about the nature and proper place of black people in America," according to Toll. And "during the sectional crisis," he suggests, "minstrels shaped white Americans' vaguer notions and amorphous beliefs about Negroes into vivid, eye-catching caricatures as they literally acted out images of blacks and plantation life that satisfied their huge audiences."[28] By the late 1890s, some African Americans such as Bob Cole, Billy Johnson, George Walker, and Bert Williams moved away from the stereotypical portrayal of plantation blacks and into musicals like *The Gold Bug* and other productions that often ridiculed the Sambo-era stereotypes of Jim Crow segregation.

Despite the racial implications of minstrelsy, these shows, which included Northern performers and composers such as Stephen Foster, influenced future performers such as Al Jolson and Eddie Cantor. The many thousands who attended minstrel shows in opera houses for decades and the large numbers of touring minstrel show troupes, whether well-known groups such as the Christy or Haverley Minstrel Shows or smaller troupes such as Lucier Minstrels and Guy Brothers' Minstrels, attest to the popularity of minstrelsy. In Leadville, Lincoln, and even in northern Vermont, the wagon show/circus show with Whitmore and Clark minstrels and their "forty five horse and forty five men" minstrel shows drew large crowds. McCabe and Young's Operatic Minstrels with "thirty artists and thirty performers, a magnificent brass band, more new songs, more new specialties, more new dances" was advertised in the *Fremont Daily Herald* in May 1891 as "the famous Conqueror of Fun and music."[29] The popularity of minstrel shows continued in the twentieth century in rural opera houses in places like Enosburgh Falls, Vermont, where traveling minstrel groups such as the Victory Minstrels performed in the 1920s and later when such shows were locally produced. For many fans of minstrelsy, the lure was the fun and music, as McCabe and Young's Operatic Minstrels advertised.[30]

The popularity of music from minstrel shows to serious opera is evident in the programs of opera houses. Band concerts and performances by musical prodigies such as Blind Boone and by opera companies such as the Emma Abbott Grand English Opera Company were perennial favorites in small towns. While larger cities like Omaha could attract well-known stars like soprano Adelina Patti, small-town opera houses provided not only programs by regional traveling companies, but also by local choral and musical groups, including the immensely popular local bands. Clearly music has been a mainstay for the opera house.

CHAPTER 9

What the Public Wants

Samuel Johnson had it right when he said, "The Drama's laws the Drama's patrons give / For they that live to please, must please—to live."[1] The audience has been a key player in determining the types of performances offered in theaters and opera houses, particularly in the early nineteenth century. People through the ages have sought to be entertained and uplifted by theater, but what constitutes entertainment or uplift for one age may not suit another. The interactions among actors, playwrights, managers, and audiences help create and sustain the basically social nature of theater.

As George Washington and aristocratic audiences of the eighteenth century enjoyed their romantic plays, even saucy ones, and Shakespeare's works were revised to please their tastes and also offer a sop to the many Puritanical antitheater factions, early-nineteenth-century audiences enjoyed romantic and poetic plays. This was the beginning of the long procession of melodramas, starting with the hit *Uncle Tom's Cabin* in 1852 and Dion Boucicault's *The Octoroon* in 1859. Both these shows looked at the role of slavery and the broader issue of law in a democratic society through the lens of melodrama. By the late 1800s, amid the profusion of entertainment options, melodrama dominated theater. *East Lynne, Under the Gaslight, Beacon Lights, The Drunkard*, and *The Span of Life* were everywhere, titillating audiences with their breathtaking escapes and chases where the heroine was always rescued. In *The Span of Life*, for example, acrobats made a human bridge for the heroine to escape from the Arab chief and a shameful life in his harem.

Changes in audience behavior reflect the dramatic shifts in values from one epoch to another. In early theater, whether in *rederijkers* in the Low Countries, midway performances at regional fairs, early street theater, or even most theater until the 1850s, attendance at plays was a lively occasion with much give-and-take between the audience and performers. Audience appreciation of Shakespeare is a barometer of changing tastes and audiences. Until the mid-nineteenth century, Shakespeare's plays were perennial hits, performed in taverns and parlors, courthouses, military garrisons, early theaters, and opera houses. Shakespeare was a part of everyday culture: almost everyone knew the Bard's works. All classes attended theater during this time, although they were seated in different sections. So it is not surprising, given the participatory atmosphere of early theater, that an actor in a Shakespeare play had to be on his toes. If he missed a line or changed some words, the audience would hiss, stomp, or whistle. Joseph Jefferson recalled almost fondly the "hissing and jeering" of vocal audiences when he missed a line in the 1840s, compared to the passive and decorous audiences of the 1880s.[2]

After the Civil War, as theater was being transformed into high art for the refined classes, Shakespeare was recast from a popular playwright, whose plays were enjoyed by all, to a playwright for highbrows. By the end of the nineteenth century, Shakespeare was no longer embedded in the culture and education of the public as he had been for earlier generations. A long-standing oral tradition was replaced by a more literary tradition. The influx of immigrants from cultures where English theater and Shakespeare had not been part of their heritage, combined with pervasive changes wrought by rapid urbanization, including growing social stratification, transformed not only Shakespeare but also theater, theatergoing, and audiences in general.

Going to the theater or any performance is a sociable occasion where audiences collectively laugh, gasp, and weep. These spontaneous emotions reflect shared experiences and also the prevailing values and attitudes of a particular era. As the nineteenth century proceeded, audience reactions were being tamed along with culture and theater. George William Curtis's experiences at two New York performances in 1863 illustrate this point. Curtis, then editor of *Harper's* magazine, took a friend to two major theaters with well-known actors, but with very different audiences. Niblo's Garden was "crammed with people. All the seats full, and the aisles, and the steps," with some on chairs, others hanging on the balustrade, to see Edwin Forrest, whose muscular performance "was a boundless exaggeration." The audience responded emotionally to Forrest's moving performance; Curtis reported that young women near them cried. "They were not refined, intellectual women. They were, perhaps, rather coarse. But they cried good hearty tears." For Curtis's friend, one act was all he could take. But then at *Othello* in the Winter Garden, they found Edwin Booth performing "a pale, thin intellectual" Iago to a cultivated audience, who watched with "refined attention rather than eager interest."[3]

Theater that was once open to all classes had become fragmented; it was no longer shared neutral turf. Rather it became stratified into different types of performances for different classes: ethnic plays, operas, classics, popular lectures, vaudeville, and minstrel shows for the working class; legitimate theater for the middle class; and operas and symphonies for the wealthy. As the country became increasingly urban and more ethnically diverse, the divides between highbrow and lowbrow, rich and poor, native and immigrant, and urban and rural were becoming more pronounced. The shock of the 1849 Astor Place Riot in New York was a warning of the growing divide between highbrow and lowbrow theatergoers. The feisty American actor Edwin Forrest's feud with the refined English actor William Charles Macready aroused such wild anti-English and anti-patrician feelings that the Bowery Irish stormed the theater and attacked Macready, his fellow actors, and their upper-class supporters such as the Astors. This raucous occasion turned into a full-fledged riot that had to be quelled by the militia after more than twenty people were killed.

Although those living on the rural frontier did not have to cope with the exclusivity and social climbing of big-city theatergoers and the dramatic divide between classes, they did feel the tensions of changing times. Their response was to seek comfort in familiar things. But the tone set by New York City permeated the entire country. Whether in Fremont, Nebraska or Lexington, Kentucky, theaters were compared to those in New York. Theatergoing like New York's became a social, almost voyeuristic event where one could see and be seen. Fortunately, especially in cities, there were increasing options, with theaters, concert halls, opera houses, hippodromes, and lecture halls offering diverse entertainment for all classes and tastes.

In small towns and rural areas, that diversity did not exist. The opera house, often the only entertainment hall in town, served all social strata with all types of performances, such as magicians, plays, operettas, and all the local plays, choruses, and school events. These audiences wanted entertainment and uplift as urbanites did, but their tastes often were less sophisticated and their standards less demanding. The breezes of refinement, however, blew their way around the country. In small places, new, larger opera houses would have boxes, balconies, and parquets like big-city theaters, and their wealthy patrons would dress up just like big-city patrons. But while offerings were fewer than in the cities, mainstream drama sooner or later came their way, thanks to hundreds of traveling troupes and improved rail service.

People sought entertainment that simplified their lives and showed how traditional virtues of courage, honesty, and hard work could overcome the threats posed by societal changes. Melodrama emerged as the answer. From the early nineteenth century, with offerings by John Howard Payne and Mordecai Noah, Americans took to melodramas. By the end of the 1800s, melodrama was so popular that troupes were performing hundreds of melodramatic favorites to enthusiastic audiences throughout the country.

The Irish-Anglo expatriate jack-of-all-trades Dionysius (Dion) Boucicault became the master of melodrama, as he knew how to blend sensation with a variety of moral themes that resonated with young, optimistic Americans in both his acting and, most significantly, his playwriting and managing. After his London success of *Assurance*, Boucicault came to the United States in 1854. At first he acted, but soon he began writing almost two hundred "rough and tumble" plays, which spilled out, he said, "as a hen lays eggs."[4]

Beginning with *The Poor of New York* (1867), his plays included *The Octoroon* (1859), *Belle Lamar*, *The Collen Braun* (1860), and *Rip Van Winkle*, which he adapted for Joseph Jefferson III. In *The Poor of New York*, Boucicault was able to Americanize what had originally been a French play about a middle-class family fighting a greedy banker as it struggled to survive during the 1857 financial panic. While the woes of poverty and urban life are explored with histrionic skill to produce tears and sympathy for the downtrodden, he cleverly focuses on the city with a rhythm and comic touch that would later be evident in early silent films.[5] Boucicault's message that things will work out and that you can make your own future won him the hearts of Americans. He empowered the innocent and the voiceless as he stoked their belief in human dignity and the system of justice, despite real-world troubles. He successfully lobbied for copyright laws for drama, fireproof scenery for theaters, and a profit-sharing program for playwrights, which confirmed his belief in a system of justice where individual actions can be rewarded and enterprising citizens can improve the state of the world. This optimistic idea that "you can make your own destiny" was a timely American theme. Instead of being daunted by changes, you could manipulate these new situations to make a better life for yourself. The message was that corporations, banks, and rampant laissez-faire attitudes, which seemed overwhelming to many at that time, need not crush you.

That simple, optimistic message of self-empowerment cast in moral tones was accessible to everyone. If you kept the faith and were righteous, you could overcome the many hurdles in everyday life like unfaithful husbands, drinking, and gambling. Feminine virtue and traditional, often rural, values would provide the moral basis for a good life in an era of physical, social, and economic uprootedness. Those themes, compounded with dramatic stage effects for fires, storms, train wrecks, and chases, made the hundreds of melodramas like *East Lynne, Under the Gaslight*, and *The Drunkard* box office successes.

"Sensations are what the public wants," Boucicault recognized early on, and they remained a critical part of the formula for a successful melodrama.[6] Thirty years after seeing *Uncle Tom's Cabin* in the Red Cloud, Nebraska Opera House, Willa Cather could still hear the barking bloodhounds on that Nebraska stage. Generations of people remember the classic railroad scene of a man tied to a railroad track but freed by the heroine just before the train approached in Augustin Daly's 1867 *Under the Gaslight*. But the popularity of such plays depended on their sensational scenes with themes that captured people's hearts and minds and confirmed their belief in themselves and their country.

Uncle Tom's Cabin, the hit of the century, was an all-American play. Unlike many popular plays, operas, and operettas, which were written or acted by foreigners or expatriates, *Uncle Tom's Cabin* was adapted from a best-selling book by an American on an American theme and had its first performance in an American opera house, albeit a "museum." Early performances of the play were in the tradition of much early theater in America: a talented family organized as a small stock company struggling for recognition in a small city, Troy, New York, just north of Albany on the opposite bank of the Hudson River.

The trajectory of *Uncle Tom's Cabin* was astonishing. It was likely seen by more people than any other play in the history of American theater. In 1902, one-and-a-half million people were thought to have seen it just in that year alone. By 1912, 250,000 performances are estimated to have occurred. Its run in Troy was considered extraordinary: "no play had ever had so many performances in so short a time in so small a place."[7] It was also a success abroad.

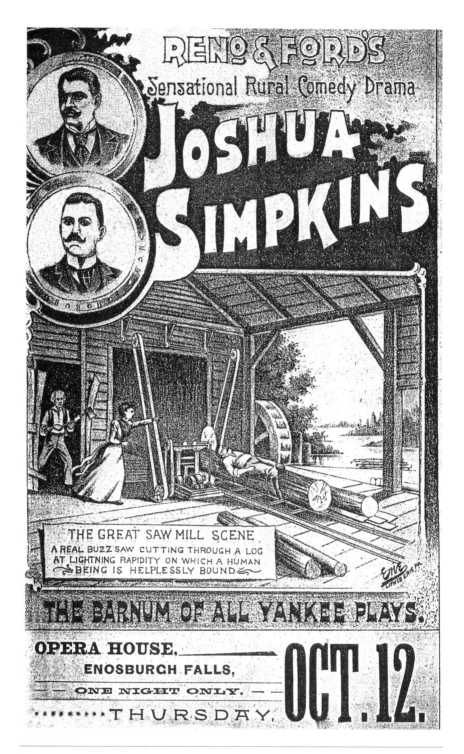

Sensational dramas like Joshua Simpkins with its dramatic sawmill scene, "The Barnum of All Yankee Plays," could provide a break from the tedium of daily chores in remote rural hamlets. *Enosburgh Historical Society and Janice Geraw*

In London six versions of the play were being performed in December 1852, before the play arrived in New York. Later it was popular in Paris.

It was probably in small-town opera houses that most people saw *Uncle Tom's Cabin*, as troupes performing only that play, referred to as "Tommers," went everywhere, often for one-night stands. The best known "Tommers" numbered 50 in the 1870s, 77 in the 1880s, 136 in the 1890, and 500 in 1900. Towns would have several shows a year, so many that in 1880 a Lancaster, Pennsylvania newspaper reported that after the tenth *Uncle Tom's Cabin* production that year "no more are wanted."[8] The productions were petering out by the 1910s, although Leon Washburn's Tom Company advertised its "Fifty-Fourth Annual Tour of Stetson's Show" in 1925.

Adapting Harriet Beecher Stowe's *Uncle Tom's Cabin* for the stage was the idea of George Howard, manager of the Troy Museum and the husband of a competent actress, always called Mrs. George Howard. They were the parents of then-four-year-old Cordelia, whom Howard thought would be a good Eva. To adapt Stowe's book into a play, Howard hired his twenty-one-year-old actor cousin of his wife and museum company member, George L. Aiken, for forty dollars and a gold watch. Aiken is said to have taken a week to complete the adaptation. The result of his efforts was a four-act play, first produced at the Troy Museum on September 27, 1852, with a running time of three hours and fifteen minutes. That Aiken version and his later revision of the play, which eventually came to six acts and thirty scenes, remained the most respected version of the play. Both Mrs. Howard and "Little Cordelia," as the Troy Museum advertised Howard's daughter, were considered excellent actresses. George Germon's performance as Uncle Tom was also heralded. Aside from being the playwright, George Aiken also played George Harris for three months before leaving for Boston, where he acted in the National Theatre.

The Troy Museum, formerly Peale's Museum, on the corner of River and Fulton Streets in downtown Troy, a prosperous, small industrial city in 1852 with a population of 29,000, was similar to many "museum" theaters: a building with an auditorium, but also filled with "natural and artificial curiosities" including 300 stuffed animals and birds, cases with hundreds of insects and mineral specimens, and life-sized figures of national heroes like Washington and Lafayette. Paintings and a "splendid cosmorama" were also available to the Troy Museum visitor.[9] The advertisement in the *Troy Daily Times* for the first production of *Uncle Tom's Cabin, or, Life among the Lowly*, "The New Drama from Harriet Beecher Stowe's popular work," listed Uncle Tom being performed by

Mr. G. C. Germon, St. Clair by Mr. Howard, George Harris by Mr. G. L. Aiken, Eliza by Mrs. G. C. Germon, Topsy by Mrs. G. Howard, and Eva by Little Cordelia Howard. The doors opened at 7:00, the play began at 8:00, the admission was twenty-five cents, children half price, the gallery twelve and a half cents, box seats twelve and a half cents extra, "Orchestra spring seats and cushioned Arm Chairs 25 cents extra."[10]

An advertisement for the first performance of the extremely popular *Uncle Tom's Cabin* at the Troy Museum, Troy, New York. *Troy Daily Times*, September 27, 1852. *Troy Public Library, Troy, New York*

Despite competing entertainment at the nearby Morris Place Concert Hall of the "Magnificent Diorama of the Burning of Moscow" with "an amusing scene in VENTRILOQUISM by Mr. Gallagher," the Troy Museum's production of *Uncle Tom's Cabin* was featured in the *Troy Daily Times*'s "Editorial Splinters":

> The representation of Uncle Tom's Cabin last evening at the Museum brought forth tears from many an eye. The part of Uncle Tom, by Mr. Germon, was a beautiful piece of acting, and Mrs. Howard was quite clever in her performance of Topsy, a wicked "colored gal." The scenes between little Eva and Uncle Tom were very affecting, and were witnessed with the most intense interest. The play is a good rebuke to those ranting abolitionists who are continually talking about slavery yet who don't do anything to either free the slave or better his condition. The piece will be performed again this evening, and we would advise all to go and see it.[11]

Three days later, the newspaper considered *Uncle Tom's Cabin* "the best play that has been brought out upon the Museum boards for a long time. Manager Howard is reaping a fine harvest from it. Go and see the play."[12] Soon the newspaper reported "the Museum is thronged every night with the most respectable audiences, who witness the play with great satisfaction."[13] That version of the play was only the first two-thirds of the novel, ending with Eva's death, but after Trojans requested Mr. Howard for a "further dramatization," Aiken then adapted the last third of the novel, which was produced on October 29 as *The Death of Uncle Tom, or Religion of the Lowly*. Soon thereafter the newspaper stated that the new play "is even considered by some superior to *Uncle Tom's Cabin*."[14] Several weeks later, despite "opposition . . . election excitement, and amusements generally," the new version had "drawn good houses for the past three weeks and has pleased and delighted all who witnessed it."[15]

By November 15, the "whole of Uncle Tom's Cabin and the Death of Uncle Tom" was presented. The starting time was moved up to "1/4 to 8" due to the length of the double-play performance. Probably Howard's most important logistical decision was to abandon the custom of farces and entertainments as entr'actes and afterpieces. Howard had already omitted the entr'actes for the first version of the play during September and October, but continued afterpiece farces such as *A Kiss in the Dark, My Wife's Come*, and *Love in Livery. Uncle Tom's Cabin* kept going in Troy, reportedly one hundred nights, with many "last nights" and special benefits for Mrs. Howard and "Little Cordelia," while the *Troy Daily Times* continued to extol the performances and urge Trojans to see it. "Mr. Howard never made a more successful hit when he procured a dramatic version of Mrs. Stowe's popular work. It had been witnessed each evening for the past eight weeks by our citizens, and each time with increased delight."[16]

The next year, when the play went to New York, its performances converted the National Theatre from a theater patronized by prostitutes and their compatriots to a "Temple of Moral Drama" where even ministers felt they could take their parishioners. The play continued to attract thousands of theatergoers. In no time *Uncle Tom's Cabin* was everywhere. P. T. Barnum, recognizing the commercial opportunities in using Conroy's version of the play, converted it into a spectacular. Minstrel shows used parts of it; Christy and Woods made one-act versions of the Aiken play into *Life among the Happy* and eventually it was a full-blown opera. It even spawned anti-Tom plays in the South, the only part of the country not overrun by Tommer troupes.

The abolitionist message of the original play was smothered as the Tommer shows became more and more spectacular, as a November 1893 advertisement confirms: "40 people, 3 palace cars/20 ponies, donkeys, and burros/8 original plantation jubilee singers/A pack of man-eating Siberian bloodhounds, including Ajax, the $5,000 beauty/Eva's golden chariot, costing $3,000.... Two bands of music."[17] Many of the shows displayed poor theater: Willa Cather slammed Rusco & Swift's production in Lincoln, Nebraska in a review for the (Lincoln) *Journal* in September 1894 as "one of the worst."[18] Like many Tommers, its company was made up of "mongrel non-descript actors, a very sleepy and sometimes pretty little girl and a few hungry-looking curs that have become stage-struck."[19] Reviewers reported Topsy sounding like "a cricket with laryngitis," Uncle Tom being obese, Eva as a saccharine child, and the animals taking center stage. The quality of the performances of the many different troupes and productions obviously varied, but clearly there were many who enjoyed the play. Robert Bosworth, a respectable actor playing with Minnie Maddern Fiske, told of going in 1902 with a group of friends to a black group's performance of *Uncle Tom's Cabin* in a "funny little theater" in Davenport, Iowa prepared to "laugh, but remained to pray for we saw an exquisitely beautiful, dignified and marvelously pathetic and sweet performance."[20]

The phenomenal success of the melodrama was attributable to its message, its high emotions, its relevance, the Aiken script, some good acting, and savvy promotion. It aroused the conscience and heart of Americans at a time when the country was wrestling with the gnawing problem of slavery and later with the pains of Reconstruction. Mr. Howard, the impresario of the Troy Museum, recognized the book's and play's important abolitionist message and was anxious to popularize "anti-slavery opinion," according to reminiscences by his daughter Cordelia, who went on to be a well-respected actress.[21] "It is important to recognize," *Uncle Tom's Cabin* scholar Thomas F. Gossett reflects, "that *Uncle Tom's Cabin* as a play was largely responsible for major changes in the way Blacks were perceived."[22] Whether or not that held for the small-town operagoer in the hinterlands of South Dakota, the abolitionist message certainly offered moral uplift in much of the country. And no doubt farmers in Nebraska, miners in Colorado, shopkeepers in Iowa, and housewives everywhere wanted to feel that they were participating in the mainstream of the country and in this new American drama—its dilemmas, its ideals, and its entertainment.

George Aiken's exceptional adaptation of the book proved critical to the success of the play, as Aiken was able to take the riveting dialogue from Harriet Beecher Stowe and weave it with contemporary idiom, so the images and timely message were convincing. Coupling that message with such melodramatic elements as the exciting flight/pursuit and the plight of the innocent victims with all the staging for such dramatic effects made for a thrilling evening. *Uncle Tom's Cabin* offered the opera house patron a message, some sensation, and the assurance that right would triumph.

It is also a success story of the opera house. The play had its origins in an opera house, albeit in the guise of a "museum," and its genesis in Troy reflects the ingenuity, industry, and talent of many small stock and touring companies performing in opera houses. Mr. Howard had an eye for an important play with a message that resonated with the public—even the "respectable" public in Troy, who did not ordinarily patronize the Troy Museum. Furthermore, he organized the varied talents in his family into a worthy company. Howard and his company were considered respectable, too: it was noted that Mr. Howard had played in the temperance play *The Drunkard*; Mrs. Howard was "universally admired not only for her brilliant talents upon the stage," according to the local newspaper, "but for her high moral worth and amiable quality personally."[23] Mr. Germon was referred to as a man of faith.

As with many early acting families, such as the Drews and the Drakes, it seemed everyone in the Howard family was involved in productions: Cordelia as Eva, Mrs. Howard as Topsy, Mr. Howard as St. Clair, and George Aiken as playwright and George Harris; the Howards' distant cousins, Mr. and Mrs. Germon, played Uncle Tom and Eliza. When the play was expanded with *The Death of Uncle Tom*, twenty-five roles needed to be filled. The extended Howard family, nine in all, came to the rescue. Mrs. Howard's mother Mrs. Emily Fox played the spinster, Mrs. Howard's brother played Phineas Fletcher, and Mrs. Fox's nephew and distant cousins also performed. The family members, especially Cordelia and Mrs. Howard, received widespread accolades for their acting from serious reviewers. Mr. Howard, on the other hand, was recognized for his savvy management. His decision to produce *Uncle Tom's Cabin* only six months after the novel was published proved to be his major accomplishment. And for thirty-five years, until 1887, the Howard family continued presenting its popular *Uncle Tom's Cabin*.

"Howard knew his business," Harry Birdoff, an *Uncle Tom's Cabin* scholar, notes. Mr. Howard knew how to produce tears and laughs.[24] He could intensify the melodrama of the chase with the orchestra's rushed music; offer comic moments with Mrs. Howard's dance; and sing many songs himself, all of which he wrote except for Stephen Foster's "Old Folks at Home." The amusement, morals, and excitement of the play were clearly appreciated by audiences. Thousands laughed and cried. When Harriet Beecher Stowe saw the Aiken version in Boston, her companion, Francis Underwood, a founder of the *Atlantic Monthly*, reported that she "scarcely spoke during the evening; but her expression was eloquent—smiles and tears succeeding each other through the whole."[25]

These Tommer shows continued to travel to opera houses, as did a parade of performers from opera companies to Chautauquas, boxing exhibitions, and oddities like midgets and dancing bears. After the turn of the twentieth century, keeping opera houses alive was difficult. Like any business, opera houses and the theatrical world were hit by the bumps of depressions like the one in 1893, local economic problems like the booms and busts of mining in the Rockies, and geographical disadvantages such as poor railroad connections. Opera houses also had to contend with inventions such as the radio, telephone, and car and the emerging interest in sports like baseball, which meant that people did not have to rely on the local opera house for all their entertainment. Now they could drive to a city for bigger shows with bigger stars or stay at home and listen to national radio programs also featuring bigger stars than would come to a small town.

The opera house buildings themselves had constant problems. Many burned down, done in by dangerously flammable gaslights and heating arrangements, but they often were rebuilt—amazingly—in a matter of months. Many existing opera houses were upgraded with new heating and electrical systems and others were totally remodeled many times. The Fulton Opera House in Lancaster, Pennsylvania was remodeled in 1856 and 1873, then again in 1904 and 1921. Stiffened fire regulations, spurred by the devastating fire in Chicago's Iroquois Theater in 1903, in which more than 600 people were killed, caused many struggling opera houses and theaters to close down as they could not afford the necessary costs of meeting new fire codes.

Even in the heyday of the opera house, with thousands of traveling theater troupes and performers in the late 1800s and early 1900s, new types of entertainment, such as vaudeville, burlesque, and motion pictures, were fast gaining popularity and forcing changes in the programs and operations of opera houses. How opera houses adapted to these threats depended on the size and location of the town in which the opera house was located, the imagination of its manager, the commitment of its owner, and whether it had signed up with a New York booking agency or syndicate. Most small-town opera houses struggled to make ends meet, even in good times, so when new threats like movies loomed, it was often their death knell. Many tried to blend movies with local fare, whether local high school plays, wrestling bouts, or community band concerts and limited traveling fare, to stay alive. Systemic financial problems always plagued such opera houses because these small towns never had large enough audiences. Many times the original backers moved away, tired of the venture, or died, so new management had to be found with the necessary financial resources. In such unsettled times, the unsung but critically important manager of the local opera house might "retire" or move on to another theater. Everyone from those intricately involved in opera house management to townspeople and performers were affected by the struggles of local opera houses.

In Fremont, Nebraska after the opera house owner, James W. Love, died, his theater-loving daughter, Para, became comanager in 1900, arranging for some popular plays like *The Taming of the Shrew* with Charles B. Hanford, which packed the house. Another performance, *The Evil Eye*, so crowded the opera house that "the stairs and halls of the building were congested with nearly suffocating humanity."[26] Mixed in were the traveling Innis Band, seventy-five artists strong, and the Grandest Minstrel Show, complete with a parade and "colored ladies drum corps." Para Love sold the opera house in 1903 to Louis P. Larson, who added his name, so it became the Love-Larson Opera House. It continued for thirteen years with fewer plays, but with local events such as high school plays and some movies such as the Ireland Brothers Entertainment Company's *Scenes from Fairyland*. It changed hands several times in the next few years and by the 1920s the building was converted to apartments. In the early days of the opera house, Fremonters could enjoy the Boston Symphony and *Richard III*, but as the twentieth century unfolded, they could go to the movies instead, since three movie theaters were built there between 1911 and 1915. A hundred years later the Fremont Opera House is coming back to life, as it is undergoing renovation to be a performance art center with programs focusing on children's and family theater.

The fate of Leadville, Colorado's Tabor Opera House, which was well promoted thanks to the tireless energy of Horace Tabor, paralleled the boom-and-bust cycles of mining in the Rockies. The opera house opened at the peak of the silver boom in 1879–1880 when Leadville had a population of twenty-nine thousand and Mr. Tabor was worth ten or twenty million dollars, depending on one's source, enabling him to toss many silver dollars to popular performers.[27] Fourteen years later, the disastrous 1893 collapse of silver mining was the downfall of Leadville. Tabor and the opera house never recovered. Tabor lost everything. His opera house was the last piece of property that he was forced to give up in 1893, but it was soon bought by the Weston family, who kept operating it as a theater and community center during difficult times in the 1890s. They sold it in 1901 to J. H. Herron, who quickly sold it to the Elks Lodge, which also continued it as a theater until 1955, when Florence Hollister came to the rescue and bought it. Since then the once prized opera house has functioned haltingly and by 2015 its future became uncertain as new owners were sought.

The ways that Iowa's many opera houses coped with the continuous changes facing them are detailed in the invaluable research of George Glenn and Richard L. Poole. The different types of touring companies performing in Iowa towns indicate a hierarchy of the towns, which probably existed in most states. In 1901–1902, large cities like Sioux City and Davenport would get the companies with the latest Broadway hits, such as Bronson Howard's *Shenandoah* and William Gillette's *Sherlock Holmes*, in which he also performed, as well as companies with well-known stars:

Ethel Barrymore and Richard Mansfield. Some of these shows would get to smaller Iowa cities like Dubuque, Mason City, and Iowa Falls, but most of the fare in these cities would be lesser programs like *Ten Nights in a Bar-Room, Go-Wan-Go Mohawk*, and, of course, the perennial favorites *Way Down East* and *Uncle Tom's Cabin*. Such opera houses in Iowa were not bereft of opportunities for plays and operettas, as many regional groups then toured, such as the Al Gorel Company, the Dick Ferris Company, the Andrews Family Opera Company, many Tommers, and three Iowa companies: the Trousdale Family Players, the G. D. Sweet Famous Players, and Terry's *Uncle Tom's Cabin* Company. And then there was as well a wide assortment of events, ranging from midget performances to medicine shows.

In this twilight period of the opera house, a new sensational extravaganza, *Ben Hur*, opened on Broadway in 1899 and toured the country until 1916. Not only did *Ben Hur* add a blockbuster to the rather dismal array of performances then available, but also it broke the tedium of fading melodramas like *East Lynne*. One of the most elaborate plays of that period, the Klaw-Erlanger production had a massive cast with twenty-two speaking principals, a chorus of eighty, and more than a hundred supernumeraries. A religious drama in which Ben Hur, a Jew and galley slave, battles a Roman, Messala, whom he defeats in a chariot race, escalated sensation to a new level. The ice floe drama of *Uncle Tom's Cabin* seemed almost tame by comparison. Not only did *Ben Hur*'s chariot race provide intense excitement, but it challenged stage technicians. It could require eight horses and two chariots on treadmills, with moving walls to provide motion, fans for wind, and a rolling panorama for spectators. For religious input, Ben Hur converts to Christianity after Jesus cures his sister and mother of leprosy, which Walter Pritchard Eaton, the *New York Herald Tribune* drama critic, dubbed "pasteboard piety." In fact, Eaton was puzzled about the popularity of *Ben Hur*, as he found it "a thing of bombastic rhetoric."[28] Whatever New York critics thought, *Ben Hur* was a hit as a play and later in two different film versions, in 1925 and 1959. In Lexington, Kentucky, a pantomime version was produced in 1896, with thirty-two parts not including the fifteen Roman soldiers, thirteen Priestesses of Apollo, eight Nymphs of Daphne, ten members of the Arabian Girls' Frolic, four Egyptian Fandangos, and three Spirites Fantasie.

With the strong arm of the syndicates, even legitimate theater was changing. Cities with syndicate theaters were exposed to good drama and good actors. Large numbers of touring companies, sometimes advertised as stock companies, were offering one-night stands in many small opera houses and weeklong engagements in larger places. A city like Lexington, Kentucky, which did sign up with a New York booking agency, had fewer performances and shorter stays, but with quality actors nonetheless. Top New York stars became a steady commodity at the Lexington Opera House: Otis Skinner played in Robert Louis Stevenson's *Prince Otto* in 1901, followed by Maude Adams, Mrs. Minnie Maddern Fiske, Tyrone Power, Lillian Russell, and later Katharine Cornell and Helen Hayes. Mixed in were a variety of entertainments: boxing bouts, lectures, minstrel shows, follies, circuses, and moving pictures. For theaters and most small-town opera houses, which were not connected with the Syndicate or to one of the large New York booking operations, these times were trying. The decline of the road company and the role of the syndicates were devastating blows to townspeople all over the country who enjoyed seeing a big-time star or play once or twice a winter. In the 1910s, stock companies struggled with low budgets while trying to play Broadway hits of the past, but their actors were often second-rate and the plays third-rate—not the route to popular success.

Competent opera house and theater owners and managers recognized the commercial opportunities of the new types of entertainment like vaudeville and burlesque, which they tried to blend into their traditional programs. But often the opera house, struggling to stay alive and lure audiences, slipped into a lower caste of sleazy burlesques, movies, and musicals. In Lancaster, Pennsylvania, the Law and Order Society tried to stop the burlesque shows and even arrested the Fulton Opera House manager. Many opera houses also had competition from new theaters devoted primarily to popular vaudeville, variety, or burlesque as entrepreneurs saw the promise of new theaters for this new entertainment. Four vaudeville theaters emerged in Lancaster between 1900 and 1910, one on the roof of the F. W. Woolworth five-and-dime store.

Motion pictures were the greatest threat. Ever since the appearance of Edison's Kinetograph, patented in 1891, and the Vitascope, first demonstrated in 1895, the prospect of seeing moving pictures was on the horizon. Actually, the step of silent films could have been skipped if Edison had succeeded in filming and recording a Metropolitan Opera performance, as he had hoped to do. Opera houses experimented with some early attempts at moving pictures. A three-reel passion play was shown in 1897 at the Thorpe Opera House in David City, Nebraska, after which movies were played periodically with pianists providing accompaniment. The Jeffries-Fitzimmons

This shows a 1896 poster for Vitascope, "Edison's Greatest Marvel," a harbinger of the demise of opera houses. 1896. *Library of Congress, Prints and Photographs Division, LC-DIG-ppmsc-03761*

prizefight at Coney Island was shown by cinematograph in 1899 at the Lexington Opera House, which continued to have live performances of plays and other entertainments for longer than most opera houses.

Many opera houses and theaters had both live entertainment and motion pictures, but trying to keep a balance of movies and live performances was difficult as the technical and artistic quality of movies improved and the quality of traveling troupes' shows lagged. Granville, New York's opera house, which opened in 1901, later than many, began with an ambitious program of plays with celebrities (Richard Mansfield, Minnie Maddern Fiske, Neil Burgess, and James O'Neill), but eventually showed mostly films such as the "seven-reel drama of everyday life," *Her Reputation*, and some adaptations of plays such as David Belasco's *The Warrens of Virginia*, using the Pember Orchestra for musical accompaniment.[29]

Despite local interest in Paris, Kentucky's Grand Opera House, by 1916 the days of enjoying Bizet's *Carmen* were over when it became primarily a "moving picture theater" and vaudeville house with occasional band concerts, minstrel shows, and school and church plays—and so it remained until the 1950s. That pattern was repeated in all parts of the country. Movies became the featured attraction as the marquee of Telluride, Colorado's opera house indicates. The Putnam Opera House in Bennington, Vermont introduced motion pictures in May 1915 on an eighteen-by-twenty-foot screen, which it proudly announced was almost as big as the largest screen in the world, the eighteen-by-twenty-four-and-a-half-foot screen at New York's Hippodrome.

The popularity of motion pictures continued as the days of seeing James O'Neill or Charlotte Cushman at an opera house vanished. At the movies, audiences might more likely see top stars and have a wider choice from cartoons to comedies. It was also cheaper to go to the movies than to the opera house, sometimes half the cost; movies might cost ten cents compared to twenty-five cents for the opera house. Operating a movie theater was also less expensive than operating an opera house, as the capital outlay and overhead were lower than all the costs of dealing with traveling troupes, not to mention the risks involved. For advertising movies, the same superlatives were being employed that opera houses had used twenty years before: "greatest picture ever," "sensation of the decade," "not to be missed."

Movie theater entrepreneurs now were building elaborate temples for the new entertainment in different architectural guises such as ornate Egyptian or grand, high-style symphony halls. The opera house, which had been an architectural gem in a town, was being outdone by the new lavish movie theater. Some new movie palaces were costly ventures. Omaha's Rialto Theater was built in 1918 for $750,000, more than six times what Boyd's Theater had cost in 1890. In 1909, Nebraska had only 51 movie theaters, but by 1917 there were 298, 7 in Lincoln alone and 2 in the small town of David City, with a population of less than three thousand. The new excitement was evident even in the names of some of the eight movie theaters built between 1906 and 1915 in Lancaster, Pennsylvania: Dreamland, Gem, Theatatorium, Bijou, and Wonder's Theater.

The major loss was live performances, which for many decades had provided excitement and passion for audiences, actors, and managers of opera houses as well as for towns. There was a magnetisim about a live performance. "Nothing takes hold of a child like a living person," Cather wrote in recalling the Emma Abbott Grand English Opera Company's "creditable" performances with a "good voice or two . . . a small orchestra, and a painstaking conductor, who was also the pianist. What good luck for a country child to hear those tuneful old operas sung by people who were doing their best."[30] Moving pictures were not the same for Cather, as she wrote to the editor of the *Omaha World-Herald* in 1929. "Moving pictures may be very entertaining and amusing, and they may be, as they often claim to be, instructive; but what child ever cried at the movies, as we used to at *East Lynne* or *The Two Orphans*?" She continues her defense of live entertainers: "only living people can make us feel." For her, especially as a child, her everyday life would vanish, as she was swept into the trials and tribulations of actors in live productions. The "searching" power of a play is missing in movies, which Cather viewed as just a "picture of a play" that "might appeal to a tired business man."[31]

Cather was not alone. For the actor Jack Burton, the succession of performers, from minstrel shows to traveling stock companies with their gripping melodramas as well as the lecturers and the many comedy companies, enthralled him as a child in Aurora, Illinois's opera house. When movies replaced all the live performances in 1913 at the Aurora's Grand Opera House, "there was no dialogue, no comic punchlines, no background music, no spontaneous song. What mechanical reproduction lacks most was a true sense of drama," Burton reminisced. "Recorded sound and vision lacked immediacy, intimacy and spontaneity." In contrast, the old opera house's "homemade music" and mixture of amateur and professional plays with school and church activities produced a variety and excitement that still stirred him in 1965, seventy years after his days at the Grand.[32]

Iowan Fred Oney Sweet, thinking back in 1940 of the pleasures at the old Hampton Opera House, bemoaned the advent of movies and loss of live actors, who had been replaced by "leading ladies [who] smile photographically for the Hampton audiences just as they do for those in the cities from coast to coast."[33] The live entertainers at opera houses introduced excitement that broke the tedium of dull winter days in small places.

The performances of these live entertainers were only part of the excitement they stirred in small towns. As the touring companies became temporary residents of these towns for the period of their stays, sometimes as long as a week, their very presence introduced an aura of fame and mystery of faraway big cities to the permanent residents of these small places. From the moment the advertisements for the shows of the touring group were displayed, to the arrival of the troupes by train, to their stays in local hotels, meals at local restaurants, and the performances themselves, an eagerness took over the town, as Willa Cather recounts:

> The excitement began when the advance man came to town and posted the bills on the side of a barn, on the lumberyard fence, in the "plate glass" windows of the drug stores and grocery stores. My playmates and I would stand for an hour after school, studying every

word on those posters; the names of the plays and the nights on which each would be given. After we had decided which were the most necessary to us, then there was always the question of how far we could prevail upon our parents . . . [then] if the company arrived by night train, when we were not at school, my chums and I always walked a good half mile to the depot to see that train come in. We found it delightful to watch the theatrical company alight, pace the platform while their baggage was being sorted, and then drive off. . . . If by chance one of the show ladies carried a little dog with a blanket on, that simply doubled our pleasure.[34]

No wonder decades later Willa Cather remembered so vividly the thrills and entertainment of the traveling stock companies performing in Red Cloud.

The contagious energy of the traveling troupes, actors, and performers of all sorts—all live—traipsing around the country in the heyday of the opera house is hard to imagine. Endless tent companies, WCTU lecturers, feminist advocates, small circuses, athletes, magicians, jugglers, and fire-eaters persevered with their trades and arduously traveled by wagon, train, van, and cars. Consider the logistical challenges of the hundred-animal County Circus coming to Lexington, Kentucky in 1893 with ten baggage cars, ten Pullman sleepers, two day coaches, and two diners—and performed a mile-long parade for the third act. Such performers, considered a lower caste of performer than those found in newer plays in New York, were not covered by many critics nor were they trying to innovate or advance the state of the art. Their commitments and passions, however, should not be underestimated. They were worked hard, enjoyed their craft, and provided entertainment in times when few other entertainment options existed. Their versatility required skills, imagination, and energy; they had no handlers or public relations firms; they created their own sets and costumes; they wrote their own shows and acted in them. That is commitment.

George Washington enjoyed *The School for Scandal* in Philadelphia as Quakers were shutting down theaters; New Englanders were surreptitiously staging plays in "museums." Soldiers in garrisons were performing plays. And early pioneers in prairie towns were building opera houses. This quest for entertainment—for smiles and tears—proves the enduring nature of this basic human need. How performers and opera houses, as part of the theatrical world, strove to meet this need reveals many undercurrents in American life. Persistent tensions—urban versus rural, highbrow versus lowbrow, international versus domestic, native versus foreigner, industry versus agriculture, local versus outsider control—were aggravated in this time of change. The independent traveling theater troupe, the conscientious opera house manager, and even the celebrity performer could not operate as freely in 1900 as they did in 1870 before the monopolistic practices of the New York theater world dictated who would play where. Likewise, audiences changed as the population grew and became more multicultural. Urban theaters were being segregated by type, class, and location as people became more divided by class and money. Some might consider many of these changes producing more varied and "sophisticated" fare for the public, while others saw a lowering of standards as monopolistic forces influenced and, in many cases, controlled mass entertainment.

When there was no other auditorium in town and no other means of live communication and entertainment, the opera house was a hub of the community. It was a social institution where people went to "meet and chat, to gossip and joke, to see and be seen, and in short have a pleasant time," as historian James Dormon described antebellum theater in the South.[35] "I just remember there were friends there" and the shows were "something to look forward to," Hilda Vasey of Cozad, Nebraska in thinking about her teenage days attending the local Allen Opera House.[36] And in Iowa in the late nineteenth and early twentieth centuries, opera houses were considered the center of local life, "an essential cultural attribute." All those magicians, Tommers, traveling troupes, lecturers, and circuses provided critical connections among townspeople and between townspeople and the cultural/entertainment world of the East or even the Old Country, as well as among the entertainers themselves.[37]

Those connections and the passion of all involved, which stirred the Drakes to drift down the Ohio River in their ark and then move from place to place with horses and wagons, kept small opera groups like Emma Abbott's performing in poorly heated or stifling halls night after night in different cities to varied audiences; persuaded Mark Twain that lecturing was enjoyable; and sustained all those magicians, circuses, Tommers, and theater, opera, and musical troupes. While on the road, the well-known stars—Sarah Bernhardt, Joseph Jefferson, Maude Adams, Helen Hayes, and John Philip Sousa—suffered the same missed connections, train wrecks, variable performing halls, poor hotels, and inadequate food as all the other performers. But their travels were not without rewards.

Travel woes: John Philip Sousa's band delayed by a train wreck between Spokane and Portland, 1899. *Library of Congress, Music Division*

"Once you are launched," actress Julie Opp Faversham reminisced, "the road . . . possesses a lure distinct, perennial, and gripping."[38] And for the audiences, that era of thousands of theater troupes and stars traversing the country, along with the rich array of other performers, produced live and "gripping" entertainment in thousands of small American towns and cities.

PART THREE

In Town

Public Halls and Public Roles

CHAPTER 10

Business Connections

To Oscar Wilde, the prairies seemed like a piece of blotting paper.[1] While they may have appeared empty and vast to Wilde, who was accustomed to the crowded, centuries-old towns and intimate countryside of late-nineteenth-century England, the prairies at that time were indeed like blotting paper. They were fast absorbing enormous numbers of new settlers, who were creating countless settlements and even cities like Kansas City and Omaha. When Wilde toured the United States in the 1880s and 1890s, the continents' grasslands were filling up. Between 1850 and 1900, the combined population of seven states—Iowa, Nebraska, Kansas, Missouri, Minnesota, North Dakota, and South Dakota—rose from 880,000 to 10.3 million. Omaha's population exploded from 1,885 in 1860 to 140,452 in 1890, and Chicago grew in one hundred years as much as Paris had in two thousand years. New rail lines, speculative builders, and even states aggressively lured Eastern adventurers, malcontents, and backcountry New England farmers, tired of rocky soil as well as oppressed immigrants from Europe, eager for democratic ways and good farmland. Wisconsin was so eager to attract immigrants that in 1852 it stationed an immigration commissioner in New York to inform newly arrived foreigners on what the state could offer them and how they could get to Milwaukee. The state's efforts paid off, and by 1890 35 percent of its residents were German-born.

A pervasive optimism in the second half of the nineteenth century bolstered this phenomenal growth, which brought new economic life and transformed values to many older Eastern and Midwestern cities and towns. That same optimism also fired up new settlers in the Western territories. Faith in the future, evident in the sprouting of opera houses, was most dramatic in the recently settled "blotting-paper" sections of the country. The promise of plentiful land, independence from the oversight of land-lords or lords, and a fresh start spurred adventurous pioneers. "After all, there is something fascinating in the thought of the opening up of a new life," Nebraska settler Mollie Dorsey Sanford stated in the late 1850s.[2] That new life was full of promise in a world of economic rewards, personal ful-fillment, and bustling towns. In Murdo, South Dakota, the Huston family started the town's first restaurant in 1873. When the Milwaukee Railroad came through town, they thought Murdo "was going to be a city about the size of Chicago, the way people talked. The town was mapped out and lots put up for sale. They sold for anything anyone bid for them."[3]

Convincing a railroad to plan its route through a town became the linchpin for a town's success in the eyes of its boosters. McPherson, Kansas, a county seat settled in 1872, began negotiating alignments with different railroad companies in 1873 to bring a line to the town in hopes of making it a candidate for the state capital. The town spent $65,000 for grading, railroad ties, and bridges to entice a railroad. However, it was not until six years later that the Marion & McPherson Railroad came to McPherson, while a branch of the more important Union Pacific arrived nine years after that. Neither railroad succeeded in making McPherson the state capital, but that did not dim the optimism of the town's leaders.

That optimism, or just plain boosterism, spurred railroads to serve towns, as well as to realize civic improvements such as paved streets, town halls, courthouses, schools, and opera houses that could transform raw land into something civilized. A new opera house could help to put a town or city on the map and instill respectability and a sense of permanence—precious com-modities for hustling towns. New communities on the rough-and-tumble frontier were trying frantically to establish themselves as settled and refined places and also to appear bigger and better than neighboring towns.

In the mining community of Central City, Colorado in 1866, long before it had an opera house, local lawyer B. B. Wade expressed this longing for sophistication in a pamphlet published by the *Miners' Register*:

> This is our mission: in this mountain clime
> A better truer mode of life to win
> T'erase the vestiges of vice and crime
> To welcome culture and refinement in.[4]

When Central City finally erected its opera house in 1878, the *Evening Call* pronounced it "the finest temple of the muses west of the

Missouri … and its audience representing the wealth, beauty and intelligence of the mountain towns … who for the first time viewed what may be looked upon as Central's pride."[5] Abundant pride in a new opera house echoed in many mining gulches across Colorado. Langrishe and Dougherty's 1861 theater in Parkville was considered "the largest and best building of the kind in the mountains," according to the *Miner's Record*. The *Leadville Daily Chronicle* went a step further, touting its new Tabor Grand Opera House in a first-page story as "the Finest Edifice in the Land."[6]

For more settled places, the opera house, like other municipal improvements, confirmed a town's maturity and cultural sophistication. This sense of a town becoming more urbane is reflected in town historian Benjamin Cowell's description of Peoria, Illinois' civic improvements around 1880:

> Prosperity was in the act of lifting Peoria out of the mud, not only metaphorically but literally. Street paving had only ceased to be a dream …. Adams Street rejoiced in cedar blocks *a la* Chicago … Civic enterprise, as such, had begun to show its head in the erection of a new courthouse…. That with the Union Depot, Chamber of Commerce and Grand Opera House, put every citizen on stilts, where he could really look out and speak the world.[7]

The handsome 1890 opera house in the established town of Paris, Kentucky was celebrated by the local newspaper as "a gem of the builder's art" and a "beautiful temple devoted to the historic art." Here a group of local stockholders, not a single entrepreneur, was responsible for the development of their opera house, making the building "our Opera House," according to the *Kentuckian-Citizen*, "not Clay's, Hinton's or Ferguson's, but ours the people's house." The newspaper continues:

> The town pride swells … we have in this house a happy realization so long the chimera of the dreams, which in nightly visions haunted the restless brain and ambitious soul of him, whose time, talent, and energy, have been so willingly lent to the accomplishment of that which today is the pride of our people—"a thing of beauty, a joy forever."[8]

Kearney, a booming town in west-central Nebraska, favored with the first intercontinental railroad, boasted of many big-city accoutrements such as a water system, electric street railway, and gas plant, but no opera house. The shame of attending plays and entertainments in a remodeled skating rink prompted thirteen prominent Kearney men in 1890 to form the Kearney Opera House Company, charged with building an opera house worthy of the then-prosperous city. The new structure, designed by the well-known St. Louis opera house architect J. B. McElfatrick and built by an Omaha construction firm, took a full year to construct— longer than most opera houses, which seemed to go up in a matter of months. The grandeur of this new opera house was worth the wait. Like

Kearney, Nebraska's grand opera house, photographed by Solomon DeVore Butcher, about 1910. Built in 1891, the building survived until 1954. *Nebraska State Historical Society*

many opera houses built in boomtowns and advertised as the "best in the state," "the biggest from Chicago to San Francisco," or as "grand as *any* theater in New York," Kearney's opera house was considered "the most imposing structure in Nebraska outside Lincoln and Omaha."[9]

In this prairie town, opening night at the opera house on May 1, 1891, with a twenty-eight-member cast performing *Mr. Barnes of New York*, was a dazzling occasion. Ushers were in "full dress," the ten-piece orchestra was at its best, and for the first-nighters the sight of so many gilded decorations brought forth "bursts of admiration," according to the *Kearney Daily Hub*. To indicate the importance of the occasion, Governor James E. Boyd, Secretary of State Allen, State Treasurer John E. Hill, Labor Commissioner Philip Andres, and Commissioner George Humphrey attended the opening. President Benjamin Harrison was invited but sent his regrets. Governor Boyd told the audience that when he had chased buffalo in Kearney thirty-two years before, he never imagined "such a town nor such a theater." And, indeed, that is how many proud Kearneyites and citizens of other "blotter-paper towns"—as Oscar Wilde called them—felt when their new opera houses were opened.[10]

Fremont, a fast-growing agricultural and business center in eastern Nebraska, boasted a population of eight thousand in the 1880s and, like many such new places, aspired to attain a sense of identity. And that is what its opera house brought Fremont.[11] The town was proud of the handsome edifice: "A building of this character is more to the city than a structure of equal cost and size and appearance designed for many other purposes," noted the *Fremont Weekly Herald* on December 20, 1888, opening day of the opera house. It was a grand hall, three stories high, with over a thousand seats of which 465 were "opera chairs." Fremonters recognized the significance of "theatricals" for a civilized society, the local newspaper continued, "and of course whatever tends to elevate their character is to that extent a public blessing."[12] Townspeople enjoyed thirty to forty performances a year and formed an opera house orchestra and a dramatic club, the Fremont Dramatic Company. The local newspaper carried a column, "Stage Glints," which reported the gossip about such leading actors as Richard Mansfield, Sarah Bernhardt, and Edwin Booth, whose death was announced in a front-page article. As the opera house and theater grew in importance in town life, Fremonters felt increasingly proud of their city and its connection with cultural worlds.

The Oriole Opera Company, a Fremont, Nebraska theater group, performs
The Chimes of Normandy at the Love Opera House, June 11, 1895. *Louise May Museum*

Only fifty years after statehood, these opera houses became a touch-stone of civilization in Nebraska.[13] That held for cities and towns of all sizes. Many opera houses throughout the country were very small. Only 20 percent of the Nebraska communities with opera houses in 1900 had a thousand residents or more, and many had around two hundred. By 1900, Vermont had a remarkable number of small towns with opera houses: Vergennes with a population of 1,753, Enosburgh with 2,054, Londonderry with 961, Hyde Park with 1,472, and Fair Haven with 2,999. Whether towns were small or large, railroads were essential for the operation of opera houses; for example, in Nebraska in the 1880s, three-quarters of the towns with opera houses had railroad connections.

Aside from these opera houses becoming important symbols of civic achievement, they represented a major undertaking for their communities and an indication of the towns' maturity. The early days for these settlers required hard, lonely work just to meet the bare needs of survival; but as settlements developed into towns and prospered, they could afford opera houses. Such halls ranked with other town assets, as real estate companies' maps would picture opera houses along with the city hall, hotels, and courthouse.

In Algona, Iowa, as in many farming towns on the new frontier, the scramble to establish a town was a rough-and-tumble affair. In 1855 Asa Call settled in Algona, which became the county seat of Kossuth County. He built a block house and laid out plats for future arrivals' lots before the federal government had even legalized ownership of the 320 acres that settlers possessed. Warding off challenges from outside promoters trying to designate the nearby town of Irvington as the county seat, Call was rewarded by being selected to the county board as "judge." That was just the beginning of Call's prominent role in Algona. Along with an inner circle of leaders, he ran the town. Call's brother Ambrose, a later arrival in Algona, joined this inner circle and wasted no time in becoming a large landowner, president of the First National Bank, and publisher of the Algona *Pioneer Press.* Through the newspaper and his other connections, Ambrose lobbied for an opera house. In 1892 he attained this goal by establishing the Call Opera House, which he considered one of his most notable achievements. As Easterners fought off Puritan hard-liners, Asa and Ambrose Call and other opera house promoters had to contend with rigid Methodists concerned that these new cultural centers would lower moral standards and disrupt the social order.[14]

Though Asa Call no doubt envisioned Algona's need for a hall of culture and entertainment, the potential economic benefits of an opera house to Algona, and indirectly to Call, did not escape his attention nor that of many opera house promoters. In settlement after settlement in the mid- to late nineteenth century, the desire for an opera house was heralded by town promoters—land developers, businessmen, and newspapers. This was clearly the case in three opera house towns in Kansas: Olathe, McPherson, and Garden City. In each of these communities, the overriding incentives for building opera houses were economic, and hoped to be a lure for new residents.[15] In these early settlements, like many other frontier areas, land speculation could lead to profitable investments. So it is not surprising that opera house proponents and land developers were one and the same.[16] At a time when the population tended to be transient, opera house developers were not only permanent residents of towns but also their business elite. They strove to take advantage of every opportunity to enhance their towns, whether railroads, schools, banks, public utilities, land development—or opera houses.

In these three ordinary towns "where nothing very monumental occurred, no extraordinary people were produced," as historian Ricky Tyler observes, the opera house was a business endeavor.[17] It was often located in a business block dominated by commercial space for rental income. The Stevens Opera House in Garden City, built in 1886 by John A. Stevens, became a regional attraction in the southwest corner of Kansas, luring theatergoers from as far away as Colorado and Oklahoma. These tourists could stay at the adjoining hotel Stevens built, shop in his stores, and even purchase property from him. The McPherson Opera House, established by a company of local stockholders in 1889, rented its two upper floors for use as county offices and the courthouse for five years. In Olathe in the northwest corner of the state, Colonel J. E. Hayes, a banker, state treasurer, and hotel owner, was considered the most philanthropic of these three Kansas opera house developers, although he did benefit from the rental income for the retail space in his 1880 Hayes Opera House.

Combining philanthropic and business interests was not uncommon. In some cases, major or at least nonlocal corporations built opera houses in

The McPherson, Kansas Opera House is restored and active. *McPherson Opera House*

towns where they derived obvious benefits. In Akron and Merrill, Iowa, the American Life Insurance Company of Des Moines constructed opera houses after the towns met the company's challenge that it would build an opera house in towns where residents purchased a certain amount of the company's insurance. More commonly, however, local businesspeople and professionals with a clear stake in the economic welfare of their towns spurred the development of these halls. Usually these were "over the store" second- and third-floor opera houses, with ground floors providing rentable space for stores, offices, various businesses, and, in some cases, municipal offices. In many places in the United States, such as Red Cloud, David City, and Minden, Nebraska, merchants occupying the ground-floor retail spaces built the hall above. In fact, at the acme of opera house development in Nebraska from 1879 to 1917, when more than 95 percent of the state's opera houses arose, the largest number were constructed by commercial property owners and/or managers who sold general merchandise, followed by real estate/loan/insurance professionals and druggists/physicians.

Some Nebraska opera house owners already controlled or managed leisure enterprises such as saloons, liquor stores, or hotels, so they just added the management of opera houses to their existing businesses. In David City, for example, Martin Novotny made a stab at running opera house–like theatricals in his tavern, and opera house entrepreneurs Fred Funk in Lincoln and H. P. Larson in Fremont both made their fortunes in the wholesale liquor business.

Farmers, however, rarely became opera house entrepreneurs, as they had neither the time nor the inclination to get involved in managing such concerns. An exception was in Omaha, where a prominent local agricultural businessman, pork packer James E. Boyd, built Boyd's Opera House. Although local businessmen who backed opera houses had achieved success in their careers and usually were members of a town's economic elite, their opera house ventures were rarely financial winners. They created and operated them out of a sense of civic duty, but "it didn't pay the bills," observes Nebraska opera house scholar D. Layne Ehlers.[18] Sometimes that civic duty was combined with a recognition of the civilizing role of women. William H. Diller gave an opera house to Diller, Nebraska to memorialize his wife; William B. Thorpe developed an opera house in David City to please his wife and daughter. Some opera house proponents who made their fortunes elsewhere, such as Edward H. R. Lyman, returned to their hometowns to provide houses of culture. Northampton,

Massachusetts was Lyman's hometown, and when he retired there he built the 1891 Academy of Music, a place "suitable for lectures, concerts, opera, and drama for the public good."[19] Lyman, who had been impressed by state-owned theaters in Germany, gave the Academy of Music to the city of Northampton in 1892 after the state legislature authorized towns to accept such gifts. Similar pride and civic duty propelled many such local philanthropists to build opera houses, theaters, or music halls in their hometowns.

An important voice promoting opera houses—and, in fact, crusading to improve the quality of life in towns—was the local newspaper. Often owned and run by a member of a town's inner circle of businessmen, the text of a local newspaper, not surprisingly, could sound like press releases from the chamber of commerce. Aware of the need for cultural development and interested in the civic welfare, Peoria, Illinois' Eugene F. Baldwin, editor of the town's newspaper, became the primary promoter for the town's 1882 Grand Opera House. He was successful in persuading other Peoria businessmen to join him in creating the elegant opera house.

In McPherson, Kansas the local newspaper pressed for organizing a fire protection company, public utilities such as electricity and telephone, public amenities such as parks and trees, and higher-quality entertainments. In 1889, when the opera house opened, the two local newspapers in McPherson, the *Democrat* and the *Republican*, boasted of the wonders of the building itself—massive double doors, polished granite columns, and colored glass—and praised the opening-night performance of *The Chimes of Normandy*. "From the moment Serpolette entered the stage until the last curtain call, the audience was captivated by the cast of more than 40 actors and actresses," the *Republican* reported.[20] The newspaper continued its praise for the opera house's public benefits for McPherson and the foresight of its promoters: "The persons that conceived the erection and completion of this building deserve a great amount of praise from the people of McPherson, there being no finer, with the exception of one, in the state ... McPherson will now be visited by the better class of entertainments."[21]

Speeches at the premiere performance of Gilbert and Sullivan's *The Mikado*, according to the local newspaper, the *Daily Irrigator*, acknowledged the community's indebtedness to John A. Stevens, the donor of the Stevens Opera House in Garden City, Kansas. At that inaugural performance, a local judge recognized the miraculous role of an opera house in advancing a small town:

> He spoke of the mariners on the sea who unexpectedly came upon an island that was not known, being on neither map nor chart: that our beautiful city, its rise, growth and prosperity was as surprising to everyone as the emerging of the island in the sea. Art is here displayed to please the eye and science exhibited in the building of the beautiful structure. We can tell of the religious meetings and the political conventions that will be held within these walls. Senators may be chosen here and governors named.[22]

In Red Cloud, Nebraska, the local newspaper also took on the role of promoting an opera house. The *Red Cloud Chief* commenced its pitch in April 1883, two-and-a-half years before the hall was completed: "One of the greatest needs of the City of Red Cloud, is an Opera House, and we are glad to say that there is a movement afoot to secure the erection of a first class one, though we, by request, refrain from giving any particulars at the present time."[23] By December 1883, the *Chief* wondered what had happened to its plea for an opera house: "We need an Opera House. Who will build it?" But a year later the *Chief* could report that the excavation for the basement of the building had begun, and then six months later that "Ross & Sanford have been awarded the contract for building the new Opera House for [local merchants] Morhart, Fulton and D. G. Mizer."[24] By October 1885 the *Chief* could proudly announce, "the Opera House is now complete, and together with the Red Cloud National Bank, are the handsomest buildings in the city."[25] The opera house was lit with gas, the *Chief* boasted, by "over forty jets, including the footlights," all fed from a tank in the back alley that was "seven or eight feet under ground, which makes an explosion from extraneous causes practically impossible."[26]

The newspaper continued its role of boosting the new opera house by declaring that the opening performance in October 1885 featured "one of the finest theatrical companies in Chicago . . . some of the best plays of the day." Due credit went to storekeepers Morhart, Fulton, and Mizer "on giving the people a good hall."[27] And for more than a hundred years, the Morhart hardware store remained in the building until the Morhart family donated the structure to the Willa Cather Pioneer Memorial and Educational Foundation in 1991.

While tens of thousands of new opera houses were built in fast-developing states like Iowa and Nebraska, opera house fever was everywhere. New York City opened its grand Metropolitan Opera House in 1883 and Paris its famed Opéra National in 1875. New England towns were forgetting the Puritan dread of theater as they enlarged their town halls to include opera houses, as in Brattleboro and Barre, Vermont. Towns farther west, such as Bozeman, Montana, and farther south, such as Dothan, Alabama, were building brand-new city halls incorporating opera houses. Larger and more elegant opera houses replaced old theaters and opera houses in southern towns like Lexington and Maysville, Kentucky. Not only were towns scrambling to validate their civic and cultural worth by erecting prized opera houses, but they competed with one another to achieve the biggest and grandest hall.

Cities and towns boasted that their opera houses were the most expensive, were the best from St. Louis to San Francisco or the best on the East Coast, had the best acoustics, were the first built in the state or the first municipally built in the country, or were the longest in continuous operation. Whether in Granville, New York or Leadville, Colorado, shows from New York were always featured. Theater companies assumed that entertainments that were popular in big cites would also be popular with rural audiences. Such urban fare made these small-town audiences feel sophisticated and up-to-date.[28] Within cities and towns of all sizes, an in-town highbrow/lowbrow competition often existed among opera houses for the best companies and most elite audiences. Even cities like Charlottesville, Virginia and Burlington, Vermont, which were ahead of the crowd in constructing public halls for entertainments and public events, felt the need to upgrade their older halls in the late nineteenth century.

Burlington's city hall had long served as the local theater, but when John Purple Howard decided in 1877 to build a large commercial building encompassing an entire downtown block, the community urged him to consider including a theater. Complaints of poor acoustics, safety problems, and the small size of the public space previously used as a theater in the municipal building finally convinced Howard to provide "the citizens of Burlington a suitable and attractive place for concerts, lectures, theatrical and literary entertainments, and other amusements of a high-toned and elevated character."[29] And so the Howard Opera House came into being. It opened in February 1879 with a season of "high-toned" opera, beginning with the Strakosch Opera Company's presentation of Donizetti's *Lucia di Lammermoor,* followed by Verdi's *Il trovatore.* These performances set off an opera craze in Burlington as items from opera glasses to kid gloves were featured in local stores. Restaurants, hotels, and stores were swamped by local residents and out-of-towners attending the opening night, creating such street congestion that extra police were needed. The quality of performances at the Howard Opera House by well-known actors such as Helena Modjeska, Joseph Jefferson, Fanny Janauschek, and E. H. Sothern meant Burlington was not a cultural backwater. The town's appreciation of Howard's gift to the cultural life of Burlington was expressed in 1890 by Daniel L. Cady, a student at the University of Vermont and a frequenter of the opera house:

> Thanks to the man whose generous heart,
> Went out to Culture and to Art,
> Nor from the lowly stood apart;
> Who so adorned fair Learning's seat,
> Gave Art a temple so complete,
> Nor left the poor upon the street.[30]

Another college town where opera house fever stirred public interest in updating an earlier opera house was Charlottesville, Virginia. After first benefiting from the southern advantage of early "theatricals" in local taverns, Charlottesville in 1852 built a town hall as "a large and commodious building … for Lectures, Concerts, etc." As this town hall was completed shortly after the Central Railroad connected Charlottesville with Richmond, traveling actors and troupes could easily reach the town.[31] Located across from the historic Albemarle County Courthouse, the neoclassical brick hall, with handsome long windows and pilasters, had a simple interior with movable benches, two interior stairways to the galleries, and a stage with two curtain sets hung from the proscenium and flydecks.

For thirty years, with an interruption for the Civil War when the Charlottesville Silver Coronet Band left and the town hall was converted to a factory producing knapsacks and uniforms for Confederate soldiers, this hall remained the entertainment center of the town. A parade of well-known performers such as the Norwegian violinist Ole Bull, opera singer Adelina Patti, and actor Joseph Jefferson took to its stage, along with sundry entertainments like minstrel shows, band concerts, ventriloquists, and a group of Aztec dwarfs, who had previously entertained the

Fillmores at the White House. Considered the center of community life in the 1850s, this town hall was a catalyst in stimulating Charlottesville's downtown and strengthening its culture. "Here will ultimately be the center of art and culture in the South," predicted a returning University of Virginia graduate in 1860.[32] After the Civil War, the town hall continued to offer entertainers, musicians, plays, lectures (including a talk on prison life of Confederate soldiers by the university's chaplain), and even a demonstration of the telephone by a Stevens Institute professor who wired music to the phone from the local railroad station.

The antiquated conditions, including the small stage and flat floor in the thirty-year-old drafty building, were brought to the attention of Charlottesville residents when Joseph Jefferson bypassed the town in 1879 for Lynchburg's new opera house. "We learn that the opera house in Lynchburg is yielding fine returns," the local newspaper, the *Jeffersonian Republican,* stated in 1886.[33] Staunton, too, benefited from its new opera house, built in less than a year, the newspaper reported. "In many respects we have an advantage over both our sister cities. We should by all means have a suitable opera house," the newspaper urged.[34] It did not take much urging for the residents of Charlottesville to realize their town hall was not only inadequate but also out of date.

Jefferson Levy, then owner and steward of Thomas Jefferson's mountaintop home, Monticello, responded to the plea for an improved opera house and bought the town hall from the Town Hall Company in 1887. By the next year he had transformed the hall into a respectable theater, the Levy Opera House, with a much larger stage, an orchestra pit, a raked floor, theater chairs, boxes, more dressing rooms and sets, and a better box office. Charlottesville now joined the mainstream of towns and cities with an up-to-date opera house that could mount the latest entertainments. Performances at the updated Levy Opera House included musical shows; orchestras such as the Boston Symphony; operas and operettas; plays with large casts, including Joseph Jefferson; stars such as Fanny Janauschek; entertainers of every sort; and animal shows, even one with ten horses. A newer and even more up-to-date opera house was built on West Main Street in 1895, eclipsing Levy's hall. Today even though the days of theater troupes performing at the Levy Opera House are long gone and its building is now a publicly owned office building with a restored exterior, old-timers still refer to it as the "Levy Opera House."

When the early town leaders promoted the idea of a local opera house, they hoped it would put the town on the map and also lure a railroad line to the town. They saw it as a commercial venture connecting the town to wider worlds and also providing cultural and entertainment benefits. However, they might not have imagined what a lasting civic role the opera house would have in a town and how it would generate community energy and engagement.

CHAPTER 11

Public Places and Civic Events

Opera houses in most rural towns were virtually community halls. As they were often the only large gathering place—and also neutral turf—in small towns, many public events took place in these halls. While some opera houses were in town halls, most were built, operated, and managed by local entrepreneurs. And many of the privately built and operated halls seemed like public halls, as their programs included so many community events. In some instances, private opera house entrepreneurs transferred ownership of their opera houses to the towns, as in Enosburgh Falls, Vermont where a local pharmacist and patent medicine magnate (creator of a popular cure for horse infirmities), Dr. J. B. Kendall, built an opera house and then gave it to the town.

As rural areas, frontier regions, towns, and cities grew and prospered in the late 1800s, people found themselves with more free time to get together for social events and entertainments. Social clubs, church groups, and fraternal organizations were formed in many places, but such groups were tainted with exclusivity as they were not open to all sectors of the public or were associated with institutions with set philosophies and sometimes prejudices—like fraternal associations such as the Elks, Moose, and Woodmen of the World. The opera house's neutral turf meant it was open to all who could pay the entry fee. However, opera houses, especially in the South, typically had separate but not necessarily equal sections for the "colored," usually in the balcony, and, if there were several balconies, it was the highest balcony. The colored balconies usually had separate entrances, sometimes reached by outdoor stairs. Nonetheless, the overarching neutrality of the opera house, combined with its intended purpose of providing space for activities for the entire community, meant it became a significant public place for the townspeople.

Opera houses with a flat floor and unbolted chairs allowed for considerable flexibility, which meant that these halls could be converted into theaters, concert halls, roller-skating rinks, dance halls, and exhibition halls. Today it is hard to imagine the breadth of activities in these buildings, which included poultry shows, bicycle races, political rallies, masquerade dances, elections, high school graduations, magicians, boxing bouts, dancing bears, and town meetings. These events punctuated the year at the opera house, especially during the winter months when farmers' workloads were light. Before schools built gymnasiums for sports and auditoriums for plays and graduation ceremonies, and before towns had large halls for meetings, elections, and conventions, the opera house served as the town's public building, whether it was privately developed and operated or town-built and run.

Blending public and private activities stands out as a distinguishing feature of opera houses, especially in buildings that combined both an opera house and a town hall. Here residents could attend plays and concerts in the opera house part of the building or get permits and access services from the police, fire, and health departments and the all-important town clerk in the municipal part of the building. Following the example of early New England meetinghouses with their public and private functions, the opera houses combined in town halls could be found throughout New England as well as in all sections of the country by the late nineteenth century—and in different configurations. In some towns the opera house and town hall were in separate sections of the building, as in Lebanon, New Hampshire where the opera house occupied the main building facing the town green with municipal offices off to the side. In most places, the town offices were located on the ground floor with the opera house on the upper floors, as in Stoughton, Wisconsin and Claremont, New Hampshire. Sometimes the auditorium occupied the ground floor with the city offices upstairs; in other places, the municipal offices were scattered throughout the building. In the present-day Vergennes Opera (Vermont) House the fire department is in the back, and, until recently, the police department was on the second floor, just outside the opera house, which is also used for town meetings and activities.

Claremont, New Hampshire's 1897 City Hall and Opera House faces the town square. Both the city offices and the opera house continue to share space in the same building. Note the impressive fly gallery. *Sheafe Satterthwaite photograph*

Aside from day-to-day town business, these opera houses also have been used for special town activities: primaries, elections, town meetings, political conventions, even military drills. In New England, the most significant local public event in these opera houses, especially the combined opera houses and town halls, would be the annual town meetings held every first Tuesday in March—as they still are in Vermont opera house towns such as Hardwick, Irasburg, Londonderry, Vergennes, and Woodstock. Political meetings and even state party conventions took place in these halls over the years. In six months from 1876 to 1877 the Fremont, Nebraska opera house hosted the state Republican convention, three local Republican meetings, and two Democratic meetings. In 1877 Trenton, New Jersey's opera house was the site for the Democratic state convention.

Election nights were particularly exciting occasions at opera houses before news came to one's living room via radio or television. Anxious crowds awaiting returns filled opera houses on election night. In Alexis, Illinois, a telegraph was installed in its opera house to convey the returns in the 1900 election. Not to be outdone, Rushville, Illinois's opera house flashed the national election returns for the same election onto a large canvas stretched on the stage as soon as news was received from both the depot and grange Bell telephones. After the returns were in, victory parties, sometimes ecumenical in celebrating victors from different parties, might be held in the opera house. Leadville, Colorado's Tabor Opera House, which Horace Tabor was anxious to develop as a community center as well as a house of culture, hosted victory parties for both Republicans and Democrats in 1880.

Patriotic events were important civic occasions where townspeople could share their pride in their town and nation. For new and distant townsfolk, celebrations of patriotic holidays helped them feel engaged with a growing, united country. Fourth of July events attracted large, enthusiastic crowds in towns everywhere; in fact, the Fourth was often the biggest annual public occasion for a town. Activities usually started in the afternoon with parades, band concerts, and political orations and went into the evening hours with potluck dinners and dances, many taking place at the local opera house. Other patriotic days such as Memorial Day were occasions to express patriotism toward the new country.

At New Jersey's 1877 Democratic State Convention in the Old Taylor Opera House in Trenton, General George B. McClellan was nominated for governor by acclamation. Illustration by George A. Bradshaw from *A History of Trenton, 1679-1929. Library of Congress F144.T7T65*

The remote town of Leadville, Colorado, ever trying to erase its image as a rough mining town, thrived on patriotic events. The 1880 Declaration Day ceremony at Leadville's opera house attracted a full house and disappointed many townspeople unable to get in. One of Leadville's most momentous patriotic occasions was President Grant's visit in 1880, shortly after the railroad reached the town. More than five thousand people, bands, and a hundred-voice choir welcomed him. He went to the Tabor Opera House, appropriately spiffed up for the visit with a special box and the seats taken up by Leadville's leading citizens, to see one act of *Our Boarding House* before attending a reception at the city hall and then staying at Horace Tabor's Clarendon Hotel adjacent to his Opera House.[1] As Grant was the only president to visit Leadville, his sudden death in 1885 was an occasion for the town's outpouring of sympathy at the opera house, the event billed as a nonpartisan citizens' memorial.

Benefits, including special performances of plays for worthy public causes such as the town's poor, firemen, injured policemen, veterans, and local schools, were common events in opera houses. Opening night for *The Victims of the Bottle*, the first play ever presented at the new Table

Willa Cather's early foray into theater as the merchant (with top hat) in *Beauty and the Beast*, at the Red Cloud Opera House in 1888. This performance was a benefit for the victims of the blizzard of '88. *Willa Cather Foundation and Nebraska State Historical Society*

Rock (Nebraska) Opera House in May 1893, was also a benefit to buy instruments for the local band. The Tabor Opera House held fundraising benefits for Leadville's firemen to attend the state firemen's convention, and several standing-room-only events to support Irish causes such as the Irish famine victims. Another full house came to hear Irish patriot Michael Davitt of the Irish Land League praise Leadville for being the first American city to respond to every solicitation of the Land League for funds. As late as 1919, the Enosburgh Falls (Vermont) Opera House held a benefit of two nights' performances of *A Private Part* for "war work." At the Red Cloud Opera House, Willa Cather performed in *Beauty and the Beast*, raising forty dollars to benefit Blizzard of '88 victims.

Although not for public causes, benefits for actors and troupes frequently took place in opera houses. Such benefits, often at the end of a run of performances, would honor an actor or troupe, and in many cases help meet a troupe's financial exigencies, such as paying the local hotel bill. At the end of *Uncle Tom's Cabin* on November 26, 1852, George Howard announced a benefit performance for Mr. G. C. Germon, who had played Uncle Tom. Several days later Howard held a benefit performance for his accomplished wife, always referred to as Mrs. Howard, who had played Topsy in *Uncle Tom's Cabin* but was already the lead in another play, *Rosina Meadows; or The Village Maid*. Without such benefits, many troupes could not have survived financially.

The opera house served as an adjunct of the local school in small towns throughout the country. Here were held all large public-school events: debating contests, elocution performances, plays, and, most important, high school graduations. For bright students in small towns, like Willa Cather of Red Cloud, Nebraska and Hamlin Garland of Osage, South Dakota, the high school graduation at the local opera house was especially significant, as here the traveling actors, lecturers, and even magicians' tricks had transported these two writers to unknown and bigger realms far beyond their hometowns. These bright graduates, however, knew their graduation was a turning point; their years of schooling and evenings at the opera house were over and they probably would no longer be part of their childhood hometowns.

Hamlin Garland carefully recorded—with both sentimentality and philosophical objectivity—his graduation in the New Opera House. He recalled, "never again shall I feel the same exultation, the same pleasure mingled with bitter sadness, the same perception of irrevocable passing of beautiful things, and the equally inexorable coming on of care and trouble, as filled my heart that night."[2] His oration on *Going West*, a timely topic for him as his father and family were about to move yet again, was "very excited and very florid." He recalled "a slight current of sympathy coming up in me, and in the midst of the vast expanse of faces 'he' began to detect here and there a friendly smile." His excessively lofty tone bothered him, but he "had written with special deliberate intent to go outside the conventional grind of graduating orations . . . feeling dimly, but sincerely, the epic march of the American pioneer." Then came the "usual hurried and painful farewells of classmates. . .some never again to meet."[3] And indeed, like many promising students from these towns, Hamlin Garland was drawn by the magnet of the big cities in the East.

Similarly, Willa Cather's graduating class of three in 1890 held its commencement exercises in her hometown opera house, where she gave the valedictorian's address, "Superstition vs. Investigation." "Miss Willa Cather treated the audience to a fine oration . . . which was the masterpiece of oratory," the *Red Cloud Chief* reported. "The young lady handled the subject with that skill that showed at once her knowledge of and familiarity with both history and classics of ancient and modern times. Her line of thought was well carved out and a great surprise to her many friends."[4] And her thoughts and studies soon were further molded by the University of Nebraska, Lincoln, and later Pittsburgh, and then especially New York. But Red Cloud and its Republican River Valley were always part of her life and writings.

Graduations and school programs continued to be held at opera houses until the construction of competing venues for activities and the introduction of such new entertainments as the radio, movies, and later television for home enjoyment. These changes clearly reduced the public's dependence on the multipurpose opera house. Ever since Edison's inventions of the Kinetoscope and Vitascope, the old-style opera house had been threatened. Many of them limped along until the 1930s, when Works Progress Administration and other federal Depression funds built new schools with auditoriums, which replaced the opera houses. Barre, Vermont's Spaulding High School graduations were held in the Barre Opera House until 1939, when they were moved to the new municipal auditorium. And that was the case in town after town as the many school programs, graduations, and sports events that for years had been regular features of the opera house transferred to new and well-equipped school auditoriums and gyms.

Before radio and television, speakers of every stripe walked the stages of local opera houses. Even in the earliest days of mining, before the appearance of an opera house, the gulches near Central City, Colorado attracted large crowds to hear lecturers. A crowd of 2,500 heard Horace Greeley speak there in 1859, and a few years later a large audience braved the bitter February cold to hear humorist Artemus Ward.[5] By the mid- to late nineteenth century, travel talks and lantern-slide lectures became immensely popular. The renowned North Pole explorers Admiral Robert Peary and Commander Donald MacMillan and many lesser-known lecturers told of their travels. These programs captivated audiences curious to learn about the rest of the world.

Equally frequent speakers at opera houses were politicians, some-times presidents or presidential candidates. Even in the 2012 presidential campaign, both party candidates spoke in New England opera houses: Obama in Lebanon, New Hampshire and Romney in Rochester, New Hampshire. Columbus, Georgia residents learned more about Al Smith than they might have wanted to know when President Roosevelt spoke at the Springer Opera House while staying at nearby Warm Springs. William Jennings Bryan lived out of a suitcase, as he appeared during his three presidential and many other campaigns in opera houses from Columbus, Georgia to Calumet, Michigan to Leadville, Colorado to Red Cloud, Nebraska. Sometimes he made three appearances in the same town. With no television spots possible, the fall months before elections would be busy times for campaigning politicians at opera houses. In October 1898 in Table Rock, Nebraska, the Hon. E. J. Burkett, Republican candidate for Congress, spoke, and then the Hon. George Hibner discussed the Free Silver Republican positions. Two years later, two Republican meetings were announced: one with R. Rusicka, editor of the *Pokrok Zapuda*a, speak-ing to the Bohemian citizens; and the other with the Hon. Norris Brown, considered a particularly eloquent political speaker in Nebraska, appearing with the added attraction of flambeau and marching club demonstrations.[6] And when politicians were not campaigning for themselves, major public officials campaigned for them. President Theodore Roosevelt's progres-sive forestry chief Gifford Pinchot promoted the candidacy of Wisconsin Senator Irvine Lenroot in 1920 at Stoughton, Wisconsin's Auditorium, later called Stoughton Opera House.

Enlisting a major politician to speak at the opening night of an opera house confirmed the importance of that venue. The biggest political prize, of course, for a town's opera house was a presidential visit. President

William Howard Taft made two trips to Vermont opera houses. In 1909 at the Vergennes Opera House he spoke at a celebration of the 300th anniversary of the discovery of Lake Champlain, and then in 1912 he addressed an overflowing crowd at (now Old) Manchester, Vermont's Music Hall, where he supposedly shook hands with seven hundred people before spending the night at Hildene, the nearby home of President Lincoln's son, Robert Todd Lincoln. Though presidents were the first choice for openings of opera houses, governors were the next best as in the opening of Kearney, Nebraska's opera house in 1891 and Bennington, Vermont's in 1892, when Governor Levi F. Fuller delivered the dedicatory speech. Just a visit by a leading politician would be permanently etched in the history of an opera house. Even today, tours of the Tabor Opera House in Leadville feature the box where President Grant sat during his brief visit in 1880.

Well-known writers, some with "educations," like Mark Twain and Oscar Wilde, and others with agendas, such as Henry Ward Beecher, Susan B. Anthony, and Samuel McClure, spoke at opera houses in large and small places everywhere. Mr. and Mrs. Henry Ward Beecher even made it to Leadville in 1883, where they enjoyed the town and the "beauty of the countryside," but because of the high altitude Mr. Beecher gave only two lectures and no sermon.[7] Depending on the interests of the towns, the types of speakers differed considerably. Barre, with its internationally known granite works and stone-cutting expertise, attracted an early interest from trade unions, hence its opera house featured an array of radical speakers. Eugene V. Debs in 1903 spoke on the industrial revolution; Emma Goldman in 1907 addressed more than five hundred people; and as late as 1926 Dorothy Thompson Lewis and Sinclair Lewis spoke to an enthusiastic crowd.

More common were the upright speakers on temperance, who competed with William Jennings Bryan for ubiquity in the flush days of opera houses—even in towns with no saloons like Watseka, Illinois, where ax-wielding Woman's Christian Temperance Union (WCTU) member Carrie Nation held forth. The national secretary of the WCTU would also venture to small Nebraska towns such as David City to lecture. Sometimes the WCTU would offer "Entertainments," which were so popular in Salem, New York in 1894 that they were repeated the next week. The Epworth League was equally active in Methodist-dominated towns. Table Rock, Nebraska's small opera house held three Epworth lectures in one winter on topics like "Travels in Europe," "Ghosts," and "Life and Experience in the Penitentiary," which followed Bishop Bowman's talk on travels in India. The bishop was a hit, as few had ever seen a bishop before: his "appearance was in harmony with their ideas of what a bishop should be," a local historian reported.[8] With no television or radio, activists in the nineteenth and early twentieth centuries effectively used opera house lecterns to reach many publics.

"If times were good at all, we had a dance every Saturday night, and, oh, how fine they were!" Colorado settler Anne Ellis reminisced in 1929 of earlier days.[9] And, indeed, the need to socialize, to get together, see one's neighbors and have some fun, maybe dance or sing, was ever-present, whether in isolated farm areas or in fast-growing cities. Diaries and books recount the good times spent at socials and dances at neighbors' houses, picnics, sleigh rides and skating in the winter, Fourth of July fetes, harvest festivals, and ballgames.

Newly settled pioneers in the emerging West reported dancing to be among their favorite pastimes. Dancing, however, remained one of the Methodists' and some other denominations' forbidden activities. Nonetheless, dancing seemed to take place everywhere.[10] In Kansas, a British visitor in the 1870s reported that "staid social gatherings" turned into dances "after the Methodists had gone home."[11] For Hamlin Garland, dances seemed to be the most popular entertainment for his parents' generation in Osage, South Dakota. When his parents danced together to Daddy Fairbanks's fiddling, "this seemed a very wonderful performance, for to us they were 'old'—far past such frolicking." Daddy Fairbanks, whose fiddling was not "even 'middlin' was a joy to watch," recalled Garland. "With fiddle under his chin he took his seat in a big chair on the kitchen table in order to command the floor. 'Farm on, farm on!' he called disgustedly ... and the dance was on.... He beat time fairly well and kept the dancers somewhere near to the rhythm."[12]

During this same period social clubs, church organizations, fraternal lodges, and opera houses started to emerge as areas grew, people prospered, and there was more free time to get together with friends. Social events, in fact, became highlights of the year at the opera house. Dinners, dances, balls, harvest festivals, and band concerts filled many long winter evenings. On holidays, and for all sorts of public occasions such as the celebration of an election or the completion of a new bridge, dances took place in barns in the summer and in opera houses in the winter. During one year, 1895–1896, in David City, Nebraska, four major dances were held at the Thorpe Opera House: a St. Valentine masquerade ball, a fire department masquerade ball, a Ladies' Aid Society charity ball, and another fire department ball, this time the Nineteenth Annual Ball. In Salem, New York, the stern Scotch-Irish Presbyterians did not seem to object to the many "socials" and dances that were held every three or four weeks at Proudfit Hall. In one month, February 1897, there were five "social" events: Marion's Ball, the Mid-Winter Social, the Men's Ball, King Winter's Carnival, and the Masonic Ball. Firemen must have enjoyed dancing, as they sponsored innumerable dances in small-town opera houses. Dances, however, were organized by many different local groups, as diverse as the Switchmen's Union in Williamstown, Massachusetts (temporarily a Boston and Maine railroad shop town) and the Bohemians in Table Rock, Nebraska. Dances, of course, could only be held in flat-floor small-town opera houses, not in the fancy opera houses with raked floors in larger, more sophisticated towns and cities.

Musicians were essential for dances, many other social occasions, and innumerable opera house performances and events. Small, three-piece orchestras would play at opera houses. Because they provided background music, their refined talents and tireless efforts rarely received the public notice or appreciation they no doubt deserved. On the other hand, local bands, often less refined than the orchestra musicians, were extremely popular and seemed to abound in towns and cities in the late nineteenth century. "The bands play here all the time," Mollie Dorsey reported soon after she arrived in Denver in 1869.[13] Towns were proud of their bands, many formed in the New England states before the Civil War. Vermont had at least thirty bands by 1869. "The country seems to be inundated with bands," James S. Smart, editor of the *Washington County* (New York) *Post*, noted in 1866.[14] Neatly uniformed bands with the town's or band's name boldly printed on the large drums played at many opera house festivities: Fourth of July celebrations, high school graduations, balls, Christmas parties, concerts, and innumerable patriotic events.

In Vermont, fierce competition existed among bands to perform at county and state fairs, sometimes for prize money. In Woodstock, Vermont, four bands competed for $175 in prizes. Often with ten to twenty instruments in a band, their boisterous music was popular at far more than official activities. They would serenade sleigh rides, provide the music for balls, entertain at concerts, and liven up any gathering, as opera house programs indicate. Like actors in a company, camaraderie built up among band members as they associated with one another and also with their towns, which they proudly promoted.

Montpelier Military Band performed in White River Junction, Vermont for the Vermont State Fair about 1893. Fellows, the Photographer, White River Junction, Vermont. *Vermont Historical Society Library*

As unlikely as it might seem today, the local opera house in the late nineteenth and early twentieth centuries was once a sports arena for school, community, and professional athletes in those towns with flat-floored opera houses. Basketball, boxing, wrestling, bicycling, and roller skating, not usually associated with houses of culture, were common and popular events in opera house towns with no large, flat auditorium. Wrestling and boxing, both as school sports and as professional matches, took place in the same opera houses that hosted Joseph Jefferson and the Metropolitan Opera. In fact, 7,000 people watched a Roeber and Crane wrestling match at the Metropolitan Opera House. Nebraska towns reported boxing bouts with such well-known professionals as Jack Dempsey. The holes used for the rope stakes around the boxing ring where John L. Sullivan and James "Gentleman Jim" Corbett fought are still visible on the fancy raised stage at the Leadville opera house and feature in its guided tours. Corbett and Sullivan, along with other boxers, even toured the country in their latter years in vaudeville and legitimate theater shows.

.Roller Skating.

at the

..New Opera House..

Wednesday Evening and Saturday Afternoon and Evening

Beginners Night---Every Thursday
Those wishing to learn Roller Skating should attend.

Prices:

Wednesday Evening--Admission 10c; Skates 15c
Saturday Afternoon--Children 5c; skates 10c
Adults 10c; Skates 15c
Saturday Evening--Admission 10c; Skates 15c

METROPOLITAN OPERA HOUSE
ATTENDANCE 7000

Sports at large and small opera houses. Roller skaters were invited to the New Opera House in Yale, Michigan and 7,000 people watched Ernest Roeber win a wrestling match at New York's Metropolitan Opera House. Roeber and Crane Bro's Vaudeville-Athletic Company advertisement n.d. *The Yale Expositor, Yale Michigan, February 1, 1917 and Metropolitan Opera: Library of Congress, Prints and Photographs Division #21438*

Not everyone welcomed such athletic events at their opera houses: Burlington, Vermonters questioned whether boxing and wrestling, appearing in the late 1890s, were appropriate activities for their Howard Opera House. However, Enosburgh Falls, a small town near the Canadian border in northern Vermont, still proudly remembers the Plouff family's athletic sons, who got their early start in boxing and basketball in the 1940s on the boards of the town's flat-floored opera house. The oldest, Armand, stood out as New England's heavyweight boxing champion for six consecutive years, fighting under the name "Kid Roy." He put on boxing bouts at the opera house and also coached his two younger brothers, Homer and Paul, who never reached Madison Square Garden but boxed in public matches at the opera house. These events attracted 150 to 200 people, some of whom would toss fifty-cent pieces, so the boys might make forty to fifty dollars a night. Basketball also appealed to Homer and Paul, who reported that they "grew up on the basketball court" at the opera house, where they were responsible for seeing that the furnace was filled with wood.[15] They were allowed to play basketball after school until dark as long as they swept up when they finished. Paul recalled moving the heavy rows of five or six chairs fastened to wooden strips. Since 1892 the Enosburgh Opera House has been in continual use, but after 1947, when a school gymnasium was built, it has no longer served as the town's athletic arena

The craze for roller skating matched the craze for melodrama in many opera houses. Popularized in New York City in the early 1860s by James L. Plimpton, roller skating quickly took the country by storm and was the rage by the 1880s. Initially, Plimpton thought this new sport would appeal to the upper classes, and it did. Wealthy New Yorkers were roller skating in Newport in the summers, but that exclusivity was forgotten as soon everyone was roller skating. Sales of roller skates in 1885 reached over $20 million. It became such a popular activity that Sunday skating was considered a cause for a noticeable drop in church attendance.

Some towns built their own rinks,[16] but for towns without rinks, the flat-floored opera houses served the purpose. Roller skating was becoming as big a hit as *East Lynne*. Estabrook's Opera House in Manchester Center, Vermont opened in 1884 and featured roller skating on its upper floor, accompanied by a variety of bands and special skating exhibitions. The same year, the new owners of Cambridge, New York's older opera house, Ackley Hall (over Ackley's drugstore), trying to compete with the more recent house in town, Hubbard Hall, latched onto the roller-skating fad and installed a floor for roller skating. A festive opening night with music by Professor Nichols and local bands launched Ackley's roller-skating sessions, which took place every night except Sunday and Thursday, when prayer meetings took place on that same floor. The new, slicker floor challenged skaters, "providing more spills to entertain the on-lookers," according to local historian Dave Thornton.[17] However, the challenging new floor did not deter residents from forming skating clubs.

In Salem, the next larger town north of Cambridge, roller skating was so popular that the floor for skating on the top floor of the 1882 Fairchild Building was worn out in two years. New owners replaced the floor and improved the facilities, renaming it the Crystal Palace Skating Rink at a grand opening attended by four hundred people. The rink soon had its own skating waltz, "Gliding in the Rink."[18] As the only place in town where large numbers of people could be accommodated, many public and social events were held at the Crystal Palace until the building burned down in 1889.

Soon to follow was the craze for indoor bicycling. Cambridge's Ackley Hall, like many opera houses, capitalized upon this new indoor sport, featuring bicycling evenings and races. While bicycling must have required rather tight turns in small-town opera houses, indoor bicycling was enjoyed everywhere; in fact, it took place in major indoor facilities in large cities like New York's Madison Square Garden. The first Madison Square Garden, built in 1879 at Madison Avenue and Twenty-sixth Street, was designed as a velodrome. It had an oval bicycle-racing track with banked curves and attracted top racers, who could annually earn up to $100,000, the equivalent of today's generous salaries for football and basketball stars. Madison Square Garden remained the most important bicycle racing track in the country for several decades until the fad for bicycling faded. However, New York City armories continued as a venue for bicycle races, with indoor seven-day bicycle races held through the 1940s.

Such sporting fads—whether roller skating, boxing, or bicycling events—provided physical exercise, excitement, and opportunities for socializing when opera houses were often the only large indoor space in small towns.

The opera house offered room for many events requiring large spaces, including even church services. The blending of secular and religious activities was not uncommon in New England, as early meetinghouses served as all-purpose community buildings—all purposes, that is, except for banned theater and entertainment.

Rockingham, Vermont's austere eighteenth-century meetinghouse with its pigpen box pews is sited, like many early settlements, on high ground, an example of an early community center where both church services and the town meeting took place.[19] It served in that capacity until the main settlement moved downhill to Bellows Falls on the Connecticut River, with its thriving water-powered industries and a new publicly funded town hall and opera house. In the early theocratic days in New England, meetinghouses such as Rockingham's were public buildings where church services were held. However, such publicly funded church buildings were no longer tolerated after the constitutional separation of church and state. They were then taken over by a church, abandoned, and converted to other uses, or became solely town halls. In some towns, church services were held in the town hall. For four years from 1854 to 1858, St. Michael's Episcopal Church held its services in Brattleboro's town hall, referred to as the town house, which ran lyceum programs and was enlarged in 1896 to include an "opera house." Hancock, New Hampshire's 1820 meetinghouse has continued its dual role in the town's civic and religious activities. Jointly owned by the town and a church association, the first floor has spaces for civic activities such as town offices, until relocated in a new building, and a large meeting space where the town meetings are still held. The second floor has been used continuously for church services. In Williamstown, Massachusetts, the opera house was originally the Methodist church, but when a new church was constructed in 1877, the building was fitted with a stage and gallery and became Waterman and Moore's Opera House.

New England was not the only region in the United States where religious and secular activities coexisted in the same building. In the Colorado mining town of Leadville, the Episcopal church moved its services temporarily from the local schoolhouse to the newly opened Tabor Opera House. In Menomonie, Wisconsin, the Unitarian Society has held its services in the Mabel Tainter Memorial Theater for 125 years: from 1889, when the theater was built, until the summer of 2014, when the society moved to new quarters. For particularly timely sermons or special services, Crete, Nebraska's Congregational church in the 1880s used Band's Opera House, since it could accommodate far more parishioners than its church building.[20]

Combining entertainment and religion was not always well received, as the Reverend Fraser Metzger of Randolph, Vermont discovered when the *Sunday Boston Herald* attacked him for sharing his Bethany Parish

House with the town's Chandler Music Hall in a 1907 article, "Should a Pastor Manage a Box Office?"[21] The Reverend Metzger saw his ecclesiastical role differently than the *Boston Herald* did. He defended his association with the music hall and its "theatricals." For him, "the church should not cease on Sunday…but that it should be an element of good for the general public," and Chandler Music Hall was a building "dedicated to the largest usefulness and the most beneficent influence possible."[22]

Despite some questions then and now about the propriety of blending church and entertainment, church services are held again at opera houses and theaters where they do not conflict with ongoing programs and can produce some needed additional income. "The steady income from a trouble-free renter was great," according to one online 2007 commentator, who endorsed renting an opera house for church use on the League of Historic American Theaters chat-line.[23]

For many towns the multipurpose opera house served as a local meeting place for professional organizations as well as for fairs and exhibits, especially agricultural exhibitions. Farmers' institutes held their meetings and conferences in the opera house, whether in Williamstown, Massachusetts or Watseka, Illinois. When Brattleboro, Vermont decided to enlarge its public hall into a well-appointed opera house, it designed a large front area on the second floor for exhibitions where poultry was often featured. In fact, poultry exhibitions continued until the 1930s in Enosburgh Falls, Vermont. Agricultural exhibits, garden shows, and harvest festivals remained for years popular programs at rural opera houses. Sewing schools were held in Williamstown's opera house, while county teacher institutes, veterans' organizations' reunions, and specialized professional groups' meetings, such as the Illinois Detective Association conventions, took place in Watseka's opera house. Even opera houses' many traveling medicine shows peddling miracle cure-alls might be considered professional and educational institutes, even though their entertainment value was probably greater than their medical advice. Orvis's Music Hall in Manchester, Vermont would waive its $60 fee for community events, church services, and graduation ceremonies of the local high school, Burr and Burton Seminary. Calumet, Michigan's municipally owned opera house was available for $40 per night for any entertainment approved by the city council.

Paternalism, pride, and the need to provide amenities to attract and retain employees encouraged the development of opera houses in company towns, which were often located in remote places—even in Death

Valley, California. The opera house in Death Valley Junction, its correct town name, was the original community hall in this company town of Pacific Coast Borax Company. The six-building Spanish colonial adobe U-shaped town, built in 1923–1924, included a hotel, company offices, dormitory, store, and Corkhill Hall. The Tonopah and Tidewater Railroad, which replaced the twenty-mule team for hauling out the "white gold," as borax was called, brought in supplies for the town and entertainments for Corkhill Hall. While Pacific Coast Borax owned the town until the 1950s, Corkhill Hall was where all public events took place including dances, town meetings, church services, and movies. However, not until the arrival of Marta Becket in 1967 did the hall become the Amargosa Opera House (Amargosa was the name of the earlier mining town at this site). Becket, an energetic and independent dancer, choreographer, and artist from New York, sometimes called the "ballerina of Death Valley," painted colorful murals on the walls of the building and held performances, sometimes to a totally empty house, for more than forty years until 2012. Now spurred by Becket's interest in continuing the hall for artists and classical performances, the building and the twenty-three-room hotel are owned by the nonprofit Amargosa Opera House, Inc., in a ghost town in a very remote area, making it one of the most unusual opera houses in the United States.[24]

More typical are the company-town opera houses in Appalachia. Here the coal companies' golden days coincided with the peak era of opera houses, from 1890 to 1930. In that period almost every Appalachian mining town had an opera house.[25] Coal towns depended on rail lines for their economic welfare—and also for bringing touring performers and lecturers to company-town opera houses. After successful geological explorations, these coal companies would invest in a site and develop it as a tightly knit working and living environment. Coal-mining towns often were isolated, so attracting and retaining a dependable and usually nonunion workforce became a concern for the companies. Owning everything above and below the ground meant that the coal companies ran everything in town, from schools, housing, stores, churches, and police and fire departments to recreation facilities, including opera houses. The extent and quality of these amenities and services varied from company to company. But the opera house, often allied with other recreation facilities such as bowling alleys, was built when families started settling in a company town, a process similar to the mining towns in the Rockies.

The company store, like the small-town general store, became the center of community life in these coal towns, as it was the place both to shop and visit with friends. In some towns, the opera house was even located in the company store building, as in Stearns, Kentucky and Nelsonville, Ohio. U.S. Steel, in its model town of Lynch, Kentucky, built an all-purpose recreation building, called the "Victory Building," which included a restaurant, dance hall, bowling alley, meeting rooms, and a 450-seat theater. The provision of entertainment in these halls, whether plays, pool, lectures, or movies, provided obvious benefits for paternalistic companies anxious to control the behavior and influence the work habits of employees and their families. Companies no doubt hoped that wholesome entertainment in recreation centers and opera houses might avert the dreaded social problems of alcoholism and prostitution—and also cultivate socially acceptable and, most important, productive workers.

Calumet, a copper mining town at the northern point of Michigan's Upper Peninsula, enjoyed the good fortune of such a rich vein of copper that deep mining was not necessary. At its peak in the late nineteenth century, when its population swelled to twenty-six thousand, almost half the country's copper came from Calumet, then called "Red Jacket." Its handsome town hall was built in 1886 and its opera house in 1900. Although the town and region were dominated by the Calumet and Hecla Mining Company, the largess of this company is often overestimated. Some people assume that public buildings like the opera house were built and given to the town by the then-prosperous company. But that was not the case. The town built both buildings. The company leased the land for the opera house, but the town borrowed $25,000 to enlarge the town hall, so a "modern opera house" could be built in the existing town hall with "proper offices for the village officers and the common council," as reported in the *Copper County Evening News* in 1898.[26] The sandstone-and-brick building, designed by Michigan architect Charles Shand and completed in March 1900, eventually cost more than $70,000. The town considered it worth the expense.

Opening night on March 20, 1900 brought out the region's "wealth, beauty, culture, and refinement" to see *The Highwayman*, performed by a New York opera company.[27] Even though the Calumet and Hecla Mining Company's financial involvement in the development of the opera house was limited to leasing the land on which the hall was built, on opening night the superintendent of the company's Bigelow mines hailed the opera house's lasting benefit to the town and his "disbelief" that such a grand theater could have been built for $70,0000.[28] The Renaissance-style opera house was indeed grand. Twenty-four-karat-gold leaf details on the Turkish red walls, tapestries, marble stairs, and a massive copper chandelier adorned its interior. It had a large stage, many well-appointed dressing rooms, excellent acoustics, and seats for twelve hundred people. Those in the parquet circle or orchestra sat on green cushioned seats, but for those in the first balcony it was wooden benches with backs, and then in the second balcony, benches with no backs—however those seats, usually occupied by the miners, cost only ten or twenty cents.

For forty years, the Calumet Theater and Town Hall remained a venue at this northern tip of Michigan for a parade of the world's best-known actors, from Sarah Bernhardt and Helena Modjeska to James O'Neill and Douglas Fairbanks Sr., and a host of other entertainers like Houdini and John Philip Sousa, some of whom appeared many times. According to a 1901 program, "leading people in each and every one of these companies united in pronouncing the theater the prettiest and most advantageously arranged of any play house they have ever played in."[29] The usual entertainments and community events as well took place in the opera house over the years. In the 1920s, it adapted to the new era of motion pictures and later became a theater for summer stock; now it is a venue for a variety of cultural programs. This off-the-beaten-path town still boasts of the days when some of the country's leading performers trod the boards in its opera house, reflecting again the pride that towns have taken in these public entertainment halls and, in Calumet, nostalgia for its once-prosperous mining days.

Whether it is an opera house in Calumet, in a town hall, or in a privately owned building, the blending of public and private activities stands out as a unique feature of the small-town opera house. Some of these halls even have benefited from local public funding for their staffs and operation. As a result of the varying degrees of public support and civic involvement, the small-town opera house has served as a community hall in many places.

CHAPTER 12

Challenges

Sometimes it was just the "village virus," but an opera house could be plagued by the same rifts, tensions, and problems that inevitably intrude in the life of any town or city. These problems might be the town's highbrows versus lowbrows, farmers versus townsfolk, one side versus another—or just the Lake Wobegon–like pettiness of a small place. As opera houses were built to provide cultural uplift and add respectability to a town, it is not surprising that highbrow-versus-lowbrow rifts occurred. Such a rift might develop into a geographical divide if the town's more affluent and cultured residents and its less affluent and blue-collar residents were clustered in different parts of the town or on different sides of the railroad tracks. The fare at the opera house could seem elitist to some townspeople and parochial to others. Those who found opera house activities tiresome were often reflecting the dreariness they saw in their hometowns, like Carol Kennicott's realization that Sinclair Lewis's Gopher Prairie was imbued with a "dullness which God made."[1]

The schisms between farmers and townspeople appeared when rural settlements were organized into towns. With their new banks, stores, grain elevators, lumberyards, hotels, and public buildings in compact town centers, developing towns fostered an urban lifestyle distinct from that of their rural neighbors in dispersed, outlying areas.[2] Schisms between townspeople and country dwellers or merchants and farmers remained a common occurrence. For the farmer on outlying land holdings, it was a challenge just to survive, as his livelihood was ruled by forces beyond his control: the weather, bankers, railroad rates, and even world markets.

Townspeople often did not comprehend how their lives and economic livelihood depended on farmers and agricultural prosperity, whether in marketing their produce or seeking their business. For the farmer, just the trip to town to visit an opera house, bumping along rough roads in a carriage after a day of hard, physical work was a challenge. So it is not surprising that farmers in Nebraska were not avid patrons of these town centered halls, nor were they involved in their management, according to listings in the 1888–1889 *Nebraska Gazeteer and Business Directory*.

This schism between farmers and townspeople is confirmed in the history of Ellendale, North Dakota's 1909 opera house, which local business leaders built with the explicit goal of offering entertainment to the surrounding region. Instead of primarily serving the town's elite, "the town owed it to its farming community to provide some place of amusement and expressed the belief that the farming community would appreciate and patronize such a place," according to the *Dickey County Leader and Ellendale Commercial*. And the farming community did patronize this modest opera house with all its varied activities, including twice-yearly two-week stints of Shakespeare, Gilbert and Sullivan, and other comic operas performed by stock companies. The *Leader* reported that it was "especially pleased at seeing so many of our farmer friends present enjoying this new play house.... The large attendance at the performances, justified ... the belief that an opera would be appreciated by our farming constituency."[3] As the county population outnumbered Ellendale's population of 1,389 by seven to one in 1910, it was clear that Ellendale's leaders knew that the opera house could not survive without those county farmers. Listed on the National Register of Historic Places in time to celebrate its hundredth anniversary in 2009, the hall continued functioning until the 1970s.

Throughout the year, Saturday was the day farmers went to town. Eleanor Patchen's mother in the Sandhills of Nebraska, recalled "going into town on a Saturday afternoon and staying around until late in the evening, visiting, shopping, and then going to a dance and returning home late at night by wagon."[4] With leisure time increasing for both farmers and townspeople, railroads bringing theater troupes and entertainers to towns everywhere, and opera house schedules geared to the farmers' slow winter months, attending opera house programs became a social and cultural opportunity for both townspeople and farm families.

As towns matured, especially in the Midwestern states, and the "village virus" emerged, well-known sons of the Midwest, such as Sinclair

Lewis and Hamlin Garland, felt the need to escape from what they felt was the smothering smallness of their hometowns. Carol Kennicott, striving to spark some intellectual verve into the humdrum life of Gopher Prairie, was rebuffed by her doctor husband when she asked about a lecture hall: "As for a lecture hall, haven't we got churches. . .better to listen to an old-fashioned sermon than a lot of 'geography' and books and things that nobody needs to know." An overriding dullness obsessed Carol and her soul mates in other small towns:

> It is an unimaginatively standardized background, a sluggishness of speech and manners, a rigid ruling of the spirit by the desire to appear respectable. It is contentment . . . the contentment of the quiet dead, who are scornful of the living for their restless walking. It is negation canonized as the one positive virtue. It is the prohibition of happiness. It is the slavery self-sought and self-defended. It is dullness made God.[5]

Sinclair Lewis escaped from Sauk Centre, which for him represented "universal similarity—that is the physical expression of dull safety." And it was everywhere in small towns. "Nine-tenths of American towns are so alike that it is the completest boredom to wander from one to another. Always, west of Pittsburg, and often, east of it, there is the lumber yard, the same railroad station, the same Ford garage, the same creamery, the same box-like houses and two-story shops."

Matching the similarity of buildings, which smeared a respectability on townscapes, Carol Kennicott "felt herself ironed into glossy mediocrity," as did thoughtful and questioning people in other rural Midwestern towns.[6] Carol was trapped in that "glossy mediocrity," but others were able to escape to larger and more sympathetic milieus. Willa Cather's Thea Kronborg in *The Song of the Lark* was able to extricate herself from a suffocating small town as her singing lessons and eventual career took her to Chicago, Dresden, and New York, much like Willa Cather's escape from Red Cloud to Lincoln, then Pittsburgh, New York, and beyond. "The story," wrote Cather in 1932, "set out to tell of an artist's awakening and struggle; the floundering escape from a smug, domestic, self-satisfied provincial world of utter ignorance. . . . What I cared about, and still care about was the girl's escape; the play of blind chance, the way in which commonplace occurrences fell together to liberate her from commonness."[7]

Childhood experiences made an indelible impression. Sinclair Lewis, Hamlin Garland, and Willa Cather never completely broke free from their Midwestern small-town backgrounds, which were woven into their writings. Cather admitted in 1893 that her early years growing up in Red Cloud, no matter how confining, provided "all the material for her writing."[8] The opera house seemed entwined with her childhood memories and her novels like *Lucy Gayheart, Obscure Destinies,* and *The Song of the Lark.* Lucy Gayheart was inspired to return to Chicago by the Andrews Opera Company, whose performances Cather had seen at the Red Cloud Opera House. Again the opera house came to the rescue when Mr. Templeton tried to console his ailing wife by taking her "to hear a company of strolling players sing *The Chimes of Normandy* at the Opera House."[9]

Aside from the feelings of despair and the isolation of small towns that the Carol Kennicotts and aspiring children like Hamlin Garland felt, there were also economic, social, and cultural cleavages in small towns with competing opera houses. In Manchester, Vermont, a small but substantial rural town at the base of Mount Equinox, a clear division existed between the Music Hall and its patrons, who lived uptown on the hill in Manchester Village, and Estabrook's Opera House in the Factory Point section by the depot. As the name implies, commercial establishments like mills and marble works and the town's businesses were at Factory Point. The Orvis company, known originally for manufacturing fly-fishing rods and in the late twentieth century expanded to an upscale sport and clothing store, was intricately involved in Manchester Village activities in the mid- to late nineteenth century. C. F. Orvis developed the classical, porticoed, and fashionable Equinox House hotel, and in 1868 Franklin H. Orvis built the Music Hall alongside the Equinox and next to the Manchester Hotel, operated by Franklin's sister-in-law, Charlotte Orvis. Franklin Orvis, like many opera house developers and as a state senator, was an important man in town and the state. He bought the entire block on Main Street with the Manchester Hotel and called it Equinox Junior. For $16,000, Franklin Orvis was able to pack into his Music Hall a billiard room and four bowling lanes on the first floor, a 500-seat auditorium with a stage on the second floor, and a connection to the Manchester Hotel on the third floor.

For forty-four years, the Music Hall provided a range of entertainments, from concerts, plays, operas, pantomimes, variety shows, and stereopticon shows to political talks—the fare that graced most opera houses. While the Music Hall opened with a concert by the Mendelssohn

Quintet Club of Boston, theatricals by the Equinox Crowd, a group of local thespians, were the featured events there for many years. Dances broke up the long winters, as did the Grand Masquerade Ball in 1872, hosted by a committee of seventy-six men, with 125 couples attending, a social highlight, according to the town's histories.

Music and monologues were popular with Music Hall audiences, especially those by the local Hoyt sisters, Grace and Frances, who with their brother toured with John Philip Sousa in Europe during World War I. Such homegrown talent was the mainstay of the Music Hall in its early years, as it would take New York City troupes almost ten hours to reach Manchester on the daily Rutland Railroad train from New York City. In 1887 the train ride was reduced to six hours and later in 1905 to even less than six hours. The Music Hall continued for decades with all-day Old Folks' Concerts, and in the early twentieth century moving pictures accompanied by live piano music were featured. After a final dance by the fashionable Ondawa Club in 1912, the Music Hall was converted to additional rooms for the adjacent hotel.

Competition, however, first emerged for this uptown Equinox crowd when the Factory Point Dramatic Club presented *The Gun Maker of Moscow* and *Stage Struck Yankee* in 1882. Sensing a broader market for an entertainment venue in Manchester, in 1884 Emerson Estabrook remodeled his boardinghouse with a dining room and a confectionary into Estabrook's Opera House on Main Street in Factory Point, now Manchester Center. On the third floor he added a stage and dressing rooms, although roller skating was also a featured activity. Estabrook advertised his third-floor skating space as the "Best Floor in the State," where one could skate for two hours for ten cents.[10] The split in the town was clear: the gentry up on the hill at the Music Hall were playing billiards or bowling and the others were skating at Estabrook's. But the crowd at Estabrook's also was exposed to live music, provided by the Farmers' Cornet Band and Bower's Rink Band.

After train service improved to Manchester and his hall was upgraded with a marble carriage stepping-block in front, Estabrook was able to attract more out-of-town talent such as the Boston Opera Company, Josh Billings and his "serio-comic lectures," and monologues such as *The Flea* and *A Brisk Package*. Estabrook's Opera House flourished until a fire destroyed it and its entire block in 1893. However, three years later, it was rebuilt as the Union Opera House, which survived until the 1960s with benefits, an annual minstrel show, lyceum courses, state and local meetings, and as a voting place. This downtown opera house in one form or another kept going for almost eighty years, establishing itself as an important town hall for public activities such as elections. The more fashionable uptown music hall provided entertainment for almost fifty years before being absorbed by the commercial world of tourism, still a major economic mainstay of that part of town today.

Cambridge, New York, a town on the other side of the Taconic Range from Manchester, also had two competitive opera houses serving diverse needs and publics at different times on opposite sides of town. Ackley Hall was built in the west end of town by pharmacist Henry Ackley in 1869, located on the third floor of the building housing his first-floor drugstore. Hubbard Hall, on the east side, was built in 1878 by Martin Hubbard, president of the Cambridge Valley National Bank and owner of the entire block where the opera house and his lumberyard were located. Before Ackley added the third floor for entertainments, most major speakers such as Frederick Douglass and Susan B. Anthony spoke at a Presbyterian church; entertainments and dances were held at Union Hall. Ackley Hall, wrote editor James S. Smart of the *Washington County Post* and a booster of Ackley's initiative, "will supply a want long felt in this Village, and one which has stood in the way of first class troupes, preventing their visiting this place."[11]

The new hall, which could seat 550 with additional camp stools for overflow, opened in November 1869 with a ceremony of shadow pantomimes, a concert by the Cambridge Band, and a talk by the Methodist minister, all presided over by editor Smart, who declared the new hall "one of the finest north of Troy."[12] In December, the Cambridge Lecture Association launched its program with a talk by the Boston abolitionist Wendell Phillips, which attracted the largest audience to gather in one building in the town's history, followed in the new year by major lecturers, first Mark Twain on the Sandwich Islands and then social reformer and suffragist Susan B. Anthony. Aside from these lectures, Ackley Hall's first year included the oratorio *Esther* sung by the Cambridge Valley Choral Society; what must have been a religious performance by the Scripture Tableaux Company, narrated by the Methodist circuit rider M. H. Meeker; a lecture by the controversial and radical millionaire George Francis Train; and the commencement exercises of Cambridge's Washington Academy. For eight more years, this third-floor opera house over Ackley's drugstore remained the main hall in town.

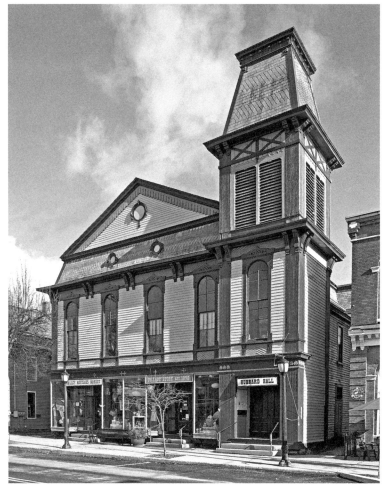

Cambridge, New York's two opera houses: Ackley Hall and Hubbard Hall. *Ackley Hall* (top photo). *Cambridge Historical Society, Ken Gottry; Hubbard Hall, George Bouret* (bottom photo)

Dissatisfied with this hall on the western side of town and no doubt disdainful of its roller-skating crowd, Martin Hubbard decided to build an even grander hall on his property on Main Street on the eastern side of town in 1878. Hubbard, a major figure in the economic life of Cambridge, who had opposed a union school for the entire town and instead built a new school for the east-siders, may well have seen the construction of Hubbard Hall and its first-floor commercial space as a way of keeping his employees working during the depression of 1878, speculates Benjie White, the persevering executive director of Hubbard Hall for thirty-seven years. Built in less than nine months, Hubbard Hall is a Second Empire mansard-style frame building with an almost belfry-like tower whose staircase, located to the right of the first floor's two retail stores, provides access to the second-story opera house. The opera house has a flat floor, a balcony, ornate Victorian gas chandelier, stenciled walls, chestnut woodwork, and a turn-of-the-century stage curtain. Martin Hubbard wanted a grander hall and he built one.

Henry Ackley saw the handwriting on the wall and sold his investment in the hall shortly after Hubbard Hall was completed. Lectures and traveling shows, previously at Ackley Hall, were now coming to the new Hubbard Hall instead. To compensate for this loss, the new owners of Ackley marketed the then-popular sport of roller skating, "go as you please" racing, and indoor bicycling, which was not feasible outdoors on Cambridge's unpaved roads many months of the year.[13] Ackley Hall's conversion to a skating hall came about when Wiley and Van Nostrand rented the hall and installed a new slick floor for skating, which proved extremely popular. However, the skating came to an abrupt end when, on the morning of December 23, 1884, a fire raged; with freezing conditions thwarting the local firemen, Ackley Hall and its entire commercial block were destroyed.

Hubbard Hall was then the only hall in town for both west- and east-siders. That is where the high school graduations as well as the local dances and benefits took place, where a host of speakers including Chautauqua lecturers held forth, where *East Lynne* and many other melodramas were played, and where all the traveling troupes performed. Hubbard Hall continued as the center of Cambridge's cultural activities until the 1920s. It was brought back to life in 1978 by a serious theater professional and Cambridge native, Benjie White. Today Hubbard Hall thrives as an important regional theater with its own stock and opera companies and an array of art programs like dance classes and chorale instruction. It is the anchor of a new regional performing arts center campus, with an art gallery on the ground floor of the hall and studios and lecture space behind the hall in the old freight buildings formerly serving Martin Hubbard's lumber yard. Not only is the 136-year-old Hubbard Hall thriving today, but, remarkably, as the last functioning opera house in Washington County, it has survived many vicissitudes that felled at least eight other opera houses in nearby towns.

Tensions within towns were not based solely on social and cultural differences. Just the physical location of an opera house could cause frictions. Fremont, Nebraska was a thriving town of more than seven thousand and served as a railroad junction when the Love Opera House was built in 1888 to replace an opera house that had burned the previous year. Fremont's grid-patterned downtown had two important streets: Main Street, with adjacent streets for shopping and offices, where the earlier Shed Opera House was located; and Broad Street, a major street with a hotel and civic buildings. Broad Street won out as the site for the new opera house, as it seemed the more important thoroughfare, with street-car and hotel access as well as proximity to the railroad. However, over the years Broad Street became State Highway 77, with heavy through traffic en route to Lincoln, only fifty miles away. The large hotel was demolished, and newer public buildings such as the post office were built nearer Main Street, now designated a historic district. If the opera house were on Main Street today, its resuscitation would probably be easier as it would fit into the retail district with its older buildings and small-scale businesses. Large, multi-axled trucks now rumble by the Love-Larson Opera House on Route 77, and the streetscape has become a shadow of its old self with many missing teeth where once-impressive buildings, like the hotel, formerly stood. Although the handsome opera house currently sits disconnected from the revived downtown, renewed efforts are being made to revive it as an active theater.

Intertown opera house rivalries spurred town after town to compete with their neighbors over which town's opera house was most significant in the area. In Illinois, the rivalry between two opera house towns, Rushville and Beardstown, demonstrates the extent of such competition. Rushville's 1882 opera house tried to outdo Beardstown's 1872 opera house by installing a fly gallery, which made for quick scenery changes as the sets were raised and lowered rather than being lugged on and off stage. Beardstown responded eleven years later by upgrading its opera house with frescoes, golden upholstered seats, velvet curtains, electric lights, and its own new fly gallery. Rushville tried to keep up, installing

electric lights, and then in 1900 added frescoes to the decor. But no matter what improvements these competing opera houses undertook, they
could not keep up with the times. Newer movie theaters and changed
times were making the opera house, no matter how up-to-date, an obsolete institution.

Noticeably absent in this discussion of schisms that affected opera
houses is the most dominant schism in this country: the enduring segregation of African Americans. Although the opera house heyday was
after the Emancipation Proclamation of 1862 and the Civil War, black
Americans were treated as though they were on the bottom rung of a
caste system for another hundred years. In public places like theaters and
schools and on public transportation, primarily in the South, African
Americans were second-class citizens—whether going to the back of the
bus, attending segregated schools, or using separate entrances and sitting
in segregated areas in theater balconies. Not until the Civil Rights Act of
1964 were these barriers made illegal.

In many of the newly developing states like Iowa and Colorado as well
as the older, established New England states, African Americans were
fewer in number than in the South, so segregation and explicit racism
were less overt problems. In 1890, when opera houses were sprouting up
throughout the country, the census recorded that the "colored" population in Iowa was .06 percent, in Nebraska .08 percent, and in Colorado
1.5 percent. In Vermont, the 1890 "colored" population was only .25 percent.[14] Even in these states with these small numbers, separate events for
"colored" citizens would be mentioned in New England town histories,
such as a Thanksgiving evening dance in 1888 at Southworth's Hall in
Williamstown, Massachusetts.

Many pioneers in the Midwest and beyond came from New England,
and they brought with them the abolitionist values that had dominated their former region. Also recent immigrants were not tainted
with American racial prejudices. While these parts of the nation were
free of much racial prejudice, they, like most Americans, enjoyed minstrel shows, mostly performed by out-of-town companies. In upstate
New York, Salem's Proudfit Hall had "never seen such an immense crowd
of people as packed every inch of available space" for Mr. Hi Henry's
minstrel show in 1894, for which "words fail to do justice to the emi-
nently satisfactory performance," according to the *Salem Review-Press.*[15]
However, as traveling companies dwindled in number, minstrel shows,
especially in remote places, were often locally produced. For more than

fifty years, a minstrel show with local performers was an annual event at the opera house in Enosburgh Falls. Such minstrel shows were universal entertainment, not seen as condescending or prejudiced, as they surely would be today.

In the South, it was a different matter, as attitudes toward the black population and the number of black people differed considerably from those in the North and most of the West. In Kentucky, black people in 1890 made up almost one-fifth of the population and almost two-fifths in Lexington's Fayette County's population. Here as elsewhere in the South, theaters had separate entrances for blacks or "colored" as the lettering stated, sometimes indoors but often by an outdoor stairway such as a fire escape. The uppermost balcony, with bare and backless seats, often just benches, was for blacks. This theater segregation, like all aspects of segregation, was permanently etched in the memories of African Americans. Even the 2009 *New York Times* obituary of the prominent historian John Hope Franklin mentioned his memory of sitting in the segregated section of the Tulsa opera house when he was young.[16]

Minstrel shows and black performers such as Blind Boone were often hits with both black and white audiences in Southern opera houses. Wilson and Rankin's Mammoth Minstrels, for example, were featured the night after the August 1887 opening of the new opera house in Lexington, Kentucky. There Lexingtonians could hear George Wilson sing songs such as "Don't Ask Me," "No, Naughty Boy," "Can't You Guess?" and "Wedding Bells." While interpretations of Southern attitudes toward such minstrel shows and talented black performers vary, there is no question that stereotypical images of Sambo or of an obsequious Uncle Tom often dominated.

The all-time favorite show, *Uncle Tom's Cabin*, which played several times a year in small-town opera houses in the Midwest, was performed in the South after the Civil War and then by a "daring Tommer company."[17] One production of *Uncle Tom's Cabin* in Louisville shortly after the Civil War met such hostility that later productions cut many of the antislavery lines and converted it increasingly into a comedy and melodrama. Indeed, the play was once advertised as "Morsels of Ethiopian Mirth, Fun and Frolic."[18] Often Tommer troupes were forced to cancel performances because of local hostility, as townspeople threw rotten eggs at the cast, damaged posters and scenery, and even drowned out performances with local bands playing "Dixie." Southern newspapers would publish tirades against the play, and many chapters of the United

Daughters of the Confederacy petitioned local theater managers to cancel upcoming *Uncle Tom's Cabin* performances.

Lexington, Kentucky's theater manager responded to such a petition in 1901 by stating bluntly that "the war has been over about thirty-six years."[19] Kentucky also distinguished itself by having the first black actor play Uncle Tom in this country, a decision Gustave Frohman made in his 1876 Richmond, Virginia production, long before New York performances, commencing in 1916, used black performers. However, Kentucky regressed with 1906 legislation making any play "that excites racial prejudice" illegal, with violators eligible for fines and prison sentences. Although never enforced, such legislation would certainly have dampened the interest in Tommer troupes performing in Kentucky. By the early 1900s, the sociopolitical message of the play had been so overtaken by the melodrama that the United Daughters of the Confederacy's concerns seemed less relevant.

Towns and cities, especially in the South, in border states, and in cities with large African American populations, often had theaters for African American audiences in the first half of the twentieth century. These theaters, many with names like Lincoln, Dixie, Apollo, and Hiawatha, were operated and owned by both African Americans and whites and featured movies as well as plays and vaudeville. Some of these theaters had been built for white audiences and were converted to theaters for blacks. It is estimated that 1,500 African American theaters existed between 1900 and 1955. For these populations in Kentucky, Louisville had seven such theaters, three dating back to the early 1920s; Lexington had three, and seven other towns each had one. In Virginia twenty-three towns and cities had theaters for blacks of which twelve were in Richmond, one in an opera house. Chicago with a large black population had forty-nine black theaters while Massachusetts, a state with a small black population and not so tinged with segregation policies, had only one such theater in Roxbury, a predominantly black section of Boston. For millions of African Americans, who previously climbed outdoor stairs to reach a top balcony with often bare benches, the existence of these theaters provided them with entertainment in a separate but equal manner in the period before civil rights legislation.[20]

Segregation by color was the most egregious type of exclusion that existed in theaters in the nineteenth and early twentieth centuries, but it was not as pervasive as segregation by price. From the earliest days of democratic theater, when all classes would attend plays, the occupants of boxes, balconies, and the pit were different folk, divided not just according to social class but by the price of the ticket. The 1737 Footman's Riot at the Drury Lane Theatre in London demonstrated the stratification of eighteenth-century theatergoers when the aristocracy's footmen rioted after the gallery assigned to them was eliminated because of complaints about their noise and obstreperous conduct. The aftermath of that riot, and the gradual transformation of audiences' active participation with actors to more passive and sedate theatergoing, meant that theater patrons were becoming spectators seeking more moral uplift than participatory entertainment. By the later nineteenth century when American opera houses blossomed, the audience had shed most of its former participatory activities, but segregation by price and class still persisted as well as segregation by race in the South, in border states, and in many cities with large numbers of African American residents.

CHAPTER 13

Immigrants

When Willa Cather reflected upon her childhood in Red Cloud, Nebraska, she remembered it was the immigrant neighbors who instilled in her the first "real feeling of an older world across the sea." The massive infusion of immigrants in the nineteenth and early twentieth centuries transformed the life and culture of many towns and cities. By 1890 Red Cloud had a mix of Germans, Czechs, English, Irish, Swedes, and Danes, but many immigrants tended to cluster. Almost half of Chicago's population in 1890 was foreign born. Some places became known for their immigrant populations such as Lindborg, Kansas, referred to as "Little Sweden," and Milwaukee, called the "German Athens in America." These foreign-born newcomers brought with them a love of culture that helped to dilute further any lingering Puritan fears about the moral dangers of theatergoing. More and more Americans wanted to attend the plays and operas that Eastern sophisticates and now these new immigrants were enjoying.

The impact of these waves of newcomers was especially noticeable in the new communities emerging on Oscar Wilde's "blotting paper." Here settlements absorbed burgeoning numbers of immigrants from Europe as well as emigrants from the Eastern states. It is not surprising that Willa Cather chose Scandinavian Thea Kronborg as the heroine in *The Song of the Lark,* for many of her neighbors in the Red Cloud area were immigrants. "We had very few American neighbors—they were mostly Swedes and Danes, Norwegians and Bohemians," reminisced Cather in 1913.

I liked them from the first and they made up for what I missed in the country. I particularly liked the old women, they understood

my homesickness and were kind to me. . . . These old women on the
farms were the first people who ever gave me the real feeling of an
older world across the sea. Even when they spoke very little English,
the old women somehow managed to tell me a great many stories
about the old country.[1]

Sinclair Lewis's Carol Kennicott also was struck by the genuineness of
the older generation of immigrants in Gopher Prairie:

> She remembered the feeble exotic quality to be found in the first-
> generation Scandinavians; she recalled the Norwegian Fair at the
> Lutheran Church. . . . There, in the *bondestue,* the replica of a Norse
> farm kitchen, pale women in scarlet jackets embroidered with gold
> thread and colored beads, in black skirts with a line of blue, green-
> striped aprons, and ridged caps very pretty to set off a fresh face,
> had served *rommegrod og lefse* sweet cakes and sour milk pudding
> spiced with cinnamon. For the first time in Gopher Prairie Carol
> had found novelty. She had reveled in the mild foreignness of it.
>
> But she saw these Scandinavian women zealously exchang-
> ing their spiced puddings and red jackets for fried pork chops and
> congealed white blouses, trading the ancient Christmas hymns of
> the fjords for "She's My Jazzland Cutie," being Americanized into
> uniformity, and in less than a generation losing in the grayness
> whatever pleasant customs they might have added to the life of the
> town. Their sons finished the process. In ready-made clothes and
> ready-made high school phrases they sank into propriety, and the
> sound American customs had absorbed without one trace of pollu-
> tion another alien invasion.[2]

Carol, like Willa Cather and many others bothered by the dullness and
uniformity in their small towns, savored the untarnished Old World
customs and manners of first-generation immigrants. From the 1870s to
the 1910s, when both Cather and Lewis were growing up, immigration
was profoundly affecting the country. In those four decades, 20,541,754
immigrants were added to the US population.

In Nebraska, the immigrant population accounted for almost 20 percent of the state's population in 1890. And they came from many different countries. In sparsely settled 11,210-person Webster County,
Nebraska in 1890, where Willa Cather grew up, fifteen different nation-
alities were represented: the Germans were the largest group, followed by

English-speaking immigrants from Canada, Ireland, and England, and then Scandinavians, Bohemians (later called Czechs), and a mixture of others in lesser numbers. Though these immigrants were no doubt scattered throughout the county, they would come to Red Cloud, the county seat, for their business transactions, making Red Cloud's influence seem greater than the town's population numbers might suggest, especially to a young child like Cather. In ten years from 1880 to 1890, the state's population more than doubled. Of all the states, Nebraska had by far the highest percentage of Czechs. Most lived in small towns or farms until the 1920s, when their distinct ethnic identities faded as they started acculturating to American ways. During the same period, from 1871 to 1910, the nation's population more than doubled from almost forty million to almost to ninety million.

While many in the first wave of Czech immigrants to Nebraska in the late 1860s and early 1870s left the old country for religious and political freedom, later Czechs were escaping Austrian military service or seeking better economic opportunities. And not all came directly from the old country. Some came first to Iowa, Wisconsin, and Eastern states and cities. For instance, Knox County, Nebraska was settled by eight hundred families from Cleveland and Chicago. Central to the Czech settlement in Nebraska was Vaclav L. Vodicka, who arrived in Omaha in 1868 and became a land agent for the Burlington and Missouri Railroad from 1877 to 1885, luring Czech settlers to his locale. As better homestead land was quickly patented, the railroad land grants, especially near the Missouri River, were eagerly sought by immigrants arriving after the 1860s. Vodicka, who spoke both English and Czech, was instrumental in helping Czechs obtain this land. Railroads had enticed immigrants with reimbursements for freight and travel, discounts for improvements, and premiums for swift installment payments.

While interest in culture and, specifically, opera houses was influenced by all European and some Asian immigrants, German immigrants often receive most of the credit for the flowering of culture in the newly settled areas. Around 1850, a wave of musically inclined Germans arrived in Peoria, Illinois and were soon organizing concerts, first in churches and then in small halls. As their concerts became increasingly popular with townspeople, they needed larger halls, eventually fulfilled by the 1,200-seat Rouse's Opera Hall. In Iowa, German immigrants, who accounted for 7 percent of the state's population in 1890, stimulated early interest in theater and even staged German productions of Goethe, Schiller, and Molière performed by professionally trained actors.[3]

Such cultural transfusions by newly arrived immigrants were made in all parts of the United States. The New England mill town, Claremont, was described in the Works Progress Administration (WPA) New Hampshire guide as a "music-loving town, due in part to the large number of foreign-born inhabitants and their children."[4] In Columbus, Georgia, his European background and interest in culture no doubt spurred Alsace native Francis Joseph Springer in 1871 to build the handsome Springer Opera House, which is still an active opera house. The construction of this cultural institution soon after the Civil War was made possible by Springer's successful wholesale grocery business. At that time only a handful of French and German immigrants lived in Georgia.[5] In the older, established Hudson River town of Poughkeepsie, the third major event to christen its grand Collingwood Opera House, built in 1869 with 2,000 seats on three levels and an unusual portable flat floor, was the Germania Masquerade dance, sponsored by the local German cultural association.[6] Although the event was considered a social risk by Poughkeepsie's establishment, which looked with scorn on the Germans in their town, it points out the role that newer immigrant groups played in the cultural life of long-established Eastern cities.

Germans comprised about a third of Milwaukee's population in 1880. They embedded themselves in the city's commercial and industrial activities and, importantly, introduced their love of music, literature, theater, and intellectual pursuits. A horticultural society, the *Garten-Verein*, was organized in the 1850s, the Free Thought movement emerged, singing groups like *Liederkranz* proliferated, and by 1900 operas were performed daily during the summer in Schlitz Park, itself named for a brewery founded by a German immigrant. The city's cultural life benefited from the largess and cultural dedication of some of its prominent German residents. Heinrich Kurz in 1868 built the Stadt Theater, a 900-seat theater for German drama, the first in the Midwest, which evolved from vaudeville into serious plays by Ibsen, Goethe, and Schiller. Rival theaters including the Grand Opera House appeared, but the Stadt Theater held on, with Ibsen plays a mainstay until 1895 when it burned down. The next chapter in German theater in Milwaukee was led by the beer tycoon Frederick Pabst.

When Frederick Pabst first converted the Grand Opera House into his large German theater and then in 1895 rebuilt the Stadt Theatre after the fire, Milwaukee was considered the "Deutsch Athens" of America. Pabst and Otto Strack, a German-born architect who was the supervising architect for Pabst's brewery, toured opera houses in the Midwest and were especially impressed by Adler and Sullivan's Auditorium Theater in Chicago, not only for its design but also for its technical equipment. Strack combined his European flair for ornate decoration and baroque design with his practical bent for technology in the Pabst Theater. This sumptuous and massive sandstone German Renaissance Revival opera house, with gilding and marble and all the latest technological inventions such as fireproof curtains, electric lights, and even an air-conditioning system using fans and ice, served as an important cultural institution for the Germans in Milwaukee, presenting theater and music from the motherland until 1935. A star like Fanny Janauschek, the famed Czech actress, made several visits to Milwaukee to perform at the Pabst Opera House.[7] Such a palace gave evidence that German immigrants had achieved social and economic success in the New World.

For Czechs, theater also loomed large, especially in Willa Cather's home state of Nebraska. This love of theater accounts no doubt for local drama societies as one of the earliest organizations Czech immigrants founded in the state. Nebraska's first Czech theatrical performance in Nebraska is reported to have been *Rekrutyka v Kocourkove* (Recruiting in Kocourkove), performed in 1869 by the Reading and Dramatic Society at a makeshift theater of boards laid over two sawbucks with calico curtains for drops, at the farm of Jan M. Svoboda near Crete. That was the beginning of fifty years of rich Czech theater in the state. Czech theater could be found in Nebraska cities such as Omaha, but mostly in small towns where Czechs had clustered such as Schuyler, Niobrara, Verdigne, and Clarkson—and, of course Wilber.

After 1900 the halls for Czech activities and plays in Nebraska were usually built by voluntary societies like Solkol and Zapadni Ceska Bratrska Jednota (ZCBJ) and always had a stage and often elaborate curtains of homeland scenes. Local interest in theater depended on the leadership and commitment of local Czech leaders. The town of Wilber became an early hub of Czech theater with the arrivals in 1877 of both Frank Sadilek from Omaha and Josef Schuessler from Chicago where he was a member of Alois Prokop's traveling troupe. Most of the productions in Nebraska's Czech halls were by local actors, but there were touring troupes like Prokop's and Frantisek Ludwik's company from Prague. To indicate the popularity of theater for the Czechs in that state, Ludwik's Prague troupe in 1893 played in twenty-seven American cities and towns of which twelve were in Nebraska. When the troupe returned to the United States in 1917, it performed in forty Nebraska towns. Some towns had theater groups in the 1880s and 1890s, but there were latecomers, who organized community halls for theater in the 1910s. Wilber outdid all other Nebraska towns as its theater continued for sixty-five years until 1942.[8]

Music also loomed as an important part of their cultural heritage. The saying "Who is a Czech is a musician" seems to have held true, as the Czechs transplanted their fondness for music in their new Nebraska settlements.[9] That interest continued as Willa Cather, on a visit home in 1912, learned that six hundred prosperous Bohemians had just left Omaha for a "great music festival" in Prague.[10]

The early programs of opera houses in Red Cloud and Table Rock do not reflect the ethnic diversity of those towns, as the Czechs and other immigrant settlers had not yet established their own cultural and civic activities. They probably had difficulties with the English-language programs and might not have felt welcome. When the Czechs did establish their own ethnic opera houses and theaters, they differed from those of their American neighbors. Productions tended to be locally produced and their opera houses were more civic than business ventures. The motivation for Czech theater, especially in small towns, was to preserve the Czech language and culture, in contrast to American theater and opera houses, which, more often than not, were driven by commercial interests. Most Czech halls built after 1900, usually by the ZCBJ, the most important Czech benevolent society in the early twentieth century, were simple, rectangular, flat-floored buildings with a raised stage at one end for dramatic performances.[11] However, their richly designed curtains displayed scenes, towns, and allegories of their motherland, unlike curtains in American opera houses with romantic views of the Alps, Venice, and places with no connection to the towns or townspeople where the opera houses were located.

Czechs clustered in Nebraska towns such as Clarkson, Wilber, Crete, and Table Rock, where they carried on their traditions, usually in music and theater. Uprooted and in unfamiliar settings, these Czech immigrants quite naturally wanted to hold on to their ethnic identity, so in their new communities they tried to re-create at least an image of their Bohemian heritage and setting.[12] Southwest of Lincoln, the small town of Wilber in Saline County, with seventeen hundred people, has enjoyed its Czech heritage ever since geology professor Charles D. Wilber, for whom the town was named, helped Nebraska in the 1870s attract "high-quality" European immigrants, including Czechs.[13] One such "high-quality" Czech immigrant who settled near Wilber was John Herman, a member of the Czech Diet in 1848, who came to this country in 1853 with considerable wealth, which was largely lost in Wisconsin land speculation but recouped again in Nebraska. The Czech heritage celebrated in Wilber in the late nineteenth and early twentieth centuries included fairs, parades, and plays at the opera house. Willa Cather is reported to have visited Wilber before she completed *My Antonia,* as did many Czech authors and politicians. After World War II, as younger Czechs became acculturated, their interest in the Czech heritage waned. However, since the 1960s a three-day Wilber Czech Festival (now attracting tens of thousands), a Wilber Czech Museum, and a Miss Czech Slovak U.S.A. Pageant have helped revive interest in Czech culture and history.

In Colfax County, Nebraska, located in the east-central part of the state with wide, high-grass prairies, Czechs outnumbered by far any of the twenty other immigrant groups in 1890; they made up more than half the immigrants and about 16 percent of the county residents. By 1910, in fact, almost a quarter of Colfax County's population consisted of foreign-born Czechs. The county was settled originally in 1868 by two Czech families with other Czechs soon following, among them Blanche Popichalova, who stimulated interest in Czech theater. The county's small towns—Tabor, Howell, Richland, and Clarkson—and neighboring rural areas, as well as the county seat of Schuyler, gradually attracted more and more Czechs.

Typical was Clarkson, which had a village population in 1890 of only 147 in a precinct populated by less than a thousand in rolling farmland. This small village now calls itself the "Center of Czechland" and boasts two recent Czech Slovak national queens. The town's wide, several-block-long Main Street is lined with small shops; doctors' and dentists' offices; and a bakery, featuring kolache and strudel, which serves as a local gathering place in the morning. At the end of Main Street, somewhat separated from the commercial buildings, sits the opera house, a solid brick structure resembling a municipal office building. Built in 1915 by the ZCBJ Lodge Zapahni Svornost and for fifty years managed by the ZCBJ, the Clarkson Opera House is the community-gathering place for meetings, dances, concerts, plays, movies, and Czech-language entertainments. Unlike most opera houses, which are on the second floor of commercial buildings, Clarkson's and most Czech halls and opera houses, run by Czech fraternal organizations, are solely for Czech theater and activities. That means that the theater or public hall has usually been on first floor and that is the case in Clarkson.

In 1963, the Veterans of Foreign Wars leased the building for its programs from the ZCBJ, but in 2002 the nonprofit Clarkson Community Opera House Inc. obtained the building for community entertainments. This nonprofit entity has stimulated interest in the town's Czech heritage and protected the opera house's six magnificent stage curtains with Old World Bohemian scenes and the proscenium. The reborn hall has mounted events like an annual Czech Festival and has again become a community center.

In Pawnee County in the southeastern part of Nebraska, with far fewer immigrants than Colfax, the 325 Czechs comprised a minority in 1890. The opera house in the village of Table Rock did not feel the influence of of its minority Czech population until 1924 when the ZCBJ bought the building for its own activities. Until then public entertainment and community events at the opera house had catered to a majority of English-speaking citizens. The Table Rock Dramatic Club, an all-American group, was a major force in the new opera house and one of the early troupes to perform there. A few events were advertised for the Czechs. Dances by "community Bohemians" were specifically mentioned in the local newspaper, *Argus*. Of twelve nondramatic events at the opera house in 1898, two

The 1915 Clarkson Opera House, Clarkson, Nebraska continues to serve the town and its Czech population. 2004. *Author photograph*

Bohemian dances were listed, one by the "community Bohemians" and the other by "Bohemian ladies."[14] A newspaper advertisement during the busy political time of October 1900 noted that the "Bohemian citizens of this vicinity" were invited to an address at the opera house by R. Rusicka, editor of the *Pokrok Zapadu* (Progress of the West), in which "one of their own countrymen [would] discuss the political issues."[15]

Table Rock, with twelve hundred people in 1894, good farmland, and an unusual rock formation for which it was named, had a precarious start. The initial development company, the Table Rock Site Company, was unable to lure as many settlers as it hoped. That company was then bought out by the Nebraska Settlement Company in 1857. However, even that company had troubles as the financial panic of 1857 and floods of 1858 reduced its two hundred families to fifteen. Yet in spite of all its problems, Table Rock soldiered on with a flour mill and sawmill, creamery, brickyard, and most significantly the Atchison and Nebraska Railroad's arrival in 1871. In 1889 G. R. Martin started acquiring lots facing the town square for an opera house, which was completed in 1893. Like many small-town opera houses, this three-story building had shops on the ground floor separated by a wide double-door that opened to steep stairs leading to the second floor, the main floor of the opera house. Here was a flat-floored auditorium with a stage and a high ceiling allowing for a balcony and a stage loft. To maximize the rental income, there was a dental office on the second floor in the front under the balcony. By 1899, the opera house building and the entire block were fitted with Conklin acetylene gas, so the hall's lighting was very much improved.[16]

The programs at the opera house in Table Rock were similar to those of many towns neither on a main rail line nor large enough to attract many well-known traveling troupes and lecturers. But that did not mean there was a paucity of varied entertainments. The local Table Rock Dramatic Club staged performances such as *New York Book Agent, White Mountain Boy,* and *Fruits of the Wine,* supplemented by performers from nearby towns such as the Tecumseh Ticklers and the Dubois Columbia Band, which produced a nautical temperance play, *Turn of the Tide.* In addition to the many dances and church suppers were the array of events: temperance lectures, hypnotists, band concerts, Epworth League talks, Woodmen's programs, Mother Goose festivals, Ladies of the Cemetery Association suppers, politicians' talks (including, of course, William Jennings Bryan), Norris Brown political party dinners, and high school graduations like 1894's, with the class motto "Honors Wait at Labor's Gate"

and six graduates, each of whom gave an oration. Out-of-town entertainers were alternated with local events: minstrel shows, Blind Boone,
the Pond-Berlin Theatrical Company, Johnnie and Ida Pringle, and in
1898 two *Uncle Tom's Cabin* troupes, Burk's Big Uncle Tom's Company,
"one of the finest organizations now traveling," and Frank E. Griswold's
Railroad Uncle Tom's Cabin Company.[17]

December 1900 forecast a gloomy future for the opera house, as two
featured out-of-town troupes failed to show for their engagements. Local
activities continued at the opera house along with medicine shows,
dances, and social functions, but around 1917 the hall started showing
moving pictures. When a movie theater opened in Table Rock, it seemed
that the end was near for the opera house as a major venue for social and
cultural events. However, that was not the case. In 1924, the local Czech
fraternal organization, Lodge Premysl Otakar II, No. 84 (ZCBJ) bought
the Table Opera House for $2,000 and brought it back to life as a center
for Czech activities.

For thirty-nine years, the ZCBJ operated the opera house, eight more
years than the Table Rock natives had. Here it held meetings, dances,
a Czech school, and plays. As in the early opera house days, the fare
was not high culture but it provided entertainment and a way for local
Czech farmers and townspeople to socialize. It is clear that the Czechs
were a proud and separate community within Table Rock. They even had
their own cemetery. Most of the Czechs who settled in Table Rock in
the 1870s spoke Czech and taught their children to speak Czech. Few
of the first generation's children attended high school; only four Czechs
graduated from high school from 1888 to 1913, while in a second generation, from 1913 to 1928, sixty-nine graduated. As in many Czech
communities in Nebraska, Czech remained the dominant language for
these newcomers. It was a potent symbol of national identity. Because the
Czechs had been constantly warring with German influences, the Czech
language assumed an importance for them in their homeland and again
when they relocated to the new country. The language and cohesiveness
of these recent arrivals no doubt prevented these Czechs from greater
participation in Table Rock cultural activities and entertainments at the
opera house.

In 1963, the ZCBJ Lodge donated the building to Gordon Bethel and
Howard Howell, who operated businesses on the ground floor. However,
two years later, these businessmen deeded the opera house to the town
historical society, which converted it into the Old Opera House Museum.

With shops on the ground floor and a museum on the second floor, Floyd Vristaka, as president of the historical society, has conscientiously curated the museum with artifacts of the opera house era such as old wooden chairs, the small stage with gilded proscenium, a painted backdrop of a forest scene, and mannequins in nineteenth-century dress. Authenticity has even included the chair and equipment of the dentist who had rented one of the front rooms on the second floor. A nearby building has become an adjunct to the museum for its considerable archival materials. Vristaka is a Table Rock native, local businessman, former state legislator, local ardent historian—and a Czech descendant. Although Table Rock's Czechs were much smaller in number than the Czechs in Colfax County, their culture has contributed to the county and to their opera house. The transfer of Table Rock's opera house from the Table Rock natives to the Czechs to the local historical society indicates the blending of Czechs into the mainstream of Table Rock. It also points out that the younger generations, especially, are less interested than earlier generations in a fraternal organization like the ZCBJ, or in identifying overtly with their Czech heritage, as they blend into mainstream American society. Through the interest of Floyd Vristaka, Gordon Bethel, and many others in the heritage of their town, Table Rock has retained its opera house and other buildings on the town square as a reminder of the heyday of its opera house, the role of its Czech residents, and of a past era in the town's history.[18]

Immigrant groups with no opera house or fraternal lodge of their own often used local opera houses for their programs. The Norwegians' Ibsen festival was held in Stoughton, Wisconsin's opera house; the Italians of Barre, Vermont's Italian operas were performed in the Barre Opera House; and the music-loving Welsh sang in opera houses and halls around the slate-rich border country straddling Vermont and New York just south of Lake Champlain. Here in the mid- to late nineteenth century, a rich node of slate quarries had attracted Welsh miners, who began in 1850 singing in concerts and then in cultural festivals known as *eisteddfods* in large and small towns. As slate villages like Granville, New York and Poultney, Vermont prospered, so did their Welsh musical activities. By 1870 *eisteddfods* were held regularly, with competitions in singing, oration, declamation, and composition. Not only did the occasions provide opportunities for the Welsh to enjoy their music and bond with each other, but they exhibited a well-deserved pride in their Welsh heritage. The Welsh also proved to their fellow townspeople and others in their communities that they were respectable and worthy citizens. In Fair Haven, Vermont, the local newspaper reported patronizingly that the Welsh audiences at an *eisteddfod* were well behaved and could be "an important part of our population; we are glad to receive them to citizenship in our country."[19]

Across the continent in the Rockies, in another mining settlement, the Cornish and their love of music stimulated interest in one of the country's best-known opera houses and one that features opera, the Central City (Colorado) Opera House. Though the early Cornish miners were not necessarily interested in opera, they organized many local singing and instrumental groups and were reported to have been involved in the construction of the Central City opera house.

Throughout the country where ethnic groups settled, cultural and social halls, sometimes called "opera houses," were established so these groups could continue the familiar music, theater, and traditions of their homelands and also attempt to perpetuate these traditions for their children. On the West Coast, Japanese immigrants, socially

Early musicians, probably Welsh miners, at the Central City Opera House in Central City, Colorado, n.d. The Welsh were famed for their singing even on their walks to work. *Denver Public Library, Denver, Colorado*

isolated in cities like Seattle, organized their own ZCBJ-like institutions such as Nippon Kan Hall, started in Seattle in 1907 and completed in 1914. "One needs to know the solidarity and social isolation of the Japanese community to appreciate what the Nippon Kan meant to it. It was, in reality, the hub of the Nihonmachi world and its people," recalled Minoru Masuda, a Nippon Kan Hall attendee. Although built later than most opera houses, the flat-floored Nippon Kan Hall served the same functions as other ethnic cultural halls—a place for plays, political debates, benefits, social events like the annual celebration of the emperor's birthday, and many weddings. In addition, the building contained a hotel. Like most opera houses, its ground floor housed retail stores. The plain, unpretentious exterior of this multipurpose clubhouse belied its vibrant interior.[20]

Traditional Kabuki, ancient Japanese plays, and traditional *odori* dances were featured at Nippon Kan Hall with the aim of instilling homeland values in ensuing generations. Most of the performances were by amateur members of four local dramatic groups, which on weekends gave several performances a month for an admission fee of seventy-five cents, but actors from Japan and even Japanese actors from Hollywood also appeared on the boards of the hall. Even the stage was designed to replicate ethnic traditions. It sat on rollers, similar to a railway turntable, and turned around with the scenery and actors for each new scene. The stage also had a small extension like a runway, and the space where the stage and runway met was occupied by percussion instruments that accompanied movements on the stage and provided sound effects to dramatize the entrances and exits from the stage in Kabuki theater. Performances began with the curtains opening to the accompaniment of wooden sticks being clicked together at a faster and faster tempo by a man on the side of the stage. Nippon Kan Hall continued as an important ethnic institution in Seattle "so people could forget that they were living so far from home," reminisced Seattle resident Miyohi Yorita. Its operation, however, was interrupted by the Japanese attack on Pearl Harbor and the subsequent banishment of Japanese Americans to internment camps.[21]

New settlers from abroad have left their imprint on civic life and culture as well as in opera houses in the towns and cities where they settled. For many, the isolation, the hard work necessary to survive, homesickness, and American prejudices kept alive their memories of the old country. Prejudice, today often focused on Hispanic immigrants, was directed in the late nineteenth and early twentieth centuries at other immigrants who now are mostly assimilated in American society. Yet only a hundred years ago, Henry Cabot Lodge, then a congressman from Massachusetts, introduced legislation to limit immigration because he saw late-nineteenth-century Italian, Polish, Asian, and Russian immigrants as threats with their "wholesale infusion of races whose traditions and inheritances, whose thoughts and whose beliefs are wholly alien to ours."[22] Yet whatever the motivation, whether pride in the culture of their homeland, a love of music, or the need to bond with fellow countrymen, immigrants celebrated their culture in opera houses in major cities like New York and Milwaukee and in small towns like Clarkson and Wilber, Nebraska. Continuing that interest in ethnic identity in younger generations, one of the motivations for the ethnic opera house, has become increasingly challenging, as the younger generations become Americanized and want to move on.

CHAPTER 14

Symbols of Pride

"Local glories," as opera scholar John Dizikes called small-town opera houses, stand out as visible symbols of a town's civic pride. In Iowa, as in many states where almost every town came to have at least one opera house, townspeople felt immense pride in these halls. "It was *theirs*, it was beautiful, it was bigger and better than anybody's else, it attracted better entertainment and served the community. It was after all, the 'Opera House,'" George Glenn and Richard Poole noted about Iowans' attachment to their local opera houses.[1]

Whether grand or simple, public or private, their distinctive architecture, elegant interiors, and key locations made these opera house buildings local landmarks in both their early days and now their comeback years. Frequently embedded in a commercial block on Main Street, some might face the county courthouse on the town square as in Minden, Nebraska. Others might stand alone dramatically on the brow of a hill or perched on a cliff overlooking a harbor and ocean, as in Stonington, Maine, or on a riverbank, like the Goodspeed Opera House in East Haddam, Connecticut. In Derby Line, Vermont the opera house and library even sit on an international border.

For decades, some of these halls survived fires, floods, economic booms and busts, and changing styles of entertainment. However, by the mid-twentieth century, many of these opera houses, along with their downtowns, were deemed anachronisms and were abandoned. If not torn down, these cultural institutions stood as ghost-like presences, reminding townspeople what their town had been. Concern about the abandonment and uncertain future of these architecturally significant local monuments, probably more than a desire for cultural events, fueled the initial interest in their restorations in the 1970s. In fact, the opera house was often the first property in a town to be listed on the respected National Register of Historic Places, as the Wheeler Opera House was Aspen, Colorado's first listing on the National Register in 1972. This interest in and appreciation of the architecture of these halls happened to coincide with the broadening of the historic preservation movement's scope to encompass the social and economic benefits of individual buildings as well as groups of buildings on Main Street. That early concern with architecture, followed by a greater appreciation of the historic cultural and social functions of these halls, helped galvanize local activists to bring the halls back to life as community theaters and art centers.

Towns and small cities often witnessed a progression of opera house buildings, from the simplest one-story buildings to larger, multi-story opera houses, culminating sometimes in luxurious grand opera houses. Keokuk, Iowa, for example, had three successive opera houses, built in 1870, 1893, and 1912. These multiple generations of opera houses reflect a town's improving economic and social status and especially its aggrandized self-image. Fires and natural catastrophes forced many towns to replace earlier halls, but prospering towns wanted larger halls that they considered appropriate for their advancing social and economic status. Pueblo, Colorado enjoyed plays and operas at four opera houses: an adobe building; a Turnverien Society hall leased to John (Jack) Langrishe's company; DeRemer's Opera House, a skating hall with a stage adequate for Emma Abbott's Italian operas; and finally the grandest of them all, the 1,200-seat Pueblo Grand Opera House built in 1890 for more than $300,000 (about $8 million today). Although DeRemer's house burned down in 1899 and was quickly rebuilt, it did not measure up to the town leaders' image of their booming city. What Pueblo needed was a grand opera house "commensurate with her late marvelous successes," city leaders were told at the first meeting of Pueblo, Colorado's Grand Opera Association in 1888.[2] And that they got two years later in the Adler and Sullivan–designed Grand Opera House, the largest theater in the state and certainly one of the handsomest. Aside from trumpeting a city's wealth, investments in opera houses and particularly in grander halls in the late nineteenth century confirmed the acceptance of theater and entertainment as a respectable and indeed necessary civic amenity.

The blossoming of opera houses coincided with a new interest in art, music, architecture, and theater, which mirrored the confidence and energy of the United States in the decades after the Civil War. As the changing styles of painters, musicians, and architects were publicized, they were sought by aspiring publics, including the town leaders and entrepreneurs promoting local opera houses. Art and architecture provided a new patina of respectability for prospering cities and towns as well as for their new socially ambitious residents. Whether built by a nouveau riche industrialist or a booming new city, a building designed by nationally known architects confirmed material achievements and cultural aspirations. This growing acceptance of the need for beauty and art was overtaking the earlier rigid moralistic attitudes toward cultural and creative activities. For the opera house, the taut, spare lines of the New England frame meetinghouse were replaced with a staggering array of architectural styles, many eclectically combined in a single building garnished with fanciful details. Architects such as Richard Morris Hunt, H. H. Richardson, Stanford White, Daniel Burnham, and Louis Sullivan became familiar names to educated Americans. Though most of their buildings shared a sense of symmetry, their styles varied and included elements of the Second Empire, with mansard roofs and dormers, smooth surfaces, florid details, pediments, and columns; squat Romanesque fortresses with rough boulder-stones; and plain functional buildings in the "form follows function" school. The Executive Office Building in Washington, DC, is a prime example of Second Empire–style fortress stone buildings in a derivative of the German Romanesque style, which appeared in the Midwest in places like Menomonie, Wisconsin and Pueblo, Colorado. These solid and impressive Richardsonian structures helped validate cultural buildings, such as libraries and opera houses, as worthy public buildings. Some scholars have ventured that these muscular, rusticated buildings, "built for all time," emulated the enduring engineering feats of ancient arched Roman aqueducts.

The Colonial Revival style eventually succeeded the Second Empire as a popular style for public buildings such as courthouses, fancy opera houses, and capitols. This revival of early American colonial styles introduced a certain quietness, as in the classical portico in an enlarged colonial hall such as Lebanon, New Hampshire's city hall and opera house.

With the ebb and flow of architectural styles in this heady time, it was difficult for small places to keep pace with changing styles. That meant most opera houses exhibited a mix of styles or vernacular architecture—in fact, a veritable encyclopedia of styles. Bellows Falls, Vermont's German Romanesque opera house is anchored by an Italianate tower; Aspen, Colorado's Romanesque Wheeler Opera House displays Italianate details; and medieval touches and neoclassical lines blend in with the Greek temple–like architecture of the opera house in Hudson, New York.

Nationally known architects designed few opera houses and certainly not those in remote, rural towns. In fact, few rural opera houses had the benefit of architectural advice. Most opera houses in small places were simple buildings developed by a local businessperson relying on local builders without the benefit of a guide or pattern book often built in the vernacular of their region and time period. Boat builders are said to have helped construct the one-of-a-kind Boothbay Harbor Opera House, and miners in Colorado gulches pitched in to build some of their early opera houses. Without any architectural guidance, the small town of Grainfield, Kansas added a touch of elegance to its simple local stone and brick opera house by affixing a factory-produced ornamental iron front, probably ordered from a catalogue. Larger places in later years, depending on their prosperity and ambitions, would call on a prominent local or regional architect or, when bursting with affluence, a nationally known architect or firm.

The detached one-story opera house, located in a small town, proved the most popular, expedient, and cheapest structure to build, but not the most

Opera houses come in all sizes. The Freeman Opera House, Sargent, Nebraska.
Collection of Andrea Faling

enduring. These simple frame buildings, often the first in a succession of opera houses in the same town, often succumbed to fire, floods, and disasters, so few remain today. Interestingly, they were considered less of a fire threat than higher buildings and met many of the new fire regulations enacted after the devastating 1903 Iroquois Theater fire in Chicago. In Nebraska more than half its opera houses built after 1900 were ground-floor theaters, most in villages with fewer than five hundred people.

These ground-floor halls had other advantages. They could easily be converted for movie showings and other events as well as to commercial or manufacturing uses. Those without balconies were more likely to be oriented to community activities, such as meetings, dances, sports, and social events, rather than theatrical productions. Some were extremely simple, like Sargent, Nebraska's, but the modest exterior of others could belie an almost elegant interior, such as the Thrasher Opera House in Green Lake, Wisconsin, a town with fewer than a thousand residents. From the exterior, this small-frame, rectangular, freestanding building, built in 1909, looks like a nondescript commercial building in a rural town. Its double

The 1901 Thrasher Opera House in Green Lake, Wisconsin has been restored and is now an active entertainment venue. *Author photograph*

doors offer the first hint that the building housed something more than a local business. Inside the raised stage, raked floor, tin ceiling, beaded board wainscoting, narrow balcony, and decorative stenciled pattern along the top of the sidewalls let people know it is an opera house. Such details would not be unusual for a small town's ground-floor opera house. Carefully restored, Green Lake's Thrasher Opera House has an active organization and many volunteers that operate its year-round programs.

As towns became more prosperous, these small halls became more elaborate. The proscenium became wider and higher, backstage space for dressing rooms was provided, and stenciling proliferated and balconies were added. Ironically, the new and often lavish movie theaters were mostly first-floor entertainment spaces similar to the modest one-story opera houses they drove out of business.

The second-floor opera house in a two- or three-story commercial building on Main Street was the most pervasive building design, especially in the last decades of the nineteenth century. Here the entertainment hall would be on the second floor, often with a balcony in three-storied buildings. Rent-paying retail establishments occupied the building's ground floor, defraying the cost of operating the rarely lucrative opera house. Many of these simpler opera houses were embedded in a commercial block of buildings on a linear main street, sometimes facing the town square with its courthouse or municipal buildings, thereby integrating them into the commercial and civic center. The exterior of a building offers clues that an opera house was once located within it. These details include a higher roofline than adjacent buildings, a stone tablet above the door with the name of the opera house, its donor, and the date of construction above the door, or a triangular pediment at the roofline. Double doors between two ground-floor businesses are yet another clue, as are large second- or third-floor windows.

Willa Cather's Italianate Red Cloud, Nebraska opera house, built in 1885, is a typical example of this common opera house design, with the second-floor opera house above stores, double doors, and a pediment identifying the building as an opera house built in 1885. Inside the double doors of this common opera house architectural style, wide, bare wooden stairs rose, sometimes very steeply, to the second floor. At the top of the stairs were the ticket window and a small lobby space. Sometimes rental space occupied the front of the lobby space, as in Table Rock, Nebraska's opera house, where the local dentist rented an office. A door opened from the lobby to the entertainment hall, which extended to the back of the

The 1885 Red Cloud (Nebraska) Opera House, now houses the offices of the Willa Cather Foundation, gallery space, and the auditorium of the old opera house on the second floor. *Author photograph, edited by George Bouret*

building. In small towns like Red Cloud, this entertainment space was a rectangular room approximately 65 feet by 80 feet with a flat floor and movable seats. At the far end of this space was a raised stage with a handsome proscenium with scene wings and a drop curtain. Aside from stenciling, often on a tin ceiling, and modest decorations, the major attraction was the curtain with local advertisements bordering an exotic foreign or romantic scene. The lighting was initially candlelight, but by 1880 most halls were lit by gas jets along the walls. A potbellied stove provided heat in the winter, the busy season for the majority of rural opera houses.

These halls could be uncomfortably hot in the summer. Larger opera houses devised ways to cool their halls, but they were rarely successful. Facilities for the performers, including dressing rooms, tended to be small spaces on either side of the stage. As there was no pit for the orchestra, the musicians sat directly in front of the stage. With no balcony and no columns, the audience had an unobstructed view of the stage. The chairs for the audience were also simple, uncushioned, sometimes collapsible, and not fixed to the floor, thus providing flexibility for a variety of events.

Numerous variations of these second-floor halls existed. Options included a painted proscenium, various scenery wings and flat grooves, curtain tracks, and rigging for roll drops, fancy or advertising front drops, and a trapdoor necessary for the ever-popular and exciting melodramas. In a three-story building, balconies provided more seating, often simple and bare, sometimes just a few rows in the back of the hall. Some opera houses, like Hubbard Hall in Cambridge, New York, had a larger entertainment space because their stairs were located in a belfry on the side of the front façade. Whatever the configuration of these small halls, they provided an intimate space conducive to live and participatory events in which audiences were drawn into the drama or entertainment.

As the demand for entertainment swelled at the end of the nineteenth century, more substantial opera houses replaced the older, humbler halls that had been felled by fire. These larger and fancier halls announced that a town was thriving and eager for culture and entertainment. A local Andrew Carnegie often would take it upon himself, sometimes even hiring an architect, to provide the new up-to-date hall, usually a brick or stone building.

Aspen, Colorado's opera house benefited from the largess of Jerome B. Wheeler, who was married to an heiress of Macy's department store in New York City. He moved to Aspen because his wife's health required mountain air, withdrew from his involvement with Macy's, and got swept into the then-lucrative silver mining business. The resulting Richardsonian Romanesque Wheeler Opera House, designed by the well-known Chicago architect Willoughby J. Edbrooke and built in 1889, anchors a prominent downtown corner in Aspen. Although the hall was over the traditional ground-floor commercial establishments, Aspen's opera house, like Leadville's, introduced another level of luxury to the mining gulches and silver-enriched mining towns. Wheeler's entertainment space was grand, replete with a raked floor, fixed seats for 500, decorative stenciling, and a full horseshoe balcony.

Other larger opera houses like Bennington, Vermont's Putnam Opera House were architect-designed and important landmarks in their towns, but not as sumptuous as the Wheeler. Maysville, Kentucky cherished its long history of theater with several generations of opera houses culminating in the Washington Opera House, built in 1898–1899 to replace an earlier hall that burned to the ground. The new Washington is a symmetrical three-story building with a ground-floor theater and two balconies, the top balcony with spare seating reserved for "coloreds." Cushioned, fixed seats, a raked floor, a handsome proscenium, and an elaborately tiled lobby make Maysville's opera house as elegant as a town of 5,500 could dream of. However, the comfort of the seats and the quality decoration diminishes on the higher levels. Maysville's exterior made of local stone, accentuated with horizontal courses of lighter stone, stands out on Main Street as an important local building—and institution.

The massive, grand Love Opera House, built in Fremont, Nebraska in 1888, reflected the prosperity of the town when it became the largest railroad transfer station in the state and its population doubled in a decade to 6,747. Designed by Omaha architect Francis M. Ellis, the four-story red brick building is divided into three vertical sections separated by light-colored sandstone pilasters, arches over windows, horizontal stripes, and pressed-brick checkerwork. Above a central Roman arch window were etched the words "Opera House." Unlike most opera houses with a central entrance, Fremont's had three entrances: a wide, central entrance to the first-floor commercial establishments and two entrances on either side leading to stairways for the theater. The house seated 1,075, with 465 comfortable, velvet-covered "opera chairs" and four balcony boxes with five chairs each. Its interior was lavishly designed in various shades of brown with maroon and blue frescoing along the walls, culminating with a frescoed proscenium arch. This grand main space had stained-glass windows, brass-rod balcony railings, and a handsome dome. The luxurious stage (26 feet by 32 feet) with a fly gallery, foot and border lights, drops and bridges, trapdoors, eleven sets of scenery, and twelve feet of space under the stage provided up-to-date facilities for touring performers and troupes as well as a resident theater company and orchestra. Located close to Omaha and with excellent rail service, Fremont's well-equipped opera house attracted performers who otherwise might not stop in such a small place. The broad range of performances and affordable tickets made theatergoing a popular activity in Fremont. The local newspaper even carried a theater column.

The substantial Love Larson Opera House in Fremont, Nebraska, built in 1888, is now awaiting restoration and revival. *Author photograph*

   This generation of larger opera houses in the late nineteenth century was not only elegant to the eye but also provided facilities for performers and audiences that were far more sophisticated than the earlier, smaller halls. These newer halls were stage-oriented with raked and tiered auditoriums, fixed and cushioned seats, bigger stages, fancier and larger prosceniums, wide wing spaces, better lighting arrangements, bigger dressing rooms and, of course, more trapdoors. "The house is supplied with every convenience," reported the *Kentuckian-Citizen* in describing the new opera house in Paris, Kentucky. Aside from all the fancy accoutrements of a larger hall, Paris provided a "waiting room for ladies, which will prove a great convenience to the country ladies," indicating that its patrons came from well beyond the city limits.[3] Although these larger halls were not quite as pretentious, and gilded as the grand opera houses, they stood out as the grandest and most elegant entertainment halls in their respective towns and cities. Only the mansions of the town's plutocrats might outdo them.

   These buildings were built to last, and they have. Throughout the United States these larger halls, especially the brick and stone opera houses like Maysville's, Aspen's, and Claremont's, are actively used today, mostly for theatrical performances, musicals, concerts, movies, and civic activities, especially in town-hall opera houses.

In the late nineteenth century, as prosperous cities were building massive opera houses—notably New York's 1883 Metropolitan Opera House and Chicago's 1888 Auditorium—so were smaller, more remote places like Oshkosh and Menomonie, Wisconsin and thriving cities like Denver, Colorado, Lexington, Kentucky, and Galveston, Texas. These impressive halls usually were called "grand opera houses" (or "Grands"), but, imitating New York's impressive hall, some cities like Grand Forks and Philadelphia named their new opera houses "metropolitan" rather than "grand." Whatever their name, these large halls, designed by well-known regional or even nationally known architects, stood three or four stories high in a prominent site, either freestanding or occupying a whole block. In smaller cities, the Grands were usually devoted solely to opera house functions with no commercial space on the ground floor. However, in larger cities like Denver and Pueblo, Colorado and Kearney, Nebraska, the grand opera houses might be encased in capacious downtown buildings called the "opera house building" (or block) with commercial space in different arrangements. In both Denver's and Pueblo's wide structures, office space was located on the sides of the buildings, while in Kearney's narrower and taller building, offices were on several floors. One of the best-known examples of encasing a grand theater in a shell of a building is Chicago's Auditorium, where shops, offices, and even a hotel surround its theater.

The interiors of these Grands could be dazzling: marble, gilt decoration, murals, possibly even cherubs and cupids cavorting around the walls, elaborate chandeliers, ornate boxes (often on two levels), two or three balconies, raked floors, and velvet cushioned "opera chairs," some with hatracks and even holders for canes and umbrellas, a permanent stage with full dressing rooms, advanced lighting and scenery facilities, an orchestra pit, and sometimes as many as five trapdoors.

Certainly the most influential American opera house, over many decades, was and is New York City's Metropolitan Opera House (the "Met"). In 1966 it moved to an up-to-date building at the Lincoln Center for the Performing Arts; neither that building nor its 1883 predecessor on Seventh Avenue achieved the architectural distinction of Garnier's 1875 Paris Opera or more recent iconic landmarks in Sydney, Oslo, and Copenhagen. The Met's original building, known today as the "old Met," was enormous, with the country's largest proscenium and an auditorium seating 5,780, even larger than Milan's La Scala. Organized and built by the Metropolitan Opera Association, comprised of New York's powerful financiers and industrialists, the building was nonethelesss utilitarian.

Today, images of the dazzling diamond horseshoe boxes come to mind when thinking of the Met's building, but that exuberant ornamentation was not in the original design. Its architect, J. Cleaveland Cady, described the building displaying "a simple dignity that will not be tiresome or uninteresting as the years go by."[4] Occupying an entire block from Thirty-ninth Street to Fortieth Street and from Broadway to Seventh Avenue, it did not appear at first glance too different from nearby office buildings. Essentially it was a three-part building. The marquee was the giveaway of the entrance to the opera house, which was in the squat building between two office buildings. The two side buildings had shops on the ground level, with ballrooms and bachelor apartments on the upper floors and a tall, extensive production/fly gallery space in the rear. There were no fanciful details on the exterior, just arched windows above the entrance and large arches at the street level. Nor was it in a prominent location like many European opera houses or even on a fashionable street like Fifth Avenue. In contrast, Garnier's Paris Opera stands nobly as an island at the Place de l'Opéra. Smaller American cities, however, often located their grand opera houses in conspicuous sites near town squares.

The utilitarian appearance of the Metropolitan resulted from an unlikely situation considering its moneyed stockholders: financial constraints. Initial estimates of $600,000 rose to $1,525,000, causing the stockholders to wonder about proceeding. They did, but Cady was careful. For him, three criteria drove his design: to provide boxes on two tiers for the seventy shareholders, each paying $15,000 for a box and then $1,500 per year, with boxes of the same size and "equally advantageous";[5] to provide generous space for the stage, accessories, actors, and audience, including comfortable and spacious seats, as Cady recognized that "opera performances can be long"; and to pay attention to fireproofing and safety, involving the use of masonry, little wood, expensive steel trusses, attention to exits, a sprinkler system, water availability, and staircases in towers with ceilings precluding grand entrances.[6] Meeting these needs, Cady found "there is little money left to make it 'A Noble Work of Art' or 'A Monumental Work.'"[7]

Despite all the fireproofing, the building was gutted by fire in August 1892 when a workman dropped a cigarette in the paint room, which then ignited discarded scenery. Cady's fireproof curtain, which might well have prevented such a serious fire, was no longer used. When it was rebuilt the next year and then renovated ten years later, the Metropolitan acquired the lavish ornamentations, so popular in this Beaux Arts era, which were missing in its original design.

New York's 1883 Metropolitan Opera House, designed by J. Cleaveland Cady, and Paris' 1875 Opera House, renamed the Palais Garnier to celebrate its famed architect, Charles Garnier. Top photo: *Metropolitan Opera House: Library of Congress, Prints and Photographs Division LC-D4-18310;* Bottom photo: *Palais Garnier: Author photograph*

A grand opera house signaled a city's confidence and prosperity. These large, elaborately decorated buildings announced to the world that a city, however small, had riches and cared for culture. What was considered "grand" depended not only on the size and monumentality of an opera house but also how a city or town viewed itself and what image it wanted to project. Many places like Fremont, Nebraska could boast of opera houses with many features of a grand opera house, but they did not call them "grand," while other places may have been too boastful in calling their halls "grand."

Pueblo, Colorado was a boomtown that did build a grand and handsome opera house. Like many towns, Pueblo launched its drive to build a large hall after the earlier DeRemer Opera House was ravaged by fire in 1888. At the first meeting of the Grand Opera Association in 1888, the city's power brokers were told by Judge T. T. Player that "Pueblo must have an opera house at once" and to accomplish this goal they must "go down into their pockets and help forward this the most important enterprise for the permanent good of the city that has yet been undertaken. . . . That an opera house was an indication of advanced civilization and refinement on the part of the people in whose city it was erected."[8] And in two years, those power brokers came through. The land was donated, the money raised, and the four-story opera house building, consuming a whole block, was erected. The size of the Opera House Block, as it was known, matched the feeling of prosperity that Pueblo was enjoying in the late nineteenth century with its thriving steel mills and railroad activity. The city was then referred to as the "Pittsburgh of the West."

More important than the size of the Grand Opera Block was its architecture. Pueblo chose one of the country's most illustrious architectural teams, Chicago's Dankmar Adler and Louis Sullivan; in fact, Pueblo's "Grand" stands out as the only small-city opera house built at this time that could boast of being designed by such renowned architects. Although Adler and Sullivan were best known for their early high-rise buildings in the 1890s such as the Wainwright Building in St. Louis, they had previous experience in theater design. They were the architects of the Academy of Music in Kalamazoo, Michigan in 1882; the rebuilt McVickers Theater in Chicago in 1885; and the epochal Auditorium Theater with 4,200 seats in Chicago's Loop in 1889, at its time the largest building in the United States. After learning of Adler and Sullivan's successful Chicago's Auditorium Theater, Pueblo's Opera House Association investigated the possibility of Adler and Sullivan designing Pueblo's opera house. Adler and Sullivan took on the Pueblo commission, which was the firm's second-largest commission.

The Pueblo Opera House, a massive red sandstone hall, was completed in 1890. A squat building of essentially four floors reminded some (and maybe Sullivan, who was fond of Florence) of a Florentine palazzo. Even its tower seemed like a Florentine campanile. For others, the building hinted at the Prairie School of architecture made famous by Frank Lloyd Wright. Like Chicago's Auditorium, which housed offices and a large hotel, Pueblo's opera house was embedded in a large opera house block with offices and commercial spaces around two sides of the building. This architectural landmark was where theater, entertainments, and social events took place for decades.

There were seats for one thousand, a large stage, and the latest in mechanical and stage equipment. For the theatergoer, the absence of pillars supporting balconies meant sight lines were not obstructed. This innovative engineering feat in Pueblo was the first of its kind in this country and the model for later Adler and Sullivan theaters like the Schiller Theater in Chicago.[9] Its interior dazzled theatergoers with gold ornamentation, much of it in gold leaf, with electric lights making it a "blaze of light."[10] Even its arched entry was ornamented with the words "Grand Opera House" and the heads of Shakespeare and Verdi on its spandrels. All this ornamentation was supervised by another Chicago firm, although Sullivan is thought to have been directly involved with much of the interior design, especially the proscenium. Some architectural historians like Henry Russell Hitchcock suggest that Frank Lloyd

Pueblo, Colorado's 1890 Grand Opera House, designed by Chicago architects Sullivan and Adler, was a precursor of the low-slung prairie architectural style. *History Colorado*

Wright, who was on the staff of the Adler and Sullivan firm at the time the Pueblo building was designed, may well have worked on the opera house. Wright's windows in his Charnley House in Chicago, which seem similar to Pueblo's, help to bolster Hitchcock's suggestion.[11]

Despite its fortress-like appearance, making the building appear fire-resistant, it is startling that a fire on the freezing morning of February 28, 1922, when firefighters were thwarted by frozen hoses, destroyed this gilded opera house. Compromises in the fireproofing plans, a negligent cleanup after a grocery organization's ball, and maybe a cigarette, have been considered as possible causes of the fire. Not only did Pueblo lose one of its most prominent buildings but, like many other boomtowns, it never became the great city its boosters hoped it would be. When the opera house opened in October 1890, a Pueblo newspaper opined: "The change wrought in the appearance of the city within a few years reminds one of the stories of the Arabian nights, the romance of Aladdin's lamp.... There are many of us living today who will see here a great manufacturing city whose wealth and influence will be second to none in the magnificent empire of the West."[12]

While Pueblo's population hovered in 1890 around 25,000, classifying it as a city, other small cities like Oshkosh, Wisconsin (population 22,000 in 1890) and Dubuque, Iowa (population 30,000 in 1890) were also keeping up with the larger cities by building grand opera houses. Oshkosh, with booming lumber mills earning it the name "Sawdust City," erected a grand opera house in 1883 after affluent business leaders decided the existing Wagner Opera House did not match their aspirations. The local newspaper reported these leaders wanted "a more metropolitan place of entertainment." The new hall, designed by local architect William Waters, who is credited with designing more than 150 private and public buildings in Oshkosh, displayed ample opulence. Blending Romanesque and Queen Anne styles, this hall with marble, gilt, and hand-painted curtains could seat 1,224 with 921 fixed seats plus additional chairs and "jump seats" that unfolded from the walls and ends of the seats. After several renovations and reopenings financed both by city and private donors, Oshkosh's Grand Opera House continues to bring live entertainment and culture to that Wisconsin city. The C. D. Hess Opera House Company's ballad opera, *The Bohemian Girl*, inaugurated the hall in 1883, followed by an array of stars including Sarah Bernhardt, Harry Houdini, and Mark Twain.

As elegant as some of the larger late-nineteenth-century opera houses in prosperous American towns seemed, they were outdone by other late-nineteenth-century grand opera houses in the United States and certainly by European and Italian opera houses like Milan's 1778 Teatro alla Scala or Venice's 1678 Teatro San Giovanni Gristomo. With five levels of boxes, sculpted and gilded ornaments, and sumptuous ceiling paintings and chandeliers, it seemed as though no surface had been "left undisturbed" in the effort to create Venice's palatial theater.[13] As remote as Venice was from small American cities, the precedents of opulent European opera houses no doubt inspired many ambitious American opera house developers.

Locating opera houses in a multipurpose public building, however, is a distinctly American phenomenon. Although most opera houses have been in private buildings, many can be found in town halls, sometimes cheek-by-jowl with the town's police and fire departments, and library. These multipurpose public buildings appeared early in New England, but could be found in the latter part of the nineteenth century in other parts of the country. Some, like the building in South Londonderry, Vermont, frugally added space to its existing town hall to accommodate opera house functions. But most interesting is how deftly New Englanders were able to adapt their buildings as well as their religions to changing times, making entertainment an acceptable activity deserving space in the town hall as well as taxpayers' money. In some of these combined town halls and opera houses like Bellows Falls, Vermont's and Camden, Maine's, the opera house managers today are town employees. These town halls with opera houses are early examples of public support of the arts; ironically, this occurred in New England with its history of Puritanical strictures on theater and entertainment.

New England's meetinghouses provided a precedent for the numerous opera houses in towns' public buildings. As a place for public assembly serving dual roles as a town's religious and secular building, the meetinghouse was the most important building in a town. From the mid-seventeenth century to the mid-nineteenth century, about two hundred meetinghouses were built in New England. Most of them served communities with fifty to one hundred families and provided venues for religious and civic events, from baptisms to town meetings.

When the public assembly functions left the meetinghouse, the new town halls abandoned some of the architectural features of the old meetinghouses while adapting others to new settings. The distinctive interior layout of many meetinghouses with the pulpit and entrance across from each other on the shallow side of the building was replaced with the more elongate, traditional church or public hall layout with the altar or stage at the end of the long axis. However, the belfry of the meetinghouse remained a feature of nineteenth-century town halls cum opera houses and some private halls, although it was usually converted into a clock tower. No doubt such a vertical element emphasized the building's

The tower of the Rockingham Town Hall and Bellows Falls Opera House dominates its downtown. *Sheafe Satterthwaite photograph*

importance in a town and distinguished it from other nearby buildings, just like the campanile in Florence and in many European cities. In new and old towns and cities, the municipal building outranked any other building for its universal use and recognition, so a tower only confirmed its importance. Places like Claremont, New Hampshire, Bellows Falls, Vermont, and Stoughton, Wisconsin illustrate the significance of the town hall/opera house tower in those communities.

As New England's mills were churning out textiles, the prosperity of mill towns like Claremont, New Hampshire made possible the creation of substantial, architect-designed opera houses. Claremont chose the New York City architect Charles A. Rich, a graduate of nearby Dartmouth. This Renaissance Revival opera house and city hall stands out as the town's major civic building, appropriately facing the town square. The ground floor with arched doorways and gilded decorations still houses the city offices while capacious stairs on either side of the ground-floor lobby lead to the opera house two flights above.

From its early New England precedent, the combined town hall/opera house became increasingly popular in Midwestern states like Wisconsin and Illinois, but could be found in places as diverse as Bozeman, Montana and Dothan, Alabama. Time, distance, and heterogeneous settlers, including many immigrants, diluted much of the rigidity of religious strictures on theater and entertainment for newcomers to the West in the mid- to late nineteenth century. Therefore, combining civic affairs, culture, and entertainment in one public building did not jolt many newcomers' previously held beliefs. And these combinations of town halls and opera houses substantiated their boosters' civic pride, as in Calumet, Michigan, boasting today of its hall as the "only municipal theater in the United States," although its 1900 opera house was hardly the first nor the only municipally owned theater at that time.

In 1890 Bozeman, Montana celebrated the opening of its city hall and opera house, just a year after Montana became a state and seven years before Bozeman was incorporated as a city. When its city hall and opera house building was first conceived, Bozeman was bursting with confidence and even aspiring to become the state capital. However, constructing the building in the young settlement, then with 3,000 people, involved many controversies, several bond issues, and a final cost of $45,000, more than four times the $10,000 estimate. The first architect, Byron Vreeland, drew up the plans in three weeks, but he died as the controversies dragged on and was replaced by George Hancock.

Once built, the three-story brick Second Empire style building soon became the civic, social, and cultural center of the city. Here were housed all the city's services as well as its cultural facilities. The firehouse, police department and jail cells, and city offices were on the first floor. The opera house, library, and offices for the city attorney and marshal were on the second floor, and the tower was used for drying the fire hoses. Additionally, there were offices for rent. The opera house flourished for several decades with three or four events a week. Famous actresses like Helena Modjeska as well as varied entertainers and troupes performed at the opera house, which served also as a venue for school plays and graduations, political rallies, and lectures.

Like many opera houses in the early 1900s, the construction of a new school auditorium, competition from movies, and the building's deteriorating physical condition, even after a 1914 remodeling, meant Bozeman city hall's opera house was no longer the prime entertainment venue in town. By 1916, it was renamed the Municipal Theater and attracted speakers like Clarence Darrow. Gone, however, were the days when the opera house was the center of the city's social life, with a wooden footbridge over Main Street from the second floor of the newly opened Bozeman Hotel to the second floor of the opera house, so ladies attending opera house performances did not get their dresses sullied. The National Guard rented the hall in the 1920s for drills and removed the seats, which were reinstalled for a short spurt of activities in the late 1920s. However, the opera house did not survive long. The city continued using the building for its fire, police, and business activities until 1966 when this grand 1890 city hall and opera house succumbed to the wrecking ball of urban renewal and the city hall was relocated in a new building.

Fortunately, information on the architecture, layout, and history of Bozeman's 1890 city hall and opera house did not vanish when the building was torn down, as was the case with most opera houses and even city halls. Careful drawings, photographs, and a history of the building were prepared in 1965 by the federal Historic American Building Survey (HABS), the United States' oldest and foremost preservation program, started in 1933 and overseen by the National Park Service. With these drawings, one can see details that would have been lost in history, including descriptions of all the doors and windows, the 100-foot flagpole topped with an eagle, and floor plans showing how the hook and ladder, jail cells, city attorney's and assessor's offices, and opera house could all fit in this one building. These drawings illustrate how efficiently such diverse activities were planned and how carefully the aesthetics were considered.[14]

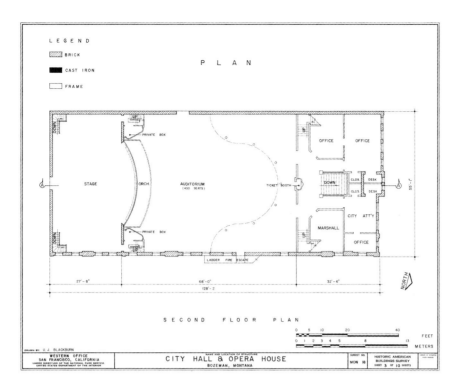

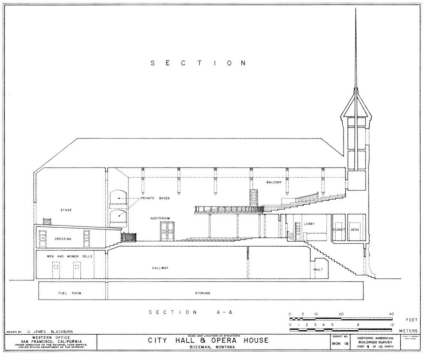

Bozeman, Montana's 1890 City Hall and Opera House Historic American Buildings Survey drawings. Upper: second floor plan with opera house. Lower: longitudinal section of the entire building showing city offices and opera house. *HABS MONT, 16-BOZ,1*

In Wisconsin, a remarkable number of cities built opera houses in their city halls in the early 1900s, spurred, no doubt, by the reformist efforts of its Progressives and Socialists to meet the state's educational and cultural needs. These buildings reflect the strong commitment to public governance in Wisconsin at that time. "This building belongs to the people," Mineral Point Mayor J. P. Parmley proudly stated at the February 15, 1915 dedication of the city's new municipal building housing the city hall, opera house, and library. Present at this ceremony were the secretary of state's Free Library Commission; several ministers, including the Reverend W. F. Phillips, who spoke on the "Wholesome Influence of Drama"; and other local dignitaries. Mayor Parmley, in his dedicatory address, boasted that the new city hall "was surpassed by no municipal building in Wisconsin" and that "it was a pleasure to him to deliver it into the hands of the people of the city, whose building it is."[15] This civic building, housing all the city's official and cultural activities, continues to function today as it did in 1915, although subsequent interior improvements included the restoration of its opera house, originally called "The Auditorium." Settled by Cornish miners who worked the local lead veins, Mineral Point, a small hill town nestled in the rolling country of south-central Wisconsin, was not alone in expressing pride in its new municipal building designed by Madison architects.

Stoughton, a city south of Madison with a large Norwegian population, houses in one building all its city hall offices and its opera house, referred to as "the auditorium." Built in 1901 to replace what Stoughton mayor O. K. Roe considered a "tumble down rookery" of a city hall, the new Romanesque building was built to last. Its interior includes elaborate chandeliers, gold-leaf fleurs-de-lis framing the proscenium, and opera chairs with hat racks and footrests.[16] Interestingly, the opposition to incorporating the auditorium in the new city hall was won over on a design issue: if the building did not include the revenue-producing auditorium, the city would end up with a squat, one-story city hall. Thus, Stoughton got its impressive city hall and auditorium. One hundred years later, the hall was restored and the City Hall Auditorium was renamed the Stoughton Opera House.

City halls like Stoughton's were prominent buildings in their cities: large in size; in prominent locations, with imposing architecture; and often with clock towers dominating the city's skyline. Stoughton's clock tower, with its four faces bringing the building height to 100 feet, seems even higher given its siting on the brow of a small hill. Stoughton followed the most common layout for opera houses with the performance hall on the upper floors and city offices on the first floor, similar to the privately built second-story opera houses with stores on the ground floor. Mineral Point, on the other hand, neatly divided separate civic activities in different sections of its building, each with direct access to the street.

The combination opera house and library is another variant of civic and cultural activities taking place in a single building for public use. Unlike the town hall/opera house, which was usually built and funded by the local government, the library and opera house was more likely the gift of a local philanthropist: Andrew Tainter in Menomonie, Wisconsin; Martha Haskell and her son Colonel Horace Haskell in Derby Line, Vermont; and, of course, Andrew Carnegie in Allegheny City, Pennsylvania. These cultural halls are functioning today, but now require public funds to supplement their original endowments. Due to the pride of the initial benefactors in their towns and their interest in establishing a significant local cultural institution, these library/opera house buildings remain imposing architectural monuments in their towns.

Straddling the American-Canadian border in Derby Line, Vermont and Stanstead (formerly Rock Island), Quebec, the Haskell Library and Opera House stands out as a uniquely located opera house. This handsome structure, built deliberately to serve both countries, now celebrates the accurate location of the international border with a diagonal black line traversing the floor of the hall. Through the decades Canadian and American interests in both the library and opera house have blended well together. The building has two mail addresses, one for each country, and one entrance on the American side of the building. Since 9/11 with heightened border concerns, its international location has become more of a concern. Canadians now are advised to park on the Canadian side of the border and "return to their country of origin" on leaving.

The benefactor of the building and another female promoter of opera houses, Margaret Stewart Haskell, enjoyed a long-standing interest in the arts and even had a small theater for plays and readings on the third floor of her house. She wanted this combination library/opera house to be a cultural and educational center for remote communities on the border. It has been that but, like most opera houses, the Haskell has not been a financial success. With little experience in the management of opera houses, the Haskells hoped the income from the opera house would be used "for the support and maintenance" of the library.

Embellished with its stained glass windows, mosaics, rare native woods, tin ceilings, and fireplaces, this formidable stone building provides substantiality in these border communities. In fact, the rococo opera house exudes a gilded quality with its horseshoe balcony, handsome proscenium, murals, ubiquitous painted and plaster cherubs, and well-preserved curtain and scenery, the only surviving work of the renowned Boston artist Erwin LaMoss. Ever since its inaugural performance in 1904, the opera house has hosted an incredibly diverse mix of plays, concerts, lectures, and even hearings for Canadian/American court cases in the 1900s. One musical performance, the Vermont Symphony's concert in the Made in Vermont Festival, has become an annual event at the Haskell. Since 2005 the opera house has had an international theatre company in residence, the Queen of the Northeast Kingdom Productions, presenting summer seasons of productions.

The festive nature of the opera house portion of this building contrasts with the more restful library with fireplaces and quiet nooks for reading books. This bilingual library continues to serve communities on both sides of the border, not only with books but also with educational programs. Mrs. Haskell and the other donors of these handsome cultural institutions recognized the symbiotic relationship of the written word, music, and theater and the need for them in places of all sizes, but particularly in remote small towns.

The diversity of these opera houses in public buildings is matched by their important role in their communities. In contrast to most privately developed and managed opera houses struggling to survive with limited public funding, the opera house in a city hall or even one combined with a city hall and library confirms a city's commitment to culture. In many of these opera houses in city halls, their construction and maintenance as well as the salary of the opera house manager are publicly funded. That is an aberration in the United States. Such a deviation, similar to European support of its opera houses, offers an example of how some small and medium-sized cities treat culture as a public service and public asset.

Most American opera houses sprang up in towns because of the vision and dedication of local cultural entrepreneurs. For these private opera houses, lone Andrew Carnegies were often the benefactors, but the public opera house by contrast usually resulted from the efforts of a committee of local town fathers and entrepreneurs.

Such private ventures depended on the initiative and largess of town leaders like W. P. Thorpe, a banker and real estate entrepreneur in David

The international 1904 Haskell Opera House and Library in Derby Line, Vermont and Stanstead, Quebec has the American/Canadian boundary line painted on the opera house floor. 2004. *Author photographs*

City, Nebraska; Franklin Pember, a lumber millionaire in Granville, New York; or Horace Tabor, a silver-mining tycoon in Leadville and Denver, Colorado. Aside from providing their towns with public halls, these philanthropists had the satisfaction of their opera houses often being named for them: the Thorpe Opera House, Pember Opera House, and Tabor Opera Houses. Their philanthropy often extended to many other critical civic improvements. In Leadville, Tabor determined "to make Leadville a first-class city" by establishing the Bank of Leadville, of which he was president, in addition to a gasworks, waterworks, fire department, telephone company, newspaper, and even a local cavalry company.[17] His philanthropy could be found in every good cause in Leadville, whether schools, churches, or the local hospital. Franklin Pember, Granville, New York's first millionaire, built a citywide water and sewer system as well as a library and natural history museum, which continue to function today.

Culture-seeking wives prodded some of their husband entrepreneurs like Thorpe and Pember. Also, a sense of Victorian noblesse oblige and that basic American quality of betting on the future no doubt spurred these men to make large contributions that they thought could improve their towns. Thorpe, Pember, and Tabor probably approved of their opera houses and other public projects forever authenticating their wealth and fame. Tabor felt his Denver Grand Opera House was as opulent as money could buy at that time. That quest for opulence in opera houses was not restricted to local benefactors in small American towns. In Venice, the Grimani family, in its ornate Teatro San Giovanni Gristostamo, even featured a chandelier with the Grimani coat of arms that would light up the theater before and after performances. For the Grimani family, that opera house in Venice heralds their fame, as Tabor's and other American entrepreneurs' opera houses do.

When an opera house bears the name of a town, it usually means that it was developed by a committee and/or financed by public subscription, as in Paris, Kentucky, Kearney, Nebraska, and Pueblo and Central City, Colorado. Although private ventures, these community halls assumed a more public nature than the entrepreneurially built halls. In Paris, Kentucky, the Bourbon Opera House did not result from the largess of prominent local patricians like the Clays, but rather the hall belonged to the people of Paris and Bourbon County. It was the "people's house." In Midwestern towns like Woodstock, Illinois and Stoughton and Mineral Point, Wisconsin, opera houses in buildings housing most or all their municipal offices bear the name of the town. These are public buildings. Occasionally an opera house might be named for a prominent person, organization, or situation not associated with the promotion or development of the opera house, like the Fulton Opera House in Lancaster, Pennsylvania, named for its famous native son, the steamboat inventor Robert Fulton; or it may recognize important service to the town, as in Maysville, Kentucky where its Washington Opera House honors not George Washington but the local fire brigade, the Washington Fire Company, which tried valiantly to save the earlier opera house in a devastating fire. In Wamego, Kansas, opera house philanthropist J. C. Rogers was so enthralled by the 1893 Columbian Exposition that his 1910 opera house was named the Columbian Opera House.

Toward the end of the nineteenth century, when more opera houses and theaters were being built and recognized as prominent cultural institutions, a market for theater architects emerged. Many of those who responded were local or regional architects. Colorado's Robert S. Roeschlaub designed the nearby Central City Opera House; Michigan's Charles K. Shand Calumet, Michigan's town hall and opera house; and Massachusetts's George G. Adams, Barre, Vermont's opera house and Rochester, New Hampshire's opera house. An international team of architects, including James Ball from Stanstead, Quebec and Gilbert Smith from Boston with Stanstead, Quebec contractor Nathan Beach, designed and built the Haskell Opera House.[18] Often the local architect of an opera house was unknown outside his town or region. And frequently, there was no architect.

The local builders responsible for the design and erection of many early and small opera houses are rarely named, despite public interest in these buildings. Even in those instances where hearsay attributes the building to local groups like sawmill workers in Woodland, Maine or miners in Central City, Colorado, there is little documentation about them. Troy, New York illustrates the anonymity of the architect or even the history of the building in which an important opera house was located. Little is known about either the history or design of Troy, New York's museum, located in a downtown office building, which opened in 1828 but became famous in 1852 when the all-time favorite *Uncle Tom's Cabin* was first performed there. By contrast, the history and design of the Troy Savings Bank Music Hall are well known and documented, as it was designed by the successful New York architect George B. Post, known for many important buildings including the

New York Stock Exchange. Built in the iron-making heyday of Troy in 1875 and still recognized for its remarkable acoustics, this handsome hall with the Troy Savings Bank on the ground floor and the Music Hall upstairs follows the layout of the small-town opera house whose commercial establishments occupied the ground floor with the hall on the upper story or stories.

With the late-nineteenth-century crescendo in opera house construction, some architectural firms began specializing in theater design, such as John Bailey McElfatrick and his firm J. B. McElfatrick & Son and Leon H. Lempert and his firm Leon Lempert and Son Theatrical Designers. McElfatrick, born in Harrisburg, started his architectural career in Pennsylvania but soon went west, establishing an office in St. Louis and later in New York. Often called "the father of American theaters," he ignored the English and European theater layout and instead planned continuous main-floor seating with deep balconies, no projecting stage apron, excellent sight lines, and up-to-date fireproofing.

From 1885 to the 1930s, the Lempert firm, another father-son operation, designed innumerable theaters and opera houses, especially in upstate New York, as the firm was based in Rochester. In New York State alone, the Lemperts designed seventy-three theaters, with Leon H. Lempert Sr. responsible for the firm's opera house commissions. Most of their opera houses were built in the 1890s, many in small upstate New York towns like Granville, Seneca Falls, and Albion. Leon H. Lempert Jr., however, designed the later theaters, primarily movie theaters, in larger cities such as Buffalo, where the firm won commissions for nine theaters, and Rochester, with fourteen. They ventured beyond New York to New England, New Jersey, Ohio, Pennsylvania, West Virginia, and across the border to Ontario.

Hiring an architect was a clear signal that a town was feeling flush, exemplified in the boom times of silver mining in Leadville, where Horace Tabor hired local architect George E. King, along with J. Thomas Roberts, the builder, to design and construct the 1879 Leadville Opera House, then considered one of the country's grandest. Later, as towns and cities became more prosperous, they would go farther afield to find suitable architects, especially as more and more architects were specializing in opera house and theater architecture in the later nineteenth and early twentieth centuries. Chicago architectural firms, the New York Lemperts, and the St. Louis McElfratricks were responding to mushrooming demand for opera houses and later for movie theaters. Pueblo, Colorado hired Chicago's Sullivan and Adler firm; Lexington, Kentucky chose another Chicago firm, Oscar Cobb and Son, with a record of designing two hundred theaters; and when Al. Ringling wanted to endow his hometown of Baraboo, Wisconsin with a luxurious theater, he chose yet another Chicago architect, George L. Rapp, whose firm had designed four hundred theaters. The well-known out-of-town architects received generous accolades when their halls opened. They also brought enormous prestige to the towns and philanthropists who hired them. However, no American architect of opera houses has received the fame accorded Charles Garnier, the young designer of the 1875 opera house in Paris; his statue still graces the front of this landmark opera house, now known as the Palais Garnier.

The extravagance, in fact, of many opera houses constructed in the late nineteenth century is often a surprise. Murals, frescoes, chandeliers, fancy woodwork, boxes, handsome seats, elegant stairways, and velvet adorn these halls in large and small cities. A capacious stairway is one indicator of the wealth of a town and the extravagance of the opera house. Rather than a set of steep treads and risers prevalent in small second-floor opera houses, grander halls may have curving stairwells, sometimes two arching from both sides of the lobby, reminiscent of Garnier's Paris opera house where there are traditions of fashionable patrons displaying themselves and the latest styles of dress. Even the small Goodspeed Opera House in Connecticut features a single red-carpeted staircase.

The architecture and interior designs of America's opera houses and theaters have understandably commanded considerable attention, ranging from landmark designations to professional books and even chamber of commerce pamphlets. However, some design and many structural elements, which are technically essential, are not necessarily visible. Acoustics is one such element. In the golden days of the late nineteenth century, an opera house's acoustics, usually the result of no specialized professional advice, was described in superlatives in notices, press releases, and advertisements—and today good acoustics turns out to be an important selling point in reviving opera houses.

After Beth Klosterman and several other women in 1979 climbed twenty-five steep steps to the second-floor hall of the Thorpe Opera House in David City, Nebraska, with its leaking roof, bats, broken

plaster, and remnants of the old balcony, they were struck by the building's "near perfect" acoustics. Although they all worked with the youth
center on the building's first floor, the second-floor opera house hall had
been off-limits until their curiosity was aroused by news that the hall
was slated to be converted into two floors of apartments. The acoustics
as well as the twenty-foot ceiling, the stage, and early curtain convinced
Klosterman that this space should be returned to its former life as a
community opera house. David City already had three performing arts
stages, two at local schools and the other at the city auditorium, but the
poor acoustics at these buildings hampered the quality of the schools'
musical and theater productions.[19] Reviving the opera house with its
splendid acoustics seemed to Klosterman a logical answer to this problem. Unable to convince city and county officials of the merits of her
idea, Klosterman purchased the building herself and launched a thirty-
year endeavor to restore the opera house as a hall for cultural and civic
activities and also as an architectural attraction.

Curtains and scenery never receive much attention from theatergoers;
it is the play and the actors that matter most. Yet these background features are an integral part of any performance and of the hall itself. From
the seventeenth century when the Venetian painter Canaletto's father
was a scene painter for opera houses until today, curtains and scenery
used in opera houses have displayed the considerable pride that towns
took in their opera houses. Curtains also have stories of their own, especially in small rural opera houses where they reflect the fantasies and
romance of townspeople and artists. Sometimes, scenery was important
enough to be advertised as an attraction of the opera house, an instance
being Fremont, Nebraska's Love Opera House, which boasted that it
had "The Finest Scenery in the State."[20]

Depending on the sophistication of the opera house, a variety of
curtains, drops, wings, and flats could be used. Four essential settings
were needed in most opera houses, especially small ones: front room,
back room, forest, and town. Such scenes could be produced by flats,
which later were replaced by roll drops or wings. Made of heavy canvas
and dropped either at the front of a stage or used as backdrops for a
play, these curtains displayed scenes of fanciful places like Venice or
the Alps.

Early peripatetic troupes, whether Flemish *rederijkers* or Americans
like Noah Ludlow or Sol Smith, brought along whatever they needed
in the way of backdrops and scenery. Later traveling troupes might

LOVE'S OPERA HOUSE

— IS THE —

Finest and Most Complete in the State

Four-story and Basement of Pressed Brick and Stone.

Fifty-five feet by 126 feet. Complete in every respect.

With all modern improvements. 1,050 Opera Chairs.

Stage 32 1-2 feet by 52 feet. Curtain 20 by 26 feet.

THE FINEST SCENERY IN THE STATE.

Well located as to hotel and street cars.

COST, $44,000.

Robert McReynolds,
Lessee and Manager,
Lincoln, - Neb.

J. W. LOVE, Owner,

FREMONT, NEB.

Opp. 104.

Love's Opera House in Fremont, Nebraska advertised that it was not only the "Finest and Most Complete in the State," but it also has 1,050 opera chairs and "THE FINEST SCENERY IN THE STATE." *Nebraska State Gazeteer and Business Directory,* 1888–1889, published by J.M. Wolfe, Omaha 1888, p. 224

also provide their own costumes and sets, making opera houses and theaters adjacent to railroad lines especially convenient in locations like Lancaster, Pennsylvania and Grand Forks, North Dakota. Unlike today, when costumes are supplied by the theater company, for many years actors provided their own costumes. The local opera house or theater, however, usually provided backdrops and curtains. The painted canvases were not just passive backdrops for plays; they could also be critical in the staging of scenes when great lengths of canvas could be rolled out to coincide with a chase through the countryside. In the late nineteenth century, an elaborate opera house like Horace Tabor's in Leadville boasted eight curtains with scenes depicting a forest, gardens, a palace arch, a chamber set, a New England kitchen, a prison, a Leadville streetscape, and a drop curtain with a landscape scene adorned with a life-size portrait of Tabor himself.

In small Vermont towns, performance spaces, sometimes above stores, in Grange buildings, and, of course, in town halls, offered a more limited number of curtains than in Leadville. However, these smaller halls displayed an array of romantic scenes: racing chariots in a Roman amphitheater graced the curtains in Westminster and Guilford and romanticized European lake scenes with castles and elaborate lighthouses were painted on the curtains in Moretown, Hardwick, and Reading. Castles and the Rhine River were perennial favorites as were distant Italian mountains and the Mediterranean coastline. The street scene in Saxtons River's curtain seemed almost surreal, with highly geometric buildings—and no sign of human life. Local or regional sites did appear on some curtains: nearby Lake Fairlee in Fairlee and Lake Willoughby in Irasburg; Mt. Ascutney in Brownsville and West Windsor; and Concord, Massachusetts's famous North Bridge in Woodville, New Hampshire. The generic and romantic European woods, mountains, and street scenes painted on most curtains must have seemed exotic in rural farm towns in 1900.

These romantic curtains expressed the fanciful wishes of the townspeople or local patrons who paid for them, combined with the imagination and skills of hundreds of local and regional artists, many unknown, as well as some painters specializing in scenery for theaters. Vermont's ambitious project of conserving painted curtains, under way since 1988, has discovered that local artists painted many of the more than 170 curtains found in opera houses, town halls, granges, and theaters.

One of the most prolific Vermont curtain painters was Charles Washington Henry, who with seventeen members of his extended family painted fifty curtains in Vermont and New England from 1885 to 1915. Although he had not traveled far from New England, when painting curtains he let his imagination carry him to faraway places like the Italian Alps or to ancient activities like Roman chariot racing. His family's artistic talents also included music, so the Henry family became a traveling troupe, like Sol Smith's in the South, with horse-drawn wagons and Model T cars carrying all the tools of its trade. Green Mountain denizens, however, were ecumenical enough to hire out-of-state curtain painters, like New Hampshire resident Robert Naves, and other scenery painters from as far away as Chicago, Omaha, Troy, Brooklyn, and Boston. In fact, due perhaps to their professional skills and materials, these out-of-staters' curtains seem to have lasted better than those of local itinerant artists.

Boston's well-known O. L. Story Scenic Company painted curtains in seven Vermont towns, mostly romantic European lake scenes, all framed with fancy swagged draperies. Only a Barnet curtain portrayed a New England scene, a lake with paper birches prominently featured in the foreground. A photograph of this conserved O. L. Story curtain with a basketball net in front of it confirms that multiple activities including sports continue in such halls. A listing for the O. L. Story Scenic Company, usually with advertisements, appears from 1872 to 1934 in the *Boston Business Directory* and, as the years went on, these advertisements included more services and skills. At first the firm offered "Scenery for Theaters, Halls, etc, Scenery to Let … Made to Order"; then its advertisements included more offerings such as "Drop Curtains & Scenery for Halls & Theaters. Photographic Backgrounds and all kinds of Large Watercolor Paintings for Decorations and other purposes. Made to Order" and "Dealer in all kinds of Stage Fixtures & Supplies." By 1911, the advertisements were lengthier, as their scope of work expanded: "Drop Curtain Scenery, Portraits & Pictorial Paintings for Public Decorations, Decorative Panels, Friezes for Interior Decorations, Oil Portraits, Photographic Backgrounds, Theatrical Properties & all kinds of stage supplies."[21] In 1912 the company added fireproof asbestos curtains to the company's repertoire, reflecting the national concern about fires.

The restoration of theater curtains in Vermont, initiated and undertaken by Christine ("Chris") Hadsell's Vermont Painted Theater Curtain

Project, has not only uncovered many curtains, long forgotten and stashed away in the attics and backrooms of opera houses, granges, and halls, but has reawakened interest in the state's opera houses and their former lives. Discoveries of these curtains, their restoration, and the publicity about this successful project are spurring towns to bring their old opera houses back to life, both in Vermont and elsewhere. Across the Connecticut River in Woodville, New Hampshire, Chris Hadsell's project restored a curtain depicting the Old North Bridge in Concord; this curtain was rescued from the Woodville Opera House when it was converted to apartments for the elderly. Subsequently, the curtain was given to neighboring Haverhill's Alumni Hall Cultural Center at a packed-house ceremony in December 2006.

Advertisements for local businesses adorned the borders of many curtains in opera houses, granges, and even stages in town halls like Pawlet, Vermont as well as through New England and in the Midwest. No doubt it was a way of paying for these curtains. Sometimes the advertisements covered the whole curtain, but usually they were on all four perimeters of a centered painted scene. Other advertisements might be spread along the top or bottom of the curtain and some were even top drapes for a centered romantic painting.

Unlike many opera house curtains that portrayed romantic landscapes with no connection to a town or its residents, opera house curtains in immigrant settlements featured scenes, places, and allegorical tales from the Old Country. The curtains in the opera house in the dominantly Czech community of Clarkson, Nebraska are a good example. Here the town's Czech theatrical heritage is evident in its proscenium and six magnificent stage curtains, which are proudly, and carefully, guarded by the contemporary Clarkson Community Opera House. The depictions reflect Bohemian scenes familiar to old-timers, including a village scene, a castle, a forest, a city, and two garden scenes. Particularly noteworthy are Karlstejn Castle set high on a hill above a winding village street, an idealized village scene of a gable-house-lined street found in many Bohemian villages; and an allegorical scene of Prince Svatopluk instructing his sons on his deathbed, with a moral that it is easier to break a bundle of sticks than an individual stick, thereby extolling the strength of communal efforts. The moral in Prince Svatopluk's instructions resonates today in small places like Clarkson trying to sustain their ethnic heritage and also strengthen their sense of community through activities at its opera house.

A curtain at the Clarkson Opera House, Clarkson, Nebraska, displays the famous Gothic Karlstejn Castle in Bohemia, only twenty miles from Prague. The gothic castle, built in 1348, stored the Imperial Regalia and Czech crown jewels. *Author photograph*

Even for performers, curtains can be meaningful. After the Vermont Symphony Orchestra's final performance at the Haskell Opera House in the border towns of Derby Line, Vermont and Stanstead, Quebec in September 2011, violinist Julie Marden with many other orchestra members stayed to watch the ritual lowering of the drop curtain with Erwin LaMoss's painting of Venice—his only surviving curtain. "It's a lovely memory," Marden reminisced. "There was something meaningful about standing behind the audience watching that beautiful curtain go down for the winter after we had just performed."[22]

In contrast to visible curtains, many opera house performances, especially plays and operas, benefit from invisible, behind-the-scenes technicians, who rarely receive publicity. Yet their clever devices have been essential in producing the exciting and magical stage effects needed in innumerable productions. Chases, storms, and escapes, so essential to the popular spell-binders of melodrama, as well as trapdoors for magicians and treadmills for races, were made possible by the ingenuity of these technicians.

Even the seating arrangements in some opera houses required engineering skills. To accommodate the varied activities that took place, from plays and performances best seen from seats on a raked floor to sports and dances requiring a flat floor, some houses, like Vermont's Barre and Bellows Falls and New Hampshire's Rochester, could adjust the floor to either a raked or a flat position. When the Bellows Falls Opera House in its Town Hall opened in 1887, the 1,000 opera chairs, 125 incandescent lamps, and steam heat were mentioned in the *Burlington Free Press and Times*, but the highlight of the new building was its floor, which "could be raised to any angle."[23] With a complicated system of motor-driven shafts, belts, gearshifts, and tension rods connected to girders underneath the floor, Rochester's opera house floor could be inclined or flattened by several feet in less than an hour.

When the restoration of the 1908 Rochester, New Hampshire City Hall and Opera House was launched in 1996, so many volunteers offered to help in reactivating the floor-changing mechanism that a lottery was held. A year later the mechanism, clogged with ninety-year-old oil and worn by age and neglect, was back in operation. Poughkeepsie, New York's 1869 Collingwood Opera House featured a different and mechanically less complicated flat-floor arrangement. Its floor was portable and could be installed in sections over all the orchestra seats with "considerable labor," according to the *Poughkeepsie Eagle News*. Such mechanisms and arrangements for providing flat floors have been replaced today by sophisticated machinery that will be used in Middlebury, Vermont's Town Hall Theater, whose seats stored on the side of a hall can telescope into raked positions, much like bench seating in gymnasiums that fold out or in.

Often overlooked, but important to the success of performances, were ingenious stage effects. Train wrecks, violent storms, exploding volcanoes, hair-raising escapes, and races punctuated the popular "fire and flash" melodramas.[24] With little sophisticated equipment, the technicians or managers in small opera houses used considerable ingenuity to produce these stage effects. An 1800 Boston theater's performances included the storming of a citadel, the destruction of the Persian fleet, a volcano eruption, and combat. By 1884, patrons at Fremont, Nebraska's opera house watched a continuous three-quarter-mile horse race in Neil Burgess's *The County Fair*. With practice and improved techniques, stage effects became more sophisticated and complex, climaxing in the twentieth-century extravaganza *Ben Hur*. Considered one of the most spectacular productions ever, *Ben Hur* employed a cast of more than twenty principals, a chorus of eighty, even more supernumeraries, and eight live horses, who galloped away on two treadmills in its famous chariot race in the extravagant Klaw-Erlanger Broadway production. Lexington, Kentucky's opera house was remodeled so the *Ben Hur* chariot race could be staged in 1896 with a cast of hundreds of people—and live horses. Even drama critic Walter Pritchard Eaton, who slammed *Ben Hur*, recognized its "mechanical excitement."[25]

Lurking behind the scenes, technology produced the most dramatic effects. The benefits of lighting, on the other hand, were more apparent. Lighting not only illuminated the overall hall so theatergoers could see the way to their seats, but was critical in assisting stage effects such as spotlighting the heroine. Lighting benefited from late-nineteenth-century scientific advances, especially electricity. The elaborate Pabst Theater, built in 1895, prided itself on being the first theater in this country to have an all-electrical lighting system. Candlepower and then gaslight, which appeared in the mid- to late nineteenth century, were crude means of lighting, accounting for many theater fires. Gaslight was an enormous improvement over candlepower as it offered a more constant glow and also the possibility of limelight and spotlights, so important in theater. Producing a spotlight had previously required a Rube Goldberg arrangement with a lens radiating a blowtorch flame. With gaslight, the stage was much brighter, so attention was focused on the stage, eliminating much of the earlier voyeurism of audience members checking out other audience members. By enabling audiences to concentrate on the performances, the new gaslights may well have reduced some of the unruly conduct so common in early theaters. But gaslights had their hazards, including a distinctive odor. The introduction of electricity provided varied light with more control and safety, although early electric lights could be noisy and sometimes emitted a harsh light compared to the softer light from gas and candles. Heating theaters, another technical hurdle for theater managers, produced many problems—and fires.

For the theater manager, an invention like electricity was a technological advance in which he had no part and that his theater used as much as it could afford. These benefits were seen by all in the theater. Backstage technology, a showcase of an opera house manager's imagination and ingenuity, was different. The behind-the-scenes technology, responsible for most of the theatrical effects and vital to the excitement of many productions, remained a mystery to most theatergoers, unless failures occurred. Here the ingenuity of the theater manager and stagehands flowered.

Backstage was a true Rube Goldberg paradise. There you might think you were looking at the riggings of a yesteryear schooner with ropes, winches, weights, and pulleys, all necessary to pull curtains up and down, open trapdoors, operate treadmills, and arrange ramps. And all the noises and effects—claps of thunder, rain, waterfalls, stampeding horses, ships bounding over waves, and chariot races—resulted from clever gadgetry. Revolving barrels with stones of different sizes could produce the sound of rain or a heavy storm, the heavier the stone the heavier the storm. Distant thunder might result from a cartful of weights being rolled backstage or by shaking a metal sheet with wooden ends, and louder thunder by cannonballs being dropped down a run into switchback troughs. For

A "rabbit hutch" for producing claps of thunder. Cannonballs bang down the trough, sometimes from an upper floor. *Cornell University Library, Masking America Digital Collection. "Behind the Scenes of an Opera House," Gustav Kobbe, Scribner's Magazine, vol.4, issue 4, 1888, p. 452.*

snow, confetti flew to the ground from containers being jerked around above the stage. Treadmills were used for races such as the famous *Ben Hur* chariot race (which required three treadmills) and Eva's escape on the ice floe in *Uncle Tom's Cabin*. Rolling scenery could enhance a sense of movement during an escape. People and scenery could appear and disappear, thanks to a trapdoor. Ramps could help provide the effect of racing. No wonder the magicians' shows were so entrancing.

Copying the press releases of the traveling troupes, local newspapers would promote the spectacular features of forthcoming performances, such as Lincoln J. Carter's "marvelous ferry boat scene" in *Under the Dome* at the Beardstown, Illinois opera house in 1900. Due to the "most intricate mechanical effects ever placed upon the stage," which were protected by twenty-five patents, Carter was evidently able to produce "an absolute perfect counterfeit of a ferry boat ride." But that was not all. Carter also promised "storms, tidal waves, legislatures, three scenes in Washington, sinking shops and a dozen additional scenes."[26] In small and large towns, such home-brewed spectacles certainly broke the tedium of daily life.

Theater purists often scorned the spellbinding stage effects produced by these ingenious gadgets as merely appealing to the senses, not the mind and soul. Even before stage managers turned plays into spectaculars, complaints about the lowering of standards were heard, as reported by Noah Ludlow in the early 1800s:

> Degraded Drama, nursed by viscious taste,
> Has thrown off diamonds to adorn with paste,
> Huge pots of paint, dutch metal, glittering foil,
> Usurp the stage, its classic boards to soil.
> The poet's gift has proved a sorry failure,
> He's been deposed by fiddler and by tailor.[27]

Similar disdain is heard today about the fare at opera houses being "entertainment," not theater.

Whether performances at opera houses were high art, vernacular theater, or plebeian entertainment, these fiddlers, tailors, and tinkers added excitement, essential to the production and popularity of entertainments, especially melodramas. Americans liked the suspense, drama, and spectacles that these inventive scenic effects provided, with thunderclaps rendered by stones rolling down troughs or chariots fighting on treadmills. Such scenic effects helped to keep opera houses alive year after year.

Often neglected, but critical to the success of opera houses, as well as to their role in the life of their communities, were opera house managers.

Many became the sole arbiters of the types of performances, lectures, and plays staged at an opera house—until New York syndicates and operators shrank these managers' responsibilities to mere booking agents. The entrepreneur or committee who developed the opera house usually trusted the manager to make the artistic and most of the business decisions. And rightly so, since numerous managers were fired up with a passion for theater and entertainment; some may well have been closet actors. Early managers, in fact, were often actors such as John (Jack) Langrishe, who organized Colorado's Gold Circuit; Luke Usher with his Kentucky circuit in Frankfort and Lexington; and, of course, all-purpose actor-managers like Sol Smith and Samuel Drake, who performed, managed, and, in some cases, even built their theaters.

Although public attention tends to focus on the architecture and décor of opera houses and on past performers, especially by well-known actors such as Joseph Jefferson and Sarah Bernhardt, it was managers who kept opera houses alive. Yet they are rarely mentioned. Many of them persevered for years. Claremont, New Hampshire druggist Harry Eaton managed the Claremont Opera House for thirty-two years in the early twentieth century when theater stock companies and traveling troupes performed in small cities. George Fox ran Brattleboro, Vermont's opera house for its exciting first twenty years from 1897 until 1917, when he showed the film *The Birth of a Nation,* a looming premonition of Hollywood's popularity and the ensuing decline of such halls.

In Granville, New York, Thomas Boyle was the longtime and highly successful manager of the Pember Opera House, a latecomer built in 1901. Boyle arranged all the programs, sought the entertainers, managed building maintenance, and organized railroad-excursion trips to the theater. Realizing a circuit of theaters could attract higher-quality performers to the Pember, he assumed the management of nearby Vermont opera houses in the town of Poultney and the small city of Rutland. Boyle welcomed all sorts of civic and patriotic benefits and charged no admission fee for children, who hung around the lobby unable to scrape together the money to purchase tickets. Unlike so many opera house managers, Tom Boyle was recognized locally for his contributions to the cultural and civic life of one town.[28]

Managing opera houses seemed to be a matter of genetics: the management passed from father to son in Lexington, Kentucky, and from father to son and then to daughter-in-law in Burlington, Vermont. In Lexington, Charles B. Scott competently managed the Lexington Opera

House from the time it opened in 1887 until 1923. Scott was assisted by his son, Harrison, who took over the reins from his father in 1923. In the early years this opera house presented plays by well-known playwrights like Bronson Howard and A. C. Gunther and performed by famous actors like Joseph Jefferson, Patti Rose, and J. K. Emmet. In his later years as both manager and the Syndicate's Lexington representative, Scott was able to attract top-flight shows en route from Cincinnati to Louisville and preseason trial runs with performers such as James O'Neill, the Barrymores, Helen Hayes, and Maude Adams. When Harrison became manager in 1923, motion pictures threatened live theater and, consequently, opera houses, so his reign was short compared to that of his father—for only three years, from 1923 to 1926. The skilled management of this Scott father-and-son dynasty certainly helps account for the long-standing respect accorded the Lexington Opera House.

Managerial skills rather than an interest in theater got Kilburn B. Walker his job as manager of the Howard Opera House in Burlington, Vermont. Walker, who came to the city as a stonemason, was hired first by the banker John Purple Howard as a mason and then as building superintendent for the construction of the opera house, which he handled so well that Howard made him the manager of his new opera house, which opened in 1879. With no training for this new job, Walker's first years involved considerable learning, beginning with squabbles over the lack of tickets for overflow audiences at the opening show and later at the highly popular performance of Joseph Jefferson in *Rip Van Winkle*. Walker, however, turned out to be a quick learner. Working with the syndicates and understanding the tastes of Burlingtonians, he organized steady programs of forty-five productions a year in the ten-month season, with fourteen musicals (which were Burlingtonians' favorites), eight comedies, thirteen serious plays and melodramas, and untold concerts, lectures, and meetings. He benefited from an extremely competent staff: two musicians for the orchestra, Bert Waterman and George Sherman, and a painter, Joseph Piggott, who limned twenty sets of every conceivable landscape and architectural subject. Piggott aroused such admiration that the opera house held a benefit performance for him.

Walker, whose business acumen outranked his diplomacy, continued to manage the Howard Opera House for six years until 1885, when his son, Willard K. Walker, took over, having probably assisted his father. Improving the interior decor seemed to be high on Willard's list. He completely redecorated the opera house, brought in a New York painter, and, most important, installed electric lighting. His first theatrical coup was to snare Richard D'Oyly Carte's production of *The Mikado* from England. Burlingtonians were pleased with his future bookings, though Willard was often out of town as an advance man for a show on a Western tour. He had even more bookings than his father: seventy-six each year between 1885 and 1899. His health failed and in 1898 he died of typhoid. While Willard was ill or traveling, his father would fill in for him, acting as "interim manager" and legal lessee. The son's death, however, did not end the days of the Walkers' management. In 1899, Willard's wife, Lena Belle Walker, took over as manager. Mrs. Walker proved to be a good businesswoman, introducing amateur nights, ladies' nights, and even coupon tickets with prizes, all of which helped produce successful seasons. However, the glory days of the Howard Opera House came to an end in 1904 after public health concerns arose about the building's plumbing and safety, especially with toughened fire regulations after the disastrous Chicago theater fire. But the final blow was the construction of a new opera house in Burlington.

The Walkers' triumvirate "presided over the birth, growth, and decline of a significant part of Burlington's cultural environment," observed University of Vermont theater historian George B. Bryan, known for his scholarly probing of Burlington and Vermont theater.[29] Civic pride and a faith that these halls could provide culture and entertainment, maybe some profits, and, importantly, make their towns better places to live spurred on the managers Walkers, Scotts, and Boyle; entrepreneurs; town leaders; and many others involved in keeping opera houses alive.

In a time when the nation was exploding with expanding frontiers, millions of immigrants, life-changing inventions, burgeoning towns and cities, and all the uncertainties of such changes, the opera house served an important role in communities. They were distinctly American institutions displaying a sense of civic responsibility and community destiny. Their multipurpose nature distinguished them from opera houses in other parts of the world. Where else in the world could one roller skate in an opera house? Or hear William Jennings Bryan or vote for president? Or think that a second-floor hall might bring a rail line to town and make it the county seat or state capital?

PART FOUR

Born Again

Revived Opera Houses and Their Communities

CHAPTER 15

The Phoenix Rises

Bumpers of lobstermen's pickup trucks, out-of-towners' Volvo station wagons, and locals' Ford compacts on Deer Isle, Maine display the bumper sticker "Incite Art—Create Community." A visitor might think Deer Isle's famous Haystack arts and crafts school would be responsible for this public display of interest in art and community. Not so. It is the Stonington Opera House and Opera House Arts that have stirred this new interest in art and community.

Perched on a granite cliff overlooking the harbor and public fishing pier at the eastern tip of Deer Isle, in the small town of Stonington, the opera house once again is offering year-round cultural and social events for Deer Isle and neighboring towns. On and off for more than a hundred years, Stonington's opera house has provided a place for dances, plays, public meetings, school events, and performers. Despite fire, changing tastes, a diminished population, a decaying building, a new school auditorium, and threatened sales, the Stonington Opera House has not only survived, it is flourishing today. With a current population of just over one thousand, Stonington today is a shadow of its former self a century ago, when its granite quarries and fishing industries prospered, its population swelled to five thousand, and its opera house could seat a thousand.

Although it is a gritty town with hardworking quarrymen and fishermen, some artists and intellectuals, and numerous summerfolk, Stonington has had a building for entertainment since 1893, when Charles B. Russ built a dance hall on the site of the current opera house.

Like miners in Leadville, Colorado, mill workers in Claremont, New Hampshire, and farmers in Minden, Nebraska, the need for escape from the drudgery of hard work as well as the urge to have some fun fueled the development of entertainment halls, sometimes euphemistically called "music halls" or "museums" and later "opera houses."

Stonington's opera house has had its ups and downs, like those in so many small towns. Despite all the societal changes from the late nineteenth century to today and new ways to be entertained, Stonington's opera house tried to keep up with the shifting fads of popular entertainment. The original 1893 dance hall was expanded in 1895, but was quickly transformed into an impressive opera house with balconies, a high scene tower, and a thousand seats with a ground-level store. For fifteen years, until it was felled by fire, this opera house thrived with local entertainment, public activities like school graduations, and performances by national traveling troupes that came to Stonington by steamboat from the mainland town of Rockland. Two years later, when it was rebuilt, times were not so propitious for the opera house or for Stonington. Nationally, movies featuring well-known stars were replacing second-rate traveling theater troupes, and steel was replacing Stonington's granite as a popular building material.

The new opera house, still a prominent building overlooking the harbor, was designed to meet the needs of a declining population. It had room for only 250 folding chairs but was adaptable for plays, school functions, town meetings, varied sports events such as basketball and roller skating—and movies. By 1918, silent films were shown, by 1929 talkies, and then in 1940 a Simplex system for film projection was installed, so movies became the entertainment staple of Stonington. Town meetings continued to be held in the opera house until 1952, and high school graduations until 1947. Seats were bolted to the floor in periods when it was primarily a movie theater or meeting room, but were quickly unbolted in the 1960s when roller skating and dancing resurfaced as popular activities. Ever since the 1940s, its existence was uncertain because of intermittent use and its deteriorating physical condition. After sales and rescues in 1979 and the 1980s, the opera house floundered, with its last full season of movies in 1992. Then for seven years it was empty and falling down, until four enterprising New York theater enthusiasts decided to revive it as a community cultural institution.

Although the Stonington Opera House has always been a landmark, its physical presence has been more commanding than its architecture. A hulk of a building, it looms high above the main street with a large, white-lettered "OPERA HOUSE" sign announcing to the world what it is. Over the years it has lost its exterior balconies, widow's walk, and many details, so it stands out as a large, bare-bones structure. Propping up the sagging structure and bringing it up to code and to Actors' Equity standards was an early and high priority for the new owners in 1999. Its spartan exterior, however, belies the year-round, humming activity inside the building since its resuscitation by the New York foursome's nonprofit organization Opera House Arts (OHA). Concerts, plays, musicals, play readings, local variety shows, circus bands, accordion rallies, films, "Souper Sundays" movies with local food, an annual Shakespeare play, and a jazz festival are but a sampling of the opera house's offerings.

Equally important are OHA's many community activities and involvements. Ex-staff members such as Judith Jerome and founding executive director Linda Nelson became embedded in the community: Jerome was the librarian at the Stonington Public Library and Nelson taught filmmaking at the local school, served on the island school board for a three-year term, and was a member of the Stonington Economic Development Committee and the Stonington Lobster Working Group. The OHA has run a digital media studio, art workshops for area teachers, and an arts camp, and it has sponsored a Shakespearean actor-in-residence at the middle school. With support of the town selectmen, hundreds of volunteers, some important grants, and the energy, talents, and commitment to the community of Opera House Arts, the opera house is again a multicultural center for Deer Isle natives and visitors. As Nelson said, it takes an island to run an opera house.

Fortunately, the island's commitment to the opera house remains strong as OHA enters a new chapter. Linda Nelson, having launched the successful revival of the orpa house, resigned as OHA's producing artistic director in January 2015 to become the assistant director of the Maine Arts Commission. After a five-month national search, Opera House Arts selected Meg Taintor, a Boston-based arts director with considerable experience in theater and arts management, to succeed Nelson. Taintor has worked as a director, producer, and teacher, and also with community organizations, which should provide a good foundation for her work with Opera House Arts, the towns of Stonington and Deer Isle, and for the opera house.

Stonington, Maine's Opera House today and the foursome that brought it back to life. From left to right: Carol Estey, Linda Nelson, Linda Pattie, and Judith Jerome. *Opera House: Author photograph. Opera House Arts: foursome photograph 2008*

Stonington beat the odds. Many opera houses, however, could not withstand the overwhelming pressures of new entertainments, new technologies, new and better local competing facilities, dwindling numbers of often inferior traveling performers, and a more mobile population. With fickle tastes ever questing for new entertainment, it was difficult for small halls to compete with Hollywood, whose stars came to towns everywhere on celluloid.

Aside from this tsunami of changed tastes and new technologies, the small-town opera house was beset with natural disasters. Fire was always a major threat, first from candles, then from gaslights, electrical problems, or cigarettes. Of the seventy-seven opera houses, theaters, and entertainment halls in New York City recorded by Isaac N. Phelps Stokes in 1918, almost 25 percent had major and some multiple fires. A donkey in *Uncle Tom's Cabin* tripped over an oil-filled footlight in the Florence (Kansas) Opera House in 1884, causing a fire on the stage, which was miraculously extinguished in time for the performance to proceed. Even after a second fire seven years later, which destroyed much of its wooden interior, the hall was back and functioning in a few weeks.

Many halls were not so lucky. A careless patron dropping a cigarette caused the fire that destroyed Peoria, Illinois' stately Grand Opera House in December 1909. Even a stolid stone building like Pueblo,

Colorado's Sullivan and Adler opera house was gutted by fire in 1922 after the fire department's efforts were stymied by freezing temperatures. Two fires ravaged the Bellows Falls Opera House and Town Hall, first in 1912 and later in 1925. Bennington, Vermont's opera house, the pride and joy of its benefactor Henry W. Putnam, carried on until 1958 when an electrical fire ignited the entire Harte Block in which the opera house was located. Even with modern electricity, opera houses in the down years were subject to fires, as many were abandoned and even those struggling to survive were not scrupulously maintained.

In town after town the new school's modern gymnasium or the new town auditorium, with modern stage technology, plenty of seats, and even large parking lots—and meeting all local codes—sidelined many old opera houses. In Salem, New York, Proudfit Hall's role as the town's auditorium for school activities and public events was usurped when the consolidated school with modern gym and auditorium was built in the late 1930s. Brattleboro, Vermont did not miss its old Town Hall/Opera House when a newer, but not nearly so grand, auditorium appeared.

In David City, Nebraska, the 1943 municipal auditorium built with local bonds and a federal grant was the death knell for its opera house. With up-to-date facilities for sports, dances, and plays in this new auditorium,

Fire in an opera house, a painting by Lawrence W. Ladd, about 1865-1895. *Smithsonian American Art Museum, Gift of Herbert Waide Hemphill, Jr., and museum purchase made possible by Ralph Cross Johnson*

the opera house ceased to function as an entertainment and community center, but limped along with different owners and different uses. At times it was totally empty. When its owners threatened to convert the interior for apartments in 1979, it was acquired by civic leader Beth Klosterman, who has spearheaded its revival. Barre, Vermont's opera house was not felled by the city's new municipal auditorium, also built in the Depression in 1939, but it lost many of the public activities that had taken place there. These new town auditoriums, many built in the 1930s, stole the shows and activities formerly held at the local opera house. It was public funding, both local and federal, that built these new municipal facilities, in contrast to the philanthropy of private donors who built, ran, and maintained so many of the late-nineteenth-century opera houses.

As their functions withered, opera houses were abandoned, demolished, or converted to other uses. Paris, Kentucky's Bourbon Opera House was replaced with a garage and tire company. Brattleboro's opera house in its town hall was bulldozed to make way for new shops when its town offices moved to spacious quarters in the old high school. Some that dodged the wrecking ball were transformed to incongruous uses. For a period before its restoration in 1923, Lexington, Kentucky's opera house, respected for its excellent shows organized by the Scott father-son managers, became a warehouse for automobiles; gas pumps were at the curb, and its entrance was converted into a tire store and gas station office. Housing replaced the interiors of the opera house in Trinidad, Colorado and in Fremont, Nebraska's Love-Larson Opera House. Baraboo, Wisconsin's second-floor opera house, facing the town square and courthouse, was side-lined by the luxurious Al. Ringling Theater, which Ringling, as a native son, presented to the town in 1915. Today the old opera house building survives, but its hall is a restaurant. Converting the large, flat floors of abandoned opera houses into warehouses or storage space seemed to be common. East Haddam's Goodspeed Opera House, now well known for its musicals and handsome building on a riverfront bluff, housed the state's Department of Transportation vehicles in its down years in the late 1940s and 1950s.

Many mothballed and altered opera house buildings that escaped demo-lition are still standing and even have new lives as venues for perform-ing arts and cultural activities. Others have become historical museums or have blended in a row of anonymous city buildings, sometimes a bit taller than the other buildings, as in Fair Haven, Vermont, or in Millersburg, Kentucky, distinguished by a surviving triangular pediment. Then there

An opera house that has experienced hard times. Jaffa Opera House, Trinidad, Colorado. about 1889. Built in 1883 by merchant brothers, Henry and Sullivan Jaffa, the stone-and-brick building with ground-floor stores and second-floor opera house with a large oval stained-glass skylight. Converted to apartments, it has faced demolition, but is still standing. *History Colorado*

are opera houses so disguised, one would never guess that traveling theater troupes and nationally known lecturers had once performed there. Not until the Vermont Painted Theater Curtain Project started searching for old stage curtains did some Vermonters realize that their town halls had served as the community's opera houses for many years. Now they are learning about the good times that were had in these buildings.

Though fires and competition from new public auditoriums caused the demise or alteration of innumerable opera house buildings, motion pictures were the greatest threat. To keep opera houses alive, enterprising managers realized that they would have to adapt their halls to the new world of movies, first showing silent films interspersed with regular opera house fare and eventually transforming the halls into full-fledged movie theaters to meet the ever-growing popularity of cinema. For opera house managers, movies were less expensive than plays, so they could offer cheaper ticket prices for movies than for live performances. Also, small first-floor opera houses with their easy access and egress seemed especially safe after the scare of the 1903 Chicago Iroquois Theatre fire and its over 600 deaths.

Small and large opera houses joined the movie bandwagon. Bellows Falls, Vermont's opera house in its town hall changed its name to "Town Theater" to reflect the addition of movies, first run by the Sunshine Theatre Company, then in 1920 by the B. F. Amusement Company, which added a new marquee with 632 lights in 1931, as if in Times Square. Today it once again has up-to-date movie projection equipment, although it also serves as an opera house for live performances. Movies were mixed in with some straggling minstrel shows at opera houses like the Bourbon Opera House in Paris, Kentucky in the 1940s. Moving pictures, often with a piano player, were shown on the second floor of David City, Nebraska's Thorpe Opera House beginning in 1900, but moved to the first floor after the Iroquois fire. "Caesar went 1,000 miles to see Cleopatra—will you go to Kearney? It cost him an Empire—it will cost you 25 cents, fifty cents, 75 cents, and $1.00," advertised the Kearney Opera House in the nearby town of Minden's newspaper, the *Minden Courier*, hoping to lure Minden residents to make the twenty-mile trip to Kearney to see the smash hit *Cleopatra*. Although the small town of Minden had its own opera house, it could not necessarily get a big hit like *Cleopatra*.[1]

Minden's opera house even had in-town competition from a new movie theater, the Gem Theatre. After David City, Nebraska, a small town forty miles from Omaha, welcomed a new movie theater in 1916 and then another in 1917, its Thorpe Opera House, which had been booking touring companies and soloists almost every month, had only a handful of programs from 1918 to 1920. By 1917 the state capital, Lincoln, boasted seven theaters, but only two offered live performances. In cities, movie houses could be very grand and glittering "palaces," making the opera houses' red velvet curtains, decorated opera chair seats, gilded chandeliers, and frescoed ceilings pale in comparison. In Omaha the new Rialto movie theater was built in 1918 for $750,000, more than six times what the Boyd Opera House had cost in 1890.

Like many opera houses, Minden's responded to these changes not only by showing films but also by organizing more lectures and dances. In 1919 two jazz orchestras provided the music for dances with tickets costing $1.25 for dancers, fifty cents for spectators, and free admission for returning veterans. Capturing an interest in Hawaiian music that same year, the Minden Opera House programmed a series of themed events: a Hawaiian String Orchestra that played "the plaintive airs of the sunny south Seas Island, hula fox trots, dreamy waltzes, and yacki hacki one steps"; a play, *A Night in Honolulu*; and on New Year's Eve, the musical comedy *Honolulu*.[2] Whatever the artistic merits of these events, exposure to the sunny islands must have lifted the spirits of these hardy Nebraskans during the long, cold winters, just as Willa Cather a few miles away was transported to distant places by performances in her town's opera house. But no longer did the manager have to deal constantly with all the logistics of traveling companies; instead, he was organizing local programs, dealing with distributors, and receiving films in metal containers.

By the mid-twentieth century, most opera houses were considered relics of bygone days, so their loss to the wrecking ball was seen as bringing in new opportunities. The pent-up demand for housing and consumer products, after long years of hardship during the Great Depression and World War II, created a pressing national need for new housing, highways, and infrastructure. Veterans were returning and the downtowns of old cities and towns seemed tired as suburbs swelled with sprawling housing developments, even large-scale Levittowns, shopping malls, and new road systems. Federal aid through favorable Veterans Administration (VA) and Federal Housing Administration (FHA) mortgages enabled eager veterans and other home buyers to purchase suburban houses. The construction of new highways with Interstate highway grants (with 90 percent federal funding) moved people and goods to the new suburban developments and beyond. Riding the crest of this popular federal assistance came another federal program to deal with urban problems, urban renewal. Created with the hope of replacing straggling inner-city neighborhoods, tired downtown office buildings, and pokey Mom-and-Pop shops with up-to-date housing, offices, and malls, urban renewal grants initially were greeted enthusiastically. Public officials, especially big-city mayors, thought these federal grants, which assisted in condemning rundown business and housing districts and in constructing new apartment towers and commercial buildings, would help to modernize their cities—and make them favorable alternatives to the burgeoning suburbs.

This renewal mentality became contagious in the late 1950s and early 1960s. Big chunks of cities were bulldozed along with well-known landmarks like New York's landmark Pennsylvania Station, designed by McKim, Mead and White in 1910. Grand Central Station just missed the wrecking ball, thanks to the protest of a bevy of high-powered New Yorkers, including Jacqueline Kennedy Onassis. Caught in this wave of urban renewal were theaters, large and small, in downtowns of cities and towns everywhere. Some owners of old opera houses, which had been limping along, realized that they too should stay abreast of the times. On their own, they could replace these seemingly redundant buildings with something new and modern, or at least give them face-lifts. The renewal bandwagon was on a roll until citizens in many blitzed cities, joining scholars and critics like Jane Jacobs and Martin Anderson, recognized—and publicized—how the "Federal Bulldozer" was destroying the life and soul of their cities.[3]

Today, with a growing respect for the role of distinctive buildings and activities in bolstering the livability and aesthetic appeal of a place, it is hard to understand the apathy that let individual landmark buildings as well as whole districts of distinctive buildings be torn down in the 1950s and 1960s. Yet for many people, such old buildings represented yester-year, not tomorrow. Many opera houses vanished with scarcely any public fuss as new and up-to-date buildings replaced them. When the dominant and much-loved Bourbon Opera House in Paris, Kentucky (named for Bourbon County) fell to the wrecking ball, there was no public outcry, as it was in such bad repair.[4] By 1953 when Brattleboro, Vermont let its opera house be demolished, the town had two movie theaters and the new high school's large auditorium, so the town had more than adequate spaces for entertainments, concerts, and lectures. While there may be some nostalgia today for the town hall/opera house, there was little public alarm about its demise at the time of its demolition. With public needs like high schools often deferred during the long years of the Depression and then World War II, and with public interest in modernizing downtowns, it is understandable that Brattleboro's opera house, like many others, quietly disappeared. Protecting old buildings was not a priority until several decades later.

Few historical plaques exist for lost opera houses. Current residents do not know where the demolished opera houses were located, or in many places if they ever existed. Only an earnest researcher might discover the site of Troy, New York's Museum or where Brattleboro, Vermont's or Williamstown, Massachusetts' opera houses once stood. They have faded into that bleary oblivion of unnoteworthy history.

Not until the 1970s and 1980s did attitudes toward historic preservation and protecting opera houses start to change. In 1976, a national organization concerned with the protection and restoration of theaters, the League of Historic American Theatres, was organized with help from the East Haddam, Connecticut's Goodspeed Opera House staff. Threatened opera houses were starting to garner supporters, just as Grand Central Station had. Sometimes sentiment rallied the troops opposing the demolition of an opera house, or serious concern for the building's architecture and the urban fabric of a town. Often, too, there was hope that the opera house could resume its past role as a place for cultural events. Historic preservation was emerging gradually from a movement of local historians and architects trying to save individual buildings as museums. In the 1960s a breakthrough occurred when groups of buildings were recognized for their collective architectural and cultural qualities rather than for the landmark status of individual buildings. This new approach to historic preservation, called "tout ensemble," considerably broadened its role in civic design. First applied in New Orleans, it was soon accepted throughout the country. Equally important for historic preservation were revisions in the 1970s to the federal tax code, which, instead of benefiting those who tore down historic buildings, now provided tax benefits to those who restored them. Historic preservation then became economically as well as aesthetically attractive.

Cities such as Charleston, South Carolina and Savannah, Georgia, which slept through urban renewal, found their intact older downtowns in the 1980s and 1990s becoming popular places to live and visit. Defenders of threatened opera houses were equally prescient, but mainstream political, economic, and social forces, whether national or local, often overwhelmed them. And that was true in England as well as the United States. In England, a committee interested in saving theaters, CURTAINS, found that 85 percent of the country's one thousand theaters, which included music halls and "flat floor-halls," in use between 1900 and 1914 had been demolished or "irretrievably altered."[5] This English committee, like its US counterpart, the League of Historic American Theatres, was formed in 1976, when public consciences were jolted by the growing number of early theaters, including opera houses that were disappearing due to neglect or to the wrecking ball.

By the 1990s, when the Waterman and Moore Opera House in Williamstown, Massachusetts was threatened with demolition, attitudes toward conservation of distinctive buildings had matured to the point where citizens mounted a robust protest. Built as a Methodist church, it was moved in 1845, converted to a music hall in 1877 after the Methodists built a new church, and transformed into an opera house and community center in 1890. When it became a music hall, the building was raised, a first floor was inserted, a stage took the place of the former sanctuary, and space was added backstage. At the time it became an opera house in 1889, its façade was remodeled. The only other change made to the building was an extension in 1918 for the new, motorized fire truck for the Gale Hose Company, which was housed in the building.

From the mid-1870s through the mid-1950s, the opera house served as a center of community and social life. Aside from providing space for many college and town plays, concerts, entertainers such as Groucho

Marx, silent films, the Williamstown Summer Theatre in the 1930s, and grange and fraternal society activities, the building also served as the town hall. Here the town offices for all the town departments were located for more than forty years, town meetings and almost twenty elections were held, the health department immunized thousands during an influenza epidemic, and state guardsmen drilled.

Until 1912 when Williams opened Chapin Hall, the college's auditorium, designed by Ralph Adams Cram, both the college and the town used the opera house as a public hall for dramatic productions, dances, and lectures, including one by Ralph Waldo Emerson, whom the college banned from lecturing in its chapel in 1865. The opera house was the community center; in fact, "no other building served so many portions of the population for so many years in so many ways," one defender of the opera house recalled.[6]

By the early 1950s, the opera house was no longer being used for civic and cultural activities, and its owner, the Taconic Lumber and Hardware Company, rented it to such groups as the Visiting Nurse Association. Eventually the opera house space on the upper floors became a warehouse. Not surprisingly, Williams College, on the lookout for additional space, eyed the site of this underused opera house as a good location for an art studio building, and the adjacent bank was eager for more parking spaces. Both these important local institutions got what they wanted, but only after a nasty fight.

The college and the bank bought the building with the clear goal of demolishing it. As keeping the building in situ was never really in the cards for these powerful suitors, the only way of saving the building was to have it moved. The prospect of moving the building gained strong support within the town from its board of selectmen and from the Massachusetts Historical Commission, which recommended the building for the National Register of Historic Places, but too late. With a complicated purchasing agreement, limited time, the need to raise tens of thousands of dollars to move it, and the overarching power of a college, the valiant efforts to save the building failed. In March 1992 the building was demolished, and four years later the college's Spencer Studio Art Building opened on the opera house site.

The fate of the Waterman and Moore Opera House is similar to that of many other opera houses. Taken for granted for many years, idle opera houses like Williamstown's had not received much public attention or historic preservation protection until contracts for their demolition were almost signed. The Waterman and Moore Opera House had not been listed on the Massachusetts or National Register of Historic Places, nor was it located in a historic district. It also had not received any state or national funding, permits, or protection under the demolition-delay law. These actions might have helped the defenders of the building obtain state or federal help, justify the historic worth of the building, or devote more time for publicity and fund-raising. The efforts to save the opera house did arouse the town's awareness of its historic and cultural heritage and the need to undertake careful preservation planning and protection.

This story is but one of many failed attempts to save an opera house. Twenty years after the demolition of the Waterman and Moore Opera House, long-forgotten opera houses are being seen again as valuable local historic resources and are being revived as important community and multiart centers. Indeed, the phoenix is rising in many places. Minden, Nebraska has revitalized its opera house, making it a key attraction at its courthouse square; Maysville, Kentucky, a town on the Ohio River where Drake and his troupe landed in the early 1800s, has brought back its Washington Opera House with so many events that residents are finding themselves going there every week; Newberry, South Carolina's revived opera house is drawing people from Columbia, Greenville, and Augusta; Hudson, New York's old Town Hall/Opera House, now functioning as an art center, began the restoration of its second-floor opera house in fall 2015; Vergennes, Vermont has restored its opera house in the town hall for year-round cultural events; and Cambridge, New York's Hubbard Hall, with its repertory group, opera company, and a myriad of plays and events has become the linchpin in a downtown arts development project. This is just a sampling of some revived opera houses in small towns with populations under ten thousand, several with fewer than three thousand.

The interest in opera houses today is driven by basically the same compelling motivations, individual enjoyment and civic place-making, that fueled the promoters of these halls in the late nineteenth century. In 1881, when the citizens of Newberry, South Carolina voted for a bond issue to construct an opera house, they wanted a place for plays and entertainment as well as a seat of government. In 1996, after years of disuse and decay, the opera house was rescued by Newberry citizens, who established it again as a center for entertainment as well as a catalyst for the revival of the city's downtown. Its initial construction and the more recent restoration were driven by similar interests. And that has been the case with most opera house revivals. Whether publicly or privately built, early opera houses provided space—often the only public space in town—for entertainment and social, public, and school events, signaling the town as a civilized place. Now, as these halls are being restored with space for entertainment and culture, they are once again civic place-makers; this time they are trying to put the town on the map by helping to revive its dormant Main Street.

With the many technological options for home entertainment, one wonders why so many small opera houses are being resuscitated. When the talents of contemporary Joseph Jeffersons and Sarah Bernhardts can come directly into one's living room, why get involved with communally created plays and concerts? Yet there is a groundswell of local cultural activities today as people again quest for community, culture, and individual fulfillment. In the nineteenth century, with the physical isolation of so many small villages, there was a natural urge to connect with a larger world and enjoy the entertainments and culture others were enjoying. Also, socializing with neighbors and friends mattered when there were no daily telephone chats. Instead of the earlier geographical isolation or loneliness of a smothering small town like Carol Kennicott's Gopher Prairie, which she felt was ironing her "into glossy mediocrity," now ironically in today's global village, with all its social media and entertainment devices, there can be a pervasive anonymity. The seeming intimacy of electronic communication, or just first-name greetings in restaurants, is deceptive. Instead of shopping at the local store where customers bump into friends and chat with the cashier, they can order online.

When live, face-to-face encounters shrink, our sense of anonymity grows. At today's opera house we are no longer passwords or targets for telemarketing, we can express and fulfill ourselves. In a sense, we are regaining some of the old can-do optimism of the early settlers as we find a community and ourselves. At the same time these restored halls with round-the-clock activities are producing a surge of civic pride, which is reinvigorating the very towns that their earlier promoters once helped put on the map.

The stories of the revived opera houses are as varied as the places and the townspeople where they are located. Some of the survivors are nationally known in cities such as Galveston, Texas, where its Grand Opera House has been returned to its former glory as a major cultural institution, and in smaller places like Central City, Colorado, whose opera house has been reactivated with serious theater and opera with considerable help from Denverites, the University of Colorado, and many national friends.

Even those halls that have prospered, including the ocean liner of opera houses, New York's Metropolitan Opera House, have had to grapple with threats of downtimes and concerns about their future. The efforts of the new manager of the Met, Peter Gelb, to democratize through open houses, innovative programs, live telecasts throughout the country, and new pricing schedules indicate a concern that high prices, union demands, and heavy costs might restrict future audiences. New York's other leading opera company, the New York City Opera, when faced in 2010 with overwhelming financial problems, gave up its space at Lincoln Center and went on the road, "building tomorrow's audiences," within the city limits. This did not work, even though its 2012 season included performances at the Brooklyn Academy of Music's Howard Gilman Opera House, John Jay College's Gerald W. Lynch Theater, and the El Museo del Barrio on upper Fifth

Mining town Central City, Colorado's famous opera house, built in 1878 and the oldest surviving opera house in the state. It remains as an important venue for opera and only an hour from Denver. *Author photograph*

Avenue. By the end of 2013, the "people's opera," as Mayor Fiorello La Guardia called the New York City Opera, was forced into bankruptcy.

Most opera house revivals, however, are in towns with no national significance or connections with famous people or events. They are just ordinary places: rural towns; small regional cities; county seats; and cities small and large whether Wamego, Kansas; Oshkosh, Wisconsin; Gardiner, Maine; Maysville, Kentucky; or Lancaster, Pennsylvania. Being prominently located on Main Street or on the town square meant these opera houses were noticed. It also meant their decay and decline were obvious. With no specific federal, state, or private programs or even organizations encouraging their resuscitation, the fate of these once-active opera houses has rested primarily in local hands.

The recovery of these halls is a remarkable story of grassroots action by local leaders, who struggled to generate interest and support. Daunting challenges faced these community leaders. Would it be possible to resurrect their opera house physically, culturally, and economically? Was there enough public support? Where were funds to bring the building up to code, from people who were potential supporters, and how could such an operation be sustained? Even though mothballed opera houses were beset with pigeons and bats, leaking roofs, sagging floors, inadequate plumbing, and improper fire escapes, local leaders envisioned how these halls could be restored and brought back to life as community cultural centers. In Coldwater, Michigan with a population of 11,000, the Tibbits Opera House dramatically illustrates the physical changes of one opera house over a little more than a century. Built in 1882 by local cigar magnate Barton S. Tibbit, this elaborate Second Empire opera house was stripped of its handsome façade ornamentation in the 1930s for an Art Deco movie theater. It was saved from the wrecking ball in the 1960s and a temporary, protective façade was erected. Its cupola was rebuilt in 2009, and with its exterior restoration completed in 2013, it was restored to its former grandeur.[7] Similar stories are repeated in towns and cities nationwide—and while the histories of each opera house differ, some patterns emerge.

The opera house in a small, isolated town with few nearby opportunities for live entertainment and a local interest in joining friends and neighbors in communal endeavors stands out as a likely candidate for restoration. Often these remote towns' opera houses limped along with local performances, stray lecturers, vaudeville, and sometimes a regional theater troupe far longer than larger towns with more modern theaters or auditoriums. Even today many remote towns have little access to live entertainment other than their opera houses. Although some of these halls continued to function, they were

Tibbits Opera House, Coldwater, Michigan, built in 1882 and restored in 2013. The before and after for this active theater and cultural center. The before: author photograph 2011. The after: Tibbits Opera Foundation & Arts Council, Inc. Sarah Zimmer– photograph 2013. *Tibbits Opera Foundation & Arts Council, Inc.*

never financial successes, as Sol Smith and his early troupe reported his pre– Civil War performances provided "more applause than wealth." Developers of these halls in the late nineteenth century hedged their bets with ground-floor rent-paying tenants.[8] Now with limited public funding sources, today's opera house revivers in big or small places are constantly searching for innovative ways to raise money and sustain public support. Small places often with few local funding opportunities—and few local philanthropists—energetically scramble for large or small grants. Enosburgh Falls, Vermont, got an early boost from a $3,600 matching grant from the Vermont Historical Trust, and Stonington, Maine, received several grants from the National Endowment for the Arts as well as from the Maine Humanities Council and the Maine Community Foundation.

The small, off-the-beaten-path town, Enosburgh Falls, in remote northern Vermont, has also withstood mainstream pressures and not only held on to its opera house but also kept it operating almost continuously, with only a few dry spells. As in Stonington and other isolated small towns, there were few alternative places to go for movies or entertainment. Enosburgh

Falls, located in a rolling stretch of agricultural land miles from urban congestion (Burlington, the closest city, is forty miles away), was fortunate to benefit from the philanthropy of its local pharmacist B. F. Kendall's successful, cure-all patent medicines. One of his donations to the town was the Enosburgh Falls Opera House, which he built in 1892 and turned over to the town two years later. For decades, it was the hall for the annual town meeting as well as a place for traveling performers, local public events, school activities, sports meets, fairs, animal shows, and also Dr. Kendall's company's medicine shows. This was typical of most opera houses, but Enosburgh Falls' Opera House did not burn down or fade away when movies and television lured people to movie theaters or their living rooms for entertainment. The building, a large, comfortable frame structure of undistinguished architecture located off Main Street near the railroad, has been relatively unaltered through the years.

The opera house continued to carry on. Although sports events moved to the new school gym, built in 1947, and fewer traveling performers made it to Enosburgh, the Enosburgh Band kept on playing into the 1930s. Intermittent children's shows, minstrel shows, local "Kakewalk" contests, Legion dances, poultry exhibits, and musical comedies were held in the opera house through the 1940s. However, as opera house performances and events waned and the building's paint chipped and its plumbing broke down, pigeons and mice were more frequent visitors than theater audiences.

The nudge to bring the opera house back to life came from the local grange, which made the restoration of the opera house its bicentennial project. An Opera House Association was organized in 1975, with new bylaws removing the requirement that if the building burned it would be rebuilt on the foundation within a year. The association installed insulation, lighting, and a fire alarm system using a $3,600 matching grant from the Vermont Historical Preservation Society. The proceeds of its first production in 1975, *Annie Get Your Gun*, and volunteer labor offset the cost of new dressing rooms and bathrooms. Since then, performances of musicals like *Oklahoma!*, *The Sound of Music*, and *South Pacific*, locally directed and produced with local and out-of-town actors and musicians, have played to sold-out crowds from all over the county and even nearby Canada. The 1980 performance of *My Fair Lady* lists the high school's librarian, fifth- and seventh-grade students, high school seniors, Burlington residents, nurses, X-ray technicians, and foresters as members of the cast.

Local interest in the opera house in its early days is being matched today by renewed community involvement in this institution, including

Enosburgh Falls, Vermont's Opera House, an almost continuously operating hall, dating from 1892. *Author photograph*

Enosburgh High School students and alumni. Ever-popular minstrel shows have been performed by the Enosburgh High School Athletic Minstrels for thirty-two years, and the high school alumni association has produced plays like *Lil Bit of Comedy.* An annual June Dairy Day Scholarship Pageant, John Philip Sousa's band, theater/entertainment troupes that stopped in Enosburgh on their runs between New York and Montreal, and Dr. Kendall's medicine shows have been replaced by community-generated productions, providing more local involvement and direct participation in productions than ever before.

Opera houses in towns with ethnic groups particularly interested in music, like Barre, Vermont's Italians, or with commitments to perpetuate their culture like the Czech towns in Nebraska, have continued functioning longer than in many places. As younger generations have become more Americanized in these ethnic towns, efforts to celebrate ethnic heritages have stepped up. Nebraska towns with Czech populations vie to crown the Czech Queen, host the largest Czech festival, or be the Center of Czechland. To promote their heritage and to entertain, events, especially for the younger generations, are held in Czech towns' opera houses and

Political and civic activities continue in opera houses. Presidential candidate Mitt Romney spoke at the Rochester (New Hampshire) Opera House on January 11, 2012. *Jim Wilson/The New York Times/Redux*

ZCBJ lodges. These evenings can include dances, including, of course, many polkas, singers, and even bluegrass music, all to the accompaniment of Czech bands with the added lure of Czech sausages and food. Such interest in ethnic heritage exists throughout the country in towns and neighborhoods with German, Finnish, Swedish, French, Norwegian, and other immigrant settlements. This commitment of ethnic communities to their heritage and their passion for their music have helped sustain rural opera houses, music halls, and ethnic lodges. Whether future Americanized generations will consider their ethnic heritage something to celebrate or forget as they blend into the mainstream is unclear.

Opera houses, mostly in New England, which have functioned as community halls for public events and important annual March town meetings, have also often escaped the wrecking ball and are still operating much as they did in the nineteenth century. Barack Obama's campaign talks to overflowing 2008 campaign crowds in Lebanon, New Hampshire; Vice President Joe Biden's talk in 2012 in a replicated opera house in Fort Dodge, Iowa; and Mitt Romney's in the Rochester (NH) Opera House in January 2012 confirm the continued use of these halls for political activities. Utilizing New England town halls/opera houses for

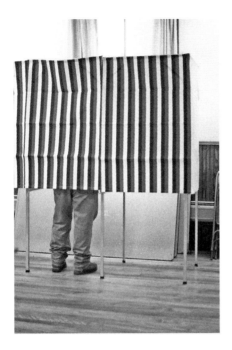

A man votes on the school budget in the Irasburg (Vermont) Town Hall and Opera House in 2006. *Holly Simpson photograph*

public and civic events no doubt results from their meetinghouse heritage. Although New England did not have a monopoly on combined town halls/opera houses, those located outside New England never had the communal mystique or sense of local ownership that New England town meetings and its meetinghouse tradition provided.

Bringing idle opera houses back to life has required a vision and a commitment from local "spark plugs," who have stirred community activists, artists, preservationists, historians, the public, and politicians. Bolstering that commitment and vision have been compelling interests in theater, music, and community. In 1888, the *Fremont* (Nebraska) *Weekly Herald* noted that "theatricals" were becoming almost an essential part of civilized society. Now more than a century later interest in theater has clearly fired up many communities, individuals, groups of individuals, and theater companies to revive their opera houses. These opera house revivals would not be as successful as they are today if it had not been for the thespian talents and drive of local theater professionals like Benjie White, Doug Anderson, and Mike Thomas and active theater groups like the Maysville Players, Lamoille County Players, and Minden Community Players. The skills and energies of these thespians have been the mainstay of the remarkable renaissance of many opera houses.

CHAPTER 16

Successes

The same excitement that Crete, Nebraska residents felt in 1877, when Band's Opera House arose in Jesse Bickle's cornfield, is in the air today as long-dormant opera houses are brought back to life in towns across the country. Then and now the success of these community halls has been due to the perseverance and vision of thespians, many volunteers, and local leaders.

The soft-spoken manner of Benjie White, the man responsible for the comeback of Cambridge, New York's 1878 opera house, Hubbard Hall, belies an enduring commitment to the role of theater and the arts in a small rural town with a population hovering around two thousand. A native Cantabrigian, White returned to his hometown with bachelor's and master's degrees in theater from Wesleyan University and experience working with the Bennington College theater program. Even as a child of five, White had shown an interest in Hubbard Hall, as he persuaded his father to get the keys to the then-empty hall so he could see what was inside the dormant but prominent building. Like so many small-town opera houses, Hubbard Hall's active years were virtually over by the 1920s. It was too expensive to get rid of or fix up, so it remained dark for fifty years. Cambridge became a rural time capsule of the early twentieth century as its population remained static at around two thousand for most of the century. Main Street reflected the town's lack of economic vitality and growth with spotty commerce: twelve empty storefronts, a dead hotel, two grocery stores, a barbershop, a bakery, a diner, and a popcorn wagon mixed in with some of Cambridge's grand houses by the early 2000s. Planning and zoning did not then exist for these independent Cantabrigians, who resisted the hand of government interfering with their private decisions. Franchised supermarkets came and went, often located off Main Street. Neither Cambridge nor nearby towns had enough of a market to attract large malls. Its local hospital, which served half a dozen towns, limped along until it closed in 2004. A sprawling central school, opened in 1950, serves as an important community institution, "a source of sociability," according to White. However, many of the town's brightest youths who went on to college headed to bigger places with more opportunities. Not Benjie White.

When White returned to Cambridge in 1976, interest in historic preservation, Main Street programs, and local arts had not yet emerged as a popular way of regenerating communities. The country was still suffering from the aftershock of the failures of the Vietnam War and the dashed hopes of urban renewal. Yet White could envision Hubbard Hall not only coming back to life but also enlivening the town of Cambridge. "And it's been fun ever since," he said with a smile that engulfed his face.[1] When the building was for sale for $20,000, White created Hubbard Hall, Inc. to buy the building in 1978. With a feasibility plan funded by the National Endowment for the Arts, Hubbard Hall was launched at a slow and steady pace. It has taken millions of dollars, thousands of hours of sweat equity, and the passion of White and many others to make it "the centerpiece of the community," noted Joe Donahoe, Cambridge resident and host of Albany public radio's *Roundtable* program. White's commitment to serious theater as well as his interest in enriching the town's coffers and culture have been the foundations of his success.[2]

White recognized that there was an audience in the region for world-class theater and music; more than half the audience drives over an hour to attend performances and concerts. Hubbard Hall has had a theater company, run by professional actors Kevin McGuire and John Hadden, producing seven to eight productions a year, including works by Shaw and Chekhov. Children's theater, variety shows, chorales, jazz fests, singing and ballet, tap and ethnic dance, groups study, rehearse, and perform throughout the year. And a very popular opera company run by Alexina Jones has been performing there since the summer of 2008.

Hubbard Hall's small auditorium allows for an intimacy that enhances all performances and activities and is quite different from Carnegie Hall or the Metropolitan Opera House. Its flat floor is adaptable for varied

Benjie White, the executive director of the thriving Hubbard Hall in Cambridge, New York from 1978 to 2014. *George Bouret, photographer*

artistic productions from theater in the round to dances. The unusually good acoustics have attracted outstanding local musical groups, such as Music from Salem and the Battenkill Chorale, and of course acoustics are important for the hall's operatic and theatrical performances. But Hubbard Hall also offers festive, fun occasions such as New Year's Eve masquerade balls, fiddling weekends, opening night celebrations, and dances. Like many second-floor opera houses, the building has rental space on the ground floor, now occupied by a community art gallery displaying regional artists' and craftspersons' work. Encouraged by the popularity and success of Hubbard Hall, some changes are evident on Main Street: the vacancy rate is down and more stores are open.

Bringing the Victorian opera house up-to-date with an elevator for the handicapped and modern plumbing, heating, air conditioning, and improved lighting has been costly. But the updating did not remove the elaborate Victorian chandelier, the original stage curtain, or the stenciled walls. In fact, Hubbard Hall looks much as it did in its heyday, which no doubt accounts for it being ranked as "exceptional" in the National Register of Historic Places' listing for the Cambridge Historic District.

White has looked beyond the confines of the opera house building to expand Hubbard Hall programs. Located near the railroad, like most opera houses for yesteryear's traveling troupes and their gear, Hubbard Hall backed up on old freight-yard buildings that had been underused for years. White saw the opportunity to convert these buildings into spaces for adjunct Hubbard Hall activities, such as dance studios, as well as to create a critical mass of art-related activities comparable to large cities' arts districts. Now Hubbard Hall Projects, Inc. consists of Hubbard Hall for its major productions and the freight-yard buildings for a multitude of art and related programs. With White's high professional standards, his understanding of the community, his determination and vision—and the support of the town and region—Hubbard Hall is an example of what can be accomplished in one small rural town. In July 2014 White stepped down as executive director after thirty-seven years, and David Snider, award-winning director of artistic programming at the Arena Stage in Washington, DC, took over the management of Hubbard Hall.

In Maysville, Kentucky, on the Ohio River, another nineteenth-century opera house has come back to life. Theater has always been part of life in Maysville, well before the North was able to enjoy plays and entertainment at real theaters and certainly before most of the country was even settled. In 1797 early residents in Mason County were attending the Theatrical Society's production of *Love à la Mode*, performed at the Mason County courthouse. From the time that Samuel Drake and his troupe landed their ark at Maysville in the early nineteenth century, the town had a series of theaters, including showboats, which docked there until the 1960s. The current Washington Opera House was built in 1898 to replace the elegant 900-seat opera house that was destroyed by fire that year. Distraught because it was unable to contain the fire, the Washington Fire Company raised $24,000 to build a new opera house, which was named for the fire company. This new Washington Opera House, like most such halls, provided a vast array of entertainment, both by out-of-town troupes and local school and community groups. As a one-night stop between Cincinnati and Lexington, Maysville also hosted many Broadway shows.

As the twentieth century proceeded, however, the Washington Opera House faced increasingly difficult times. Movies were shown at the opera house from 1908 on, but by the 1930s the opera house was forced to close for several years due to the Depression and competition from a new, luxurious fireproofed theater, the Russell, that offered movies as well as road shows.[3] The Washington Opera House soldiered on, primarily showing movies, under a series of owners until it closed in 1956. Put up for auction in 1963, the opera house failed to sell. Luckily, the previous year a local theater company, the Maysville Players, had been organized, first performing in the high school auditorium. This company was looking for a permanent space, and it rescued the opera house by buying it in 1964 as a permanent home for its own productions as well as community events. Since that purchase, the Maysville Players, Inc. assumed responsibility for the operation, restoration, and revitalization of the opera house. Its early and thorough concern for the architecture and restoration of the opera house stands out nationally. As early as 1974, the building was listed in the Kentucky Survey of Historic Buildings; by 1975, it was listed as contributing to the National Register's Historic District for Maysville; and by 1985, it had received landmark status. The Maysville Players have established an enviable record for civic and theatrical accomplishments in a small city with a population of approximately nine thousand. This theater company has enjoyed enthusiastic support since 2000 from the city's mayor, David Cartmell (a third-generation mayor), as well as recognition from the State of Kentucky, which designated Maysville one of the state's six cultural districts.

The recent reinvigoration of this opera house is due to an actor, playwright, and native son, Mike Thomas, who returned in September 2007 to manage the opera house. Like Benjie White in Cambridge, Thomas has enjoyed the challenge of bringing new life to the Maysville Players and the Washington Opera House. After acting on the road, Thomas returned to his hometown, where he recalls seeing movies such as *The Snow Queen* at the opera house and *Becky Thatcher* on a showboat in the 1960s. With "an unending passion and love for the theater," as he described it, Thomas has created a regular schedule of plays; recent seasons included Agatha Christie's *The Mousetrap*; a musical, *Nunsense*; and the annual teen production of *Seussical*. Aside from the productions of the Maysville Players, chamber music concerts, children's theater, a summer performing arts school, and many private events take place in the opera house. There are 126 people actively involved with the Maysville Players, including not only actors but also technicians, ushers, and many others needed to keep such a company going. The opera house programs reach 25,000 to 30,000 people on both sides of the Ohio River, with groups from as far away as Cincinnati coming to performances—and eating at restaurants and staying at hotels. As the Washington Opera House

The 1898 Washington Opera House, Maysville, Kentucky and Mike Thomas, producing director of the Maysville Players. *Maysville Players*

and its Maysville Players thrive, and Maysville's downtown attracts new galleries, restaurants, art studios, and even recently converted loft space, the city is hoping to become a civic and arts center.

The revival of opera houses devoted primarily to theater is occurring in all parts of the country, but perhaps this trend is most surprising in small, remote towns such as Hyde Park, located near ski country in northern Vermont. Hyde Park, the county seat for Lamoille County, has had a courthouse and town hall since the 1830s. The town hall served as a meeting place for many town and county functions, and probably entertainments as well: a stage and improved lighting were added in 1895. However, a massive fire in 1911 destroyed many buildings in the town, including the town hall. It took very little time to rebuild the hall, but this time the hall, with a raked floor, was large enough to accommodate meetings and conventions. Within a year, the town hall was ready not only for town meetings but also for Phil Ott and His Twenty-Five Merry Singers, Dancers, and Beauty Chorus. Ott's show, which attracted 500 enthusiastic people, launched the Hyde Park town hall into the realm of entertainment; in fact, the review of Ott's show referred to the hall as an "opera house."[4]

This town hall/opera house continued as the town's meeting place. Congregational services were held there while the church was under construction; schools had plays and graduations there for thirty years; and it hosted all local and traveling entertainments and town meetings until 1952, when they were moved to the local school's new, large gymnasium. The year 1952 was a momentous year for this 1911 hall. With the new school gymnasium, the town decided it no longer needed the building and planned to sell it. With the prospect of the opera house being replaced by a bowling alley, and no offers to purchase it, the village of Hyde Park voted at its 1953 town meeting to buy the building for one dollar. As the building had been neglected for years, with only an occasional play performed on its boards, it was not heretical to think of a more modern recreational facility taking its place. However, the Reverend John Knight of the Congregational church across the street from the opera house felt differently, as did a group of theater buffs, which in September 1952 performed *The Mikado* with more than seventy local people in the cast and crew as a benefit for a new furnace for the church. Pleased with the success of their first show, they successfully mounted another Gilbert and Sullivan work, *The Gondoliers,* the next year. They then organized the Lamoille County Players, and by 1954 proposed leasing the town hall/opera house from the village for a dollar a year. That offer was accepted at the 1954 town meeting, so the Lamoille County Players began their management of the Hyde Park Opera House, which has continued for more then sixty years.

Bringing the building up to code with necessary repairs such as a new furnace, sprinkler system, and upgraded electrical system, and then doing all the needed upkeep, installing new carpets, restoring the proscenium curtain, and reupholstering the seats, has been an ongoing program. Salvaged from its earlier days were some cushioned seats, which are now in the gallery, or balcony, which many opera houses have replaced as today's heavier patrons have trouble fitting into yesteryear's narrower seats. Also retained is the handsome, but initially controversial, stage curtain of Virginia's Natural Bridge with Killington Mountain as a touch of Vermont in the background. The instructions to the artist were to paint a local scene, but Charles Andrus, a prodigious commercial artist from Enosburgh Falls, soothed those who criticized him for ignoring their instructions by pronouncing that Virginia's Natural Bridge was one of the "Seven wonders of the world and this Opera House is the eighth."[5] Now the curtain is featured, along with the acoustics and good sight lines, as an attraction in this restored and welcoming building.

The opera house has become an integral part of Lamoille County. The Lamoille County Players provide an annual scholarship of $500 or more for a county or regional high school senior who has participated on stage or backstage with the Players to attend an "institute of higher learning." As proud as the community is of the restored opera house, its varied programs are what Hyde Park residents and neighbors from nearby towns really enjoy. The Lamoille County Players have been producing four plays and musicals every year; the annual favorite each autumn is *The Sound of Music*, about nearby Stowe's Trapp family. The Players' selections are all-time favorites such as *The Music Man, Annie Get Your Gun*, and *Brigadoon* as well as Agatha Christie mysteries and children's plays such as *Wind in the Willows*.

The Hudson Opera House provides another comeback story. This opera house stands taller and broader than most buildings lining Hudson, New York's Warren Street, which slopes down toward the Hudson River, where its early Nantucket Quaker settlers docked their whaling ships. A grand building built in 1855 as the city hall, featuring a large second-floor auditorium, is one of the oldest surviving theaters in the United States, according to the League of Historic American Theatres. Its first floor initially housed the Franklin Library and the First National Bank of Hudson and then the city offices, police department, post office, and common council; on the second floor is the hall, renamed the Opera House around

Hyde Park, Vermont's 1912 Opera House's curtain of Natural Bridge, Virginia, the "seventh wonder of the world" with Killington Mountain in the distance. Artist Charles Andrus claimed Hyde Park's opera house the eighth wonder of the world when townspeople questioned his choice of a non-Vermont scene. *Author photograph*

1880 when opera houses were coming into vogue. Here traveling theater troupes, lecturers, musicians, and entertainers performed; nearby artists such as Frederic Church exhibited their paintings; and many dances, fairs, graduations, meetings, and political gatherings took place. This city hall with a second-floor opera house was a community gathering place in the late nineteenth and early twentieth centuries in this city thirty miles downriver from Albany.

As in so many cities and towns, Hudson's downtown and opera house fell on hard times in the mid-twentieth century, especially in the 1960s and 1970s. Many shops on Warren Street were empty and abandoned; its newcomers were often poor immigrants, and the once-proud days when it almost became the state's capital were past. Its death knell was the move of the city offices to a new building in 1962. For thirty years the opera house was largely dark except for a few years as a Moose Lodge, and for many years it was home to pigeons and mice. The building decayed, as did much of Warren Street. Hudson was indeed a downtrodden place by the late 1980s, not unlike other Hudson River small cities such as Newburgh and Peekskill.

When you are down so low, you can only go up. That was the case for Hudson. With its depression came real estate bargains, which lured a host of artistic people, tired of New York's high rents and hectic lifestyle. Working artists, art dealers, and antique dealers arrived and started to convert Hudson's downtown into an antique haven. Amid this burgeoning commerce, the civic neglect of the opera house stood out as a festering sore. It took the threat of demolition in 1990 to mobilize Columbia County and Hudson residents to organize the nonprofit Hudson Opera House, Inc. in 1991 to investigate restoring the opera house to its former glory as a cultural and civic center. With volunteers and a part-time administrator, the organization tried to grapple with the overwhelming problems of a building left to rot, from a leaking roof to a flooded basement, along with all the preservation requirements for a building in a State Historic District. Funds were raised to restore one room, then four more on the first floor of the building, and then the roof.

Restoration was on its way, but there was a long road ahead not only to restore the building physically, but also to organize its programs. It was clear that a full-time professional executive was needed, as a 1994 planning study had recommended. That is when Gary Schiro, the spark of the opera house's revival, came in. Schiro had worked for the New York State Council for the Arts for fourteen years, providing individual grants to artists, but he spent his weekends in Columbia County. When he saw the advertisement for a director of the opera house, he realized that he could live and work in Columbia County, avoid those tough weekend commutes, and tackle the challenge of making the opera house a vital part of community life.

The first order of business was erasing the stereotypical elitist image of the old building and structuring programs that would be meaningful to the diverse population of the city and region, which ranged from Hispanic immigrants to wealthy New York City weekenders. Using the first-floor rooms, which were gradually restored for classes, lectures, and events, Schiro attracted increasingly eager attendees. Children came for hands-on art classes, dance workshops, theater projects, puppet programs, environmental activities, and storytelling sessions after school and on weekends. For adults, there have been nonstop activities, workshops, lectures, plays, readings, and exhibits. In one month, one could attend Music From China, a flamenco exhibition, a guitar concert, a Hudson Valley Literary Magazine and Small Press Fair, a blues concert, a Danish theater group's performance of *Hamlet*, two photography exhibits, and workshops in playwriting, painting, yoga, piano sing-along, *kuumba* drumming, gypsy dance, and "swap and sew" lessons. A highlight of the year is the December

Hudson, New York's 1855 opera house, once its city hall and now the opera house, is being restored and revived. Its co-directors, Gary Schiro and Tambra Dillon, review restoration plans. *Hudson Opera House*

Winter Walk, sponsored by the Opera House, which attracts thousands of
people and provides welcome patrons to local restaurants and hostelries.
The mile-long Warren Street is transformed into a festive holiday celebration with entertainment from Mr. and Mrs. Claus, marionettes, local belly
dancers, bagpipers, sitar players, the Coxsakie-Athens Community Band,
and NYC Percussionists. Food and drink are everywhere in local restaurants, outdoor food stands, and at the finale benefit dinner at the Opera
House, prepared by a Culinary Institute of America chef.

Hudson's Opera House, known as a multiarts center, is far more than a
place where the intellectual and artistic elite gather; it has become a place
where many different people enjoy marvelously varied programming. In
2014 53,000 people attended almost 900 programs, most of them free.
Thousands of students were involved in the 122 in-school programs. The
opera house's motto, "Stir the Senses," has been at work. It also worked for
the City of Hudson, as the opera house estimated it added $2 million to the
local economy and fifty-three full-time equivalent jobs to the city in 2014.
With Schiro's ten years of increased programming attracting more attendees—and building a growing constituency—the Hudson Opera House,
with $4.3 million for its capital campaign, is on its way toward its next goal:
restoring the second-floor auditorium and performing space. The contract
to begin the restoration was signed in June 2015 and the estimated completion date for the project is December 2016. Then the upstairs as well as the
ground floor will be throbbing with cultural activities.

In Vermont's oldest and smallest city, Vergennes (population 2,700),
the Opera House revival also resulted from an uphill, grassroots movement of local people, who saw what a restored opera house could do for
the community—and steadfastly worked for decades to make it happen.
The red-brick, Richardsonian arched entrance and heavily massed brick
opera house/city hall, built in 1897 to replace an earlier Greek-style col-
umned building that burned two years earlier, was the community gathering place for this then-prosperous industrial town. Here a wide array
of out-of-town and local entertainments, movies, and public meetings
(like the annual city meeting and city council meetings) took place in
the second-floor opera house, with the rest of the space occupied by city
offices, police, and fire departments. But with all the changes of the early
twentieth century, and the loss of industry once dependent on water-
power from Otter Creek and nearby Lake Champlain for transportation,
Vergennes and the opera house fell on hard times. Vergennes residents
could easily drive to Burlington, Middlebury, and Rutland, all less than

an hour away. By the 1950s and 1960s, its downtown was losing its heart as stores and offices closed and even its town square looked unkempt. For tourists or nonresidents, Vergennes became a place to drive through.

Until the union school with an auditorium was built in the 1960s, community events took place in the opera house—but in dwindling numbers. However, by the late 1960s, the opera house was in terrible shape: leaking roof and walls, crumbling plaster, no electricity, but plenty of pigeons. Repairs were estimated at $50,000, with an additional $10,000 to bring the space up to fire code, more than the city could afford. An application for a bicentennial grant from the state's Historic Preservation Office was rejected. The building continued to deteriorate until the early 1990s, when the Friends of Vergennes Opera House was organized. It was slow going at first; the city leaders were skeptical and relations with the city council were edgy.

The tide changed in 1993 and 1994. A new mayor and several council members viewed the restoration project more favorably, and Gerianne Smart became the new president of the Friends group. Smart, like Beth Klosterman in David City, Nebraska, was the spark in Vergennes. Although young and a newcomer to the area, Smart benefited from an interest in theater, having graduated from the American Academy of Dramatic Arts and subsequently having a career in advertising and public relations. She and a growing number of active members of the Friends of Vergennes Opera House worked hard to persuade city council members and other public officials of the merits of reviving the opera house. Vergennes successfully applied for a grant from the US Department of Housing and Urban Development (HUD). Projects began and money came in from donors large and small, farmers, small businesses, foundations, many residents, and government agencies. Momentum started to build. The scaffolding for the roof repairs was a sign to the outside world that the opera house might really come back to life.

Gradually the building was rehabilitated and brought up to code: the plumbing, electrical and heating systems, plaster, woodwork, windows, floors—everything was made new. Some people interested in historical accuracy were concerned about new features like chandeliers and carpets, but, as in Minden, the new features turned out to be popular additions. Almost ready for the planned reopening of the opera house in 1997, they found themselves $50,000 short of their goal. After a visit to the work in progress in 1996, Governor Howard Dean allocated $50,000 for them in the state budget, which, with the help of several senators, they received. However, the funds were not available until after the opening. With a negotiated line of credit from the local Chittenden Bank, they met their deadline and the restored opera house opened in July 1997 as planned.

For a small city like Vergennes to raise $1.2 million was a feat—and it took legions of volunteers and thousands of contributors, many with contributions ranging from $5 to $30. Now the city can again enjoy a parade of productions and entertainments, just as earlier generations did. It is not just high art. There is something for everyone, from children's theater to social dances with fundraisers such as an annual road rally. The diversity of accessible and affordable activities follows Smart's and the Friends' philosophy that the arts are a great equalizer. Everyone is equal who walks into the opera house; it is neutral turf and a safe haven.

For Vergennes and its "downtown," which is essentially two blocks on its main street, the revived opera house has been a catalyst. It woke up the city, showed what could be done with vision and determination, and stirred a new sense of pride in the community. The downtown even looks different. New restaurants and shops filled up the once-empty storefronts that lined Main Street within a year after the Opera House's opening. The town square is spruced up. Tim Ryan, owner of a plumbing and heating company on Main Street that has been in his family since 1867, sensed the change in the way people now feel about Vergennes. "It's like a snowball," he observed.[6] He in turn spent $30,0000 painting his own building.

Sustaining that momentum in operating a small community arts business is challenging and requires new programs and new approaches. After the excitement of the early days, measured and careful planning is needed to maintain and operate the opera house. That is being provided by Gerianne Smart, who is back at the job instilling sound business practices as well as ensuring its cultural programs reach the needs of a diverse community. In the meantime, three to four plays, ranging from *Much Ado about Nothing* to *Fractured Fairy Tales* to *The Diary of Anne Frank*, are produced each year by the Little City Players, and many community events from the high school's musical to the annual city meeting are held in this opera house in Vermont's oldest and smallest city.

Minden, Nebraska's rural opera house has been brought back to life, but with a very different story. Here a 1900 opera house was revived one hundred years later through a community effort backed by civic and theatrical organizations, rather than by an individual entrepreneur. Minden used more of a top-down approach to its opera house revival. Its opera house, originally the Hosteller Opera House and now the Minden Opera House, sits proudly on the north side of the town square that is dominated

The 1897 Opera House and City Hall in Vergennes, Vermont with Gerianne Smart, who has spearheaded its revival. *Author photographs*

by the county courthouse, now festooned with white lights strung from the courthouse to the edges of the square. The role of the opera house in the community life of this town of approximately 3,000 people was gradually diminished by the competition of movies, a new auditorium, and the changing tastes of different eras. Over time the opera house has seen a series of different owners, tenants, and uses, including a mortuary on the ground floor and a storage operation on its second floor from the 1950s to 1990. Dancing turns out to have been the opera house's most popular activity, with music supplied by many local bands as well as by famous bands such as Lawrence Welk's. The virtual abandonment of this prominent building in its downtown stirred Minden's community leaders to investigate how they might revive the opera house. The Kearney County Community Foundation, comprised of civic leaders, rose to the challenge and took the lead in the 1990s in mobilizing the planning and impressive renovation of the building, which was completed in 2000. Working hand-in-hand with the foundation were the Minden Community Players, organized in 1984 and enthusiastic about the possibility of an improved theater at the opera house for their performances.

The Minden Community Players got an up-to-date theater and the town a revived opera house. Recognizing the need to modernize the building, the Community Foundation decided to change features of the original building and drastically renovate its interior, which meant it was not eligible for historic preservation grants. For example, adding an exterior balcony to its front at the second-floor/theater level of the building has proved very popular for theatergoers, who can enjoy a view of the illuminated courthouse during intermission. But that did not comply with federal restoration guidelines. As a result, the foundation was unable to seek federal preservation funding and tax assistance. Instead the foundation went it alone in fundraising—and was successful in raising $2.5 million. Its goal was "to enhance the quality of educational, cultural and entertainment opportunities for our citizens" and create economic benefits. "Economic development should be stimulated as we put this new resource to work to expand our tourism potential," the Community Foundation stated, but only "if we continue to devote the same kind of creativity, hard work, and dedication that has completed the building renovation."[7] To ensure that these community benefits continue, a nonprofit organization, Minden Opera House, Inc., was established. The Kearney County Community Foundation continued as the owner and overseer of the opera house, with the Minden Community Players an active participant, first advising on the renovation, then assisting in the construction

The remodeled Minden, Nebraska opera house, facing the courthouse square and featuring a new balcony. *Author photograph*

process itself, and, most important, agreeing to produce two plays a year. The day-to-day operation initially was overseen by Ben Morey, a Kearney County native with a background in education and an interest in theater, and since 2010 has been managed by another native, Marcy Brandt, a theater major in college and formerly head of the local chamber of commerce.

Minden Community Players' three to four theatrical programs each year include mysteries, comedies, and musicals, such as Rodgers and Hammerstein's *Oklahoma!*, which are perennially popular in the Minden area, as elsewhere. Movies new and old, dances, band concerts, and children's programs such as Halloween events and storytelling fill many evenings. For instance, a free lecture series in 2008 supported by the Nebraska Humanities Council, offered talks on Nebraska history, Nebraskan William Jennings Bryan, and Danish immigration.

With the strong influence of the local organizers, it is not surprising that the Minden Opera House serves many community purposes. Its renovation was designed to provide space not only for plays and entertainments but also for community activities such as the chamber of commerce on the first floor and spaces, many named after generous donors, for galleries, shops, meetings—and weddings and parties. The hall with the stage on the second floor, named for Minden resident Ruth Armstrong, seats 276, with a reception room in the front that has a balcony overlooking the courthouse and square. But it is the ceiling mural in the theater, named for prominent Minden residents Dick and Kaylyn McBride, that is eye-catching. Here the world of Minden is depicted; its culture, its history, its landmarks, and its settlers—in particular, a local noted doctor and botanist, a banker involved with water projects, and the inventor of Flex-O-Glass and founder of Pioneer Village, a local tourist attraction. Along with depictions of early settlers are whooping and sandhill cranes, local landmark buildings, and a gold-leaf sun that becomes a full moon when the lights are dimmed. With a high-tech fiber-optic system, the ceiling turns into a starry spring night. It is an elegant monument that, not surprisingly, attracts people from many miles away.

Unlike some opera houses that stress high-art productions, Minden has designed an opera house to appeal to the townspeople and farmers of its region. The renovation has been a community project through and through. Rob Raun, a local farmer, former regent of the University of Nebraska, and former board member of the Kellogg Foundation, envisioned the renovated opera house and also solicited funds for the project. He was not alone. Hundreds of individuals and companies joined him in this effort. The generosity of a Minden resident, Vane Nied, established the Kearney County Community Foundation and the Minden Opera House benefited from a $300,000 grant from a foundation set up by his estate. The communal nature of this renovation reminds one of the earlier opera houses, often beneficiaries of the philanthropy of an individual or of a group of local businesspeople, but usually with the hope that it would benefit not only the town's culture but also its economic and social future.

A glimpse at four opera houses today along the Maine coast shows the variety of opera houses and programs reflecting the different needs and desires of disparate communities, from mill towns to summer resorts. At the easternmost tip of Deer Isle sits Stonington's opera house, whose motto "Incite Art—Create Community" accurately portrays its creative programming and active community involvement. This hands-on, year-round facility involves all ages in its programs, which include documentary films, stage productions, local variety shows, movie weekends, poetry readings, musicals, circuses, and performances by out-of-town troupes.

More than a hundred volunteers help with maintenance and operations matters, and local high-school students join the staff in summers, as do Island Institute fellows. With the influx of summer folk, clearly important sustainers of the opera house, its programs reflect their interests in more high-art programs as well as community-related shows like "Quarryography," a dance performance based on the theme of Stonington's granite industry.[8] The success of the opera house is evident in its popular programs, which sometimes are so numerous that the opera house has taken over a nearby church for overflow programs. The 1960s anthem, "People Have the Power," which is played by local bands at opera house community dances, captures the philosophy of its savvy management. By embedding itself in the community, the staff has developed a sensitivity to the community's interests, which in turn has helped create a remarkable community cultural institution in an isolated location.

Across Penobscot Bay due west of Stonington lies a stretch of communities, including Camden and Rockport, that have attracted wealthy summer residents since the late nineteenth century. The Camden Opera House in its solid and well-maintained town hall on Main Street reflects the affluence and cultural interests of the residents of this area. Built in 1894, the well-equipped opera house opened on June 6, 1894 with the Boston Opera Company's performance of "Maritama" and later that night a grand ball. Its programs over the years have included movies, balls and dances, traveling shows with well-known stars like Tallulah Bankhead and Lillian Gish, and many concerts by the Curtis School of Music. The building is also Camden's town hall, where its town offices are located and where innumerable public events have been held in its auditorium starting with the town's first town meeting in 1895.

The opera house has benefited over the years from the generosity of Camden residents such as publishing heiress Mrs. Mary Curtis Bok (later Zimbalist) as well as MBNA Bank. In the mid-1950s its floor was raked, and in 1993 the opera house underwent an extensive renovation, converting it into an extremely comfortable and well-equipped hall while retaining much of the original detail. The town clearly takes pride in and responsibility for the opera house as it funds the salary of the manager for the Camden Opera House. Its programs are not as participatory as Stonington's or Boothbay Harbor's, farther down the coast, although its resident community theater group, the Camden Civic Theater, has performed a variety of shows since the 1970s. This includes an array of nationally known performers, like the Eileen Ivers Band and comedian Bob Marley, and authors such as Pulitzer Prize winner Richard Russo have appeared at the opera house as well as family shows such as Avner the Eccentric. Unlike most opera houses, the Camden Opera House has hosted two annual conferences: the Camden Conference on International Affairs since 1987, and the Camden Technology Conference (Pop-Tech) since 1996. Functioning year-round, the Opera House holds a Maine Authors Series and Literary Festival in November. In 2013, its international film festival was awarded a National Endowment for the Arts grant. Such offerings, reflecting the traditional nature of the area, provide programs often found only in urban places.

Farther down the coast, at the narrow end of a long promontory finger, is Boothbay Harbor. Here in a hulking frame building built in 1894, which looks like an old school, is its opera house, officially called the "Opera House at Boothbay Harbor." The town originally rented the downstairs auditorium and a room for the town clerk, while the Masons and Knights of Pythias had a lodge upstairs. When the YMCA and the local school built new structures in the 1970s, the barnlike building was emptied of tenants and up for demolition. A group of local people formed a nonprofit organization and bought the building.

As in Camden and Stonington, this opera house operates all year, with its year-round population of 6,500 swelling to between thirty and fifty thousand in the summer. The office for the opera house, located on the first floor, is staffed by manager Cathy Sherrill, whose background in development has helped bring in the funds to support the opera house. The flat-floored auditorium, which seats 650, is located on the second floor, with a space in the front of the third floor now converted into a bar/recreation area. It has a comfortable feel. The place is hopping with activity, with three to five shows a week showcasing Maine artists; plays by a local troupe, the Overboard Players; one-night events such as Maine Hysterical Society comedy shows; musicals, readings; the Portland String Quartet; Wednesday night programs for children; and Youth Theater, a cooperative venture between the library and opera house. Three hundred volunteers all pitch in with theater work. "People love the place," one volunteer remarked.[9]

Biddeford, once a textile manufacturing giant, is just south of Portland. In 1895, when Pepperell Mills occupied fifty-six acres with miles of buildings and thousands of employees, Biddeford erected an impressive brick-and-granite three-story, clock-towered city hall with an opera house. This city hall/opera house was Biddeford's second opera house; the first, built in 1860, burned in 1894. Today the city hall/opera house, built in 1896, dominates the downtown. In fact, it stands out as a monument to the city's former days of glory amid the ruins of old mills, one directly across the street. The opera house, renamed City Theatre in 1955, has red velvet seats, gilded friezes, a brass chandelier, a wide proscenium, a horseshoe balcony, and, of course, a raked floor.

After its early-twentieth-century heyday when famous actors such as the Barrymores played in Biddeford, along with minstrel shows and vaudeville, the opera house converted in the 1930s to a movie house and later installed a permanent CinemaScope screen. By 1963, unable to compete with television and drive-in movies, the theater closed. In the 1970s, it was used for storage and in 1975 its orchestra pit was even filled with sand for a horseshoe pitch. The neglect of the opera house mobilized the creation in 1977 of City Theatre Associates, which has since undertaken a gradual restoration of the building with the aid of many volunteers as well as a mix of federal, state, local, business, and private support, culminating with a 2005 Maine Preservation Honor Award for its restoration.

City Theatre Associates rents the building from the city and has since offered an array of plays, musicals, concerts, and community activities, all with local actors and technicians. They reopened the theater in 1978. This is truly a community theater as all the actors and the technical staff are local residents. Its ambitious program has included musicals and comedies like *Almost Maine, The Secret Garden,* and *The Pirates of Penzance.* Aside from plays that City Theatre Associates produces, other programs, such as a summer theater for children and "Senior Acting Up," have attracted thousands of participants. With its productions and cultural events, City Theatre Associates makes an important contribution to the welfare of the people in this depressed city, whose world-renowned Pepperell Mills are now converted to the Pepperell Mill Campus with eighty apartments and ninety businesses.

Although plays and entertainments have been the mainstay of these and most opera houses, music and opera, both light and serious, have always been a part of their programs. And that is true today with the revived opera houses. What kinds of music and how often they are programmed depend on the inclinations of the opera house's owners and managers, the competing institutions and cultural groups in the town or region, and the important interests of the community. Some opera houses today rely on out-of-town performers, as in Stoughton, Wisconsin where its opera house director Bill Brehm and event coordinator Christina Dollhausen program include not only touring companies or one person shows, but many out-of-town performers, bands, string quartets, authors, singers, dancers, opera for children, and the Stoughton Chamber Singers.

An opera house known for outstanding music programs is Piper's Opera House in the mining town of Virginia City, Nevada. Piper's dates back to 1867 and its history parallels that of most nineteenth-century American opera houses: two fires and two rebuildings. Its programs were packed with all the usual fare, performed by a resident company of twenty troupers as well as by nationally known figures such as Mark Twain, Susan B. Anthony, and Lillie Langtry. Unlike most opera houses, which have changed owners many times, Piper's remained in the family from 1867 until 1997. Its revitalization and focus on music have been led by the original John Piper's great-granddaughter, Louise Driggs, an accomplished musician who lived in New Jersey before she became involved with the opera house in the 1970s. She established a summer chamber music festival with accomplished artists, and her daughter is continuing that tradition by introducing well-known musicians, jazz festivals, dance classes, and band concerts, along with plays, balls, and the usual opera house fare. However, in 1997 the Driggs family sold the opera house to Piper's Opera House Historic Programs, a nonprofit foundation, which is upgrading the building while holding school plays and graduations, cultural programs, and fundraising events. In recognition of the contributions of this opera house to the cultural life of the region and country, this mining town's entertainment hall was declared a National Treasure in 2001 by the National Park Service—and its musical programs were an important reason for this award.

In the central Vermont town of Randolph, native son Colonel Albert Chandler, chairman of the board of the Postal Telegraph Company, financed the construction of a music hall in 1907 to be combined with the town's Bethany Church Parish House. In its first year, the church's progressive minister, the Reverend Fraser Metzger, warded off criticism of his association with the music hall and its "theatricals," and the church and music hall continued their association. The hall, called Chandler Music Hall, built with chunky concrete blocks, functioned as a community opera house from 1907 until the 1930s with plays, movies, political rallies, lectures, and school events. By the 1930s, however, the Chandler could not compete with alternative entertainments in larger towns like White River Junction, Vermont and Lebanon, New Hampshire. The town of Randolph took over the Chandler in 1947 and ran entertainments and public events in the hall until the 1970s. Then the newly organized Friends of Chandler Music Hall provided another spurt of energy. This time the building was restored and brought back to life with plays, band concerts, variety shows, bazaars, and artists' exhibitions. With the building's excellent acoustics, the Friends of Chandler Music Hall organized an extensive and very popular musical program with chamber music, choral concerts, string quartets, and jazz sessions, the Cab Calloway orchestra, an a cappella teen chorus, folksingers, African music, and an annual Mud Season Variety Show. In 2013, more than twenty thousand visits were made to the Chandler in a town of around five thousand people. The Chandler, now known throughout the state for its music, was recognized by the National Endowment for the Arts with a 2013 grant for its statewide orchestral music festival, which included artists' residencies in four Vermont towns exploring the theme "My Hometown."

Musicals remain all-time favorites in small and large opera houses in all parts of the country. Sometimes managers are afraid to admit this popularity, as it might reflect their audiences' conventional inclinations. However, this distinctly American contribution to theater continues to draw the crowds. One opera house, the Goodspeed Opera House in East Haddam, Connecticut, has capitalized on the popularity of musicals to become the nation's leading center for the professional production of musicals and seemingly everything related to musical theater. The trajectory of this nationally acclaimed opera house is remarkable.

The Goodspeed Opera House began like most opera houses: the effort of a prominent local entrepreneur to provide an all-purpose building for his steamship business, his store, other local businesses, the post office, and an opera house. This 1872 building sits tall astride the bank of the Connecticut River. From the riverside it has six floors: the lowest housed William H. Goodspeed's steamship business offices; the next floors the dry goods store, a dentist, an insurance office, and other local businesses; and the top two floors were occupied by the opera house. The opera house was not grand or large. It seated 398 people and was flat-floored with movable chairs, a raked stage, proscenium boxes, a wooden-benched balcony, a small orchestra pit, and a drop curtain featuring Goodspeed's State of the Union steamer. Its fare was typical for small opera houses with the exception that Goodspeed's steamers could bring New York actors directly to his hall, so the East Haddam audiences were exposed to stars now and then. Its heyday was short, as Goodspeed died only ten years after his opera house opened. However, the programs continued with lectures, masquerades, comic operas, political gatherings, concerts, roller skating, and, in 1902, *Uncle Tom's Cabin,* its last legitimate theatrical production.

The opera house never regained its former success. In fact, in 1912 the building was deemed unsafe for public use, as there was no fire escape. Various attempts were made to resurrect it as a performance space, but all faltered. Owners came and went, and the building was used for incongruous activities such as World War I militia headquarters. By the end of the Depression the building was empty. The State of Connecticut purchased it in 1943, stripped off the front porch, and added garage doors so that state trucks and equipment could be stored on the main floor. After World War II, the state no longer used it, and in 1959 slated it for demolition. That was the alarm bell that roused local preservationists and changed the life of the Goodspeed.

The story proceeds on the track of many restored opera houses: local preservationists Mrs. Paul Kaye, Mrs. Alfred Howe Terry, and Mrs. Eugene Narducci organized the Citizens Committee for the Preservation of the East Haddam Opera House. Undaunted by headstrong state bureaucrats, they made their case directly to Governor Abraham Ribicoff, who advised them to raise $20,000 to prove their financial worthiness, which they did. They garnered powerful support from citizens, local politicians, key business executives, academicians, well-known actors and opera stars, and union leaders. More than 300 opera house supporters showed up at the state capitol for a hearing on the proposed demolition, forcing the hearing to be moved to larger legislative chambers. The preservationists won that hearing. The building was not torn down, and the women and their many supporters kept on winning. That launched the committee to worlds far beyond East Haddam—corporate boardrooms, prominent artists, respected architectural historians, and many cocktail parties with high-powered and moneyed guests in upscale Fairfield County. In May, the Goodspeed Opera House Foundation was established, with Governor Ribicoff as its honorary chairman. Within a year, more than $300,000 had been raised, so the challenge of restoring the building and reviving the opera house could begin.

So far the story is not unusual, except that the committee had access to wealthy supporters in Hartford, New Haven, and New York, so restoration got off to a speedy start. Architects were hired, plans prepared, and the building, then in shambles, was restored. The Lynde Selden family provided important leadership, financial support, and even its first managing director, Lynde Selden's son, Albert, who had a background in commercial theater and a love of musical comedies. In 1963, the opera house came back to life as an all-purpose venue offering plays, opera,

The Goodspeed Opera House in East Haddam in 2013 and in the 1950s when used by the State of Connecticut to store state trucks. Now a thriving opera house and national center for musical theater. *Left photograph: Author photograph. Right photograph: Goodspeed Musicals*

ballets, and concerts for the East Haddam area and beyond. As early as 1959, Goodspeed's newsletter provided a premonition that it might be more than a small-town opera house, maybe "an unusual cultural center, which will be important to the entire country. . .It may well become an entertainment showcase of the nation, for living in Connecticut's towns and adjoining areas is a great concentration of leaders of the performing arts, capable of making Goodspeed programs truly outstanding."[10]

Opening with the musical *Oh Lady! Lady!* was another clue to its future. The Goodspeed presented in 1964 travel lectures, vaudeville, Gilbert and Sullivan productions and a Mozart concert. The next year's successful world premiere production of the musical *Man of La Mancha* launched the opera house's future in musicals. Each year thereafter the Goodspeed produced musicals: *Maggie, Tom Piper, Good News, Where's Charley?, Shenandoah,* and *El Capitan.* In 1968 Michael Price became executive director, and his reputation as an accomplished producer of musical comedies was borne out by Goodspeed's performances of twelve new musicals; between 1969 and 1982, three of these ended up on Broadway. The opera house has continued to produce prizewinning musicals, which have won more than a dozen Tony awards, and Broadway hits. In 1971, it revised its mission to concentrate on musicals and to introduce new musicals, composers, and lyricists; to develop innovative ways of furthering musical theater; and to broaden appreciation of musical theater through educational seminars, festivals, and outreach programs. This decision to focus on one performing art indigenous to this country, the American musical, and its heritage has paid off.

Today Goodspeed is the country's center for musical theater. This small opera house with a very tight stage (27 feet wide, 20 feet deep, and 16 feet high), no fly space, and a tight orchestra pit provides an intimate theater environment for the three musicals produced each year. Some 120,000 people a year attend its musicals, which attests to Goodspeed's popularity. The opera house, the centerpiece of this enterprise, is now only part of an ever-expanding campus with twelve buildings and continually changing educational programs: a former knitting-needle factory in nearby Chester has been converted into the Norma Terris Theater for experimental musicals; its vast costume collection rents its costumes to theaters around the globe; and its warehouse-sized production center constructs elaborate scenery. Nearby a recently acquired building has been converted into a multi-purpose rehearsal studio, and across the street is a formidable library for books, records, broadbills, and scores on musicals. Aside from these buildings directly associated with the production of musicals, the campus also includes the Gelston Hotel and the Artists' Village, a cluster of seven new, environmentally sound houses for artists and scholars involved with the productions, built in 2012 cooperatively with East Haddam using private funds and a generous state Department of Economic and Community Development grant. Aside from providing much-needed housing in this rural area, the village buildings facing a small green were carefully designed to add to the New England ambience of the local historic district. Goodspeed is now not only a center, but a campus for musical theater.

Its programs are expanding along with its plant. In 2013–2014, the Musical Theatre Institute offered twelve classes and internships including backdrop painting, musical dance, and audition classes, mostly for professionals but also for high school and grade school children. Members of Goodspeed Musicals, the steady financial backers, are offered lectures, tours, and special productions. Broadening the appreciation of musicals and encouraging support have helped to make Goodspeed a leader in the field of musical theater today.

How did this come about? And could such a concentration on a single theater type or other types work for other opera houses? Focusing primarily on musicals was an early decision and a gamble. Such a gamble might not have worked if musicals had not been immensely popular or if Goodspeed had not had outstanding talent and aggressive management. Its location near Hartford and not that far from New York meant it could attract top talent and top dollars, yet it was also remote enough to provide an escape from pressurized urban life. Financial support from New York and Hartford was critical, but that was the result of an early, effective campaign gaining the support of key politicians, artists, and financial supporters. It is an unusual trajectory for an out-of-the-way small-town opera house. Art has won, but community in the traditional sense of communally focused programs has lost out.

In the early days of the opera house's revival, community support was essential. Its earliest supporters were all local, including local state legislators. The basement of the local Rathbun Library even served as rehearsal space. In its first revival years, the diverse programs and special shows at Christmas were geared to local residents. But, as musicals took over and out-of-towners filled the hall, the locals were left behind. Goodspeed today compensates for this loss by offering imaginative outreach programs, including many for schoolchildren in the region. However, even in William Goodspeed's day a rift existed in East Haddam, not between East Haddamites and outsiders but between upper and lower East Haddam. Although located less than a mile apart, each place had its own steamboat stop, hotel, bank, and schools, with the uphill East Haddamites considering themselves superior to the downhill folk until Goodspeed altered that relationship. The Goodspeed, no longer a small-town opera house offering the traditional diverse programs for local residents, has become a national institution and an example of the melding of drive, location, management, networking, and some luck.

Interest in another music form, opera, has developed in some small-town opera houses in New England. Up the Connecticut River in New Hampshire, the Lebanon opera house in its town hall also overflows with community production groups: North Country Community Theatre, Northeast Shakespeare Ensemble, Lebanon Community Chorus, City Center Ballet, Upper Valley Community Band—and, importantly, Opera North. Opera North, which originated in 1981, is nationally recognized for its outstanding summer opera festivals. Operating out of the 710-seat Lebanon Opera House, Opera North now produces two musical programs each summer, Verdi's *La traviata* and Lerner and Loewe's *My Fair Lady* in 2014, as well as a Young Artist Program that offers apprenticeships for young opera professionals. Each spring its extensive outreach program with a team of young artists fans across northern New Hampshire and Vermont, enticing children and adults with the marvels of opera. Also, during the off-season, Opera North performs opera scenes in schools and other public venues. This is serious opera, recognized by critics and appreciated by patrons who come from great distances to attend its performances. Participants in Opera North programs have joined major orchestras and opera companies such as the defunct New York City Opera and the Metropolitan Opera. Opera North, which grew out of a community theater group in Thetford, Vermont, has continued for thirty seasons as a communal operation, now with 350 volunteers, performing in Lebanon's opera house as well as other nearby opera houses, including Barre, Vermont.

Not to be outdone by a New Hampshire opera company, Vermont has had several opera companies. The Green Mountain Opera Festival, sponsored by the Green Mountain Cultural Center, is based in the Joslyn Barn in Waitsfield. Founded by Taras Kulish, the Green Mountain Opera Festival each June performs its centerpiece production in the Barre Opera House. Like Opera North, Vermont's program tries to involve the local artistic community as well as visits from well-known professionals such as retired soprano Phyllis Curtin. Aside from full-fledged opera productions, like Rossini's *La Cenerentola* and Britten's *The Rape of Lucretia* in 2014, the festival offers concerts, free master classes, and open rehearsals. An Emerging Artist Program, launched in 2007, provides classes for talented young artists, up to the age of thirty-two, to work with experienced professionals and coaches at no cost. Students can participate in opera concerts as well as take secondary roles in the festival's major opera productions.

In Montpelier, the Vermont Opera Theater has performed since 1984 a variety of operas, operettas, and programs with a wide range of music, from cabaret to classics—and also offers classes and workshops in opera and classical song. Featuring operas produced in both Boston and Montreal, the Vermont Opera Theater's program also has included *Opera Insights with Tavcar* programs, which included Tavcar's discussion of operas and their composers and performers and ended with "mini-concerts" of operas such as *The Barber of Seville, The Elixir of Love,* and *Semele.* Vermont Opera Theater's performances were held originally in the Barre Opera House and later in the Montpelier Unitarian Church. After thirty years of active highly professional performances and programs, the Vermont Opera Theater did not mount any programs in 2014 or 2015.

While Lebanon Opera House's Opera North, the Green Mountain Festival, and the Vermont Opera Theater have concentrated primarily on opera, smaller opera houses do not have that luxury, as their smaller audiences want a variety of entertainment. However, some rural places are now performing opera and even establishing opera companies. Cambridge, New York's Hubbard Hall in 2008 started an opera company, which has been inducted as a professional member of Opera America. Its repertory has included operas like *La traviata* and *Carmen*; initially one was performed each year, but there have been two a year since 2014. Plans for an opera company are also in the works for the restored auditorium in Hudson, New York's opera house. Middlebury, Vermont's Town Hall Theater since 2004 has added opera to its programs with its Opera Company of Middlebury performing works like Bizet's *The Pearl Fishers* as well as offering the Metropolitan Opera's "Live in HD" programs.

With these developments and the popularity of the Met's live HD telecasts, it would seem that serious opera is making a comeback in some opera houses. Ironically, most opera viewers today see the Met telecasts at movie theaters, which were responsible for the death of most nineteenth-century opera houses.[11] But plenty of operagoers can enjoy their own respectable and popular local opera companies. In 2014 there were more than 160 opera companies in all major cities as well as in smaller cities like Sarasota, Florida, Billings, Montana, and Roanoke, Virginia. Many of these companies were organized after the Metropolitan Opera stopped touring in 1986, and more than half have come to life since 1970. Now American opera companies outnumber German and Italian opera companies, despite a lack of state and federal support in the United States. According to a National Endowment for the Arts study, from 1982 to 2002 attendance at these companies' live opera productions grew by almost 50 percent; by 2007, almost as many people attended live opera performances as NFL football games.

Thus, opera has deep roots in America. An interesting feature of today's surge of interest in opera is the experimentation in operas at some regional companies and major opera festivals like Santa Fe's and Cooperstown, New York's Glimmerglass. Not until November 2008 did opera receive the ultimate blessing of the National Endowment for the Arts when it inaugurated its Opera Awards. The first recipients were Leontyne Price, Carlisle Floyd, and Richard Gaddes, and the eighty-one-year-old Leontyne Price, who belted out "God Bless America" at the award ceremony. Another sign of new respect for opera, or at least a recognition that opera singers have powerful voices, is recent sports events where stars have sung the national anthem: Sarasota Opera's tenor Heath Huberg at the Baltimore Orioles' 2013 opening game and the soprano Renee Fleming at Super Bowl XLVIII.

Why this resurgence of interest in opera today? Perhaps because more people are going to college, are exposed to different types of culture, and have more leisure time and disposable income. Captioning technology in opera houses and on television has made opera less intimidating. The advent of high-definition television has enabled the Met to broadcast live Met performances, with behind-the-scenes tours at intermission. These screenings in worldwide locations certainly have also helped to popularize opera. Maybe the all-encompassing nature of opera, with the power of its music, the drama of its plot, and its often extravagant staging and costumes, appeals to those whose senses have been numbed by an overload of electronic media and video games. This popularity may also be due to the amplified emotions in opera such as desire and fulfillment, anxiety, relief, despair and ecstasy, which can reach an almost subverbal realm and capture those who may find chamber music and symphonies dry and abstract.

From the early days when Galileo's father, according to folklore, told stories while strumming his lute, when vagabond troupes performed in town squares, and later when innumerable opera companies and opera houses sprang up in European cities and then in the United States, it would seem that the protean nature of opera has a universal appeal. Dion Boucicault, the energetic nineteenth-century actor, playwright, and manager, may have had it right when he thought that the public wanted sensations. And in today's small-town opera house with its flat floor, opera can be staged in the center of the floor with the audience seated on all sides, making it a more inclusive, involving experience than sitting in a remote balcony looking down on a performance, as in large city opera houses. While these community halls were called "opera houses" in the nineteenth century primarily to give them a veneer of sophistication, today these new opera companies are validating the "opera" in the names of these halls even while some opera houses are transformed into art centers as at Cambridges's Hubbard Hall.

Over the years musicals have remained one of the most popular entertainments for both participants and audiences. Doug Anderson, the manager of Middlebury, Vermont's restored Town Hall, comes to the job with a professional background in acting and directing musicals. In this college town, with Middlebury College's wide menu of concerts, plays, and

The Howard Opera House building, Burlington, Vermont still stands and dominates the city's popular pedestrianized street. Its upper floors, once the opera house, now are offices. *Author photograph*

lectures meeting many of the intellectual needs of the area, the Town Hall offers an alternative of lively culture, entertainment, and community. Its down-home group Made in Vermont, made up of local women, produces a musical evening each year. Ben Morey, ex-manager of the Minden, Nebraska opera house, rather self-consciously said his opera house audiences wanted musicals, like the classic Rodgers and Hammerstein offerings of *Oklahoma* and *Carousel*. Look at the programs of most opera houses in this country today and you will see that musicals have taken the place of yesteryear's moralistic melodramas as popular opera house fare.

The revival of many opera houses and the types of their programs reflect not only local interest but also local talent. When theater professionals manage opera houses, like Benjie White in Cambridge, New York, Mike Thomas in Maysville, Kentucky, and Doug Anderson in Middlebury, Vermont, locally produced quality performances predominate. Other small places such as Minden, Nebraska and Hyde Park, Vermont have benefited from active local theater groups, which have been instrumental in the revival and performances of those halls. The same holds for musical performances. In places such as Lebanon, New Hampshire and Randolph, Vermont, local interest in music combined with local talented musical professionals have helped spur the survival of their opera houses. When such local talent whether musical or theatrical does not exist, managers have to rely more on out-of-town performers.

The fate of opera houses in cities has been particularly precarious. Usually located on prime downtown real estate, the downtown elite—with powerful politicians, developers, and bankers—has sought to replace what seemed like anachronistic opera houses with lucrative new buildings. In only a few cities, such as Lexington, Kentucky, have opera house defenders been successful in retaining their opera houses. Some cities just outgrew their old halls. In Burlington, Vermont, the Howard Opera House building still stands; its exterior, even its street-level stores, look much as they did in 1879, but the building's interior is now divided into offices. It remains a prominent building on the popular, pedestrianized Church Street. In 1879, the Howard Opera House was adequate for the 11,365 residents of Burlington, but now with a city population of 39,000 and a metropolitan population of almost 200,000 it yielded to the 1982 Flynn Center of the Arts, which seats 1,000 and features popular programs like *Man of La Mancha*, performed by out-of-town troupes and stars.

The revival of opera houses has engaged citizens unafraid of daunting tasks with heartening high points and many desperate low points. And after an opera house has been brought back to life, sustaining enthusiasm, funding, staff, and performers is a constant challenge in any size place, but especially in small, remote towns.

CHAPTER 17

Engines for Regeneration

The developers of early opera houses and today's opera house revivers have envisioned them as bringing economic as well as cultural and social benefits to their communities. Yesteryear's developers were often the town's boosters, as in McPherson, Olathe, and Garden City, Kansas. They hoped the new opera houses would bring class and fame to their towns and also make them seem more important than their neighboring towns. These community halls became symbols of civic pride. Even though most opera houses were private ventures, their image and many public activities made them seem like public buildings. The Grand Opera House in Peoria, Illinois, for example, along with the city's new courthouse and Union Depot, made its citizens feel as though they were ready to "look out and speak to the world."[1]

Public pride in these once-grand opera houses, however, slumped as newer types of entertainment and better-equipped halls usurped their place in the public life of a community. For old-timers there were memories of good times at the opera house and shopping at familiar stores with long-known clerks, but for the younger generations those Main Street institutions represented a past era overtaken by new, larger, and more modern institutions, whether the stores at the mall or multiplex movie houses. The small-town sociability of meeting friends and acquaintances while shopping in local stores, or of laughing and crying with friends and neighbors at the varied presentations of the opera house, disappeared in this new era.

It is hard to pinpoint just how and when attitudes changed about the role of opera houses in communities—and the role of Main Street in the life of a town. Certainly historic preservationists were in the forefront of this change, as they left the confines of museums and landmarked buildings for a broader realm that blended social, economic, and cultural factors into their architectural and design concerns. The threat of neglected opera houses being demolished mobilized local preservationists and citizen leaders to protect these cultural halls. The 1977 launch of the Main Street Program of the National Trust for Historic Preservation ("National Trust") by Mary Means in the Trust's Midwest office was well timed for the revitalization of small-town opera houses. This program realized that hoisting new awnings and painting buildings were not enough to transform decaying downtowns. To revitalize these downtowns, economic, social, and political factors have to mesh, and that is what the National Trust's program set about doing. In revitalizing hundreds of Main Streets, this program helped to change the image of historic preservation. The Trust's and specifically its Main Street program's broadened approach to preservation planning certainly helped empower Main Street renewers trying to reverse the downward spiral of downtowns and, in turn, helped empower the pioneers hoping to bring their opera houses back to life as vital civic institutions.[2]

This broadened approach to historic preservation could not have taken place if it had not been for an increasingly vocal reaction to the bland-ness of the man-made world as well as the remoteness of institutions, stores, and innumerable daily transactions with mechanical voices and telephone menus. Gertrude Stein's "there is no there there" expressed what many people felt. Many people drive alone long distances to work, rather than taking trains and buses with neighbors and conductors or bus drivers whom they got to know; others telecommute, losing the random conversations that characterize office life. Shopping takes place out of town on highways lined with vast big-box stores offering deep discounts and little sociability. Entertainment comes to the customer at home via the airwaves or a hand-held machine. Children do not have the ritual of Saturday matinees with their friends, but instead watch DVDs or play video games at home. These are lonely crowds.

For these lonely crowds, it is not surprising that the urge for commu-nal sociability and creativity arises. People like working with others; they enjoy producing musicals or Shakespeare, or playing in a local orchestra or string quartet, or dancing, or fixing up the old stage curtains and operat-ing behind-the-scenes mechanics of an old opera house. And, indeed, the opera house offers opportunities for such communal creative activities with the added benefit of renewing down-at-the heels downtowns.

Town political leaders have rarely been at the forefront in today's opera house revivals. The energy and drive for the changes in attitude toward opera houses often come from single visionaries: Benjie White in Cambridge or Beth Klosterman in David City; or groups of people interested in the vitality and cultural opportunities of their hometowns as in Vergennes, Vermont and Maysville and Lexington, Kentucky. Usually these pioneers were natives, but some efforts were undertaken by outsiders, as in Stonington, Maine who quickly embedded themselves in the community. Sometimes there would be one persevering person; sometimes a community group would initiate the process but then turn it over to a professional, as in Hudson, New York; and sometimes the initiating group would continue the process, as in Vergennes. It was never a straight path, but it was almost always uphill. The vision was clear, but raising funds and arousing public interest have been difficult and lengthy challenges, especially in recent economic downturns. Fremont, Nebraska is trying to get started; Hubbard Hall in Cambridge, New York has been in the process of continuous revival and expansion for thirty years; David City, Nebraska, is struggling to take off thirty years after Beth Klosterman bought the building; and in Kentucky, Maysville has been involved in resuscitating its opera house for more than forty years.

Money is the perennial problem for the restoration and operation of cash-strapped opera houses, especially during hard times or in periods when public funding for the arts or even downtown renewals does not fit the agenda of those who advocate a smaller role for government. Persistence, imagination, and pragmatism are needed. Judy Lloyd, executive director of the Johnson Hall Performing Arts Center in Gardiner, Maine states, "we make it work by grants, town economic development funds, memberships, annual appeal, rentals, tickets and tuitions, concession sales, and the very important business sponsorships."[3]

Public funding sources are essential, but limited. Bicentennial funds were responsible for spurring many opera house revivers as in Enosburgh Falls, Vermont and Cambridge, New York. The history of a town and its institutions then attracted local public attention and the celebration of its past evolved into a public priority. The opera house, fortunately, climbed on the bandwagon of local patriotism. Grants for feasibility studies from the National Endowment for the Arts (NEA) helped in the early stages of many restoration projects as they not only provided needed money for an important first step but also validated the efforts of the volunteers as worthy public projects. These NEA grants, though often small, have been vitally important in other phases of opera house operations, not only for direct funds but also in attracting other public and private support.

In many states such as Vermont, the state arts councils have been critical supporters of opera house projects at different stages. Opera house renewers have benefited from early help from state historic preservation offices as well as from the National Park Service's historic preservation division. And grants from unlikely agencies have been discovered. Lead, South Dakota, for example, received a grant and large loan from the US Department of Agriculture's rural development agency for the purchase and restoration of its Homestake Opera House. For opera house renewers, local and regional foundations should be the first place to search for assistance, but they are usually more numerous in urban areas.

Tax policy changes have given new life to historic preservation efforts. Before 1976, the federal tax code benefited those who tore down historic buildings to replace them with something new rather than those who saved historic buildings. In 1976 that tax benefit was turned around, so the tax code has included tax credits up to 20 percent on the rehabilitation of historic commercial buildings meeting the standards of the National Register of Historic Places. This program, run by the National Park Service, the Internal Revenue Service, and state historic preservation officers, has placed no limit on the amount of credits claimed and is used as a credit against income tax liability, not a deduction. Some states have similar rehabilitation tax credits and also tax credits for state income taxes, which have been an invaluable help in the restoration of historic buildings, including opera houses. In 2004 the Historic Theatre Financing Fund, which makes millions of dollars in equity investments, was initiated by the League of Historic American Theatres with the National Trust Community Investment Corporation specifically for theater and opera house restoration. Though complicated and best handled by financially savvy professionals, this program helped historic theaters and opera houses obtain federal and state tax credits, which could then be converted into cash or equity to assist in financing restorations. Unfortunately, this promising fund was dissolved in 2008.

Whatever route opera house resuscitators take, local public support is basic for successful restoration and operation, and that requires adroit public relations, savvy politics, and diplomacy, especially in the early days when initial plans often are met with skepticism. Visible progress in the physical restoration of an opera house—a repaired roof or just scaffolding on the building—as well as inexpensive community-geared programs can help to convince the public that opera house promoters are serious and even effective. Success breeds success.

The energy and enthusiasm involved in reviving opera houses can be contagious. Even large cities herald their new theaters much as the early opera house developers did in the nineteenth century. In Philadelphia, ex-Mayor John F. Street, not known for his artistic inclinations, declared in 2007 that art and culture make a city work when he saw the benefits of many cultural institutions, among them the glitzy Suzanne Roberts Theater in a section of Broad Street now called the Avenue of the Arts. Such districts where artistic activities have clustered add a "cultural buzz" to a place, according to geographers like Elizabeth Currid of the University of Southern California, who mapped such buzzed districts throughout the country. Inspired by the work of Richard Florida, a scholar promoting the benefits of the cultural class on civic development, Currid has culled information from contemporary sources such as Twitter and Flickr.[4] For large cities, the "cultural buzz" of theaters, often with millions of dollars of local and state support, is injecting much-needed new life in their downtowns, many in serious trouble. Whether Pittsburgh, Tampa, or Cleveland, major cities are finding their theaters a linchpin in their new and popular downtown arts/cultural districts. And architects are coming aboard this bandwagon. Prize-winning architect Renzo Piano, designer of Paris's Pompidou Center and New York's new Whitney Museum, believes in the power of cultural institutions. He sees concert halls, libraries, and museums as "places where people share values, where they stay together"; in fact, for him this is the "civic role of architecture."[5]

In Newark, New Jersey, the New Jersey Performing Arts Center (NJPAC), which opened in 1997, has brought new energy to this city after many down decades. In fact, the success of the center has emboldened NJPAC to launch an ambitious development project on the eight acres not used by the center on its twelve-acre site. This project, a high-rise tower with residential units and retail space to be run by the NJPAC Development Corporation, is envisioned as providing economic opportunities to the city as well as an alternative source of income to the center. Besides this new tower opening in spring 2015, many other changes are occurring in the downtown area near the NJPAC. Military Park, a neglected park across the street from the center, has been restored and now is managed by New York's Bryant Park management group. The city's old and long-dormant department store building, Hayne's, is being rehabilitated for retail and residences, with Rutgers University taking space for arts programs and Whole Foods on the ground-floor retail space.

Prudential Financial (formerly Prudential Insurance Company) is reaffirming its century-old loyalty to Newark by building yet another large building downtown. These new additions to downtown Newark, certainly benefiting from NJPAC's presence and initiatives, combined with existing downtown cultural institutions such as the Newark Museum, the Newark Public Library, and the New Jersey Historical Society, create an impressive cultural center. Newark's popular ex-mayor, Cory A. Booker, noted that such an arts and cultural center can be a force in the creation of economic opportunity and, importantly, can help make Newark an arts capital. Luring more people to downtown Newark looms as a high-priority goal for the city. In fact, Newark leaders hope the arts center will be the Piazza Navona of Newark with round-the-clock activities including restaurants, galleries, and cafes.

In upstate New York, which brings to mind a belt of faded cities from Buffalo to Albany, Rochester is coping with some wrenching downturns after one of its major economic engines, Eastman Kodak, declared bankruptcy in 2012. With careful economic planning, entrepreneurial public/private partnerships, and academic and cultural institutions, Rochester is bucking the unemployment crisis. Kodak's 60,000-person workforce in 1982 is down to less than 7,000, but many of Kodak's highly skilled former employees, other technical workers, and many graduates of Rochester's educational institutions are infusing new economic life into the area as they start diverse business ventures. Public and private agencies such as Greater Rochester Enterprise, a regional economic development organization, has been behind these entrepreneurial efforts. The Eastman School of Music, now part of the University of Rochester, the Rochester Philharmonic, and the International Museum of Photography at George Eastman House, have been lures in attracting people to the area as well as retaining long-term residents.

The intellectual and cultural vibrancy of the area—a citywide buzzed area with deep roots—results in large part from the remarkable philanthropy and social conscience of George Eastman, the founder of Eastman Kodak. Among the institutions that Eastman started and supported were the Eastman School of Music and the Rochester Philharmonic Orchestra. He was also a major benefactor of the Mechanics Institute, now the Rochester Institute of Technology.[6] However, a lasting and less tangible philanthropy for Rochester was his progressive policies toward the employees at Kodak, such as a profit-sharing plan for each employee. Today, as Rochester tackles its economic problems, George Eastman's legacy of institutions, cultural amenities, and progressive policies provides a comprehensively buzzed district, which now is helping Rochester cope in difficult times.

These buzzed districts are not just in cities with well-known cultural institutions, but in cities and towns of all sizes with different goals, programs, and audiences. In smaller places the impact of a cultural district is equally important to that community. Schenectady, New York, a mid-sized city near Albany with a population of 62,000, is promoting culture to stimulate interest in education, economic development, and civic engagement. Philip Morris, director of Schenectady's Proctor Theater, who had already galvanized a cultural district in Jamestown, New York, sees this effort benefiting the quality of life not only in Schenectady but also in the greater Albany area.

Another mid-sized city whose arts program reaches beyond its inner city is Lancaster, Pennsylvania, sixty miles west of Philadelphia, with a population of 55,000. Usually associated with the Pennsylvania Dutch culture and its well-known farmers' market, Lancaster has recognized the arts as an economic "driver." After completing a strategic plan analyzing the educational, promotional, and community benefits of an arts "hub," LancasterARTS, a coalition of twenty-two art institutions, was created in 2007 to establish a citywide cultural program. Included in this program are chamber music, dance, singing, opera groups, the Lancaster Symphony, and the thriving Fulton Opera House, which has a long and established place in the city's cultural life. Founded in 1852 as a community hall for the town's civic, social, and entertainment needs, with performers like Norwegian Ole Bull, the opera house was rebuilt in 1873 and renamed the Fulton Opera House for its native son, the steamboat inventor Robert Fulton. For fifty years, many well-known actors, from the Drews and Barrymores to Alfred Lunt and Helen Hayes, appeared there when plays from New York and Philadelphia stopped in Lancaster before going on the road. Interest in theater continues in the renovated Fulton Opera House, which meets Equity standards with state-of-the-art technology. A 2009 report noted that 30 percent of the population attended theater in Lancaster. As the varied arts programs attract increasing numbers of patrons from both the city and county, they also add over a thousand jobs in arts-related organizations and pump $36 million into arts-related events, including classes, art purchases, parking, shopping, and restaurants. Recognizing the importance of the arts to the civic and

Lancaster, Pennsylvania's Fulton Opera House, with a statue of native son Robert Fulton in recessed window above the marquee. The Symphony offices are next door and Lancaster's famous Central Market is across the street. *Author photograph*

cultural life of the city and region, the City of Lancaster's Promotion Department in 2013 took over LancasterARTS' initiatives.

In small towns with few cultural institutions, the opera house can provide a welcome "cultural buzz" in uplifting down-at-the-heels downtowns and regions. Usually prominent buildings with distinctive architecture, these renovated halls are a source of enormous pride and economic benefits. As they lure other artistic ventures such as galleries, studios, and artists' housing, they form a critical mass of cultural activities, which in turn can attract restaurants and other businesses, just as in larger places. In small towns with second-floor opera houses, the ground floor, formerly used for commercial businesses, now may house galleries exhibiting the work of local artists and craftspeople as in Minden, Nebraska and Cambridge, New York. In other places the opera houses have expanded their operations by purchasing adjacent buildings, as the hamlet of Green Lake, Wisconsin did for its opera house's offices and the Ringling Theater in Baraboo, Wisconsin did for an art gallery, café, and offices. In David City, Nebraska, the Thorpe Opera House is planned as a first-class performing arts facility and the centerpiece of a planned community arts district referred to as "the Thorpe." The building adjacent to the opera house will house the local history center, Horacek Heritage Center, the Chamber of Commerce offices, meeting and banquet spaces; and the ongoing Boston Studio Project, a large collection of archivally preserved negatives of Butler County images. Located across from the Butler County Courthouse, "the Thorpe" is seen as an effort to preserve the history and culture of the area as well as to establish a cornerstone in downtown development.

Renovation/revitalization projects for most opera houses and adjacent buildings have not come easily. Local politicians and local residents as well as foundations, government agencies, and other funding sources have to be persuaded of the significance of such renovations. Strategic planning is essential in making the case for renovation. How and when can a theater renovation spur downtown revitalization? For Kennedy Smith, former director of the National Trust for Historic Preservation's Main Street Program, former executive director of the League of Historic American Theatres, and now a principal in the Community Land Use and Economics Group, the key to success lies in creating an inviting economic environment that provides a comfort zone to prospective investors:

> I do think that theatre rehabilitation is often a catalytic element in downtown revitalization—but only after a certain amount of revitalization has already occurred. Lenders and equity investors must feel relatively secure about their investments in theatre rehabilitation, and the physical environment must be perceived as reasonably safe before people are generally willing to patronize a restored theatre—so there has to be some basic revitalization activity before theatre rehabilitation is feasible. After that basic level of economic and physical improvement, a theatre rehabilitation can significantly accelerate further district revitalization activity.[7]

Newberry, South Carolina is a place where things were done right. The 1881 Newberry Opera House is often called the city's mythological phoenix as its renovation in the 1990s has spurred a considerable economic

Newberry, South Carolina's successful opera house hosts performances by well-known national entertainers. *Newberry Opera House*

resuscitation and physical rehabilitation of Newberry's downtown as well as a boost to its community pride.

In 1880, with a town population of only 2,342, Newberry approved by an 80 percent vote the expenditure of $30,000 for the construction of a town hall/opera house. Its opera house was not an all-purpose, flat-floored hall where school basketball games could be played, but a theater with permanently raked seats. Newberry and its opera house flourished in the late nineteenth and early twentieth centuries, when four cotton mills hummed with activity, but then, like many Southern towns, it was hard hit by the Depression, textile plant closings, and ensuing economic problems. Newberry by the 1980s found its downtown deserted and its buildings deteriorating, including the Newberry Opera House, last used as a movie theater in 1952.

The initiative to restore the Newberry Opera House came from private citizens, including women who barricaded it to prevent its demolition in 1948 and then from Dr. James E. Wiseman, who as chairman of the Newberry Opera House Foundation raised early support of $100,000 from his Newberry High School classmates and local business leaders. The foundation was fortunate to be able to sell its former office space to the city for its administrative offices, previously located on the first floor of the opera house. That sale jump started the campaign to renovate the opera house, which was announced at the opening of its doors in May 1992.

After a feasibility study was undertaken, an able and energetic arts administrator, Deborah Smith, was hired in 1992. Then things started to accelerate: grants came in, consultants were engaged, and the $5 million renovation project was begun in 1996. Another $1 million was needed for the initial operating and miscellaneous costs. With over $3 million raised from private foundations, corporations, and state and federal agencies, the Newberry City Council approved the development plan and leased the opera house and fire station to the foundation. A sophisticated plan for funding was launched. A $3.2 million tax increment revenue bond issued in 1998 by the city was critical to financing the opera house's renovation. A pledge of the revenues of the foundation and a mortgage on the building were necessary, with the security of payments from the foundation to the city, tax revenues from the redevelopment project area, and the mortgage on the opera house. This all-important tax increment financing, which sounds like a straightforward business arrangement, involved careful planning and strategies to be certain that the tax increment revenues would be available for the long haul. The hospitality/accommodation fees from new restaurants, bars, and hotels, all spurred by the revitalized opera house, have added considerable revenue to meet the city's long-term debt.

While the Newberry Opera House is an example of remarkable benefits of a revived opera house for a town's downtown, the road to its success was not without innumerable financial and political challenges. Fundraising and maintaining comfortable relations with the city council have been perpetual challenges. Yet with the conversion of the adjacent firehouse into a conference center and the development of additional nearby housing, the Newberry Opera House Foundation is trying to sustain its early momentum and to spread its benefits beyond the immediate downtown, a daunting challenge for any opera house or arts facility.

The success of this 426-seat opera house is largely due to effective planning, renovation, and programming. With interstate highway access making it possible to draw audiences from Columbia and Greenville, this small city, with a population of 10,000 in 2000, saw the possibility of providing a first-class theater that would meet Equity standards. The physical renovations were extensive: the configuration of the seating was not altered, but the stage was doubled in size, spacious dressing rooms provided, a hydraulic pit installed, and $1 million invested in lighting and sound equipment. With this upgrading and savvy management, the opera house now has a schedule of 250 performances a year by well-known performers such as Arlo Guthrie, Jimmy Webb, and the Oak Ridge Boys, as well as the Moisev Classical Ballet, the Vienna Choir Boys, the New York Gilbert and Sullivan Players, and the New Christy Minstrels. Without a resident theater group, a small place such as Newberry is dependent on traveling entertainers. However, their programs also include performances by local groups, such as concerts by the Newberry County Civic Orchestra and plays by Newberry College theater groups. Clearly the enthusiasm of the community for their opera house and its programs and performers is evident not only in sold-out performances but also in the participation of the opera house's 400 volunteers. As its administrator Deborah Smith said, "it works."[8]

Lexington, Kentucky, an established theater city, provides a different cultural buzz story, one in which its well-known opera house has become part of a major downtown convention center development project. With its 210-year history of interest in live theater, it is not surprising that the city has had two new opera houses, two remodelings, and one major reconstruction from 1850 to today. Ever since Luke Usher's theater opened in 1808, the city has had a "theater district" off and on near the current Lexington Center and Lexington Opera House.

Despite fires, threats of demolition, reuses, depressions, and many changes of ownership, the opera house kept coming back to life. The 700-seat opera house at Main and Broadway, which opened in 1850, was

Lexington's first significant opera house, attracting well-known actors such as Edwin Booth, entertainers like Tom Thumb and his dwarfs, and famous plays such as Bulwer-Lytton's *Lady of Lyons*. Opera house performances, which continued even during the Civil War, were increasingly popular in the 1870s and 1880s, benefiting local restaurants and hotels as Lexingtonians and out-of-town tourists enjoyed their evenings at the Opera House.

Lexington's opera house was destroyed by fire in January 1886, but by July 1887 a new opera house—"one of the costliest, handsomest and most convenient Thespian temples in the South"—appeared at 143 Broadway. Designed by Chicago architect Oscar Cobb, the opera house was opulent and comfortable, with upholstered chairs with holders for hats, canes, and umbrellas, and welcome cool air cool from the nearby ice factory.[9] Modern inventions were introduced such as a fireproofing system, whereby water pressure could quickly flood the theater, 250 gaslights, and an Edison light board. The building itself came in two parts, a four-story stage area, equipped for every sort of scenic effect, thirty-seven sets of scenery, a drop curtain, and a three-story auditorium with two balconies and many boxes. And its acoustics were touted as superb.

Under different owners, but with Charles Scott as manager for over three decades, the opera house continued to flourish until the late 1910s, with road shows and many Broadway plays and actors often stopping en route to Louisville or Cincinnati. In 1921 the state fire marshal ordered the opera house closed due to insufficient exits, and for two years it became an automotive facility, storing cars in the theater. A gas station and tire store used its Broadway frontage. In 1923 its owner, Charles Berryman, and its manager, Harrison Scott, managed to incorporate the New Lexington Opera House Company with the support of a hundred Lexingtonians and to remodel the theater so the opera house could function again—but not for long. By 1930, it was sold at auction, and for more than twenty-five years it persisted primarily as a movie house with ever-changing owners.

After yet another remodeling in 1955, its life was threatened with a demolition permit in 1961.Only the adjacent laundry was torn down, so the opera house survived. Another remodeling was proposed in 1970, but never materialized, so for the next few years the then-roofless building was battered by winds and rain. Yet that was not the end.

The next chapter involves big-time redevelopment by the Lexington Center Corporation, which created a downtown convention center with

The new entrance to Lexington, Kentucky's long established 1886 opera house and a band concert at the opera house in 2013. *Entrance: Author photograph; band concert: Paul Hooper/ Lexington Opera House*

a 23,500-seat sports arena. In 1974, this corporation bought the opera house, only a block from the convention center, in a complicated negotiation with the Lexington Council of Arts and then launched a major renovation of the opera house, completed in 1976. Aside from virtually rebuilding the opera house, there was an attempt to retain its former ambience: the stage was rebuilt to the old dimensions, and the old seating arrangement was kept. However, another floor was added for a rehearsal area, and more space was provided for a dance studio, modern dressing rooms, and a totally new entrance on the side of the building. Now the opera house is part of Lexington's revitalized downtown, an added amenity for conventiongoers and a renewed cultural venue for Lexingtonians. As a quasi-public institution now with a 501(c)(4) tax status, which limits it from receiving some grants, the Opera House Fund, with 501(c)(3) status, has raised more than $10 million for specific projects and an endowment for the opera house as well as support for local art groups. Concerts, children's theater, local musical productions, live Broadway performances such as *The Belle of Amherst* starring Julie Harris, and Emlyn Williams impersonating Charles Dickens have kept the opera house alive and well as a respected cultural institution, even though Lexington now has many competitive college, dinner, and amateur theaters.

In many cities, this opera house would have long since fallen to the wrecking ball. Denver's Grand Opera House, by comparison, was replaced by a massive shopping center and hotel complex whose only recognition of the former cultural center was its name: the Tabor Center. Denver's convention center, similar to Lexington's and many cities' at that time, obliterated all traces of the old opera house. There is not even a commemorative plaque. That Lexington's opera house survives today is a testament to the endurance of its long theatrical heritage and the perseverance of residents and the initiatives of city officials in recognizing the significance of this cultural institution to the city and the role it could play in late-twentieth-century downtown redevelopment.

In small places, sustaining opera houses and luring entertainers and audiences remains a constant challenge. An opera house in a city like Lexington or Philadelphia can fit into an existing critical mass of cultural institutions and activities. In a town of 2,000, the opera house is often an isolated cultural institution. In the nineteenth century, energetic opera house managers would knit together a circuit of opera houses to attract superior troupes and entertainers as well as hearty

Horace Tabor's Grand Opera House in Denver, Colorado built in 1881, replaced in 1964 by Tabor Center, a large mall-office complex. Top photo: *L.C McClure, Denver / Library of Congress LC-USZ62-116142;* bottom photo: *Author photograph*

audiences. Today, few are part of a regional network; most are isolated local multiart centers. In fact, competition between facilities in nearby towns can impede regional networking. West Virginia's historic theater trail offers an innovative alternative.[10] The state's public and private preservation agencies, convinced that cultural tourism could benefit both the preservation and use of the buildings, chose twenty-six diverse theaters located in every section of the state for its Historic Theatre Trail. Funded with the federal government's Preserve America grants, this Trail includes a range of theaters from small-town opera houses to downtown movie palaces to suburban 1950s drive-ins, reflecting the changes in entertainment venues during the twentieth century.

Two opera houses, located in very different parts of the state, follow the same life story as most opera houses. In Charles Town, a West Virginia town now popular with Washingtonians for second homes and weekend visits, its 1910 opera house in a two-story attached brick building withstood wars, the Depression, and radio. By 1948, this 500-seat opera house with a curved balcony, fly space, orchestra pit, and proscenium stage was unable to survive as an entertainment space. It was dark until 1973, when the building was donated to a local theater group that renovated it and reopened it in 1976 as the Old Opera House. Two years later it was listed on the National Register of Historic Places. Since the reopening the popular attractions at the opera house continue to be stage performances, children's programs, art classes, and shows.

Marlinton, another West Virginia opera house town, is deep in a forested area of the state. Its opera house, built in 1910 after the railroad came to Pocahontas County, served as an all-purpose hall. The new rail line could export the county's timber to distant markets and also bring traveling entertainers to the county's previously isolated residents. Plays, lectures, musicals, and minstrel shows took place in the hall along with roller skating, basketball, and religious services. The Pocahontas Opera House, a formidable three-story building built of reinforced concrete with three arched doorways on the first floor, towers over the rest of the town. Its small, intimate performance space and horseshoe-shaped balcony seats 250 people. Its early life was short as J. G. Tilton, its developer and publisher of the local newspaper, sold the building in 1914 when the lumber business crashed and he ran into serious financial problems, similar to the situation of Horace Tabor and his downfall with the silver bust. For a long period a car dealership and lumber warehouse occupied the building. In 1991 the Historic Landmarks Commission of Pocahontas

County bought the opera house, raised $5 million, and resurrected the building with community support. By 1999 it was again a performance hall for Pocahontas County. Today, along with community events such as an annual craft fair, family movie nights, and school programs, the hall is active on weekends with bluegrass bands, entertainers, jam sessions, and concerts. It is alive again as "the cultural heart of the community," the opera house's motto.

The Pocahontas Opera House is on the state's Historic Theatre Trail and also on the West Virginia Music Trail and Appalachian Waters Scenic Byway. It is not often that cultural institutions are allied with environmental projects, so partnering with the Appalachian Waters Scenic Byway indicates that Marlinton has an ecumenical approach to its cultural assets. The success of this hall is also due to broad support from residents and businesses in the county as well as the county's historic preservation officer B. J. Gudmundsson.

Among the revived movie theaters, drive-ins, and converted churches on the trail is Carnegie Hall in Lewisburg, near the fashionable Greenbrier Hotel in White Sulphur Springs. Now referred to as a music hall, Carnegie Hall was built in 1902 with a Carnegie grant as the auditorium for the Lewisburg Female Institute. Lewisburg resident James Laing, who grew up in the same town in Scotland as Andrew Carnegie, used that connection to successively persuade Carnegie to donate to the construction of classrooms and an auditorium for the school. The handsome Greek Revival building with an Ionic-order portico was taken over after the school closed in 1972 by the Greenbrier Learning Center. In the 1980s, after the center closed, a new nonprofit organization, Carnegie Hall, Inc., was organized to convert the entire building into a regional arts and education center. After over a $3 million renovation, Carnegie Hall became an active performance center hosting well-known performers like Harry Belafonte, the Celtic Tenors, Suzanne Vega, and the revived Glenn Miller Orchestra.

The variety of performance halls on this historic Theatre Trail and the continuum of entertainment history that they represent are remarkable. But perhaps most remarkable is the communal creative energy charging the revival of these halls in remote small towns in the Allegheny Mountains and elsewhere in the state. This West Virginia multitown trail shows how cultural tourism can help single performing halls gain greater visibility and better patronage by joining together with other theaters on a themed trail. With increasing leisure, more elderly people free to travel, and new interest in close-to-home cultural exploring, such a theater trail could be developed in many regions and states.

Whether in a small mountain town in West Virginia or a larger place like Lexington, Kentucky, restoring and operating an opera house is a formidable and continuous challenge. Small, remote towns where most opera houses are located do not have the plump community foundations or local corporations for financial assistance available in cities. Therefore, opera houses in such places need to distinguish themselves as especially interesting or unique to attract public attention. It could be a theme like musical theater at the Goodspeed Opera House in East Haddam, Connecticut, opera in Central City, Colorado, or music at the Chandler Music Hall in Randolph, Vermont. Focusing on cultural and heritage tourism provides another way of publicizing an opera house or series of opera houses, as in West Virginia's historic theater, or through a historic association like Willa Cather and Red Cloud, Nebraska. Regional themes for opera house trails abound: mill towns in New England, pioneers and immigrants in the Midwest, mining towns in the Rockies, and river towns along the Hudson. Even single opera houses with a unique setting like the Haskell Opera House on the Canadian-United States border, distinguishing architecture as in Menomonie, Wisconsin, or elaborate theaters like native son Al. Ringling's in Baraboo, Wisconsin can be tourist attractions for a town or region. Many places may not have such distinctive features or attractions, but have developed a critical mass of performances and cultural activities. They then can reach a broader audience. To survive, the small opera house has to reach beyond its town, as Newberry, South Carolina has proven so successfully.

The restoration of the opera house building itself can attract early public attention and prove to the naysayers that the opera house supporters' intentions were carried out. "It says yes to the future," noted Sara Garonzik, the artistic producing director of Philadelphia's Suzanne Roberts Theater. The Tibbits Opera House in Coldwater, Michigan treated its restoration work as a "yes to the future" project with its effective publicity. Through videos, large posters, and news coverage, Tibbits informed the public of its stunning progress in stripping off the opera house's inappropriate veneer and then restoring its original façade.

Such physical changes are dramatic, but the ever-important infrastructure projects like new plumbing, air conditioning, and meeting requirements of the Americans with Disabilities Act (ADA) (such as elevators) seem rather humdrum. Sara Garonzik worries about everyday sustenance of an arts institution. "Keeping up a theater has the same sex appeal as repairing old bridges."[11] That is the challenge for all cultural institutions and districts. The behind-the-scenes sweat labor, donated services, and hundreds of volunteers' efforts do not make the headlines, but they are essential to the functioning of every opera house. For the opera house managers, sustaining a community's interest, attracting funding, and mobilizing programs to appeal to a range of interests remain constant concerns. Media support has always been essential. In the early days of opera houses, newspaper editors were a community's major promoter for opera houses, urging a town to have an opera house, fussing when construction seemed delayed, and then wallowing in pride when the opera house finally opened. Today with so many different media options for publicity, incredibly diverse cultural and community programs, and many local volunteers, the small-town opera house can be an engine for Main Street regeneration.

CHAPTER 18

Like Family

Fueling the enthusiasm for renewing opera houses are the many connections that take place in live performances between actors and audiences—and also among actors and other performers. Live performances, whether plays, magic shows, or concerts, involve the audience with the immediate happenings on stage. In contrast to movies or recordings, where the audience is presented with a completed project, live performances are works in progress with the actors and audience participating and interacting. "Only a living human being," Willa Cather observed, "in some sort of rapport with us, speaking the lines, can make us forget who we are and where we are, can make us (especially children) actually live in the story that is going on before us, can make the dangers of the heroine and the desperation of that hero much more important to us, for the time much dearer to us, than our own lives."[1]

With live productions, moreover, there is often the unexpected—the improvisations, the missed line, and the added bit. Jack Burton, who acted for many years in Broadway musicals, remembered his childhood years in Aurora, Illinois, where he enjoyed melodramas, minstrel shows, operettas, and lectures at the Coulter Opera House and later at the Grand Opera House. When movies came, he missed the dialogue, the punch lines, and the spontaneity that was such an important part of live drama. The early movies were like peep shows to him, as they seemed remote; they were missing the human warmth of direct engagement and empathy. Even with stars and spectacular scenery, movies never provided that immediate engagement and spontaneity of the traveling troupes' plays at the Coulter Opera House of his childhood.

The face-to-face dramatization of everyday life and the interaction possible in live performances enabled people to escape from their daily lives and express hidden emotions. That could occur in small places, like Willa Cather's Red Cloud, Horace Tabor's Leadville, or "out-of the-way" theaters, as actress Minnie Maddern Fiske reported. Fiske, in warning high-culture actors and critics about their patronizing attitudes, remembered that "one of the most stirring performances I ever witnessed was in a little German theater out West."[2] The same engagement, spontaneity, and interaction that stirred audiences also kept actors—theater troupes, community theaters, and repertory groups—performing over the years.

In the early days audiences were almost participants in plays as they vociferously made their emotions known by jeering, mocking, and applauding. Joseph Jefferson commented that those audience chastisements, if he missed a line, kept him on his toes. Because many in the audience knew the lines to plays, especially Shakespeare's, they would not hesitate to correct wavering actors. On the other hand, most actors, and certainly stars such as Edwin Booth and Sarah Bernhardt, thrived on audience approval. When the folksinger Odetta ended her November 1991 concert with "Amazing Grace" at Randolph, Vermont's Chandler Hall, she asked the audience to join in singing with her. The response from this music-loving crowd, with its Randolph Singers who fell into four-part harmony, moved Odetta to tears.

For Charles Dickens, bonding with audiences was what he so enjoyed in his public readings. His readings gave him a welcome opportunity for a two-way, face-to-face communication with the audience. After months of writing and talking to himself, as writers do, Dickens found his fictions, which were so real to him, came alive as he shared them with his audiences. Heartened by the bond that he established with his listeners, Dickens, at his last reading in New York, expressed this appreciation of his listeners: "I shall never recall you as a mere public audience, but rather as a host of personal friends."[3]

Whether Dickens or a troupe of traveling actors spending a week at an opera house, these performers became part of the place where they were performing. They established a temporary sense of community. When Hampton, Iowa native Fred Oney Sweet reminisced about his local opera house, he remembered the touring actors being embedded in his town during their engagement. "Our romantic hero and heroines walked out streets, breathed our air, ate our food. They were not strips of celluloid packed tightly in tin boxes shipped to us from across the continent."[4] They became temporary citizens of Hampton. Cora Chandler Mueller, who lived behind the Mineral Point, Wisconsin Opera House in the 1920s, recalls chatting with visiting Broadway touring troupes when she was a youngster. Like Willa Cather and many children in opera house towns, waiting for troupes to arrive and then seeing them wander around their hometown streets were thrills. Mueller particularly remembered actress Madge Sigel, who seemed "a lovely, gracious lady with a pink-and-white complexion and brown wavy hair done in the latest style. As a child, when I saw her walking on our little street so graceful and all, I thought a princess had stepped out of a page of a fairy tale book."[5] This sense of intimacy with audiences and the public seems ironic at a time when performers sometimes suffered the stigma of being social outcasts and purveyors of immorality.

Actors have connected not only with audiences and townspeople but also with one another while performing. Their collaborative creative work, often lasting months and years, bonds them into a community. In the nineteenth and early twentieth centuries, actors bonded with fellow actors as they traveled for weeks on end performing in town after town. Their professional bonds became even more solidly cemented as they defended themselves from early Puritan attacks, followed by intermittent censuring, the Syndicates, and underlying public attitudes about their rootless, "loose" lifestyles. "It was like family," as an actor from the 1920s recalled. Of course, some early theater troupes were, in fact, literally family. The extended, well-known Drew family, which included Mr. and Mrs. John Drew, their son John, and their daughter Georgiana, who married Maurice Barrymore, acted in and managed important theaters in both New York and Philadelphia throughout the nineteenth and early twentieth centuries. The Drakes were a less well known but intrepid thespian family who set off from Albany, New York in the early nineteenth century. Samuel Drake, with his wife, who died en route, three sons, and two daughters, floated down the Ohio River to perform in the welcoming South. An even larger family, the Andrews clan, included brothers, sisters, wives, husbands, and many children in their late-nineteenth-century traveling musical ventures in Minnesota. They started as a vocal group, added a cornet band and Swiss bells, and finally grew to present grand opera in English at moderate prices. The New Hampshire Hutchinsons, consisting of Jesse Hutchinson and his eleven sons and daughters, sang their moralistic music as a family group in the mid-nineteenth century. George Howard's Troy (New York) Museum achieved national fame with *Uncle Tom's Cabin*, thanks to the talented performances of his family, including himself, his wife Caroline, his daughter Cordelia, and his cousin George Aiken. In an earlier company, Howard's mother-in-law and three brothers-in-law had also been members. But probably Joseph Jefferson's seven generations of actors holds the record for a theatrical dynasty.

While dynasties of many theatrical families were responsible for much early theater in this country, most troupes or theater productions since the late nineteenth century have been nonbiological families. "Theatrical productions create such strange, intense ad hoc communities, families really, no less effective for being short-lived," comments actor and playwright Ellen McLaughlin, who played the angel in Tony Kushner's *Angels in America*. Collaborations have long fascinated McLaughlin, as she has found them to form "even in unlikely groups." Staging a reading of *The Trojan Women* with refugees from different sides of the conflict in the former Yugoslavia, none of whom were actors, in a New York theater in the 1990s, McLaughlin found that even these participants, "several of whom were people who would have crossed the street to avoid each other in any other circumstance," bonded while performing together. They not only shared the stage, "but often times shared the same part—the roles being played by more than one actor." It seemed incredible that "despite enormous resistance and countless obstacles, the actors bonded and formed a company by the time they were acting together."[6]

Such bonding occurs in troupe after troupe, whether acting, dancing, or singing. "When you are in an opera, it means working very hard and a lot, so you become a mini-family," Christina Scheppelmann, the artistic and production director at Barcelona's Liceu opera house, noted after the death of two of the company's singers in the shocking suicide plane crash in the French Alps in March 2015.[7] The benefits of such shared experiences in singing or acting are keenly felt by the individual performer. For Peter Judd, his acting in New York has been a "joint endeavor and the focus that comes when there is a live audience."[8] When Debbie Weil, an author, digital publisher, and board member of the Stonington Opera House, was given a chance to act in a play at the opera house, she was exhilarated by the trust and camaraderie of the players, stagehands, and director.[9]

For many music and theater groups, this bonding has provided more than interpersonal benefits: it has involved them in the active operation of their halls. The Randolph Singers, who overwhelmed Odetta, have been a bonded group as well as the backbone of the Chandler Music Hall. And in Maysville, Kentucky and Hyde Park, Vermont, the Maysville Players and Lamoille County Players not only campaigned to save their opera houses but also became their owners. Many groups like Minden, Nebraska's Community Players actively participated in the planning and restoration of their local opera houses.

Around seven thousand community theaters exist today in the United States, according to the American Association of Community Theatre (AACT). As to why such groups organized and survive, the major reason is that "theatre meets needs," according to Julie Angelo of AACT. "People will create theatre wherever they are." But establishing "a formal theatre group depends upon a nucleus of dedicated people" and its survival rests on "the ability of those people to motivate others to become involved as volunteers and supporters."[10] Amateur theater groups have had a long history, but it was not until the end of the nineteenth century that such groups were organized, among them the Concord Players in Massachusetts with Louisa May Alcott; the Aurora Drama Guild in Illinois; and the oldest continuously producing community theater, the Footlight Club, founded in 1877 in Jamaica Plain, Massachusetts. The Irish Players' US tour in 1911 has been credited with stirring interest in amateur theater groups as a reaction to the poor quality of American commercial theater. And, indeed, several noncommercial theater groups were formed: the Washington Square Players in 1914, later the Theatre Guild; the Provincetown Players, where Eugene O'Neill played, in 1915; and the still-operating Neighborhood Playhouse in New York City. In some metropolitan areas, the early community theaters have morphed into professional theater groups: the Cleveland Playhouse, the Pittsburgh Playhouse, and the Pasadena Playhouse.

Puppetry, another type of performance, often mistakenly considered only for children's amusement, is increasingly popular with all ages throughout the country and around the globe—and it appears in opera houses. The life-size horse puppets produced by the South African Hardspring Puppet Company for the play *War Horse* awakened international attention to the power and artistry of puppetry. After premiering in London in 2007, the play continues to tour the world, and has been seen by millions. In the United States puppet companies using puppets, marionettes, masks, stilts, and giant figures perform a wide range of shows in theaters, schools, barns, outdoors, and even on television. Some puppeteers are nationally known like the late Jim Henson and his Muppets but most are local and regional companies that tour and also sponsor workshops, study programs, and residencies. Some have been in existence for many decades, such as Peter Schumann's Bread and Puppet Theater, which originated in 1963 on New York City's Lower East Side but is now based in Glover, Vermont. This company uses the primitive power of puppets to imaginatively probe political issues such as the Vietnam War and social conditions such as alienation. In May 2014, Bread and Puppet's *Birdcatcher in Hell* was performed in two Vermont opera houses, Bellows Falls and Barre. Many companies entertain with tales like Pinocchio, but others explore myths, folk tales, and legends; for instance, the Mettawee River Theater in Salem, New York, founded in 1980, creatively combines puppetry with dance, music, and wordplay, even "wisecracking cockroaches and philosophical turtles." The popularity of puppetry indicates yet again the public quest for live, challenging, and wondrous performances.

A rapt audience at the Bread and Puppet's performance in the Barre, Vermont Opera House, May 2014. *Mark Dannhauer*

Convinced, like many puppeteers, that theater appealed to more than urban audiences, Cornell University professor Alexander Drummond promoted regional and rural theater when he, along with the Cornell Dramatic Club, set up a stage for plays on rural life at the 1919 New York State Fair. Drummond, who started the theater department at Cornell as well as the New York State Playwriting Project, saw a potential for rural and regional theater where local rural people could write plays about the drama in their daily lives and in their communities. This homegrown theater would discuss the everyday life of these often forgotten people.

While there was considerable interest in plays by these rural folk, Drummond and his student Robert Gard were disappointed in the quality of the plays. "I knew there must be plays of the people that WERE filled with the spirit of places," Gard thought. "There must be plays that grow themselves, born of their happiness and sorrow, born of toiling hands and free minds, born of music and love and reason. There must be many great voices singing out the lore and legend of America from a thousand hilltops, and there must be students to listen and learn, and writers encouraged to use the materials."[11] Drummond, encouraged by Gard, saw the possibility of a "people's theater" spurred by their belief in "the goodness of the folklore and life of the region."[12]

To discover potential playwrights lurking in the hills of rural New York, Drummond wrote to newspapers and magazines, with the added lure of providing his advice on editing and production. He was flooded with letters and ideas. Similar ideas about regional theater were percolating around the country, in North Carolina, Montana, and especially Wisconsin. From the 1910s to the 1950s, regional and rural theater—and art—flowered. Gard, who directed the Wisconsin Idea Theater, was a leader in encouraging regional writers and public involvement in regional theater. Progressive Wisconsin provided fertile ground for the growth of such theater, which proliferated with state and university programs, extension programs, a radio program called "Wisconsin Yarns," a quarterly journal, pageants, and a Rockefeller Foundation–funded Playwrights in Residence program. The 1934 Wisconsin Drama Plan's objectives were many: encouraging dramatic art throughout the state in schools, churches, industrial groups, and social/fraternal organizations; arousing interest in folk drama, playwriting, and production; and organizing and operating small or civic theaters.[13]

Around the same time, the Federal Theatre Project (FTP), one of four art projects sponsored by the Works Projects Administration (WPA) during the Depression, was launched. It soon became the most extensive public theater project in the country. Like its sibling WPA projects in music, writing, and art, its aim was to employ out-of-work artists, writers, and directors. The program was begun in 1935 under the direction of Hallie Flanagan, a former student in Harvard professor George P. Baker's playwriting course and the administrator of a theater program at Vassar. Twelve thousand people were employed over its four-year life, producing twelve hundred performances and reaching twenty-five million viewers in forty states. Half of its employees were actors. The programs were to be free, adult, and uncensored for their political or social content.

Federal Theatre Project (FTP) groups performed many Shakespeare and classical plays, musicals, children's theater, and puppet shows as well as new plays. Although these groups operated primarily in places with unemployed theater professionals, they did tour sections of the country with a few dramatic productions. The Cincinnati group, for example, toured Ohio, West Virginia, and Kentucky, while a group from Chicago and Peoria toured Wisconsin and Illinois. Technical help, equipment,

Children watch a WPA (Works Progress Administration) performance in the 1930s.
Library of Congress Prints and Photographs Division LC-USZ62-77356

and even personnel were provided by the FTP. The New York unit was the project's biggest center, directed by Elmer Rice. Of all New York's many programs, its Living Newspapers, which adapted current issues from newspapers into plays, received the most attention and quickly ran into trouble. Despite the stated policy that the content of its programs would not be censored, Living Newspapers was considered controversial and leftist. With congressional objections not only to the left-wing tone of some of its productions but also to its administrative inefficiencies, the whole program came to a halt in 1939. However, like other WPA art programs, the Federal Theatre Project produced many noncontroversial plays that were popular with the public, and it also helped launch the careers of well-known artists such as Arthur Miller, Elia Kazan, and Orson Welles.

The existence of the Federal Theatre Project and various regional theater programs with state support validates the important role that theater can play in the lives of ordinary people and their communities. Theater can be more than entertainment and high art; in fact, these public theater programs proved that theater can have a social as well as an artistic mission involving people of all backgrounds in all places. The depression, with its WPA programs, turned out to be a high point in public support of the arts.

Today, in flusher times than the New Deal, federal commitment to the arts and cultural institutions is limp. Since 1967 there has been a federal agency, the National Endowment for the Arts (NEA), offering a host of grant programs in the arts, with a $146 million budget in 2013. That might sound like an ample bank account, but it is really pocket change when compared to the $525 billion budgeted for the Department of Defense or even the $8 billion budgeted for the Department of Commerce. The NEA is funded at a per-capita rate of 46 cents, according to Americans for the Arts, an advocacy organization. Compared to Europe, American funding for the arts continues to be infinitesimal.

Public funding of opera houses is more the exception than the rule in the United States, as J. Cleaveland Cady, the architect of the 1883 Metropolitan Opera House, discovered. "In this country, where government is not 'paternal,'" noted Cady, "aid has to be found in another quarter: the wealthy, fashionable classes, who, even if not caring especially for, nor appreciating deeply the music, find [the opera house] a peculiar and valuable social feature." Such financing, Cady concluded, "in no small degree determines the size and character of the house."[14]

In contrast, publicly funded opera houses are found throughout Europe, where culture is treated as a public service and considered almost a civic responsibility. In Paris the construction of the National Opera of Paris, later known as the Palais Garnier for its young architect, Charles Garnier, resulted from an order issued by the minister of state on December 29, 1860, declaring the proposed opera house a "public utility."[15] Confirming the public nature of this new opera house, Count Alexandre Walewski, minister of state and Napoleon's illegitimate son, laid its foundation stone. As in Paris, most of Europe has publicly funded cultural institutions. Germany generously funds three levels of opera houses—state, regional, and municipal—in marked contrast to the United States. In 2012 Germany's government expenditures on culture amounted to almost $150 per capita; even financially pinched Hungary spends $72 per capita, compared to the US National Endowment for the Arts' budget of less than fifty cents per capita. Clearly the United States shares neither the European penchant for culture nor its willingness to fund culture.

"Culture costs, but a lack of culture—Un Kultur—costs much, much more," reported not Austria's minister of culture, but Maria Fekter, Austria's minister of finance in 2013. The $236 million opera house built in Linz, Austria in 2013 illustrates this Austrian commitment to the arts by all levels of government. Ninety-five percent of the funding for this long-planned 1,000-seat opera house, which includes a theater for ballet, orchestra, and musicals as well as opera, was public: 20 percent from the Republic of Austria, 50 percent from the State of Upper Austria, and 25 percent from the city of Linz, an industrial city of 200,000 between Vienna and Salzburg. That meant only 5 percent had to be raised privately (in the United States it is usually the exact opposite).[16] Aside from the cost of construction, public funding accounts for 85 percent of the $52 million annual budget of Landestheater Linz, which is composed of the various music, theater, and dance companies that perform in the Musiktheater.

The importance of this opera house to the city of Linz is also reflected in its design and location. Its siting in a run-down section of Linz was chosen to stimulate development in that part of the city. The site links to a major city park and provides a counterbalance to Brucknerhaus, the former home of the Bruckner Orchestra Linz on the Danube. The London architectural firm of Terry Pawson, which designed the building, even relocated part of a major traffic artery so the opera house's entrance would open to the park, thereby creating "a new, common living room for the whole city," according to Pawson. That park entrance even features in the opera house's name: Musiktheater am Volksgarten.[17]

These European examples dramatically show the comparative lack of support for cultural institutions like opera houses in America. With such limited federal funding as well as scant state and local funds available for the arts, American opera house staffs and boards in small towns and elsewhere are constantly on the lookout for government programs as well as private foundations and other funding sources. Even in unlikely places, such as the Treasury Department with New Markets Tax Credits or the Agriculture Department with Community Facility Grants, some programs for small or low-income communities and their opera houses can be found. One federal initiative, Preserve America, begun in 2003, has helped places protect and use their historic and cultural assets for community revitalization and economic development through a matching grant program begun in 2005. The mission of Preserve America is not only unique, but, with the Advisory Council on Historic Preservation in the lead, involves a coordinated effort of seven federal departments. Its 50/50 matching grants ranging from $20,000 to $25,000 were for designated Preserve America Communities. Most of its grantees were small places or regions; for example, West Virginia's Historic Theatre Trail was funded by this program, which helps to account for the trail's inclusion of history, culture, and environment. Such a comprehensive program integrating diverse federal programs is rare. Preserve America is still alive and located in the Advisory Council for Historic Preservation, but its major function of helping communities with grants is no longer funded. The mechanism is still in place; all it needs is federal funding.

Aside from the limited public support for cultural institutions in general, the opera house on Main Street in a town of 2,000 has a hard time competing for either public or private funds against big city's major opera and music halls. A small town does not have the clout of big-city institutions with cutting-edge arts programs, nor does it have effective elites to lobby for it. Bigger places serve more people and have greater political recognition and more resources on which to draw compared to a rural town. Consequently, today's "large new performing arts facilities," according to University of Minnesota economist Ann Markusen, "tend to receive disproportionate shares of the public dollar."[18] Most of the NEA's grants serve city institutions, as understandably they usually make up the majority of grant applications. In the NEA's Art Works grant program in 2013, 75 percent of the recipients of its theater and musical theater grants were in large cities and only 6 percent in small towns; in its opera grant program, 74 percent of the grantees were in large cities with no grants to small-town institutions. Yet an opera house in a small place with few competing cultural venues has a greater impact on that community than an opera house in a city like New York with a plethora of symphonies, art film theaters, off-Broadway theaters, and dance studios. In a small village, the single opera house is the all-purpose cultural institution. Its impact is not only on the performers and participants but also on the local and regional economy. And there are many such towns—more than 29,263 places with populations under 10,000 in 2010 with an overall population of over 43 million people. That is more people than in all of Canada.

Do they not deserve greater assistance in enriching their cultural, social, and economic lives? Is it because the country, while sentimental about Norman Rockwell–like small places, is biased toward cities as progressive places with forward-looking people and au courant activities? The trend of shrinking rural populations and ever-increasing urbanization has been interpreted as societal progress ever since machines in urban factories started whirring.[19] However, the slower pace, healthful living, and abundant natural amenities of small rural areas have appealed to many over the years. For artists and intellectuals, who are often footloose, rural places offer a lower cost of living, freedom from the competitive pressures of the city, and abundant amenities, as Robert Frost, Edna St. Vincent Millay, Lewis Mumford, and John Irving discovered. Now with the Internet and other media, artists and intellectuals can communicate immediately all over the world from most rural hamlets and export their work and products without having to be in the city. Concerns about environmental well-being and the excessive materialism of the urban corporate world in recent decades have driven people to rural places. Vermont has become such a magnet for the "granola" types, who farm organically, raise sheep, and also enjoy the opportunities of living in a small place where they can influence its present and future through planning and environmental protection.

When Hubbard Hall in the 2,000-person town of Cambridge, New York advertised for a replacement for its manager Benjie White, who retired in 2014, it received fifty replies. Dave Snider, most recently artistic director of Washington, DC's highly respected Arena Stage, was selected. Prior to his position at the Arena, he was producing artistic director and chief executive office of the Young Playwrights Theater, also in Washington, DC. Snider was attracted to Cambridge by its lively interest in the arts, a thriving opera house, and opportunities for broadening the hall's programs. He hopes to reach new audiences, find talent and interns from nearby colleges and beyond, and even teach playwriting to tenth graders at the local high school. Aside from the professional opportunities, Cambridge appealed to him and his wife as a satisfying place to live and bring up their young children. They have quickly settled into life in Cambridge, with his wife working as communications director at nearby Bennington College, their two young children in local schools, and all enjoying an ample house on Main Street with a large backyard and stream. The same communal and professional attractions have lured other theater professionals, like Mike Thomas in Maysville, Kentucky and Doug Anderson in Middlebury, Vermont, to small-town opera houses. Their opting to work in these nonurban performance halls sends a strong signal of their confidence in the vitality of these halls and in the cultural life of small places far from Broadway.

That signal, one hopes, will be heard by public and private funding sources, which will increase assistance to opera houses in rural places. Already initiatives by the nonprofit organization Project for Public Places, now partnering with NEA, the Orton Family Foundation, and the Department of Agriculture on a Citizens Institute on Rural Design, are encouraging signs of a change of attitude toward rural areas.

Aside from the artistic and community programs of opera houses in rural places, family has often been a hidden ingredient in the success of these halls—whether family dynasties like the Jeffersons, the bonding of actors into family, or the Sniders' move to Cambridge, New York not only for the challenges of Hubbard Hall but also for the benefits of small-town life.

CHAPTER 19

Connecting Again

It's all about connecting—then and now. Then-isolated pioneers in the recently settled areas as well as all the newcomers and old-timers in towns and cities throughout the country wanted opera houses to help them connect with mainstream culture as well as with one another in their own towns. Today, as opera houses are being resuscitated, they are being reinvented as vibrant art centers and gathering places. Once again, the drive to connect with friends and neighbors is at play. This time, however, without the thousands of roaming entertainers, opera houses depend more on local artistic and entertainment energies for their performances, further strengthening a town's sense of community. "Making Art and Community Happen" is the message, echoing the motto for the revived 1878 rural opera house in Cambridge, New York.

Today's opera house revivals result from ground-up, communal energy in contrast to the earlier top-down development of these cultural halls. When Fremont, Nebraska's James Wheeler Love, and Leadville and Denver, Colorado's Horace Tabor generously gave their towns important opera houses in the nineteenth century, it was these men's initiative, funding, and management that created these cultural institutions. Today, it is rarely local entrepreneurs or philanthropists but, rather, local nonprofit organizations that are regenerating opera houses, spurred by local leaders such as Gerianne Smart, Beth Klosterman, and Benjie White, and also local theater groups such as the Maysville Players and the Randolph Singers. The local nonprofit organization has replaced the community philanthropist. This makes today's opera house more than a place where people attend plays and local events; it is their community hall.

When the artist and set designer Paul Bouchey joined his friend and professional theater colleague Dick Emerson on the production of *The Pajama Game* in 1972 at Randolph, Vermont's Chandler Hall, Bouchey found that "almost everyone in town was either in the show, worked backstage or made some contribution—large and small—to the project. The enthusiasm and dedication of people of every age and status in life in this small New England town were impressive indeed—and contagious. The hall was fast becoming a center for community focus." Emerson was struck by this "special collection of people" who congregated "with a transient, powerful impact" at the rebirth of the Chandler in 1972. "The cool, clean waters of collective endeavor, applied energy and special purpose commingled to secure and resurrect Albert Chandler's classic gem."[1] And that same local enthusiasm is found in many other opera houses such as Maysville, Kentucky's Washington Opera House, where 126 people work together as actors, ushers, technicians, and promoters to put on a single show.

The early American actor and theater promoter Noah Ludlow considered theater "an undeniable cultural force, almost a necessity."[2] The history of opera houses confirms Ludlow's assessment. It is indeed remarkable that these small halls have withstood threats from perpetual lack of funds, new technologies, fickle tastes, and monopolistic practices of syndicates. Through the years, the satisfactions of theater have been experienced by bored soldiers at remote garrisons performing Shakespeare, sedate Victorians watching spectacular escapes in the heyday of melodramas, and today's opera house patrons tapping their feet to the songs of *Oklahoma!*.

Culture and theater mean many things to many people. The characterization of opera houses' programs as entertainment, not theater, points out the highbrow/lowbrow, exclusive/inclusive, and often urban/rural conflicts that theater and especially rural opera houses have faced. Naming these community halls "opera houses" in the late nineteenth century reflected their developers' interests in adding a touch of urban exclusiveness to their often humble towns. But there is irony in how the pioneering spirit and quest for independence of these developers propelled them to leave the confining ways of the East only to find themselves adopting symbols of Eastern culture. The reality was that, while they wanted culture and uplift, they hoped Eastern culture would erase some of the inferiorities of their remote rural life.

At the same time that opera houses proliferated, many cultural activities acquired a new Victorian refinement and exclusivity. Attending plays, which had been a participatory, sometimes rowdy activity, with all classes mingling and expressing their emotions, gradually became a more sedate and private experience. Cultural activities assumed more and more of an upper-class status, creating a growing rift between highbrows and lowbrows and a clear tension between inclusivity and exclusivity. Lower classes strove to be a part of this upper-class culture, while the elite felt they had hegemony over culture and, in effect, social control. For a new town with muddy roads lined with buildings just two stories high, an opera house brought to mind the image of handsome, ornately decorated buildings filled with fur-bedecked, jeweled patrons. When the governor, three state cabinet officers, the town's elite in fancy attire, and ushers in "full dress" attended the opening night of Kearney, Nebraska's opera house, they must have felt connected to distant centers of high-class culture.

Across the Atlantic in England a different type of entertainment hall, the music hall, appeared in large and small cities at the same time as opera houses were sprouting up on America's Main Streets. By 1900 every town and city had a music hall; London boasted sixty. While music halls and opera houses shared the same goal of brightening people's lives by providing escape from the dreariness of everyday life, they were very different institutions, mirroring the different sociocultural features of the two countries. English music halls were large, boisterous places for eating, drinking, and entertainment, some seating 3,500 people, often run by major circuits similar to American syndicates in what became a business of pleasure. There the working class ate and drank while taking in bawdy and vulgar fare, which, like the American halls, had undertones of sentimentality, patriotism, and gentility. The patrons would join in singing favorites like "The Boy I Love Is Up in the Gallery." There were tightrope walkers, blackfaced minstrels, freaks, boxers, and cancan dancers along with variety shows by troupes of dedicated musicians and comedians, as England's former prime minister John Major poignantly describes in his book about his father's life as a music hall comedian and musician. For both of Major's parents, the world of the music hall, despite all its deprivations, was "full of life, with each performance a kaleidoscope of colour and contradiction: the beautiful and the bizarre; the glamorous and the grotesque; the romantic and the raffish; the comedic and the crude." At his father's death-bed, Major knew that his father was where his heart was: "back on stage" with the bright lights and "a boisterous audience cheering."[3]

Alcohol was usually associated with the English music halls. Ever since the seventeenth century when Puritanical legislation closed theaters, plea-sure seekers had been enjoying music, food, and drinks at inns and pubs. In the music hall even the musicians' and performers' wages were linked to alcohol sales. In contrast, the late-nineteenth-century American opera house featured itself a respected and respectable local institution for enter-tainment and enlightenment as well as for uplift and gentility. Just naming them "opera houses" hinted at the social and cultural ambitions of their promoters and town fathers. Here food and drink came only with the clean fun of occasional organized socials. American democratic values propelled the development and influenced the programs of the small town opera house, while England's music hall mirrored its class system. The English shopkeeper with slim chances of budging into a higher socioeconomic level was not aspiring to higher culture when he went to the music hall; he just wanted a good time with clever and often talented entertainers.

American small-town opera house developers and their fellow towns-people, seeking respectability and a touch of big-city exclusivity, were correct in recognizing opera as a symbol of culture rather than a cul-tural force. Opera itself was also becoming synonymous with exclusivity. Wealthy New Yorkers kept building newer and grander opera houses, first the Italian Opera House in 1833, then the Astor Place Opera House in 1847, followed by the Metropolitan Opera House in 1883. When 150 fancy New Yorkers built the Astor Place Opera House, new rituals of the fashionable took over. This "resort of our exclusively aristocratic Upper Ten Thousand" maintained its exclusivity by dress codes and reserved seating: "[A]n atmosphere of elegance and refinement makes itself pal-pable. . . . There is a feeling of repose, of security from rude and imperti-nent interruption," the *Spirit of the Times* reported of the new Astor Place Opera House.[4]

Exclusivity and high fashion became associated with opera-going at the Astor and other large cities' opera houses, especially for women. By the late nineteenth century theaters were seen as public places that respectable women could patronize—like the department store. As women gained more independence and ventured out on their own to shop or attend matinees, they became important consumers as well as purvey-ors of middle-class culture. Certainly women's values influenced not only the fashions and manners of theater- and operagoers but also the types of productions, with melodramas being the most obvious example. Those values reached towns everywhere as performers roamed the country and helped reduce the cultural breach between big cities and rural towns.

Even the ultimate symbol of exclusivity, the Metropolitan Opera, is trying today to be a more inclusive cultural institution with lower-priced tickets, open houses, new and innovative performances, and telecasts. Although the attendees of the Met's performances are often portrayed as dowagers and their socially elite friends, that stereotype is not a fair description of the mix of Met fans. The Met's upper balconies—and other sections of the house—are filled with avid and diverse patrons, from older Italian shoe repairmen to sweatshirted twentysomethings, similar to the tens of thousands of diverse fans for whom the Saturday radio broadcasts were a weekly ritual and also today's almost nine million telecast viewers of live operas in the six years of *The Met: Live in HD*. At the same time, opera companies with talented staffs are providing live opera to eager and also diverse audiences in more than a hundred cities, often in small opera houses.

As the Met is trying to become more democratic and many small-town opera houses are performing more erudite theater, the rift between highbrow theater and lowbrow entertainment in opera houses continues, as rural opera house fare is mostly entertainment, not theater (as a serious theater professional reminded me). Avant-garde theater and serious classical theater have not been mainstays of small-town opera houses, but that does not mean musicals have muscled out all serious plays, dance, and lectures. Despite the often-condescending attitude toward local opera house programs, an amazing amount of what might be considered highbrow offerings is available at opera houses today as more people become involved in their operations. One can see Chekhov and Shaw plays along with Martha Graham–trained dancers, Juilliard-trained singers, and Metropolitan Opera stars in small cities and rural towns throughout the country. Most of this challenging fare in small opera houses is coming not from New York or London but from local groups, trained and performing locally. Such performances can be exhilarating, as author James Atlas describes in the *New York Times* his attending an opera at Hubbard Hall in Cambridge, New York:

> I attended a performance of "The Magic Flute" in a small, 19th century town hall that seated 90 (and, I'm glad to say, was filled to capacity). Tickets were $30. I've seen Mozart's joyous opera many times, and this was the best by far. The singers were superb; the

mini-orchestra played with gusto; the makeshift costumes were touchingly inventive. How did the cast members get paid? Or did they? The production was instructive: there was a soprano from a local conservatory, an itinerant freelance tenor, a baritone working for his M.A. in musicology. Some of the staff worked pro bono.... It was an exhilarating event.[5]

Community remains an overriding feature of today's opera houses on Main Street. Community-interested people and organizations have steered the restoration of the buildings, the structuring of their programs, and their operations. With few federal or state programs or even private foundation grants, opera house revivals have been essentially grassroots, locally community-generated projects. Saving the buildings, often local landmarks, garnered early support, which has evolved into broader communal involvement in the planning, management, and operation of opera houses as well as the creation and production of its programs, whether musicals, children's theater, dance groups, or masquerade balls.

The quest for community has been a basic drive going back to Massachusetts Bay Colony governor John Winthrop's "city set upon the hill" sermon: "Wee must delight in eache other, make others' condicions our owne, rejoice together, mourne together, always having before our eyes our Commission and Community in the worke, our Community as members of the same body."[6] In a new country with a virtual tabula rasa, the pioneers' urge to settle and seek community has been extremely powerful. Often escaping oppressive situations, these settlers created a society providing freedom and independence for individuals, yet bound in an indivisible nation governed by a constitution prepared by and for its people. Thus, this federalism, one of the most enduring features of American democracy, melded two different and important traits, communal interdependence and individual self-determination.

This continuing search for civilizing community raises interesting paradoxes. We live in a shrinking global village where we can communicate with each other instantly anywhere at any hour in so many different ways, establish personal social networks and virtual communities, and share information instantly. Yet we seem isolated. We are also physically isolated as we live in gated neighborhoods, commute long distances alone in our cars, and telecommute from our homes. But for scholars of social networking like Barry Wellman at the University of Toronto, the streets and alleys in communities have been replaced by bits and bytes in this new world of "glocalization." The Internet extends the community, but are networked individuals just "portals of communication" or "engagements" for advertisers? Do we really know each other in this virtual world? Certainly we have lost much of the traditional face-to-face socializing and the public trust and respect that it can breed.

For entertainment, today's endless media opportunities would be daunting for our ancestors. Yet our communication devices do not offer live entertainment nor the pleasures of viewing or participating with others in live performances that our ancestors enjoyed. So it is no surprise that tens of thousands of people today are drawn to the opera houses. Here they can enjoy live, creative, and communal activities—rehearsing, performing, and attending events as well as tending to all the hard work repairing crumbling buildings, raising funds, and spending many nights at long committee meetings. These activities, importantly, are inclusive. They override often hidden but divisive barriers of age, race, class, income, and skills. In fact, the varied, live, and inclusive programs and activities at opera houses now provide some needed communal "glue" in a time of fractious polarizations.

That satisfying community of live entertainment, culture, and education found in opera houses is also blossoming in local programs in abandoned public buildings, community orchestras, and book clubs everywhere. In Salem, New York, its abandoned courthouse and jail are now bustling with local programs such as talent shows, musicals, a scarecrow festival for children, and an al fresco weekend celebrating the town's agricultural heritage. They want the community that such activities provide. They want to be connected with friends and neighbors; and they enjoy the joint venture of performing in plays, singing in choirs, or playing in orchestras.

The 2007 film *Young@Heart* brought to the attention of millions of moviegoers the pleasures that a chorus of elderly residents in Northampton, Massachusetts can generate for audiences in Northampton and all over the world. Begun in 1982 with people living in a senior housing project, the Young at Heart Chorus members, whose ages range from seventy-two to eighty-eight, swing and sway with music one might expect to hear teenagers sing. The fast-tempo songs make these octogenarians feel as contemporary as their music and their audiences as upbeat as these performers. Watching their director Bob Cilman push and prod these singers, one cannot but be inspired by the commitment of these geriatric men and women to learn complicated lyrics and adapt to pounding instruments. But fueling their drive to perform has been an amazing—and heartening—bonding. The group, composed of disparate people from the Northampton region, has bonded together. Their rehearsal nights have been the highlights of their week and their popular performances stir them to keep going. They share the joys of working together to get the pieces right, of singing solos, duets, or in the chorus, but they also share the losses of members who were sick, can no longer join them, or who have died. Like true performers, despite those heartfelt losses, they have carried on. The show must go on. Their pluck and enthusiasm have been contagious: one member singing while his oxygen tank ticked away like a metronome, another joining the group right after a hospital stay, and another leaning on a cane while performing. The joy of their belonging to this musical community, which has helped these seniors defy their encroaching years and accompanying disabilities, has produced cheering audiences here and abroad and brought yet another artistic success to Northampton's opera house, the Academy of Music.

Even those with minimal talents can enjoy the pleasures of performing together in an orchestra, as the Edinburgh author of *The No. 1 Ladies' Detective Agency* series Alexander McCall Smith notes in touting his and others' participation in the Really Terrible Orchestra. He wondered why serious musicians had all the fun. Smith, who had been envious of the good times his son had playing in a school orchestra, found that he, as a bassoonist, could participate in communal musical activities in the inclusive Really Terrible Orchestra. This ensemble, which gives people with limited skills a chance to perform with others, has drawn large audiences at its public concerts, even at an annual concert at the Edinburgh Festival Fringe. Its major benefits, however, are for the players, who, like Smith, may be terrible but are having fun.

For more serious musicians—or the "real musicians," as Smith called them—symphony orchestras, chamber music groups, choruses, and many jazz, folk, rock, and other contemporary music groups abound in this country. Major symphony orchestras alone number over 230 in forty-nine states, and that does not include all the local symphonies. In Washington, DC's northern Virginia suburbs alone, Arlington, Alexandria, and Fairfax each have full-blown symphony orchestras. These numerous and usually high-quality orchestras and musical groups provide opportunities for both performers and audiences to enjoy a great variety of music—and have fun, just like the Really Terrible Orchestra. The performers enjoy not only playing their individual instruments but also the collegiality of playing together. They bond like actors and many other performing groups.

The Vermont Symphony Orchestra, founded in 1935, offers quality music at moderate cost to towns throughout the state—with many performances in opera houses such as those in Vergennes, Bellows Falls, and Derby Line. Interestingly, this Vermont orchestra was the first state-supported orchestra in the country, as state funds enabled it to perform at the 1939 World's Fair in New York. Its musicians include farmers, teachers, postal workers, truckers, and lawyers along with professional musicians, and its programs are offered throughout the year with the Summer Pops and the fall Made in Vermont Musical Festival tours as highlights. Aside from exposing townspeople in every corner of the state to quality music, the musicians derive their own satisfactions from the communal synergy of playing as well as the bonding that such musical activities offer. The orchestra "definitely provides musicians with opportunities to bond, especially its tours," notes violinist Julie Marden, who adds that the orchestra's bonding is greatly enhanced on tours involving long, shared bus trips and hotel stays. But bonding, Marden adds, also occurs on stage.

The Vermont Symphony Orchestra playing (on the Canadian side of the hall) at the Haskell Opera House in Derby Line, Vermont and Stanstead, Quebec. *Vermont Symphony Orchestra*

"The music will sometimes go in interesting interpretative directions," she relates. "In the summers [at the Pops concerts], the orchestra has developed choreography to the 'Stars and Stripes Forever,' where the double bass players twirl their basses and the violinists stand up and swing their hips, and last year [2011] we even played musical chairs. During the fall tour, we can't get that lively, but we usually develop some private musical jokes or we take faster and faster tempos." At the end of a tour, a final bonding is the gift-giving to the soloist, conductor, and backstage manager. Playing in older but renovated opera houses adds to the performing experience, Marden suggests, as those houses can be "tiny and charming" in contrast to impersonal school auditoriums or large performing arts centers.[7]

In the mid-1990s, Harvard professor of public policy Robert Putnam found civic and social capital—all the networks, values, and trust needed to produce cooperation and communal involvement in this country—at a low point, as he discussed in his book, *Bowling Alone*. In his studies for this book, along with an earlier research project in Italy on the role of community and community involvement as predictors of economic and political well-being, Putnam explored basic questions of civic life. In northern Italy, communitarianism and egalitarianism, illustrated by many organizations, social clubs, soccer leagues, choral groups, and unions, strengthened civic, economic, and political life and the sense of communitas. In contrast, southern Italy, with its hierarchical and patron-client relationships, of which the Mafia is a good example, created insecurity and mistrust, which hampered civic life. Here Putnam found a decrease in civic engagement, neighborliness, trust, and "social connectedness." The title of his book, *Bowling Alone*, makes his point. More than eighty million people bowled in 1993, 10 percent more than in 1980, but during that same period there was a 40 percent drop in participation in organized leagues. Many factors are at work: more women in the workforce, more mobility, demographic changes, large-scale economic activities, and technological changes in leisure, especially television. To counter these forces and this erosion of social capital, Putnam advocates voluntary associations as a means to reinvigorate civic life. Opera houses are such voluntary associations.

On an encouraging note, Richard Florida, a scholar of urban affairs now at the University of Toronto, wrote in the early 2000s of the increasingly influential role of creativity in society in *The Rise of the Creative Class*. He sees "great promise" in the social and economic systems "that tap human creativity and make use of it as never before."[8] For Florida, the creative class includes all those using their minds creatively: artists, musicians, engineers, scientists, and "knowledge-based" professionals. The future is in the hands of the creative class, according to Florida, and, fortunately, he predicts that this class will grow in numbers and strength. Less than one-tenth of American workers were doing creative work in 1900; by 2000 that number had jumped to one-third. With factory and farm jobs decreasing and Rust Belts still suffering, many are left out of this new creative world. Gnawing inequalities and a seriously divided country result, which challenge the creative class to bring outsiders into the creative world or provide benefits for them. Talent, technology, and tolerance stand out as the key determinants of the dynamism of this creative class—and also for all those involved with opera houses.

Another voice recognizing the role of creative energy, especially its economic impacts on communities is that of Ann Markusen and her associates at the University of Minnesota's Humphrey Institute of Public Affairs. Since the early 2000s, Markusen has been discussing the "artistic dividend" that millions of artists and cultural workers provide for places of all sizes. Through creative placemaking, arts can enhance the livability and economic viability of places—and many decentralized places. In fact, they can become "creative crucibles," according to Markusen. She and her colleague David King "suggest that the productivity of and earnings in a regional economic rise as the incidence of artists within its boundaries increases, because artists' creativity and specialized skills enhance the design, production and marketing of products and services in other sectors."[9] Compared to the dividend from professional sports, the "artistic dividend" fares well, as professional athletes do not live year-round in a single place and usually do not engage in other activities such as business or teaching in the area. "Artists' contributions reach more broadly and deeply into the regional economy" than professional sports.[10] While her studies concentrate on major art hubs like Los Angeles and Boston, Markusen recognizes dispersal of artists to smaller cities and towns is a trend today as the Internet has made proximity less important.

Opera house managers, revivers, and performers like Markusen's dispersed artists are not Luddites. Many are utilizing the latest electronic technology for productions as well as programs and outreach. For instance, the restored, simple one-floor Thrasher Opera House in the small town of Green Lake, Wisconsin, with a population of less than 2,000, savvily uses its website to advertise its programs, even to embed artists' videos, sell tickets, and reach out to distant, potential patrons. Innumerable opera houses meet Equity standards and have "state of the art" facilities with up-to-date electronic capabilities. Bellows Falls (Vermont) Opera House, which had been a movie theater from the 1930s through the 1960s, can now show digital films as well as live performances. Video arts and augmented reality are being introduced as creative activities that appeal to young audiences, who might not otherwise be interested in what they perceive as "high art" programs at opera houses. The challenge of attracting young participants in opera houses has generated a variety of concerts, really jam sessions, for local bands, as in Gardiner, Maine's Johnson Hall Performing Arts Center, which organizes sessions twice a month for four bands from the Kennebec region. Opera house staffers now have online resources that enable them to quickly communicate and exchange information with their peers anywhere in the country. The League of Historic American Theatres' chatline is a gold mine of information and advice. If an opera house manager wants to know how to find new electronic letters for a marquee, whether to replace old seats, how to find historic carpet designs, how to design a box office, how to deal with certain film distributors, or how to encourage volunteers, posing the questions to colleagues via chatlines will produce a flood of answers. Certainly, all those opera house revivers, staffers, and supporters are adding to the burgeoning numbers of Florida's creative class.

These new technologies, along with Putnam's ideas on voluntary associations strengthening civic capital and Florida's vision of the role of the creative class, offer hopeful examples of ways to engage today's lonely crowds in a civic and civilized society. And, indeed, a significant step in that direction is evident in the communal and equalizing creative opportunities that revived opera houses are providing today.

When Willa Cather in 1929 bemoaned the disappearance of the opera houses in her native state of Nebraska, when Hallam's company was run out of Providence, when George Washington needed special permission from the governor of Pennsylvania to see a play on his birthday, and, more recently when urban renewal's wrecking ball destroyed hundreds of opera houses, the future of opera houses appeared bleak. It would seem a miracle to those early theater buffs, the many theater troupes and entertainers, and all the early defenders of opera house buildings that so many opera houses have been brought back to life. Indeed, the phoenix has risen all over the country.

The history of the opera house is an American story. Those "local glories" resulted from many small-town entrepreneurs' optimism, pragmatism, and energy, such essential ingredients of the American spirit. Americans had "spacious ideas," fueled by optimism and energy.[11] The opera house entrepreneurs had confidence in the future. They banked on a community hall with the proud name of "opera house" to help transform a straggling settlement into a civilized town. No lords, wealthy patrons, or heavy government subsidies were there to help, as was often the case in Europe. And the same is true today, as most revived US opera houses rely on volunteers and private money, with small grants trickling down through state arts councils and the National Endowment for the Arts. The optimism and pragmatism that fired up the nineteenth-century entrepreneur is alive today, with revivers hoping to resuscitate not only their opera houses but also their downtowns and towns.

The staying power of the arts and the passion of so many involved in producing and enjoying performances have been evident from the time when thousands of intrepid troupers and entertainers traveled by horse, coach, or train to off-the-beaten-path towns. And today, townspeople in small, remote towns are again enjoying theater and creative programs at their once-dormant opera houses.

This story also reflects the timeless quest of so many different people for cultural nourishment, especially women. Their civilizing influence and their effective nudging of men helped introduce some refinement and theater, whether in mining camps in the Rockies or in countless small places with limited opportunities for cultural enrichment. Today women are no longer behind the scenes prodding others to provide these cultural halls; they are in the forefront of local campaigns to revive opera houses. They are often the activists. But their activism would not take hold if it were not for the many audiences and supporters who enjoy the uplift, escape, and fulfillment that performances provide.

Today's interest in and enthusiasm for opera houses reflect an urge to break away from the virtual world and connect with others in live face-to-face joint ventures. Our forebears with no telephones, much less smartphones or computers, broke out of their isolation to meet friends and neighbors and enjoy entertainment at the opera houses. They wanted to connect with the world near and far. Now the urge is to disconnect from the outside world of mass-produced commercial entertainment, the proliferation of communications, and the remoteness of so many of our computerized transactions. People want to challenge the tedium of every-day life; they want to dream, create something positive, and share that with others. By so doing they forge connections and engage in community. And that is what today's revived opera houses are offering: participation in creative ventures, a community of shared interests, and a renewed civility.

Afterword

Discovering small-town opera houses, their histories, and their varied cultural, entertainment, and civic programs as well as all the people engaged with them proved a fascinating undertaking. This distinctly American institution offers a glimpse of the values, tastes, and moods of the country. It is also a unique example of the cultural entrepreneurism and place making that took place after the Civil War and is occurring again today.

This history of small opera houses has given me the chance to weave together my interests in city planning and American history, which were spurred by two Harvard professors and friends: the late John E. Sawyer, later president of Williams College, whose holistic approach to economic history helped me appreciate the dynamics of the social sciences; and William Leuchtenburg, later at Columbia University and the University of North Carolina, scholar of the twentieth-century American political scene and a tutor whose enthusiasm and vitality led me to a lifelong fascination with many aspects of American history.

The communal nature of opera houses for performers, audiences, and towns—"where art and community meet"—particularly interested me. No doubt that interest in community has been influenced by my being a single person. I am sure that I am more dependent on my neighborhood and local affiliations than my married friends. My friends, neighbors, acquaintances, and coworkers are an extended family. My own family has provided incredible support to me. I am grateful for the intellectual curiosity and independence I inherited from my parents, the late J. Sheafe Satterthwaite and Margaret H. Speer Satterthwaite, and the intellectual stimulation and advice continuously provided by my brother Sheafe Satterthwaite, who long taught landscape and land use history at Williams College. Also, I am extremely grateful for the invaluable assistance of Kenny Hersey for all his digital scanning of images, Jessica Carr for her persistent work on the listing of opera houses in the appendix, and Valery Raytchev for his invaluable computer help. Not being on the faculty or staff of an institution like a university has meant that I did not have the intellectual exchange that occurs among faculty members nor some of their benefits like JSTOR, and efficient interlibrary loans, and other logistical support.

Although I am not a theater historian, along the way I garnered considerable information on theater and entertainment history, the remarkable variety of performers, and the ways theater and entertainment have responded to changing times and audience interests. I gained a new appreciation for the powerful thespian urge of early family troupes, who traveled with all their equipment on horseback, coach, or even river rafts to perform on courthouse steps, in plantation parlors, or in makeshift theaters. Then came the late-nineteenth-century troupes traveling from town to town with tight schedules, late trains, poor hotels, and often miserly pay in straggly new communities, and now today there are hundreds of people reviving opera houses. Equally significant has been the public's yearning to be entertained and uplifted, even at times when it meant bucking prevailing moral codes.

My research took me to many opera houses; local, state, public, private, and university libraries; town and state historical associations; specialized libraries like Denver's important Western History Collection; and state historic preservation agencies. Here I found research papers, architectural and preservation reports, town meeting minutes, local newspapers, professional journals, student papers, reviews, accounting records, photographs, broadsides, and sometimes diaries. The staffs of the substantial, publicly funded state historical societies in both Colorado and Nebraska guided me to useful information and provided help beyond the normal call of duty. I discovered an array of data important to my research in local libraries like Arlington, Vermont's Canfield Library; private nonprofit organizations like the Willa Cather Foundation; private historical society libraries like Louisville, Kentucky's Filson Historical Society; county libraries like those in Mason County and Bourbon County, Kentucky; and state historic preservation offices in Nebraska, Kentucky, Vermont, Colorado, and New York. The reference librarians in my hometown libraries, the Library of Congress and Georgetown University, especially John Kimbrough, have been there whenever I needed them. I was assisted not only by innumerable helpful, patient, and interested librarians and local historians but also by many people who, learning of my project, called or wrote me with information on some particular opera house or troupe. Some friends like Leslie Johnson, an opera fan as well as an opera singer, provided me with firsthand insights into opera performances and the Metropolitan Opera audiences; and her husband, Eugene J. Johnson, an architectural historian and professor of art at Williams College, shared with me some of his research on the Venetian opera house, Teatro San Giovanni Grisostomo. An old friend, John Carnahan in Brattleboro, Vermont, a stalwart worker at the Estey Organ Museum, and his son, Paul, librarian at the Vermont Historical Society, provided me with useful information. Rebecca Bates of Berea College provided invaluable substantive and editorial advice. Insights from her childhood in a small rural town were helpful in thinking about the neutral turf of opera houses. All this help and enthusiasm spurred me on.

Fortunately, excellent scholarship is available in a variety of books on regional opera houses: George Glenn and Richard Poole's on Iowa opera houses, William Condee's on Appalachian opera houses, Ricky Tyler's work on Kansas opera houses, and most recently Brian Leahy Doyle's on Wisconsin opera houses. On the history of opera, I consulted John Dizikes's *Opera in America* and Katherine Preston's *Opera on the Road*; for the history of theater, Mary Henderson's *Theater in America* and Arthur Hornblow's *History of Theatre in America*; and for reflections on sociocultural factors like audiences and public tastes, scholars like Lawrence Levine, Richard Butsch, Bruce McConachie, and Richard Bushman. Information on individual opera houses has been hard to track down. Such information may well have been lost in fires or in turnovers of managers and owners or was considered too inconsequential to keep. However, that gap was offset by the conscientious research of some local historians on their hometown opera houses, whether in Leadville, Colorado, Mineral Point, Wisconsin, Enosburgh Falls the, Vermont, or Charlottesville, Virginia; and in a state like Vermont with University of Vermont's late drama professor George B. Bryan's impressive writings and archives. Some performers like actors Joseph Jefferson and Sarah Bernhardt, lecturers Mark Twain and Elizabeth Cady Stanton, and traveling troupe managers Sol Smith and Noah Ludlow have written vivid accounts of their travels and performances, confirming their unstinting commitment to their callings and revealing the hardships and pleasures of traveling and performing in opera houses. Dickens's bicentennial brought to light his deep interest in theater and amusements, which he—and the developers and managers of American opera houses—considered so important for the commonweal. To balance the writings by and about well-known stars, with often hefty egos, are books and articles by lesser-known troupes like Minnesota's Andrews Family Opera company, which describe the everyday world of regional entertainers and small, rural opera houses.

There have been some disappointments. Due to the multitude of opera houses, it was necessary to narrow my research to certain states, which I selected for their diversity. That meant many interesting places and people have been slighted. However, I kept coming upon intriguing opera houses, especially current revivals, in other states, which I could not resist including. In New York, the remarkable stories of Hubbard Hall in Cambridge and the Opera House in Hudson, are both being brought back to life today—in contrast to two nearby towns, Fort Edward and Granville, whose opera house buildings no longer exist. In New Hampshire, once-prosperous cities like Claremont, Lebanon, and Rochester, and in Maine Biddeford, Camden, Gardiner, Boothbay Harbor, and Stonington have restored their opera house buildings, which are now alive with varied programs and diverse audiences. I was pleased to find that some opera houses in town halls in places such as Bellows Falls, Vermont, Camden, Maine, and towns in Wisconsin treat their opera houses as public services with the opera house manager on the town payroll. Whether in Texas, Oklahoma, Nevada, Oregon, Pennsylvania, Kansas, the Dakotas, Montana, or California, I found interesting and relevant information in both yesteryear and contemporary opera house activity. Spearfish in South Dakota's Black Hills is an example. Here the 1906 second-floor Matthews Opera House was rescued from disrepair in the 1970s by Black Hills State College theater students, who repaired the building for summer theater programs. Later the Spearfish Downtown Association and the Spearfish Center for Arts and Humanities undertook a full restoration of the building and organized an arts center with films, plays, and art exhibitions. Its motto, "Your very own community theater—A vibrant century," describes their accomplishment. Nearby Lead's Homestake Opera House, which also includes a bowling alley, swimming pool, and a library, is undergoing a similar revival. Many such rich lodes, which I did not study, await future scholars.

The behind-the-scenes staff of these opera houses—the seamstresses, lighting technicians, scenery artists, orchestras, and, of course, the managers—make it possible for the shows to go on. While I discuss some managers, I regret that I did not investigate other opera house workers, especially orchestras and their members. As I concentrated on the heyday and the present, I do not discuss adequately some entertainment types such as vaudeville, which came to the rural opera houses at the end of the nineteenth century and lasted for several decades but, fortunately, has been the subject of many studies.

Tracking down diaries of people connected with early opera houses, such as those who organized them, performed in them, or attended them, proved difficult. Perhaps such diaries are still hidden in attic trunks or local historical societies. Even a published book, *I Too Lived on Main Street,* by Para Love, the theater-loving daughter of Fremont, Nebraska's opera house owner, and the papers of businesslike Franklin and Ellen Pember, who started Granville, New York's opera house, have disappeared. Observations by such people closely connected with opera houses may be considered too inconsequential to keep or make available to the public, even in collections of women's dairies and books at specialized places like the Radcliffe Institute's Schlesinger Library. Yet more quotidian information from diaries would have added vital firsthand experiences to this book.

Another research gap is information on regional and even national traveling theater, opera, and other troupes. Hundreds of traveling companies like Holman's Opera Company, Georgia Hamlin Dramatic Company, D. R. Star Dramatic Company, and the Earle Comedy Company were mainstays of many small opera houses, but it is difficult finding information and records on them such as lists of members, itineraries, accounting records, and diaries. Whether because of their vernacular nature, their lack of star power, or their minor-league entertainer status, little seems extant on them in major theater collections like the Harvard Theatre Collection. Fortunately, I did come upon some information on the Emma Abbott Opera Company and the Haverstock Tent Company, but more intensive study of other regional troupes is needed.

Researching today's revived opera houses proved incredibly heartening. Visiting them; interviewing their managers, promoters, and community supporters; and attending performances provided many pleasures. My research also reawakened my respect for the hard work and patience, perseverance and political skills, and talents and diversity of all those involved with opera houses. Like the earlier generation of opera house workers, today's are bringing culture and live entertainment to small places and in so doing are influencing the social and civic life in those places.

When I discuss these "local glories" past and present with old and new friends or professional city planning allies, their curiosity, surprise, and delight is encouraging. At first, newcomers to the topic think that opera was the mainstay of these opera houses, but their interest perks up when they learn of the diverse programs and community activities at these small halls. Fortunately, that interest seems to be on the increase. When I started my research around 2003, I contacted every state historic preservation office, but only a handful had surveys specifically on opera houses. Within a few years, however, a surprising number of states were undertaking further research and thereby recognizing the historic and cultural significance of these small halls. As these opera houses gain public attention, I hope that educational and research institutions as well as university and specialized libraries will encourage scholars to pursue further work on these remarkable "local glories."

Appendix: A Listing of Extant Opera Houses by State

The following list of opera houses was compiled by contacting the State Historic Preservation Offices (SHPOs) for each of the fifty states. (SHPOs are state agencies created by the 1966 National Historic Preservation Act to administer national historic preservation programs for states.) Most responded favorably, either by directly supplying information or by making their databases accessible. A few SHPOs had neither the time nor the resources to research this topic, or an online searchable database. In these latter instances, it was possible to ascertain extant opera houses by searching the National Register of Historic Places database for "opera house" listings. Information is listed for all but five states.

This list is intended to identify the extant opera houses in each state. Although National Register-listed buildings are more likely to survive the passage of time, an effort was made to discover how many other opera houses remain standing, and how many are still being used for performances. Many opera houses have not received any historical designation nor been nominated to the National Register of Historic Places. Many more have burned, been demolished or otherwise lost.

It should be noted that, even though many responses were received, few SHPOs had lists specifically for opera houses. Much of the information they provided was gleaned from searches for "opera house" in their general databases. Several SHPO databases contained so many listings of opera houses that it is unlikely that they are all still extant. It may be their information is outdated and some of the listed buildings are no longer standing. Some searches may have overlooked those opera houses that were renamed and used for different purposes.

The names for these performance halls, whether opera houses, halls, theaters, or auditoriums, are often interchangeable. In some instances, theaters, halls, and auditoriums offering theatrical and entertainment programs as well as community events have been listed. Opera houses being revived, but not yet operating as performance halls, were not listed as "active." Although this book and list focus on small town opera houses, some large city opera houses on state listings are included as their influence was considered significant in their states.

In the interests of refining this list of extant opera houses, any up-to-date information or corrections would be welcome at USoperahouselist@gmail.com.

Legend

Buildings are listed by state and then by county following the format of both national and state registries of historic places.

Active opera houses, those currently being used for performances and community events, are italicized.

Sources

Name Only: listings for this state were provided directly by the State Historic Preservation Office (SHPO) through its search for "opera house" or its knowledge of operating opera houses

Database: listings for this state were obtained by searching the database or website provided by the SHPO

Other Source: listings for this state were not provided directly by the SHPO

No Data: either no responses from the SHPO or it was presumed that there are no extant opera houses in the state

NR: listing on the National Register of Historic Places

NRHD: listing included in a National Register Historic District

SR: listing on a state's Register of Historic Places

Alabama

- *Fort Payne Opera House*—Fort Payne, DeKalb County (NR)
- *Blunt Opera House*—Greensboro, Hale County (NRHD: Greensboro)
- *Dothan Opera House*—Dothan, Houston County (NR)

- Montgomery Theatre—Montgomery County (NRHD: Court Square)
- Cotaco Opera House—Decatur, Morgan and Limestone Counties (NR)

Alaska (no data)

Arizona (no data)

Arkansas (name only)

- Hutchinson Building—Opera House—Sulphur Springs, Benton County
- Rogers Opera House Building—Rogers, Benton County (NRHD: Rogers Commercial Historic District)
- *Opera House*—Wynne, Cross County (NRHD: Wynne Commercial Historic District)
- King Opera House—Van Buren, Crawford County (NRHD: Van Buren Historic District)
- McNeil Opera House—Rector, Clay County (NRHD: Rector Commercial Historic District)
- Opera House, Old—Arkansas City, Desha County
- Ozark Opera House—Ozark, Franklin County (NRHD: Ozark Courthouse Square Historic District)
- Knights of Pythias Opera House—Fayetteville, Washington County

California (database)

- Reedley Opera House Complex—Reedley, Fresno County (NR)
- Napa Opera House—Napa, Napa County (NR)
- Loring Opera House, Golden State Theater—Riverside, Riverside County
- South San Francisco Opera House—San Francisco, San Francisco County
- Old Petaluma Opera House—Petaluma, Sonoma County (NR)
- Woodland Opera House—Woodland, Yolo County (NR)

Colorado

- Dickens Opera House—Longmont, Boulder County (NR)
- *Idaho Springs Opera House, Mines Theater*—Idaho Springs, Clear Creek County (NRHD)
- Silver Plume Bandstand—Silver Plume, Clear Creek County (NRHD)

- Ordway Opera House, The Old Magic Door—Ordway, Crowley County
- Louviers Village Club—Louviers, Douglas County (NR)
- Dove Creek Opera House—Dove Creek, Dolores County
- *Opera House*—Paonia, Delta County
- *Boettcher Concert Hall*—Denver, Denver County
- *Odeon Theater, Fraternal Order of Eagles Hall,* The Pullman Bar—Glenwood Springs, Garfield County
- *Central City Opera House*—Central City, Gilpin County (NR)
- Smith's Opera House—Gunnison, Gunnison County
- *Lake City Opera House*, Pitkin Guard Armory, Lake City Town Hall, Jail and Community Center/Rebekah Lodge (Hall)—Lake City, Hinsdale County (NRHD)
- Music Studio, LMC, Alder—Bailey, Jefferson County (SR)
- Opera House—Golden, Jefferson County
- Jaffa Opera House, Trinidad Opera House, Hausman Drug—Trinidad, Las Animas County (NR)
- *Tabor Opera House*—Leadville, Lake County (NRHD)
- Belmont Dance Hall, Belmont Building—Durango, La Plata County
- A & B Building, Bartholf Opera House, Arcadia Hotel—Loveland, Larimer County
- Opera House Block Building, Central Block Building—Fort Collins, Larimer County (NR)
- Mancos Opera House—Mancos, Montezuma County (NR)
- Gray Building/Novelty Theater/Opera House, Downtown Shirt Company—Montrose, Montrose County
- *Wrights Opera House*, Wright Brothers Opera Block—Ouray, Ouray County (NRHD)
- *Wheeler Opera House*—Aspen, Pitkin County (NR)
- Butte Opera House, Cripple Creek Fire Department—Cripple Creek, Teller County (NRHD)
- Dowding Building/Dowding Opera House/Windsor Opera House/Windsor Masonic Lodge—Windsor, Weld County
- Grover Opera House ~ Bivens Grocery Store—Grover, Weld County

Connecticut (other source)

- New Britain Opera House—New Britain, Hartford County (NR)
- Thomaston Opera House—Thomaston, Litchfield County (NR)

- *Goodspeed Opera House*—East Haddam, Middlesex County (NR)
- Sterling Opera House—Derby, New Haven County (NR)

Delaware (other source)

- *Newark Opera House*—Newark, New Castle County (NR)

Florida

- High Springs Opera House—High Springs, Alachua County
- J J Heard-Opera House Block—Arcadia, DeSoto County
- Saenger Theater—Pensacola, Escambia County
- Quincy Opera House—Quincy, Gadsden County
- Perkins Opera House—Monticello, Jefferson County
- Munro's Opera House—Tallahassee, Leon County
- Imperial Opera House—Sanford, Seminole County

Georgia (other source)

- Grand Opera House—Macon, Bibb County (NR)
- Degive's Grand Opera House—Atlanta, Fulton County (NR)
- *Springer Opera House*—Columbus, Muscogee County (NR)

Hawaii (no data)

Idaho

- Gorby Opera Theater—Glens Ferry, Elmore County
- Bovill Opera House—Bovill, Latah County (NR)

Illinois (other source)

- *Beardstown Grand Opera House*—Beardstown, Cass County (NR)
- Fife Opera House—Palestine, Crawford County (NR)
- Sesser Opera House—Sesser, Franklin County (NR)
- Galva Opera House—Galva, Henry County (NR)
- *Woodstock Opera House*—Woodstock, McHenry County (NR)
- Alexis Opera House—Alexis, Mercer and Warren Counties (NR)
- Phoenix Opera House Block—Rushville, Schuyler County (NR)

Indiana (database)

- Cheney Hardware/Opera House—Montpelier, Blackford County
- Clay City Opera House—Clay City, Clay County
- Leive-Parks and Stapp Opera House—Aurora, Dearborn County (NR)
- Opera House/Moss Opera House—Bloomfield, Greene County
- Commercial Building/Opera House—Linton, Greene County (NR, SR)
- Grand Opera House/Grand Theater—Linton, Greene County
- H.J. ThistleWaite Opera House—Sheridan, Hamilton County (NR, SR)
- Guyer Opera House/Lewisville Public Hall—Lewisville, Henry County (NR)
- Strattan Opera House—Gary, Lake County
- *Mitchell Opera House*—Mitchell, Lawrence County (NR)
- The Opera House—Bloomington, Monroe County (NR, SR)
- *Rockville Opera House*—Rockville, Parke County (NR)
- Opera House/Masonic Hall—Mount Vernon, Posey County (NR, SR)
- Thrall's Opera House—New Harmony, Posey County (NR, SR) (other)
- Vurpillat's Opera House—Winnamac, Pulaski County (NR)
- Liberty Opera House—Liberty, Union County
- Standard Opera House—Perrysville, Vermillion County

Iowa

- Warren Opera House Block and Hetherington Block—Greenfield, Adair County (NR)
- Corning Opera House—Corning, Adams County (NR)
- Parker's Opera House—Mason City, Cerro Gordo County (NR)
- Cresco Opera House—Cresco, Howard County (NR)
- Masonic Opera House—What Cheer, Keokuk County (NR)
- Pella Opera House—Pella, Marion County (NR)
- McHaffey Opera House—Eldon, Wapello County (NR)
- Steyer Opera House—Decorah, Winneshiek County (NR)
- Ossian Opera House—Ossian, Winneshiek County (NR)

Kansas (database)

- J.C. Merrill's Opera House—Westphalia, Anderson County
- Stores, Office & Opera House—Great Bend, Barton County

- High Street Opera House—Horton, Brown County
- Ellet's Opera House—El Dorado, Butler County (NRHD: El Dorado Downtown Historic District)
- Strong City Opera House/Strong City Auditorium/Strong City Theatre—Strong City, Chase County (SR)
- Sedan Opera House/Emmett Kelly Museum—Sedan, Chautauqua County (SR)
- *Brown Grand Opera House*—Concordia, Cloud County (NR, SR)
- Laroque Opera House—Concordia, Cloud County
- Opera House—Girard, Crawford County
- MCcune Opera House—MCcune, Crawford County
- Leland Opera House/Opera House—Troy, Doniphan County (NRHD: Doniphan County Courthouse Square Historic District)
- *Bowersock Opera House (Lawrence Opera House)/Liberty Hall*—Lawrence, Douglas County (NRHD: Lawrence Downtown Historic District)
- *Colonial Theater (Opera House)*—Junction City, Geary County
- Grainfield Opera House—Grainfield, Gove County (NR, SR)
- Opera House/Clark's Drug—Cimarron, Gray County
- Ensign Opera House—Ensign, Gray County
- Opera House—Eureka, Greenwood County
- Potter Opera House—Coolidge, Hamilton County (SR)
- Critchfield Opera House—Oskaloosa, Jefferson County
- Dighton Opera House—Dighton, Lane County (other)
- Mound City Opera House—Mound City, Linn County
- Opera House Block—Harford, Lyon County
- Florence Opera House—Florence, Marion County (NR, SR)
- Opera House—Axtell, Marshall County
- Opera House—Blue Rapids, Marshall County
- Frankfort Opera House—Frankfort, Marshall County
- Weis Opera House—Frankfort, Marshall County
- *Waterville Opera House/Waterville City Hall*—Waterville, Marshall County (NR, SR)
- *McPherson Opera House*/Mac Movie Theater—McPherson, McPherson County (NR, SR)
- The Capitol Block—Opera House/McPherson State Bank—McPherson, McPherson County
- Williams Opera House—Chanute, Neosho County

- Opera House—Carbondale, Osage County
- Howe's Opera House—Osage City, Osage County
- Opera House—Downs City, Osborne County
- Leach Opera House—Wamego, Pottawatomie County
- Shirley Opera House—Atwood, Rawlins County (NR, SR)
- Old Opera House—Manhattan, Riley County
- Grand Opera House—Topeka, Shawnee County (NR)
- Opera House Block—Smith Center, Smith County
- Old Opera House Building—Caldwell, Sumner County
- Barnes Mercantile & Opera House—Barnes, Washington County
- J.B. Dobyns Grocery & Opera House/Center Square Merchant—Yates Center, Woodson County (NRHD: Yates Center Courthouse Square Historic District)

Kentucky

- Gordon's Hall (Petersburg Opera House)—Petersburg, Boone County (NR)
- Miller Block—Old Opera House—Millersburg, Bourbon County (NRHD: Millersburg Historic District)
- Opera House—Princeton, Caldwell County (NRHD: Princeton Downtown Commercial Historic District)
- Holland Opera House—Hopkinsville, Christian County (NRHD: Hopkinsville Commercial Historic District)
- Opera House/Music Hall—Winchester, Clark County (NRHD: Winchester Downtown Commercial Historic District)
- *The Opera House & Yates Book Shop Building*—Lexington, Fayette County (NR)
- Vendome Opera House—Fulton, Fulton County (NR)
- Stewart Opera House Building—Elizabethtown, Hardin County (NRHD: Elizabethtown Courthouse)
- The Opera House—Leitchfield, Grayson County (NRHD: Court Square Historic District)
- Old Opera House/Odd Fellows Lodge—Harrodsburg, Mercer County (NRHD: Harrodsburg Commercial Historic District)
- Opera House—Henderson, Henderson County (NRHD: Stearns Commercial/Administrative Historic District)

- Miles Opera House—Madisonville, Hopkins County (NRHD: Madisonville Historic District)
- H B Thomas Building/Opera House—Horse Cave, Hart County (NRHD: Horse Cave Historic District)
- Old Opera House—Russellville, Logan County (NRHD: Russellville Historic District)
- *Washington Opera House*—Maysville, Mason County (NR)
- Odd Fellows Hall/Sauer Bros/Opera House—Lagrange, Oldham County (NRHD: Central Lagrange Historic District)
- Wades Hall/Opera House—Franklin, Simpson County (NRHD: Franklin Downtown Commercial Historic District)
- Ole Opera House—Guthrie, Todd County
- Opera House—Springfield, Washington County (NRHD: Springfield Commercial Historic District)

Louisiana (other source)

- Rapides Opera House—Alexandria, Rapides Parish (NR)

Maine

- Island Falls Opera House—Island Falls, Aroostook County (NR)
- *Portland City Hall Auditorium*—Portland, Cumberland County (NR)
- *Stonington Opera House*—Stonington, Hancock County (NR)
- *Johnson Hall*—Gardiner, Kennebec County (NR)
- Waterville Opera House—Waterville, Kennebec County (NR)
- *Camden Opera House*—Camden, Knox County (NR)
- *Rockport Opera House*—Rockport, Knox County (NR)
- *Boothbay Harbor Opera House*—Boothbay Harbor, Lincoln County (NR)
- Odeon Hall—Bethel, Oxford County
- Norway Opera House—Norway, Oxford County (NR)
- Bangor Opera House/Penobscot Theatre—Bangor, Penobscot County
- Dexter Town Hall—Dexter, Penobscot County
- Shaw's Opera House—Greenville, Piscataquis County
- Skowhegan Opera House—Skowhegan, Somerset County (NR)
- Hayford Hall/Belfast Opera House—Belfast, Waldo County (NR)
- *City Theatre*—Biddeford, York County (NR)

Maryland (no data)

Massachusetts (no data)

Michigan

- *Tibbits Opera House*—Coldwater, Branch County
- Wagner Block—Marshall, Calhoun County
- Centennial Hall Building—Marcellus, Cass County
- *Cheboygan Opera House*—Cheboygan, Cheboygan County
- Sturgis Opera House—Fowler, Clinton County
- *Blake's Opera House/Grand Ledge Opera House*—Grand Ledge, Eaton County
- Vermontville Opera House—Vermontville, Eaton County (NR)
- *City Opera House*—Traverse City, Grand Traverse County (NR)
- *Calumet Theater*—Calumet, Houghton County
- Stockbridge Town Hall—Stockbridge, Ingham County
- Portland Opera House—Portland, Ionia County
- Iron River Town Hall—Iron River, Iron County
- Brown's Opera House—Sparta, Kent County
- *Adrian Union Hall/Croswell Opera House*—Adrian, Lenawee County (NR)
- Howell Opera House—Howell, Livingston County
- *Ramsdell Theater*—Manistee, Manistee County
- Burt Opera House—Burt, Saginaw County
- Fischer's Hall—Frankenmuth, Saginaw County
- Colon Opera House—Colon, St. Joseph County
- *Detroit Opera House*—Detroit, Wayne County

Minnesota

- Mantorville Opera House—Mantorville, Dodge County (NR)
- Galligan Opera House—Lanesboro, Fillmore County (NR)
- Bank of Pine Island, Opera House Block—Pine Island, Goodhue County (NR)
- Kenyon Opera House—Kenyon, Goodhue County (NR)
- Madison City Hall & Opera House—Madison, Lac qui Parle County (NR)

- Lake Benton Opera House & Kimball Building—Lake Benton, Lincoln County (NR)
- Fairmont Opera House—Fairmont, Martin County (NR)
- Litchfield Opera House—Litchfield, Meeker County (NR)
- Opera Hall Block—Pipestone, Pipestone County (NR)
- Lockwood Opera House-Melwin Building—Northfield, Rice County (NR)
- Masonic Temple Opera House—Duluth, Saint Louis County (NR)
- Nicolin Opera House—Jordan, Scott County (NR)
- Batcher Opera House—Staples, Todd County (NR)
- Grand Opera House (First National Bank)—St. James, Watonwan County (NR)

Mississippi (database)

- Opera House—West Point, Clay County (NRHD: West Point Unified Historic District)
- Faler Opera House—Hazlehurst, Copiah County (NRHD: Hazlehurst Historic District)
- Old Opera House—Oxford, Lafayette County (NRHD: Oxford Courthouse Square Historic District)
- *Grand Opera House*—Meridian, Lauderdale County (NRHD: Meridian Historic Downtown District)

Missouri

- Opera House—Cape Girardeau, Cape Girardeau County
- Montgomery Opera House—Kahoka, Clark County (NR)
- Lohman Opera House—Jefferson City, Coleman County
- Lyric Theater/Thespian Hall—Boonville, Cooper County
- Greenfield Opera House Building—Greenfield, Dade County (NR)
- Opera Hall Block—King City, Gentry County (NR)
- Finke Opera House—California, Moniteau County (NR)
- Dougherty Auditorium/Farris Theater—Richmond, Ray County (NR)
- Opera House—St. Charles, St. Charles County
- Kiel Opera House—St. Louis Independent City

Montana

- Bridger Opera House—Bridger, Carbon County (NR)
- Fromberg Opera House—Fromberg, Carbon County (NR)
- McIntosh Block and Opera House—Kalispell, Flathead County
- Lavina Opera House—Lavina, Golden Valley County
- *Philipsburg Opera House*—Philipsburg, Granite County
- Ming Opera House—Helena, Lewis and Clark County
- Babcock Theatre—Billings, Yellowstone County
- Broadview Opera House—Broadview, Yellowstone County

Nebraska

- Thorpe's Opera House—David City, Butler County (NR)
- Surprise Opera House—Surprise, Butler County
- Lodgepole Opera House—Lodgepole, Cheyenne County
- *Z.C.B.J. Opera House*—Clarkson, Colfax County (NR)
- Army Theatre—Fort Robinson, Dawes and Sioux Counties
- Allen's Opera House—Cozad, Dawson County (NR)
- *Love Opera House*—Fremont, Dodge County
- Schneider's Opera House—Snyder, Dodge County
- Creighton Theatre—Omaha, Douglas County
- The Auditorium—Geneva, Fillmore County
- Hampton Opera House—Hampton, Hamilton County
- Tecumseh Opera House—Tecumseh, Johnson County (NR)
- *Minden Opera House*—Minden, Kearney County
- Pospeshil Theatre—Bloomfield, Knox County (NR)
- Z.C.B.J. Opera House—Verdigre, Knox County (NR)
- Martha Ellen Auditorium—Central City, Merrick County
- New Opera House—Auburn, Nemaha County (NR)
- Lawrence Opera House—Lawrence, Nuckolls County (NR)
- Steinauer Opera House—Steinauer, Pawnee County (NR)
- Table Rock Opera House—Table Rock, Pawnee County (NR)
- Gehling's Theatre—Falls City, Richardson County (NR)
- Warren's Opera House—Friend, Saline County (NR)
- Gourley's Opera House—Rushville, Sheridan County (NR)
- I.O.O.F. Hall and Opera House—Bladen, Webster County
- *Red Cloud Opera House*—Red Cloud, Webster County (NR)
- Clem's Opera House—Gresham, York County (NR)

Nevada

- *Eureka Opera House*—Eureka, Eureka County (NR)
- Nixon Opera House—Winnemucca, Humboldt County (NR)
- *Thompson's Opera House*—Pioche, Lincoln County (NR)
- *Piper's Opera House*—Virginia City, Storey County (NR)

New Hampshire (other source)

- Wakefield Opera House—Wakefield, Carroll County (NR)
- Keene Opera House—Keene, Cheshire County
- Gorham Opera House—Gorham, Coos County
- Opera Block—Haverhill, Grafton County (NR)
- *Lebanon Opera House*—Lebanon, Grafton County
- Opera House—Lisbon, Grafton County
- Littleton Opera House—Littleton, Grafton County
- Marionette Opera House—Peterborough, Hillsborough County
- Derry Opera House—Derry, Rockingham County
- *Rochester Opera House*—Rochester, Strafford County
- *Claremont Opera House*—Claremont, Sullivan County

New Jersey

- Montclair Opera House—Montclair, Essex County
- Flemington Opera House—Flemington, Hunterdon County
- Park Opera House—Asbury Park, Monmouth County
- Baker Opera House/Baker Building—Dover, Morris County (NR)
- Dennis Opera House—Newton, Sussex County
- New Opera House—Belvidere, Warren County

New Mexico

- *Shuler Theater*—Raton, Colfax County (NRHD: Raton Downtown Historic District, SR)
- Pinos Altos Opera House—Pinos Altos, Grant County (SR, NRHD: Pinos Altos Historic District)
- Elks Opera House—Silver City, Grant County (NRHD: Silver City Historic District, SR)

- Opera House—White Oaks, Lincoln County (NRHD: White Oaks Historic District, SR)
- Kitchen's Opera House—Gallup, McKinley County
- Cerrillos Opera House—Cerrillos, Santa Fe County
- *Santa Fe Opera*—Santa Fe, Santa Fe County
- Garcia Opera House—Socorro, Socorro County (NR, SR)

New York (name only)

- Keller-Palmer Opera House—Cuba, Allegany County
- Stone Opera House—Binghamton, Broome County
- *Fredonia Opera House*—Fredonia, Chautauqua County
- *Earlville Opera House*—Earlville, Chenango County (NR)
- Smyrna Town Hall Opera House—Smyrna, Chenango County (NR)
- Earlville Opera House—Earlville, Chenango and Madison Counties
- *Hudson Opera House*—Hudson, Columbia County
- *Collingwood Opera House and Office Building*—Poughkeepsie, Dutchess County (NR) (active)
- *Lancaster Opera House*—Lancaster, Erie County
- *Smith's Opera House*—Geneva, Ontario County (NR)
- Pratt Opera House—Albion, Orleans County
- Bent's Opera House—Medina, Orleans County
- Wood's Opera House—Hoosick Falls, Rensselaer County
- Opera House—Montour Falls, Schuyler County
- Opera House—Addison, Steuben County
- Purdy Opera House—Bath, Steuben County
- Frey Opera House—Hammondsport, Steuben County
- Kingston Opera House—Kingston, Ulster County
- *Hubbard Hall*—Cambridge, Washington County
- Olive Opera House—Ossining, Westchester County

North Carolina (name only)

- Mont-White Theatre Graham Opera House—Graham, Alamance County
- Hyatt's Opera House—Asheville, Buncombe County
- Opera House—Warsaw, Duplin County
- Masonic Hall & Opera House—Rocky Mount, Edgecombe County
- Oxford Opera House—Oxford, Granville County

- Stallings Building/Opera House—Enfield, Halifax County
- Bobbitt Opera House—Littleton, Halifax County
- Commercial Building & Opera House—Farmville, Pitt County
- Old Hamlet Opera House—Hamlet, Richmond County
- Opera House—Red Springs, Robeson County
- Meroney Opera House—Salisbury, Rowan County
- Opera House—Rutherfordton, Rutherford County
- Opera House/Starnes Jewelers Building—Albemarle, Stanly County (NR)
- Galloway Opera House—Mount Airy, Surry County
- Burwell Block Building-Opera House—Henderson, Vance County

North Dakota (name only)

- Maddock Opera House—Maddock, Benson County
- Ellendale Opera House—Ellendale, Dickey County (NR)
- Metropolitan Opera House—Grand Forks, Grand Forks County (NR)
- Opera House—Steele, Kidder County
- Welo Block/Opera House—Velva, McHenry County
- Opera House—Wahpeton, Richland County
- Lisbon Opera House—Lisbon, Ransom County (NR)
- Lankin Opera House—Lankin, Walsh County
- Ray Opera House—Ray, Williams County (NR)

Ohio

- Ohio Theatre—Lima, Allen County (NR)
- Hayesville Opera House—Hayesville, Ashland County (NR)
- City Hall and Opera House—Loudonville, Ashland County (NR)
- Stuart's Opera House—Nelsonville, Athens County (NR)
- Dixon--Globe Opera House--Robinson-Schwenn Building—Hamilton, Butler County (NR)
- LaSalle Theatre Building—Cleveland, Cuyahoga County
- Moreland Theater Building—Cleveland, Cuyahoga County (NR)
- The Mayfield Theatre Building—Cleveland, Cuyahoga County
- Playhouse Square Group—Cleveland, Cuyahoga County (NR)
- Variety Store Building and Theatre—Cleveland, Cuyahoga County (NR)

- Columbus Avenue Historic District—Sandusky, Erie County (NR)
- Ohio Theatre—Sandusky, Erie County
- Schine State Theatre—Sandusky, Erie County (NR)
- Vermilion Town Hall—Vermilion, Erie County (NR)
- Lincoln Theatre—Columbus, Franklin County (NR)
- Pythian Temple & James Pythian Theater—Columbus, Franklin County (NR)
- American Insurance Union Citadel—Columbus, Franklin County (NR)
- Ohio Theatre—Columbus, Franklin County (NR)
- Cedarville Opera House—Cedarville, Greene County (NR)
- Fairborn Theatre—Fairborn, Greene County (NR)
- Jamestown Opera House—Jamestown, Greene County (NR)
- Main Street Historic District—Spring Valley, Greene County (NRHD)
- Twentieth Century Theatre—Cincinnati, Hamilton County (NR)
- Majestic—Cincinnati, Hamilton County (NR)
- Albee Theatre—Cincinnati, Hamilton County
- Hamilton County Memorial Building—Cincinnati, Hamilton County (NR)
- Palace Theatre—Cincinnati, Hamilton County (NR)
- Showboat Majestic—Cincinnati, Hamilton County (NR)
- Bell's Opera House—Hillsboro, Highland County (NR)
- Woodward Opera House—Mt. Vernon, Knox County (NR)
- Marlow Theatre—Ironton, Lawrence County (NR)
- Monroe Township Hall-Opera House—Johnstown, Licking County (NR)
- Newark Downtown Historic District—Newark, Licking County (NRHD)
- Schine's Holland Theatre—Bellefontaine, Logan County (NR)
- Avon Isle—Avon, Lorain County (NR)
- Palace Theatre Building—Lorain, Lorain County (NR)
- Maumee Theater—Maumee, Lucas County (NR)
- The Ohio Theatre—Toledo, Lucas County (NR)
- Burt's Theater—Toledo, Lucas County (NR)
- Valentine Theater Building—Toledo, Lucas County (NR)
- London Commercial Business Historic District—London, Madison County (NRHD)
- Warner Theater—Youngstown, Mahoning County (NR)
- Liberty Theatre—Youngstown, Mahoning County (NR)

- State Theater—Youngstown, Mahoning County (NR)
- Palace Theater—Marion, Marion County (NR)
- Classic Theater—Dayton, Montgomery County (NR)
- Victory Theater Building—Dayton, Montgomery County (NR)
- Genoa Town Hall—Genoa, Ottawa County (NR)
- Camden City Hall and Opera House—Camden, Preble County (NR)
- Bellville Village Hall—Bellville, Richland County (NR)
- Ohio Theatre—Mansfield, Richland County (NR)
- May Realty Building—Mansfield, Richland County (NR)
- Soldiers and Sailors Memorial Building and Madison Theater—Mansfield, Richland County (NR)
- Lyric Theater—Portsmouth, Scioto County
- Eagles Building--Strand Theatre—Alliance, Stark County (NR)
- Palace Theater—Canton, Stark County (NR)
- Loew's Theatre—Akron, Summit County (NR)
- Main Exchange Historic District—Akron, Summit County (NRHD)
- South Main Street Historic District—Akron, Summit County (NRHD)
- Tuscarawas Avenue--Alexander Square Commercial Historic District—Barberton, Summit County (NRHD)
- Niles Masonic Temple—Niles, Trumbull County (NR)

Oklahoma (database)

- Opera Block—Westville, Adair County (NR)
- Opera House—Atlus, Jackson County
- Marietta Opera House—Marietta, Love County
- Ralston Opera House—Ralston, Pawnee County (NR)
- Opera House—Collinsville, Tulsa County
- *Tulsa Convention Hall (Tulsa Municipal Theater)*—Tulsa, Tulsa County (NR)

Oregon (database)

- Opera House—Haines, Baker County
- Midvale Opera House/John Day Opera House—John Day, Grant County
- Ganiard Opera House—Ashland, Jackson County (NRHD: Ashland Downtown Historic District)

- Albany Opera House—Albany, Linn County
- Vale Hotel & Vale Grand Opera House/Drexel Hotel—Vale, Malheur County (NR)
- Opera House—Vale, Malheur County
- Grand Opera House—Vale, Malheur County
- Reed Opera House & McCormack Block Addition—Salem, Marion County (NR, NRHD: Salem Downtown State Street-Commercial Street Historic District)
- Opera House—Independence, Polk County (NRHD: Independence Historic District)
- Weston Opera House/Weston Memorial Hall—Weston, Umatilla County (NRHD: Weston Commercial Historic District)
- *Elgin City Hall & Opera House*—Elgin, Union County (NR)
- Vogt Opera House/Bakitchen Bakery—The Dalles, Wasco County (NRHD: The Dalles Commercial Historic District)
- Dayton Opera House—Dayton, Yamhill County (NR)

Pennsylvania (other source)

- *Fulton Opera House*—Lancaster, Lancaster County (NR)
- Fountain Hill Opera House—Bethlehem, Lehigh and Northampton Counties (NR)
- Arch Street Opera House—Philadelphia, Philadelphia County (NR)
- Metropolitan Opera House—Philadelphia, Philadelphia County (NR)

Rhode Island (other source)

- Woonsocket Opera House—Woonsocket, Providence County (NR)

South Carolina

- *Abbeville Opera House*—Abbeville, Abbeville County (NR)
- *Dock Street Theatre*—Charleston, Charleston County (NR)
- Chester City Hall and Opera House—Chester, Chester County (NR)
- Bishopville Opera House—Bishopville, Lee County (NRHD: Bishopville Commercial Historic District)
- *Newberry Opera House*—Newberry, Newberry County (NR)
- Sumter Opera House—Sumter, Sumter County (NRHD: Sumter Historic District)

South Dakota (other source)

- Garden City Opera House—Garden City, Clark County (NR)
- Slettebak Groceries, Hardware and Opera House—Armour, Douglas County (NR)
- Wessington Springs Opera House—Wessington Springs, Jerauld County (NR)
- Selby Opera House—Selby, Walworth County (NR)

Tennessee (no data)

Texas (no data)

- Stafford Bank and Opera House—Columbus, Colorado County (NR)
- Grand Opera House—Galveston, Galveston County (NR)
- Devine Opera House—Devine, Medina County (NR)
- Thiele, J., Building—Miles, Runnels County (NR)
- Millett Opera House—Austin, Travis County (NR)
- Grand Opera House—Uvalde, Uvalde County (NR)

Utah

- Beaver Opera House—Beaver, Beaver County (NR)
- Opera House Square—Lagoon—Farmington, Davis County
- Lagoon Opera House—Lagoon—Farmington, Davis County
- Morgan Opera House—Morgan, Morgan County
- Towne Cinema/Opera House—Ephraim, Sanpete County
- Moroni Opera House—Moroni, Sanpete County (NR)
- Payson Opera House—Payson, Utah County
- St. George Social Hall/Opera House—St. George, Washington County (NR)

Vermont

- *Vergennes City Hall and Opera House*—Vergennes, Addison County
- Howard Opera House—Burlington, Chittenden County
- *Enosburg Opera House*—Enosburg, Franklin County (NR)
- Hyde Park Opera House—Hyde Park, Lamoille County
- *Chandler Music Hall*—Randolph, Orange County (NR)

- *Haskell Opera House and Library*—Derby, Orleans County (NR)
- *Barre City Hall and Opera House*—Barre City, Washington County (NR)
- *Bellows Falls Opera House*—Bellows Falls, Windham County
- *Briggs Opera House*—White River Junction, Windsor County (active)
- *Town Hall*—Woodstock, Windsor County

Virginia (name only)

- Masonic Lodge/Masonic Theatre/Opera House/Stonewall Theatre—Alleghany County
- Levy Opera House (Town Hall)—Charlottesville Independent City (NRHD: Albemarle County Courthouse Historic District)
- Opera House—Berryville, Clarke County
- Danville Academy of Music/Danville Opera House/Majestic Theater/Virginia Theater—Danville Independent City (NRHD: Downtown Danville Historic District)
- Stephens City Opera House—Stephens City, Frederick County (NRHD: Newtown--Stephensburg Historic District)
- Henry Street Opera House/Little Theatre/ Majestic Theatre/Odd Fellows Hall/Rockbridge Boot & Shoe Factory/Troubadour Building—Lexington Independent City (NRHD: Lexington Historic District)
- Lynchburg Opera House/Warner Theatre—Lynchburg Independent City
- Conner Building/Conner's Opera House—Manassas Independent City
- Center Theater/Arena Municipal Auditorium/Harrison Opera House—Norfolk Independent City
- Opera House/ Shackelford, Thomas & Gregg PLC Attorneys at Law—Orange, Orange County (NRHD: Orange Commercial Historic District)

Washington

- Sequim Opera House—Sequim, Clallam County (NR, SR)
- Seeley Theater & Opera House—Pomeroy, Garfield County (NR, SR)
- Brunswig Hotel/Grand Opera House—Chehalis, Lewis County

- Harrington Bank Block & Opera House—Harrington, Lincoln County (NR, SR)
- Opera House—Anacortes, Skagit County
- Edmonds Opera House/Masonic Temple—Edmonds, Snohomish County
- Marysville Opera House—Marysville, Snohomish County (NR, SR)
- Opera House & IOOF Lodge—Colville, Stevens County (NR, SR)
- Meyers Falls Opera House—Kettle Falls, Stevens County

West Virginia

- *Apollo Civic Theater*—Martinsburg, Berkeley County
- Davis Opera House—Huntington, Cabell County (NRHD: Downtown Huntington Historic District)
- *Keith Albee Opera House*—Huntington, Cabell and Wayne Counties
- Silas P. Smith Opera House—West Union, Doddridge County (NR)
- Rose Garden—Clarksburg, Harrison County
- *New Opera House*—Charles Town, Jefferson County (NR)
- *Shepherdstown Opera House*—Shepherdstown, Jefferson County (NRHD: Shepherdstown Historic District)
- Capitol Theater—Charleston, Kanawha County
- Capitol Music Hall—Wheeling, Marshall and Ohio Counties
- Metropolitan Opera House—Morgantown, Monongalia County
- Marlinton Opera House—Marlinton, Pocahontas County (NR)
- *Pocahontas Opera House*—Marlinton, Pocahontas County
- Cottrill Opera House—Thomas, Tucker County (NR)
- *Gaslight Opera House*—Sistersville, Tyler County
- Lincoln Opera House—New Martinsville, Wetzel County
- *Smoot Theater*—Parkersburg, Wood County

Wisconsin (database)

- Grand Opera House/Ashland Liquor Store/Ashland Gun Shop—Ashland, Ashland County (NRHD: West Second Street Historic District)
- Mellen City Hall/Opera House—Mellen, Ashland County (NR, SR)

- Portage Opera House/Eulberg Opera House/Montgomery/Rhyme's Drugs—Portage, Columbia County (NRHD: Portage Retail Historic District)
- Prairie du Chien City Hall/Grand Opera House—Prairie du Chien, Crawford County (NR, SR)
- Mt. Horeb Opera Block—Mount Horeb, Dane County (NR)
- *Stoughton Opera House*—Stoughton, Dane County
- Hazel Green Town Hall/Hazel Green Opera House—Hazel Green, Grant County (NR)
- Reed's Opera House—Lancaster, Grant County (NRHD: Courthouse Square Historic District)
- Gombar Hall; Laube Hall/Pierce True Value—Brodhead, Green County (NRHD: Exchange Square Historic District)
- Putnam Building/Broughton Opera House/McNair Block/City Hall—Brodhead, Green County (NRHD: Exchange Square Historic District)
- *Thrasher's Opera House*—Green Lake, Green Lake County (NR)
- *Mineral Point Municipal Theater*, Opera House and Library/Point Theatre/City Hall/Public Library—Mineral Point, Iowa County (NRHD: Mineral Point Historic District)
- Village Hall and Opera House/Arcadia Bowling—Fort Atkinson, Jefferson County (NRHD: Main Street Historic District)
- Concordia Opera House/B.P.O.E. Lodge No. 666—Watertown, Jefferson County (NRHD: Main Street Commercial Historic District)
- Driver's Store and Opera House/Benedicts and the Townsmen—Darlington, Lafayette County (NRHD: Main Street Historic District)
- Rodham's Opera House/Co-op Corner Store—Darlington, Lafayette County (NRHD: Main Street Historic District)
- Copeland Opera House—Shullsburg, Lafayette County (NRHD: Water Street Commercial Historic District)
- Antigo Opera House—Antigo, Langlade County (NR)
- Hortonville Community Hall/The Opera House—Hortonville, Outagamie County (NR)
- H.D. McCulloch Block/Silvermint Arcade—Stevens Point, Portage County (NRHD: Mathias Mitchell Public Square-Main Street Historic District)
- Opera House/Fox Theater—Stevens Point, Portage County (NR)
- Fifield Town Hall/Opera House—Fifield, Price County (NR, SR)

- H.T. Bailey Store and Opera House/1883 Antiques and Etc.!—Richland Center, Richland County (NRHD: Court Street Commercial Historic District)
- W.H. Pier Building & Opera House; Coffland Bros./Coffland Annex—Richland Center, Richland County (NRHD: Court Street Commercial Historic District)
- Hanchett Block/Hanchett's Hall—Beloit, Rock County (NR)
- Myers Opera House—Janesville, Rock County (NR)
- Opera Hall Block/The Opera House—Hudson, St. Croix County (NRHD: Second Street Commercial Historic District/ Opera House)
- Barton Opera House—West Bend, Washington County (NRHD: Barton Historic District)
- First Methodist Church (Wagner Opera House)/Boy's Club of Oshkosh—Oshkosh, Winnebago County (NR)
- *Oshkosh Grand Opera House*—Oshkosh, Winnebago County (NR, SR)

Wyoming

- Grand Encampment Opera House—Encampment, Carbon County
- Opera House—Rawlins, Carbon County (NRHD: Downtown Rawlins Historic District (Boundary Increase))
- Union Opera House—Rock Springs, Sweetwater County (NRHD: Downtown Rock Springs Historic District)

Notes

INTRODUCTION

1. These population figures are from the 1900 US Census.
2. Willa Cather, letter to Harvey Newbranch, editor, *Omaha World-Herald*, October 27, 1929.
3. *Saline County Union*, November 19, 1877; Street, "Band's Opera House," 57.
4. See the Afterword for further discussion of research goals and procedures.
5. John Dizikes called small-town opera houses "local glories" in his *Opera in America*, 269.

CHAPTER 1

1. Ludlow, *Dramatic Life as I Found It*, xv.
2. Cather, *Song of the Lark*, 103.
3. Cahn, *Julius Cahn's Official Theatrical Guide 1896*.
4. Paige Carlin, "End of an Era," 4.
5. Springer and Springer, *Plains Woman*, 131.
6. George B. Bryan, "Historical Who's Who of Vermont Theatre," 10.
7. *Fremont Daily Herald*, January 1, 1888.
8. Jefferson, *Autobiography*, 28.
9. Ludlow, *Dramatic Life as I Found It*, xxii.
10. Woollcott, *Mrs. Fiske, her views on actors, acting, and the problems of production*, 29.

CHAPTER 2

1. Among the many other inventions in this period changing the nature of industry and communications were the typewriter (1870) and the radio (1895). Population statistics from the decennial US Census Bureau reports.
2. *Report of the Special Commissioner of the Revenue for the Year 1869*, 2.
3. S. Lewis, *Main Street*, 234, 235.
4. Nasaw, *Andrew Carnegie*, 361.
5. "The Opera House," *Bennington Banner*, December 16, 1892, 1.
6. M. J. Lewis, *American Art and Architecture*, 120.

7. Artists such as Bingham, Bierstadt, LaFarge, Church, Durand, Homer, St. Gaudens, Sargent, Merritt, Cassatt, Eakins, and Cropsey.
8. Schlesinger, *Rise of Modern America*, 131, 132.
9. Ashley, "Beyond the Aesthetic," 38–61. This is a good history of the many efforts to improve cities through aesthetic initiatives.
10. Slote, *Kingdom of Art*, 448.
11. Wagner, *Daughters of Dakota*, 117.
12. Kolodny, *Land before Her*, 9.
13. Ibid., 152.
14. Spearman, "The American Desert," *Harper's New Monthly Magazine*, vol. 77, July 1888. Spearman, an author of twenty novels, is best known for *Whispering Smith*, which was made into a movie and a television serial.
15. Lewis, *Main Street*, 234.
16. Ibid., 235.
17. Hine, *Community on the Frontier*, 74.
18. Griswold and Griswold, *History of Leadville and Lake County, Colorado*, vol. 1, 296.
19. Rote-Rosen, "The Pember Theatre Opens." *Granville* (NY) *Sentinel*, December 15, 1934.
20. Sander, *Mary Elizabeth Garrett*, 123.
21. General Council of the City of Lexington, Kentucky, Ordinance No. 620.
22. Nasaw, *Andrew Carnegie*, 192.

CHAPTER 3

1. Butsch, *Making of American Audiences*, 64.
2. Siry, *Chicago Auditorium Building*, 79.
3. Degitz, "History of Tabor Opera House, Leadville, Colorado," 7.
4. "It Opens With 'Macbeth,'"*Boston Herald*, November 30, 1892.
5. *Kentuckian-Citizen*, December 31, 1890, from Mrs. Paul Biddle's papers. Paris is the county seat for Bourbon County, hence the name of the opera house.
6. *Chief, Red Cloud Chief* June 1885; Bergers, *History of the 1885 Red Cloud Opera House*, 1.
7. Brattleboro Town Records, Town Meeting Records, March 1 and 3, 1895.
8. It is interesting to note that Barre's earlier town halls had many commercial tenants: a dry-goods store, meat markets, printers, pool halls, unions, local newspapers, and offices for various professionals like engineers.
9. Carnegie's love of music included listening to organ music, which was almost a devotional experience for him. The organ in the Allegheny City music hall was just one of the organs he funded. His philanthropy helped over four thousand American institutions, mostly churches, purchase organs.

CHAPTER 4

1. Brady, *Martha Washington*, 189; Johnson and Burling, *Colonial American Stage*, 54, 166, 190; Shiffler, "Religious Opposition to the Eighteenth Century Philadelphia Stage." Shiffler describes the many Quaker bans on theater and then the repeals, beginning with William Penn's 1686 "Frame of Government," which considered "stage plays an offense against God."
2. Methodist Church, *Doctrines and Discipline of the Methodist Episcopal Church*, 1920, 69.
3. Johan Huizinga, *Homo Ludens*, 23.
4. Ibid., 26.
5. Prynne, *Histrio-Mastix: The Players Scourge or Actors Tragedie*, 374–375 in Morgan; Morgan, "Puritan Hostility to the Theatre," 342.
6. Gibson, *Pieter Bruegel*, 146.
7. Huizinga, *Homo Ludens*, 4.
8. Morgan, "Puritan Hostility to the Theatre."*Proceedings of the American Philosophical Society* 110: 5, 340–347 for informative discussion of the Puritans' deep-seated hostility to theater.

9. Shiffler, "Religious Opposition to the Eighteenth Century Philadelphia Stage," 223.
10. Barish, *Theatrical Prejudice*, 3.
11. Hornblow, *History of the Theatre in America*, 24.
12. Clapp, *Record of the Boston Stage*, 2.
13. Hornblow, *History of the Theatre in America*, 24.
14. Ibid.
15. Shipton, *Sibley's Harvard Graduates*, 485.
16. Hawthorne, *Blithedale Romance*, 181.

CHAPTER 5

1. Brady, *Martha Washington*, 45.
2. Dormon, *Theater in the Ante Bellum South*, 288.
3. Hill, *Theatre in Early Kentucky*, 9.
4. Ibid., 25.
5. *Kentuckian-Citizen,* December 31, 1890. From Mrs. Paul Biddle's papers.
6. Ludlow, *Dramatic Life as I See It*, 7.
7. Hepburn, *Me*, 81.
8. *New York Times*, September 29, 2013, Sunday Styles, 18.
9. Ludlow, *Dramatic Life as I See It*, 9, 45.
10. Ibid., 77, 86, 88, 89.
11. Ibid., 153, 173.
12. Smith, *Theatrical Management in the West and South for Thirty Years*, 13.
13. Ibid., ii.
14. McArthur, *Actors and American Culture*, 88. Henderson, *Theater in America*, 142. Colorado, Iowa, and Nebraska opera house information from the states' historic preservation data.
15. Schoberlin, *From Candles to Footlights*, 66.
16. A subway circuit existed in New York City in the early twentieth century. It included theaters in Manhattan, Brooklyn, and the Bronx where its 1913 Bronx Opera House with 1,900 seats has been converted to the Opera House Hotel. *New York Times*, June 1, 2015. p. A15.
17. Paige Carlin, "End of an Era," 8. Published by Kearney Daily Hub.
18. Confirming the impression that these museums were seen as inferior to real theaters, Troy's county historical society and Albany's state library have no information on the Troy Museum.
19. Hunter, *Theatre Architecture in Canada*, 17.
20. Clapp, *Record of the Boston Stage*, 3.

CHAPTER 6

1. *St. Louis Missouri Gazette*, April 25, 1839, quoted in Dormon, *Theater in the Ante Bellum South*, 249.
2. Most actors were not accepted socially. However, it should be noted that Boston's Mary Ann (Mrs. James R.) Vincent was accepted socially and, importantly, helped change attitudes toward theater.
3. *Bennington Banner*, November 11, 1892; Schanke, "Fremont's Love Opera House," 228.
4. Few post–Civil War performers wrote books describing their work and travel like Sol Smith and Noah Ludlow except for Joseph Jefferson and Sarah Bernhardt.
5. Joseph Jefferson III lived from 1829 to 1925, to differentiate him from the other Joseph Jeffersons.
6. Jefferson, *Autobiography of Joseph Jefferson*, 30; McArthur, *The Man Who Was Rip Van Winkle*, 41.
7. Jefferson, *Autobiography of Joseph Jefferson*, 457, 225.
8. Ibid., 457.
9. Cather, "Review of Joseph Jefferson in *Rip Van Winkle*," in Curtin, *World and the Parish*, vol.1, 422.

10. Ibid.
11. Jefferson, *Autobiography of Joseph Jefferson*, 459.
12. Ibid., 111.
13. Bernhardt, *Memories of My Life*, 369.
14. Huret, *Sarah Bernhardt*, 135.
15. Bernhardt, *Memories of My Life*, 433, 434.
16. Ibid., 416, 417, 419.
17. Ibid., 407.
18. Briney, "The Divine Sarah in Louisville Seventy Years Ago," *Louisville Times*, May 31, 1951.
19. *St. Louis Missouri Gazette*, April 25, 1839, cited in Dormon, *Theater in the Ante Bellum South*, 249.
20. Morris Rote-Rosen, "M. Rote-Rosen Gives History of Granville: The Pember Theatre," *Sentinel*, October 20, 1938.
21. Wilde, "Impressions of America 1882," 54.
22. Rupert Hart-Davis, *The Letters of Oscar Wilde*, 112.
23. *Fremont Tri-Weekly Tribune*, April 20, 1895.
24. Curtin, *World and the Parish*, 1:89.
25. "Oscar Interviewed," *Sunday Argus*, February 19, 1882.
26. Bryne and Kyle, "Springer Opera House History," n.p.
27. Rupert Hart-Davis, *The Letters of Oscar Wilde,* p. 94.
28. Andrews, *Charles Dickens and His Performing Selves*, 167.
29. Tomalin, *Charles Dickens*, 47.
30. Andrews, *Charles Dickens and His Performing Selves*, 167.
31. Ibid., 10.
32. Ibid., 217.
33. Twain, *Mark Twain's Autobiography*, 2:157.
34. *Baltimore Sun*, February 12, 1868.
35. See Schilke, *Dickens and Popular Entertainment*, for an interesting discussion of Dickens's interest in and support of popular entertainers.
36. Blair, *Mark Twain's West*, 424.
37. Ibid., 429.
38. Neider, *Selected Papers of Mark Twain*, 614.
39. Lorch, *Trouble Begins at Eight: Mark Twain's Lecture Tours*, 104.
40. Ibid.
41. Thornton, "Tales of Old Cambridge," *The Eagle*, June 12, 1991.
42. Lorch, *Trouble Begins at Eight*, 241.

CHAPTER 7

1. Lewis, *Main Street*, 237.
2. Eckman, "Culture as Entertainment—The Circuit Chautauquas in Nebraska," 246.
3. Gladden, "Christianity and Popular Amusements," 385, 386, 387.
4. Ibid., 388, 387, 388.
5. Rieser, *Chautauqua Movement: Protestants, Progressives, and the Culture of Modern Liberalism*, 256.
6. *Doctrines and Discipline of the Methodist Episcopal Church 1920*, 69.
7. *Doctrines and Discipline of the Methodist Episcopal Church 1939*.
8. Rieser, *Chautauqua Movement*, 257.
9. Ibid., 255.
10. Woollcott, *Mrs. Fiske*, 108.
11. Schanke, "Fremont's Love Opera House," 249, 250.
12. Ronning, "Cather and the Theater in Red Cloud," 1, 2.
13. Canfield, *Diary*, March 23, 1892, and April 11, 1893.
14. Data from University of Kentucky Library, Breckinridge Room, Lexington Opera House archives.

15. Ernst, *Trouping in the Oregon County*, 20.
16. Ludlow, *Dramatic Life as I Found It*, 568.
17. "Showboats Brought Entertainment to River Towns in the Early 1900s," *Clarion* newspaper, July 2, 1951, Filson Library archives.
18. Bryant, *Here Comes the Showboat!* xii, 2.
19. Graham, *Showboats*, 167.

CHAPTER 8

1. Sweeney, *Old Paris* (Kentucky) *Opera House*, April 25, 1958, 3.
2. Scholes, *Puritans and Music in England and New England*, 19.
3. Ibid., 204.
4. Ibid.
5. Cockrell, *Excelsior: Journals of the Hutchinson Family Singers*, 184.
6. Ibid., 184, 185.
7. Everman, *History of Bourbon County*, 62.
8. Trustees of Public Reservations, *First Annual Report*, 26.
9. Blind Tom lived from 1849 to 1908 and Blind Boone lived from 1864 to 1927.
10. Schmidt, "Archangels Unaware," http://www.twainquotes.com.
11. *Salem Review-Press*, April 27, 1894.
12. Bassett, "Minstrels, Musicians, and Melodeons," 32.
13. Ibid., 33.
14. Preston, *Opera on the Road,* 114.
15. Ibid 17n 34.
16. Ibid., 99, Appendix B, C, and D, 323, 324, 335, 336, 358, and 359.
17. Ibid., 140.
18. Curtin, *World and the Parish*, 173.
19. DuBois, "Opera on Wheels," 119.
20. Galloway, "Very American Story of Emma Abbott," 683.
21. The Andrews archives are in the Memorial Library of the Southern Minnesota Historical Center at Minnesota State University in Mankato.
22. DuBois, "Opera on Wheels," p. 120.
23. ———."Operatic Pioneers: The Story of the Andrews Family," *Minnesota History* 33, no. 8 (1953): 322.
24. Ibid., p. 325.
25. *Courier*, April 11, 1896, in Harlan Jennings, "Grand Opera in Nebraska in the 1890s," *Opera Quarterly* 11, no. 2 (1995): 100.
26. *Omaha Republican*, March 5, 1890, in Jennings, "Grand Opera in Nebraska in the 1890s," p. 111.
27. Robert C. Toll, *Blacking Up: The Minstrel Show in Nineteenth-Century America* (New York: Oxford University Press, 1974), p. 57.
28. Ibid., pp. 57, 65.
29. *Fremont (NE) Daily Herald*, May 26, 1891.
30. The Moving Image Section of the Library of Congress has short films of minstrel shows, mostly in the 1930s, some of which have been digitized. There is a film "Cake Walk," which can be seen at: http://hdl.loc.gov/loc.mbrsmi/varsmp.0367.

CHAPTER 9

1. Grimsted, "Melodrama as Echo of the Historically Voiceless," 81n6.
2. McConachie "Pacifying American Theatrical Audiences, 1820-1920" in *For Fun and Profit, The Transformation of Leisure into Consumption. 60.*

3. Levine, *Highbrow/Lowbrow*, 57, 58.

4. Bordman and Hischak, *Oxford Companion to American Theatre*, 88.

5. Gerould, "Americanization of Melodrama," 11.

6. Bordman and Hischak, *Oxford Companion to American Theatre*, 88.

7. Thomas F. Gossett, *Uncle Tom's Cabin and American Culture*, 269.

8. Ibid., 270.

9. Rutherford Hayner, *Troy and Rensselaer County, New York: A History*, 1:691.

10. *Troy Daily Times*, September 27, 1852.

11. Ibid., September 29, 1852.

12. Ibid., October 1, 1852.

13. Ibid., October 12, 1852.

14. Ibid.

15. Ibid., November 12, 1852.

16. Ibid., November 18, 1852.

17. Slote, *Kingdom of Art*, 130.

18. Ibid., 269.

19. Ibid.

20. Gossett, *Uncle Tom's Cabin and American Culture*, 381.

21. Ibid., 263.

22. Ibid., 283.

23. *Troy Daily Times*, December 2, 1852.

24. Birdoff, *The World's Greatest Hit*, 49.

25. Gossett, *Uncle Tom's Cabin and American Culture*, 266.

26. Schanke, "Fremont's Love Opera House," 250.

27. Leadville's 2010 population was 2,602, a modest number compared to the 29,040 in 1880.

28. Eaton, *American Stage of To-Day*, 21.

29. *Granville Sentinel*, November 14, 1924.

30. Cather, "Incomparable Opera House," 375.

31. Ibid., 376.

32. Burton, "Show Biz Old and New," 21 in Lewis, ed., *From Traveling Show to Vaudeville*, 21.

33. Glenn and Poole, *Opera Houses of Iowa*, 75.

34. Cather, "Incomparable Opera House,"375.

35. Dormon, *Theatre in the Ante Bellum South*, 237.

36. Ehlers, "Historical Context of Opera House Buildings in Nebraska," 90.

37. Glenn and Poole, *Opera Houses of Iowa*, 65, 73.

38. McArthur, *Actors and American Culture*, 64.

CHAPTER 10

1. Wilde, "Personal Impressions of America," in Hofer and Scharnhorst, *Oscar Wilde in America: The Interviews: Personal Impressions of America*, 180.

2. Sanford, *Mollie*, 3.

3. Wagner, *Daughters of Dakota*, 2:112.

4. B. B. Wade, *Register* (Central City, Colorado) pamphlet, May 1866, quoted in Bancroft, *Gulch of Gold*, 148.

5. Gern, "Colorado Mountain Theatre," 151.

6. Schoberlin, *From Candles to Footlights*, 66; and Degitz, *History of Tabor Opera House*, 7.

7. Reed, "History of the Grand Opera House in Peoria, Illinois," 16.

8. Biddle, *Paris, Kentucky opera house notes*, private papers, December 31, 1890, for entire paragraph.

9. Paige Carlin, "End of an Era," 1.

10. Ibid., 3.

11. Schanke, "Fremont's Love Opera House."

12. *Fremont Weekly Tribune*, December 20, 1888.

13. Ehlers, *Historical Context of Opera House Buildings in Nebraska,* 22.

14. Atherton, *Main Street on the Middle Border,* 23.

15. Tyler, "Social and Recreational Entertainments in Olathe, McPherson, and Garden City, Kansas," 221.

16. Ibid., 220.

17. Ibid., 222.

18. Ehlers, *Historical Context of Opera House Buildings in Nebraska*, 87.

19. Academy of Music, www.academyofmusictheatre.com, 1.

20. Tyler, "Social and Recreational Entertainments in Olathe, McPherson, and Garden City, Kansas," 146.

21. Ibid.

22. Ibid., 207; *Daily Irrigator,* October 7, 1886.

23. Bergers, *History of the 1885 Red Cloud Opera House,* 1.

24. Ibid.

25. Ibid.

26. Ibid., 2, 1.

27. Ibid., 2.

28. Margaret Kline-Kirkpatrick discusses the quest for sophistication in rural towns in her *Right to Recreate and the Attempt to Amuse.*

29. Bryan, "Howard Opera House in Burlington," 197.

30. Ibid.

31. Clark, "Levy Opera House—A Heritage to Honor," *The Daily Progress,* February 10, 1974.

32. Clark, *Golden Age of the Performing Arts,* 9.

33. Ibid., 20.

34. Ibid.

CHAPTER 11

1. Furman, *Tabor Opera House,* 91.

2. Garland, *Son of the Middle Border,* 230.

3. Ibid., 232.

4. Bergers, *History of the 1885 Red Cloud Opera House,* 4, 5.

5. Bancroft, *Gulch of Gold: A History of Central City, Colorado,* 194.

6. Fike, "Table Rock Opera House," 164.

7. Griswold and Griswold, *History of Leadville and Lake County, Colorado,* vol. 1, 1218.

8. Fike, "Table Rock Opera House," 24.

9. Ellis, *Life of an Ordinary Woman,* 126.

10. Vale, *Gentleman's Recreation,* 88.

11. Brown, *Gentle Tamers,* 130.

12. Garland, *Son of the Middle Border,* 94.

13. Dorsey, *Journal of Mollie Dorsey in Nebraska and Colorado Territories,* 132.

14. Thornton, "Tales of Old Cambridge," 3.

15. Geraw, "Plouff Boys," 2.

16. Hoover, "Roller-Skating toward Industrialism," 65.

17. Thornton, "Tales of Old Cambridge," 3.

18. Cormier, "Summer Paradise."

19. Instead of a central aisle with straight pews on either side, some meetinghouses had "pig pen" box pews. These pews were square or rectangular boxes with a door and bench seats on all sides for the parishioners. They were called "pig pen" boxes as they looked like pens where pigs might be kept.

20. Street, "Band's Opera House," 65.

21. Drysdale, *Not a Bad Seat in the House,* 37.

22. *National Park Service National Register of Historic Places Inventory—Nomination Form for Chandler Hall and Bethany Parish House,* 5 (history section); and Drysdale, *Not a Bad Seat in the House,* 32.

23. League of Historic American Theatres website. http://www.lhat.org.
24. Todd Robinson's 2000 Emmy Award–winning documentary film of the opera house, *Amargosa*, provides a picture of the accomplishments and determination of Marta Becket.
25. William Condee's book, *Coal and Culture*, is an excellent source of information on Appalachian opera houses.
26. *Copper County Evening News*, November 28, 1898, quoted in Case, "Calumet Theater and Town Hall," 4.
27. Case, "Calumet Theater and Town Hall," 5.
28. Ibid., 6.
29. Replica of 1901 program, "The New Calumet Theater—Only Municipal Theater in the United States," 1.

CHAPTER 12

1. Lewis, *Main Street*, 265.
2. Hudson, "Plains Country Town," 117.
3. *Dickey County Leader and Ellendale Commercial*, February 11, 1909, 1, *National Register of Historic Places Continuation Sheet Ellendale, N.D.*, sec. 8, 2.
4. McNall and McNall, *Plains Families*, 140.
5. Lewis, *Main Street*, 155, 136, 265.
6. Ibid., 268, 266.
7. Cather, *Song of the Lark*, vi.
8. Slote, *Kingdom of Art*, 5.
9. Cather, *Obscure Destinies*, 171.
10. Bigelow and Otis, *Manchester, Vermont*, n.p.
11. Thornton, "Tales of Old Cambridge," part 11.
12. Ibid., part 12.
13. Ibid., part 16.
14. US Census Bureau, *Report on Population of the United States 1890*.
15. *Salem Review-Press*, January 26, 1894.
16. *New York Times*, March 26, 2009, B12.
17. Gossett, *Uncle Tom's Cabin and American Culture*, 373.
18. Ibid.
19. Ibid., 375.
20. Smith's *African American Theater Buildings* is an excellent source for information on these buildings. This is the first comprehensive research on the topic, which opens the door to further study.

CHAPTER 13

1. Slote, *Kingdom of Art*, 448, 449.
2. Lewis, *Main Street*, 265, 266.
3. Federal Writers' Project, *Iowa: The Hawkeye State*, 148.
4. Federal Writers' Project, *New Hampshire: A Guide to the Granite State*, 127.
5. Only 2% of Georgia's population was German in 1890.
6. The portable floor could be installed over the orchestra seats providing a flat floor.
7. Fanny Janauschek (1830–1904), originally from Czechoslovakia, began her acting career in Prague and performed in Frankfurt, then in the United States. She was considered one of the last great actresses in the "grand style," according to the *Cambridge Guide to Theatre*.
8. Murphy, "Dramatic Expressions," 169–172.
9. Kucera, *Czechs and Nebraska*, 233.
10. Jewell and Stout, *Selected Letters of Willa Cather*, 164.

11. ZCBJ stands for Zapadni Ceska Bratrska Jednota (Western Bohemian Fraternal Association), founded in 1897 as a fraternal association of Czech Americans or Bohemians.
12. Screws, "Tools of Ethnic Identity," 45.
13. Kral, "History of Wilber," 1.
14. Fike, "Table Rock Opera House: Its Beginning and Early Years," 25, 26.
15. Fike, "Table Rock Opera House, 1893–1900," 165.
16. Acetylene gas or carbide was used for lighting in places not served by electrification, especially in the late nineteenth and early twentieth centuries. Its beam was clearly strong as such lighting systems were used for lighthouse beacons.
17. Fike, "Table Rock Opera House: Its Beginning and Early Years," 15, 16.
18. The Czech Heritage Project at University of Nebraska–Lincoln is an excellent source of information on the role of Czechs in Nebraska.
19. Roberts, *New Lives in the Valley*, 286.
20. Dubrow and Graves, *Sento at Sixth and Main*, 69, 73.
21. Ibid., 67, 74.
22. Lodge, Henry Cabot, "Restriction of Immigration" speech, *Congressional Record*-Senate, March 12, 1896, 2820. Lodge gave this speech when introducing a bill to amend earlier legislation and to further restrict immigration.

CHAPTER 14

1. Glenn and Poole, *Opera Houses of Iowa*, 63.
2. *Chieftain*, May, 13, 1888.
3. *Kentuckian Citizen*, December 31, 1890, Mrs. Paul Biddle's papers.
4. Cady, "Essential Features of a Large Opera House," 48.
5. Van Rensselaer, "Metropolitan Opera-House, New York," 86.
6. Cady, "Essential Features of a Large Opera House," 46.
7. Ibid., 48.
8. *Chieftain*, May 13, 1888.
9. Siry, *Chicago Auditorium Building*, 48.
10. Engelbrecht, *Adler and Sullivan's Pueblo Opera House*, 287.
11. Ibid., 282.
12. Ibid., 292; *Pueblo Daily Chieftain*, October 10, 1890, 2.
13. Eugene J. Johnson, draft of Italian theater and opera house manuscript, chaps. 8, 15.
14. The stained-glass transom has been preserved and is now in the Museum of the Rockies.
15. *Mineral Point Tribune*, February 18, 1915.
16. Nerhaugen, *Players on a Stage*, 25.
17. Furman, *Tabor Opera House*, 15.
18. The Canadian architect James Ball came from Rock Island, Quebec and the contractor Nathan Beach came from Georgeville, Quebec. Since 1995 Rock Island and Georgeville have been incorporated in Stanstead, Quebec.
19. Glass, *Prairie Opera House*, 77.
20. *Nebraska State Gazeteer and Business Directory*, 6:224.
21. "The Other Painted Stage Curtains by The O. L. Story Company," 3, 4.
22. Communication from Julie Marden to author, February 7, 2012.
23. *Burlington Free Press*, September 8, 1887, Bryan Archives, University of Vermont.
24. Grimsted, "Melodrama as Echo of the Historically Voiceless," 81.
25. Bordman and Hischak, *Oxford Companion to American Theatre*, Ben Hur entry, 68.
26. Cain, "Illinois Opera House," 5.
27. Grimsted, *Melodrama Unveiled*, 79.
28. Rote-Rosen, *Granville Sentinel*, March 20, 1941, for all quotations in this paragraph.
29. Bryan, "Howard Opera House in Burlington," 216.

CHAPTER 15

1. Kearney County Community Foundation, *Minden Opera House Commemorative Book*, 35.
2. Ibid., 36.
3. *The Federal Bulldozer* was written by Martin Anderson and published by MIT Press in 1964. Jane Jacobs wrote *The Death and Life of Great American Cities*, published by Random House in 1961.
4. Interview with Kenney Roseberry, Paris, Kentucky resident.
5. Mackintosh and Sell, *CURTAINS!!! Or New Life for Old Theatres*, 14.
6. Robert Volz quoted in *Preservation News*, June 1992, 14.
7. The website of Tibbits Opera House, www.tibbits.org, has an informative video of the construction and erection of the new cupola.
8. Smith, *Theatrical Management in the West and South for Thirty Years*, ii.

CHAPTER 16

1. Author's interview with Benjie White in Cambridge, NY, December 28, 2003.
2. *Roundtable* interview, WAMC, December 7, 2007.
3. Newspaper article, December 4, 1981, no identification, in Maysville historic preservation documentation.
4. Lamoille County Players, *The Historic Hyde Park Opera House*, 2, 3.
5. Ibid.
6. Granstrom, Chris, "Little City Turn-Around: Vergennes Makes a Comeback," *Vermont Life*, Spring 2000, 43.
7. Kearney County Community Foundation, *Minden Opera House Commemorative Book*, 1.
8. A video of the Quarryography production can be found on YouTube: http://www.youtube.com/watch%3Fv%3D2xZccJxuawO, available 2015.
9. Author's interview with Cathy Sherrill, July 2007.
10. *The Goodspeed Opera House News*, vol. 1, no. 1, December 1959.
11. Five years earlier, these telecasts were shown in only 415 theaters in 398 cities. In fact, the online magazine *The American: A Magazine of Ideas* had a lead article, "America's Opera Boom" in its July/August 2007 issue, which spelled out the astounding increase in the number of opera companies, live opera productions, and audiences.

CHAPTER 17

1. Carole Reed, "A History of the Grand Opera House in Peoria, Illinois," 16.
2. The Main Street program has become the National Main Street Center, Inc. and a subsidiary of the National Trust for Historic Preservation. Its main office is in Chicago and its website is: http://www.mainstreet.org.
3. e-mail message to author from Judy Lloyd, October 23, 2008.
4. Melena Ryzik, "Mapping the Cultural Buzz: How Cool Is That?," *The New York Times*, April 7, 2009, C 1.
5. Elizabeth Kolbert, "Postcard from Rome: Civic Duty," *The New Yorker*. January 12, 2015, 20.
6. Other Eastman philanthropies were the University of Rochester, especially its medical and dental schools, the Bureau of Municipal Research, MIT, Tuskegee, Hampton, and Mississippi State, and dental clinics in Rochester, London, Brussels, and Rome.
7. e-mail message to author from Kennedy Smith, October 8, 2008.
8. Interview, April 18, 2009.
9. www.cr.nps.gov/nr/travel/lexington. *Lexington Opera House*, 1.
10. The State of West Virginia developed a West Virginia Historic New Deal Trail at the same time as the theater trail.
11. Jesse Green, "Enter the Boosters, Bearing Theaters," *The New York Times.*, March 9, 2008, 8.

CHAPTER 18

1. Willa Cather, "The Incomparable Opera House," ed. Mildred R. Bennett, *Nebraska History* 49 (1968): 376.
2. Woollcott, *Mrs. Fiske, her views on actors, acting, and the problem of production,* 108.
3. Andrews, *Charles Dickens and His Performing Selves*, 49.
4. Glenn and Poole, *Opera Houses of Iowa,* 75.
5. Doyle, *Encore! The Renaissance of Wisconsin Opera Houses,* 161.
6. Email message to author from Ellen McLaughlin, March 18, 2007.
7. Minder and Smale, "Among Victims of the Crash, Opera Singers and Newlyweds," *New York Times*, March 26, 2015, A8.
8. Email letter to author from Peter Judd, March 3, 2008.
9. *The Spill Light,* quarterly newsletter from the Stonington Opera house, Spring 2013.
10. Email message to author from Julie Angelo, December 13, 2007.
11. Gard, *Grassroots Theater,* 33.
12. Ibid., 34.
13. Ibid., 97, 98.
14. Cady, "Essential Features of a Large Opera House," *The American Architect and Building News.* October 29, 1887, 618.
15. *Le Moniteur Universel*, Decembre 31, 1860.
16. Oestreich, "Flaunting the Spirit of Support for the Arts," *New York Times*, April 15, 2013, c 2.
17. Oestreich. "Flaunting the Spirit of Support for the Arts," *New York Times*, April 15, 2013; and letter to author from Ellen P. Caimol, Office of the Director/Press Counselor, Embassy of Austria, April 15, 2013 confirming the facts in Oestreich's article.
18. Markusen, Schrock, and Cameron, *Artistic Dividend Revisited,* 21.
19. Census Bureau figures indicate that the US urban population from 1910 to 2010 grew by 35 percent while in that same period the rural population shrank by 35 percent.

CHAPTER 19

1. Drysdale, *Not a Bad Seat in the House,* 50.
2. Ludlow, *Dramatic Life as I Found It,* ix.
3. Major, *My Old Man,* 337, 1.
4. Butsch, *Making of American Audiences,* 64.
5. Atlas, "Don't Show Me the Money," *New York Times*, September 12, 2012, Sunday Review.
6. Winthrop, *Life and Letters of John Winthrop,* 19.
7. Julie Marden, communication with author, February 2012.
8. Florida, *Rise of the Creative Class,* xii.
9. Markusen and King, *Artistic Dividend*, 3.
10. Ibid., 6.
11. Commager, *American Mind,* 6.

APPENDIX

1. The author can be reached at annthwaite@gmail.com.

Bibliography

Academy of Music Theatre. "Academy of Music." 1975. www.academyofmusictheatre. com.

Actors' Equity Association. *About Equity: A Handbook*. New York: Actors' Equity Association, 2002.

Adams, Annon. "Mr. Platt Goes to the Collingwood Opera House." In *Dutchess County Historical Society Year Book*. Vol. 78. 1993, 46–79.

———. "Oh! Those 19th Century Opera Houses. Flat Floor Events." *Marquee*. 34, no. 4 (2002): 400.

Ames, Kenneth L. *Death in the Living Room and Other Tales of Victorian Culture*. Philadelphia: Temple University Press, 1992.

Andrews, Malcolm. *Charles Dickens and His Performing Selves*. Oxford: Oxford University Press. 2006.

Archer, Stephen M. "E Pluribus Unum: Bernhardt's 1905–6 Farewell Tour." In *The American Stage: Social and Economic Issues from the Colonial Period to the Present*, ed. Engle and Tice. New York: Cambridge University Press, 1993, 159–174.

Archibald, Robert R. *The New Town Square: Museums and Communities in Transition*. Walnut Creek: AltaMira Press, 2004.

Aron, Cindy. *Working at Play: A History of Vacations in the United States*. New York: Oxford University Press, 1999.

Ashley, Amanda Johnson. "Beyond the Aesthetic: The Historical Pursuit of Local Arts Economic Development." *Journal of Planning History* 14, no. 1 (February 2015): 38–61.

Atherton, Lewis. *Main Street on the Middle Border*. New York: Quadrangle/New York Times, 1975.

Atlas, James. "Don't Show Me the Money!" *New York Times*, Sunday Review, September 15, 2012.

Axelrod, Alan, ed. *The Colonial Revival in America*. New York: W. W. Norton (published for Henry Francis DuPont Winterthur Museum), 1985.

Baker, Nora Cox. *Recollections of Childhood, and Happenings to Me*. Chadron: Chadron Normal College, n.d.

Bancroft, Caroline. *Gulch of Gold: A History of Central City, Colorado*. Boulder: Johnson, 1959.

Bang, Roy T. *Heroes without Medals: A Pioneer History of Kearney County, Nebraska*. Minden: Warp, 1952.

Banham, Martin, ed. *The Cambridge Guide to Theatre*. Cambridge and New York: Cambridge University Press, 1992.

Barish, Jonas, *The Theatrical Prejudice*. Berkeley: University of California Press, 1985.

Barry, Harold A. *Town Hall*. Brattleboro, VT: self-published, 1983.

Barton, H. Arnold. *Letters from the Promised Land: Swedes in America 1849–1914*. Minneapolis: University of Minnesota Press for the Swedish Pioneer Historical Society, 1975.

Barzun, Jacques, ed. "Shakespeare: Each Play a World." *The Selected Writings of John Jay Chapman*. New York: Farrar, Straus & Cudahy, 1957.

Bassett, T. D. Seymour, "Minstrels, Musicians, and Melodeons: A Study in the Social History of Music in Vermont, 1848–1872." *New England Quarterly* 19 (March 1946): 32–49.

Belding, Russell. "Old Town Hall—69–77 North Main 1860." Unpublished paper. Barre, VT.

Bennett, Jane A. "Entertainment in Troy in the 19th Century." *Sunday Record*. November 9, 1980, B1.

Bergers, John B. *History of the 1885 Red Cloud Opera House*. Red Cloud: Willa Cather Pioneer Memorial and Educational Foundation, n.d.

Bern, Enid, ed. "They Had a Wonderful Time: The Homesteading Letters of Anna and Ethel Erickson." *North Dakota History* 45, no. 4 (Fall 1978): 4–31.

Bernhardt, Sarah. *Memories of My Life: Being My Personal, Professional and Social Recollections as Woman and Artist*. New York: D. A. Appleton, 1907.

Biddle, Patty: research on Paris, Kentucky opera house, n.d.

Bigelow, Edwin L., and Nancy H. Otis. *Manchester Vermont: A Pleasant Land among the Mountains 1761–1961*. Manchester: Town of Manchester, 1961.

Birdoff, Harry. *The World's Greatest Hit—Uncle Tom's Cabin*. New York: S. F. Vanni, 1947.

Blair, Walter, ed. *Mark Twain's West: The Author's Memoirs about his Boyhood Riverboats, and Western Ventures*. Chicago: Lakeside Press, R. R. Donnelly, 1983.

Blouet, Brain W., and Frederick C. Luebke, eds. *The Great Plains: Environment and Culture*. Lincoln: University of Nebraska, 1979.

Booker, Susan. "Did They Really Sing Opera in the Opera Houses?: Public Entertainment in Oklahoma and Indian Territories, 1895–1907." *Chronicles of Oklahoma* 81, no. 2 (Summer 2003).

Bordman, Gerald, and Thomas S. Hischak. *The Oxford Companion to American Theatre*. New York: Oxford University Press, 2004.

Bort, Mary Hard. *Manchester: Memories of a Mountain Valley*. Tucson: Marshall Jones. for Manchester Historical Society, 2005.

Braden, Donna. *Leisure and Entertainment in America: Based on the Collection of the Henry Ford Museum and Greenfield Village.* Dearborn, MI: Henry Ford Museum and Greenfield Village, 1988.

Brady, Patricia. *Martha Washington, An American Life.* New York: Viking, 2005.

Branch, Edgar M., Michael B. Frank, and Kenneth M. Sanderson, eds. *The Mark Twain Papers: Mark Twain's Letters.* Vol. 1, *1853–1866.* Berkeley: University of California Press, 1988.

Brattleboro Town Records. *Town Meetings Records.* March 6, 1853; February 7, 1854; March 5, 1895.

Briney, Melville O. "The Divine Sarah in Louisville Seventy Years Ago." *Louisville Times*, May 31, 1951.

Brooks, Van Wyck. *The Confident Years: 1885–1915.* New York: E. P. Dutton, 1952.

Brown, Dee. *The Gentle Tamers: Women of the Old Wild West.* Toronto, NY: Benton Pathfinders Edition, 1974.

Bryan, George B. "A Historical Who's Who of Vermont Theatre." *Occasional Paper #13.* University of Vermont Canter for Research on Vermont, 1981.

———. "The Howard Opera House in Burlington." *Vermont History* 45, no. 4 (1977).

———. Papers. Archives, University of Vermont Library.

———. "Uncle Tom's Cabin and Vermont." *Vermont History* 45, no. 1 (1977).

———. "Vermont Drama: A Bibliography." *Vermont History* 46, no. 3 (Summer 1978): 175–93.

Bryne, Mary M. and F. Clason Kyle. *Springer Opera House History.* n.p., 1967.

Bryant, Betty. *Here Comes the Showboat!* Lexington: University Press of Kentucky, 1994.

Bucco, Martin. *Main Street: The Revolt of Carol Kennicott.* New York: Twayne, 1993.

Burris-Meyer and Edward C. Cole. *Theatres and Auditoriums.* New York: Reinhold, 1964.

Burton, Jack. *In Memoriam: Oldtime Show Biz.* New York: Vantage Press, 1965.

Burton, Jack. "Show Biz Old and New," in Lewis, *From Traveling Show to Vaudeville—Theatrical Spectacle in America.* Baltimore. John Hopkins Press, 2003.

Bushman, Richard L. *The Refinement of America: A Social History of the Visual and Performing Arts in America, 1890–1950.* New York: Harper & Row, 1985.

Butsch, Richard. *The Making of American Audiences: From Stage to Television—1750–1990.* Cambridge: Cambridge University Press, 2000.

Butsch, Richard, ed. *For Fun and Profit: The Transformation of Leisure into Consumption.* Philadelphia: Temple University Press, 1990.

Byrne, Mary Margaret, and F. Clason Kyle. "Springer Opera House History." *Springer Opera House First Annual Gala*, 1967.

Cady, J. Cleaveland. "The Essential Features of a Large Opera House." *American Architect and Building News* 22 (October 29, 1887): 46–48.

Cahn, Julius. *Julius Cahn's Official Theatrical Guide 1896.* New York: Publication Office, Empire Theatre Building, 1896.

Cain, Jerrilee. *Illinois Opera House: A Time of Glory.* Western Illinois University Library and Archives Collection, n.d.

Calvert, Jean, and John Klee. *Maysville, Kentucky: From Past to Present in Pictures.* Maysville, KY: Mason County Museum, 1983.

Canfield, Flavia A. "Diary 1892, 1893, 1894, 1897." Unpublished. Archives, Canfield Library, Arlington, VT.

Canning, Charlotte M. *The Most American Thing in America: Circuit Chautauqua as Performance.* Iowa City: University of Iowa Press, 2005.

———. "'The Most American Thing in America': Producing National Identities in Chautauqua, 1904–1932." *Performing America: Cultural Nationalism in American Theatre*, ed. Jeffrey D. Mason and J. Ellen Gainor. Ann Arbor: University of Michigan Press, 1999.

Carlin, Paige. *An End of an Era: A History of the Kearney Opera House, 1891–1954.* Kearney: *The Kearney Daily Hub*, n.d.

Carson, Jane. *Colonial Virginians at Play.* Williamsburg, VA: Colonial Williamsburg Foundation, 1989.

Case, Kim M. "The Calumet Theatre and Town Hall." Unpublished paper, Michigan Technical University, 1995.

Casto, Marilyn. *Actors, Audiences and Historic Theaters of Kentucky.* Lexington: University Press of Kentucky, 2000.

Cather, Willa. *My Antonia.* Boston: Houghton Mifflin, 1954.

———. "The Incomparable Opera House." *Nebraska History* 49 (1968): 373–378.

———. *Obscure Destinies.* New York: Alfred A. Knopf, 1932.

———. *O Pioneers.* Boston: Houghton Mifflin, 1995.

———. *The Song of the Lark.* Boston: Houghton Mifflin, 1937.

Clapp, William W., Jr. *Record of the Boston Stage.* 1853; reprint, New York: Greenwood Press, 1969.

Clark, Margaret F. "The Levy Opera House- A Heritage to Honor," *The Daily Progress.* February 10, 1974.

Clark, Margaret W. Fowler. *The Golden Age of the Performing Arts: The Town Hall (Levy Opera House) 1852–1912.* Petersburg: Dietz Press, 1976.

___. "The Levy Opera House—A Heritage to Honor," *The Daily Progress*, February 10, 1974.

Clift, G. Glenn. *History of Maysville and Mason County.* Vol. 1. Lexington: Transylvania Printing Company, 1936. Reprint, Kokoma: Selby Publishing and Printing, 1983.

Cockrell, Dale, ed. and anno. *Excelsior: Journals of the Hutchinson Family Singers 1842–1846.* Sociology of Music Series No. 6. Stuyvesant: Pendragon Press, 1989.

"Collection of Nebraska Pioneer Reminiscences." Nebraska State Society of the Daughters of the American Revolution, 1916.

Collins, Gail. *America's Women.* New York: HarperCollins, 2003.

Columbian Theatre Foundation. "The Columbian Theatre Museum and Art Center: Grand Opening Commemorative Guide." Wamego: Columbian Theatre Foundation, 1994.

Commager, Henry Steele. *The American Mind.* New Haven: Yale University Press, 1964.

Condee, William Farley. *Coal and Culture: Opera Houses in Appalachia.* Columbus: Ohio State University Press, 2005.

Cormier, William A. "A Summer Paradise—Salem 200 Years Ago." *Greenwich Journal and Salem Press*, February 20, 2003.

Creigh, Dorothy Weyer. *Nebraska: A Bicentennial History.* New York: W. W. Norton and American Association for State and Local History, 1977.

Cunning, Tracy. *Iowa Opera Halls and Opera Houses: Evolution of Stage-Focused Structures in Iowa.* Des Moines: Bureau of Historic Preservation for Iowa State Historical Society, n.d.

Curti, Merle. *The Growth of American Thought.* New York: Harper & Row, 1964.

Curtin, William M. *The World and the Parish: Willa Cather Articles and Reviews 1893–1902.* 2 vols. Lincoln: University of Nebraska Press, 1970.

Dalzell, Robert F. *The Good Rich and What They Cost Us.* New Haven: Yale University Press, 2013.

Daniels, Bruce C. *Puritans at Play: Leisure and Recreation in Colonial New England.* New York: St. Martin's Press, 1995.

Davis, Peter A. "Puritan Mercantilism and the Politics of Anti-Theatrical Legislation in Colonial America." *The American Stage: Social and Economic Issues from the Colonial Period to the Present*, ed. Ron Engle and Tice L. Miller. Cambridge: Cambridge University Press, 1993.

Deer Isle–Stonington Historical Society. *Image of America: Deer Isle and Stonington.* Charleston: Arcadia, 2004.

Degitz, Dorothy M. "History of Tabor Opera House, Leadville, Colorado, from 1879–1905." Master's thesis. Gunnison: Western State College of Colorado, 1935.

Dizikes, John. *Opera in America: A Cultural History.* New Haven: Yale University Press, 1993.

Donahoe, Ned. "Theatres in Central Illinois—1850–1900." PhD dissertation, University of Illinois, 1953. Ann Arbor: University Microfilms, n.d.

Donnelly, Marian Card. *The New England Meeting Houses of the Seventeenth Century.* Middletown: Wesleyan University Press, 1968.

Donovan, Josephine, *Uncle Tom's Cabin: Evil, Afflictive and Redemptive Love.* Boston: Twayne, 1991.

Dormon, James H., Jr. *Theater in the Ante Bellum South 1815–1861.* Chapel Hill: University of North Carolina, Press 1967.

Dorset, Phyllis Flanders. *The New Eldorado: The Story of Colorado's Gold and Silver Rushes.* New York: Macmillan, 1970.

Douglas, Ann. *The Feminization of American Culture.* New York: Alfred A. Knopf, 1977.

Doyle, Brian Leahy. *Encore! The Renaissance of Wisconsin Opera Houses.* Madison: Wisconsin Historical Society Press, 2009.

Draper, Benjamin P. "Colorado Theatres, 1859–196." PhD dissertation, University of Denver, Faculty of Arts and Sciences, 1969.

Drysdale, M. Dickey. *Not a Bad Seat in the House.* Randolph: Chandler Center for the Arts, 2007.

DuBois, Cornelia Andrews. "Opera on Wheels." *Gopher Reader* (1958): 119–121.

———. "Operatic Pioneers—The Story of the Andrews Family." *Minnesota History* 33, no. 8 (Winter 1953): 317–25.

Dubrow, Gail, and Donna Graves. *Sento at Sixth and Main*. Washington, DC: Smithsonian, 2002.

Dunbar, Willis Frederick. "The Opera House as a Social Institution." *Michigan History* 27 (Summer 1943).

Dupont, David. "Opera House Revivals: Renovation and Renaissance." In *Winter in Vermont*, n.d.

Eaton, Walter Pritchard. *The American Stage of To-Day*. Boston: Small, Maynard, 1908.

Eckman, James P. "Culture as Entertainment—The Circuit Chautauquas in Nebraska, 1914–1924." *Nebraska History* 75, no. 3 (Fall 1994): 244–253.

Ehlers, D. Layne. "The Historical Context of Opera House Buildings in Nebraska: The Opera House Buildings in Nebraska Study." Master's thesis, Graduate College, University of Nebraska, Lincoln, 1997.

———. "Second Floor, Brick Block: Nebraska's Opera Houses." *Nebraska History* 72, no. 1 (Spring 1991): 3–20.

Ellis, Anne. *The Life of an Ordinary Woman*. Lincoln: University of Nebraska Press, 1980.

Emboden, William. *Sarah Bernhardt*. New York: Macmillan, 1975.

Emerson, Ken. *Doo-Dah: Stephen Foster and the Rise of American Popular Culture*. New York: Simon & Schuster, 1997.

Emery, George. *The Methodist Church on the Prairies, 1896–1914*. Montreal: McGill-Queens University Press, 2001.

"End of an Era: A History of the Kearney Opera House 1891–1954." *Kearney Daily Hub*, 1954.

Engle, Ron, and Tice L. Miller, eds. *The American Stage: Social and Economic Issues the Colonial Period to the Present*. New York: Cambridge University Press, 1993.

Engelbrecht, Lloyd C. "Adler & Sullivan's Pueblo Opera House: City Status for a New Town in the Rockies." *Art Bulletin* 67, no. 2 (June 1985): 277–295.

"Enter the Booster, Bearing Theaters: Regional Stage Companies." *New York Times*, March 9, 2008, 1, 8.

Ernst, Alice Herson. *Trouping in the Oregon Country: A History of Frontier Theatre*. Portland: Oregon Historical Society, 1961.

Everman, H. E. *The History of Bourbon County—1785–1865*. Paris: Bourbon Press, 1977.

Fairbanks, Carol, and Bergine Haakenson. *Writings of Farm Women—1840–1940*. New York: Garland, 1990.

"Familiar Faces Take the State." *Connecticut Valley Spectator*, March 27, 2008.

Fanning, Patricia J. "From 'Bolshevik Hall' to Butterfly Ballroom: The Assimilation of South Norwood's Lithuanian Hall." In *Life on the Street Commons, 1600 to the Present*. Dublin Seminar for New England Folk Life, Boston: Boston University Press, 2005.

Farfan, Matthew F. *The Making of the Haskell Free Library and Opera House: The Construction Years, 1901–1904*. Selected Letters from the Haskell Archives. Quebec: Haskell Free Library, 1999.

Federal Writers' Project of the Works Progress Administration. *Colorado: A Guide to the Highest State*. New York: Hastings House, 1959.

———. *Indiana: A Guide to the Hoosier State*. New York: Oxford University Press, 1961.

———. *Iowa: A Guide to the Hawkeye State*. New York: Hastings House, 1959.

———. *Nebraska: A Guide to the Cornhusker State*. New York: Hastings House, 1947.

———. *The WPA Guide to Kentucky*. Ed. F. Kevin Simon. 1939; reprint ed., Lexington: University Press of Kentucky, 1946.

Fike, Duane. "The Table Rock Opera House, 1893–1900: A Small-Town Community Center." *Nebraska History* 58 (1977): 144–174.

———. "The Table Rock Opera House: Its Beginning and Early Years." Paper for American Theater History Course, University of Nebraska, Lincoln, 1999.

Fink, Deborah. *Wives and Mothers in Rural Nebraska—1880–1940*. Chapel Hill: University of North Carolina Press, 1992.

Fisher, Judith, and Stephen Watt, eds. *When They Weren't Doing Shakespeare: Essays on Nineteenth-Century British and American Theatre*. Athens: University of Georgia Press, 1985.

Fiske, Minnie Maddern Papers. Library of Congress.

Fitzgerald-Hume, Elizabeth. "Rights and Riots: The Footmen's Riots at Drury Lane 1737." *Theatre Notebook* 59, no. 1 (2005): 41–52.

Florida, Richard. *The Rise of the Creative Class*. New York: Basic Books, 2004.

Frick, John W., and Carlton Ward, eds. *Directory of Historic American Theatres*. Westport, CT: Greenwood Press, 1987 (for the League of Historic American Theatres).

Fried, Benjamin. "Big Things in Littleton." *Making Places* (June 2005).

Frohman, Daniel. *Encore*. New York: L. Furman, 1937.

Frutchey, Jane. "The Arts as an Economic Engine." *Maryland Life* (November–December 2007): 73–77.

Fuller, Kathryn H. *At the Picture Show: Small-Town Audiences and the Creation of the Movie Fan Culture*. Washington, DC: Smithsonian Institution Press, 1990.

Furman, Evelyn E. Livingston. *The Tabor Opera House: A Captivating History*. Aurora: National Writers Press, 1984.

Galloway, Tod Buchanan. "The Very American Story of Emma Abbott." *Etude* 9 (1935).

Gard, Robert. *Grassroots Theater: A Search for Regional Arts in America*. Madison: University of Wisconsin Press, 1999.

Garland, Hamlin. *A Son of the Middle Border*. New York: Macmillan, 1917.

Gates, Henry Louis, and Hollis Robbins, eds. *The Annotated Uncle Tom's Cabin*. New York: W. W. Norton, 2006.

General Council of City of Lexington. *Ordinance No. 620*. January 11, 1895; in Lexington Opera House program, November 2, 1896.

Geraw, Janice. "Boxing Champ 'Kid Roy.'" *Enosburgh Historical Digest* 6, no. 2 (Spring 1999).

———. "The Plough Boys: Basketball and the Opera House." *Enosburgh Historical Digest* 6, no. 2 (Spring 1999).

Gern, Jesse W. "Colorado Mountain Theatre: History of Theatre at Central City, 1859–1885." PhD dissertation, Ohio State University, Graduate School, 1960.

Gerould, Daniel C. "The Americanization of Melodrama." In *American Melodrama*, ed. Daniel C. Gerould. New York: Performing Arts Journal Publications, 1983.

Gibson, Walter S. "Artists and Rederijkers in the Age of Brugel." *Art Bulletin* 63 (1981): 426–46.

———. *Pieter Bruegel and the Art of Laughter.* Berkeley: University of California, 2006.

Gladden, Washington. "Christianity and Popular Amusements." *Century Magazine*, January 1885.

Glass, Rita M. *Prairie Opera House: A History of the Thorpe Opera House at David City.* David City: South Platte Press and the Thorpe Opera House Committee, 2007.

Glenn, George D., and Richard L. Poole. *The Opera Houses of Iowa.* Ames: Iowa State University Press, 1993.

———. "The Opera Houses of Iowa: An Introduction." *Opera Houses of the Midwest.* Mid-America Theatre Conference, South Dakota University/Kansas State University, 1988.

Goodheart, Adam. "This Side of Main Street." *Preservation* (March–April 2002): 36–4.

Gossett, Thomas F. *Uncle Tom's Cabin and American Culture.* Dallas: Southern Methodist University Press, 1985.

Graham, Philip. *Showboats: The History of an American Institution.* Austin: University of Texas, 1951.

Granstrom, Chris. "Little City Turn-Around: Vergennes Makes a Comeback." *Vermont Life*, Spring 2000, 38–43.

Granstrom, Chris. "Little City Turn-Around: Vergennes Makes a Comeback." *Vermont Life*, Spring 2000, 43.

Gratz, Rebecca. *Letters of Rebecca Gratz.* Ed. Rabbi David Philipson. Philadelphia: Jewish Publication Society of America, 1929.

Green, Jesse. "Enter the Boosters, Bearing Theaters." *New York Times.* March 9, 2008, 8.

Greiner, Tyler L. "A History of Professional Entertainment at the Fulton Opera House in Lancaster, Pennsylvania." Master's thesis, Department of Theatre and Film, Penn State University, 1977.

Grimsted, David. *Melodrama Unveiled: American Theater and Culture 1800–1850.* Berkeley: University of California Press, 1987.

Griswold, Don L., and Jean Harvey Griswold. *History of Leadville and Lake County, Colorado: From Mountain Solitude to Metropolis.* Vols. 1 and 2. Denver: Colorado Historical Society and University Press of Colorado, 1996.

Hall, Gertrude. *The Wagnerian Romance.* Introduction by Willa Cather. New York: Alfred A. Knopf, 1925.

Handlin, Oscar, *The Americans: A New History of the People of the United States.* Boston: Atlantic Monthly Press, 1963.

Haraven, Tamara K. *Anonymous Americans: Explorations in Nineteenth-Century Social History.* Englewood: Prentice-Hall, 1971.

Hart-Davis, Rupert. ed., *The Letters of Oscar Wilde.* London: Rupert Hart-David, Ltd., 1962.

Hart, James. "Dion Boucicault's Comic Myths." In *When They Weren't Doing Shakespeare: Essays on Nineteenth Century British and American Theatre*, ed. Judith Fisher and Stephen Watt. Athens: University of Georgia Press, 1985.

Hawthorne, Nathaniel. *The Blithedale Romance*. Boston and New York: Bedford/St. Martin's, 1996.

Hayner, Rutherford. *Troy and Rensselaer County, New York: A History*. Vol. 1. New York: Lewis Historical Publishing, 1925.

Heinemann, Margot. *Puritanism and Theatre: Thomas Middleton and Opposition Drama under the Early Stuarts*. London: Cambridge University Press, 1980.

Henderson, Mary C. *Theater in America: 200 Years of Plays, Players, and Productions*. New York: Henry N. Abrams, 1996.

Hepburn, Katharine. *Me: Stories of My Life*. New York: Alfred A. Knopf, 1991.

Hervon, Ima Honaker. *The Small Town in American Drama*. Dallas: Southern Methodist University Press, 1969.

Hewitt, Nancy A. *A Companion to American Women's History*. Oxford: Blackwell Publishers, 2002.

Higham, John. "The Reorientation of American Culture in the 1890s." In *Origins of Modern Consciousness*, ed. John Weiss. Detroit: Wayne State University Press, 1965.

Hill, West T., Jr. *The Theatre in Early Kentucky: 1790–1820*. Lexington: University Press of Kentucky, 1971.

Hine, Robert V. *Community on the American Frontier: Separate but Not Alone*. Norman: University of Oklahoma Press, 1980.

Hooley's Opera House Songster. New York: Dick & Fitzgerald, 1863.

Hoover, Dwight W. "Roller-Skating toward Industrialism." In *Hard at Play: Leisure in America, 1840–1940*. ed. Kathryn Grover, Amherst: University of Massachusetts Press, 1992.

Hornblow, Arthur. *A History of the Theatre in America*. Vol. 1. 1919 reprint, New York: Benjamin Blom, 1965.

Howe, M. A. DeWolfe, ed. *The Articulate Sisters: Passages from Journals and Letters of the Daughters of President Josiah Quincy of Harvard University*. Cambridge, MA: Harvard University Press, 1946.

Hubbard Hall Times. Cambridge, NY: n.p., 2002–2012.

Hudson, John C. "The Plains Country Town." In *The Great Plains: Environment and Culture*, ed. Brian W. Blouet and Frederick C. Luebke. Lincoln: University of Nebraska Press, 1979.

Huizinga, J. *Homo Ludens: A Study of the Play Element in Culture*. New York: Harper and Row, 1970.

Hunt, Hugh. *The Live Theatre: An Introduction to the History and Practice of the Stage*. London: Oxford University Press, 1962.

Hunter, Robert. *Theatre Architecture in Canada: A Study of Pre-1920 Canadian Theatre*, study for The Historic Sites and Monuments Board of Canada, n.p., 1984–1985.

Huret, Jules. *Sarah Bernhardt*. London: Chapman and Hall, 1899.

Hutton, Laurence. "The Negro on the Stage." *Harper's New Monthly Magazine*, vol. 79, no. 469, June 1889.

Jackson, Kenneth. *Crabgrass Frontier: The Suburbanization of the United States*. New York: Oxford University Press, 1995.

Jeffcoat, A. E. *Spirited Americans: A Commentary on America's Optimism—From the Puritans to the Cyber-Century*. Bainbridge Island, WA: Winslow House Books, 2000.

Jefferson, Joseph. *The Autobiography of Joseph Jefferson.* New York: Century Company, 1890.

Jennings, Harlan. "Grand Opera in Nebraska in the 1890s." *Nebraska History* 78 (1997): 2–13.

Jewell, Andrew, and Janis Stout, eds. *The Selected Letters of Willa Cather.* New York: Alfred A. Knopf, 2013.

Johnson, Eugene J. Unpublished draft of book on Italian theaters and opera houses, 2007.

Johnson, Odai, and William J. Burling. *The Colonial American Stage, 1665–1774: A Documentary Calendar.* Madison, NJ: Fairleigh Dickinson Press, 2001.

Johnson, Sally West. "Theatre Comes to Town." *Vermont Magazine*, May–June 2007.

Jones-Eddy, Julie. *Homesteading Women: An Oral History of Colorado, 1890–1980.* New York: Twayne, 1992.

Jusserand, J. J. *English Warfaring Life in the Middle Ages.* Trans. Lucy T. Smith. London: Bern, 1950.

Kearney County Community Foundation. *Minden Opera House Commemorative Book.* Minden: Minden Community Players, 2000.

Kellogg, Orleatha Gravel. *Bloom on the Land: A Prairie Pioneer Experience.* Henderson: Service Press, 1982.

King, Donald C. *The Theatres of Boston: A Stage and Screen History.* Jefferson, NC: McFarland, 2005.

Kleber, John E., ed. *The Kentucky Encyclopedia.* Lexington: University Press of Kentucky, 1992.

Kline-Kirkpatrick, Margaret. *The Right to Recreate and the Attempt to Amuse: Recreation and Leisure in the Towns of Addison County, Vermont, 1790–1930.* Middlebury, VT: Friends of the Library, Middlebury College, 1998.

Kolbert, Elizabeth. "Postcard from Rome: Civic Duty," *The New Yorker*, January 12, 2015.

Kolodny, Annett. *The Land before Her: Fantasy and Experience of the American Frontiers, 1630–1860.* Chapel Hill: University of North Carolina Press, 1984.

Kucera, Vladimir. *Czech Drama in Nebraska.* N.p., 1978.

Kucera, Vladimir, and Dolores Kucera. *Czech Music in Nebraska.* N.p., 1980.

Kucera, Vladimir, and Alfred Novacek. *Czechs and Nebraska.* N.p., 1976.

Kral, E. A. "History of Wilber." Paper presented at Nebraska SVU Conference 2000, Czechoslavak Society of Arts and Sciences.

Kral, E.A. *The History of Wilber.* Paper presented at Nebraska SVU 2000 conference.

Lamoille County Players. *The Historic Hyde Park Opera House.* n.p., 2005.

Langdon, Philip. "The Coming of the Creative Class." *Planning.* July 2002.

Laufe, Abe. *The Wicked Stage: A History of Theater Censorship and Harassment in the United States.* New York: Frederick Ungar, 1978.

Lears, T. J. Jackson. *No Place of Grace: Antimodernism and the Transformation of American Culture.* New York: Pantheon, 1981.

Lee, Nell. "Old Hall Reflects Proud Heritage." *Daily Progress*, March 21, 1981.

"Let the Town Hall–Levy Opera House Live Again in Charlottesville: A Plan for Adaptive Restoration." n.d.

Levine, Lawrence W. *Highbrow/Lowbrow: The Emergence of Cultural Hierarchy in America*. Cambridge, MA: Harvard University Press, 1988.

"The Levy Opera House—A Heritage to Honor." *Daily Progress*, February 10, 1974.

Lewis, Michael J. *American Art and Architecture*. London: Thames & Hudson, 2006.

Lewis, Robert M., ed. *From Traveling Shoe to Vaudeville: Theatrical Spectacle in America 1830–1910*. Baltimore: Johns Hopkins University Press, 2003.

Lewis, Sinclair. *Main Street*. 1920; reprint, Amherst: Prometheus Books, 1996.

Lingeman, Richard. *Small Town America: A Narrative History 1620—The Present*. New York: G. P. Putnam, 1980.

Londre, Felicia Hardison, and Daniel J. Watermeier. *The History of North American Theater from the Pre-Columbian Times to the Present*. New York: Continuum, 1998.

Lorch, Fred W. *The Trouble Begins at Eight: Mark Twain's Lecture Tours*. Ames: Iowa State University Press, 1968.

Ludlow, Noah M. *Dramatic Life As I Found It*. Ed. Richard Moody. 1880; reprint, New York: Benjamin Blom, n.d.

Lynes, Russell. *The Lively Audience: A Social History of the Visual and Performing Arts in America, 1890–1950*. New York: Harper & Row, 1985.

MacKaye, Percy. *The Civic Theater in Relation to the Redemption of Leisure*. New York: Mitchell Kennerly, 1912.

Mackintosh, Iain, and Michael Sell, eds. *CURTAINS!!! Or New Life for Old Theatres*. London: John Offord Ltd. in association with Curtains!!! Committee, 1982.

Magnuson, Landis K. "The Last Moving Floor in Action." *Design & Technology* (Fall 2006): 15–21.

Major, John. *My Old Man*. London: Harper Press, 2012.

Marks, Patricia. *Sarah Bernhardt's First American Theatrical Tour*. Jefferson, NC: McFarland, 2003.

Markusen, Ann, Greg Schrock, and Martina Cameron. *The Artistic Dividend Revisited*. St. Paul: University of Minnesota Humphrey Institute of Public Affairs, 2004.

Marrow, Clare G. "The Brattleboro Auditorium." Unpublished paper, May 1955.

Mason, Andrew. *Community, Solidarity and Belonging: Levels of Community and Their Normative Significance*. Cambridge: Cambridge University Press, 2000.

Mason, Jeffrey D., and Ellen J. Gainor, eds. *Performing America: Cultural Nationalism in American Theater*. Ann Arbor: University of Michigan Press, 1999.

Maurer, David A. "Opera House Entertained a Generation." *Daily Progress*, October 21, 1990.

McArthur, Benjamin. *Actors and American Culture 1880–1920*. Iowa City: University of Iowa Press, 2000.

———. *The Man Who Was Rip Van Winkle: Joseph Jefferson and Nineteenth-Century American Theatre*. New Haven: Yale University Press, 2007.

McCarty, R. Paul, ed. *The Fort Edward Sesquicentennial 1849–1949*. Fort Edward: Fort Edward Sesquicentennial Committee, 1999.

McConachie. Bruce A. *Melodramatic Formations: American Theatre and Society—1820–1870*. Iowa City: University of Iowa Press, 1992.

———. "Pacifying American Theatrical Audiences, 1820–1920." In *For Fun and Profit: The Transformation of Leisure into Consumption*. ed. Richard Butsch. Philadelphia: n.p., 1990.

McNall, Scott C., and Sally Allen McNall. *Plains Families: Exploring Sociology through Social History*. New York: St. Martin's Press, 1983.

McPherson Opera House Preservation Company. *The Business Plan of the McPherson Opera House Preservation Company*. McPherson: McPherson Opera House Preservation Company, 2004.

Merrill Peter C. *German-American Urban Culture: Writers and Theaters in Early Milwaukee*. Madison, WI: Max Kade Institute for German-American Studies, 2000.

Methodist Episcopal Church. *Doctrines and Discipline of the Methodist Episcopal Church 1904*. New York: Easton & Mains, 1904.

———. *Doctrines and Discipline of the Methodist Episcopal Church 1920*. New York and Cincinnati: Methodist Book Concern, 1920.

———. *Doctrines and Discipline of the Methodist Church 1939*. New York: Methodist Publishing House, 1939.

Methodist United Church. *Book of Discipline of the United Methodist Church 2004*. Nashville: United Methodist Publishing House, 2004.

Mickel, Jere C. *Footlights on the Prairie*. St. Cloud, MN: North Star Press, 1973.

Miller, Tice L. *Entertaining the Nation: American Drama in the Eighteenth and Nineteenth Centuries*. Carbondale: Southern Illinois University Press, 2007.

———. "The Image of Fashionable Society in American Comedy—1840–1870." In *When They Weren't Doing Shakespeare*, ed. Judith L. Fisher and Stephen Watt. Athens: University of Georgia Press, 1989.

"Mississippi Grandeur." *Clem Labine's Traditional Building* (August 2007): 34–36.

Mitchell, Mark D. *The St. Johnsbury Athenaeum: Handbook of the Art Collection*. Boston: University Press of New England, 2005.

Moody, Richard. *America Takes the Stage*. Bloomington: Indianan University Press, 1955.

Morgan, Edmund S. "Puritan Hostility to the Theatre." *Proceedings of the American Philosophical Society* 110, no. 5 (October 1966): 340–347.

Morison, Samuel Eliot. *The Oxford History of the American People*. New York: Oxford University Press, 1965.

Murphy, David. "Dramatic Expressions: Czech Theatre Curtains in Nebraska," *Nebraska History*, vol. 74, 1993, vol. 74, nos. 3 and 4.

Nasaw, David. *Andrew Carnegie*. New York: Penguin Press, 2006.

Naylor, David, and Joan Dillon. *American Theaters: Performance Halls of the Nineteenth Century*. New York: Preservation Press and John Wiley & Sons, 1977.

Nebraska State Historical Society. *Preservation at Work for the Nebraska Economy*. Report on Study by the Center for Urban Policy Research, Rutgers University, and the Bureau of Business Research, University of Nebraska–Lincoln. Lincoln: 2007.

Neider, Charles, ed. *The Selected Papers of Mark Twain*. New York: Cooper Square Press, 1999.

Nelson, Linda. "The Stonington Opera House: Rock and Roll." *Memories of Maine Magazine*, 2007.

Nerhaugen, Dan. *Players on Stage: Stoughton and Its Opera House 1901–2001*. Stoughton, WI: Dan Nerhaugen, 2001.

Nye, Russell. *Society and Culture in America—1830–1860*. New York: Harper & Row, 1974.

Ockman, Carol, and Kenneth E. Silver. *Sarah Bernhardt: The Art of High Drama*. New York and New Haven: Jewish Museum and Yale University Press, 2005.

Olson, James C., and Ronald C. Naugle. *History of Nebraska*. Lincoln: University of Nebraska Press, 1997.

Orcutt, Marjorie A., and Edward S. Alexander. *A History of Irasburg, Vermont*. Rutland, VT: Academy, 1989.

"Oscar Wilde Interviewed." *Sunday Argus*, Louisville, February 19, 1882.

"Paramount Importance." *Rutland Daily Herald*, April 1, 1994.

Parker, Alison M. *Purifying America: Women, Cultural Reform and Pro-Censorship Activity—1873–1933*. Urbana: University of Illinois Press, 1997.

Parks, Joseph. "Fires, Firemen and Firefighting: Fire Destroys the Harte Theatre Building and Adjoining Business, 1959." *Bennington Banner*, April 30, 2000, 18.

———. "The First Big Downtown Hotel: Building the Putnam Hotel." *Bennington Banner*. April 23, 1999.

———. "More about How Movies Came to Bennington." *Bennington Banner*. December 13, 2002, 18.

Payne, Duke. "Winding Flows Old Stoner." Unpublished paper. Paris, KY, n.d.

Peiss, Kathy. *Cheap Amusements: Working Women and Leisure in New York City 1880–1920*. Philadelphia: Temple University Press, 1986.

Pember, Ellen J. L. W. *Diary 1879, 1880*. Granville: Pember Library.

———. *Scrapbook*. 1878, 9, 80, 81, 82, 85, 89; 1904, 5, 6, 7; 1910. Granville: Pember Library.

Perry, Lewis. *Intellectual Life in America*. New York: Franklin Watts, 1984.

Plummer, Alfred, and Richard E. Early. *The Blanket Makers, 1669–1943: A History of Charles Early and Marriott (Witney) Ltd*. New York: Augustus M. Kelley, 1969.

Poggi, Jack. *Theatre in America: The Impact of Economic Forces 1870–1967*. Ithaca: Cornell University Press, 1968.

Potter, D. S., and D. J. Mattingly. *Life, Death and Entertainment in the Roman Empire*. Ann Arbor: University of Michigan Press, 1999.

Powers, Ron. *Mark Twain: A Life*. New York: Free Press, 2005.

Preston, Katherine K. *Opera on the Road: Traveling Opera Troupes in the United States, 1825–1860*. Urbana: University of Illinois Press, 1993.

Ramsay, Allan. *Mr. Law's Unlawfulness of the Stage Entertainment Examin'd*. 1726; reprint, New York: Garland, 1974.

Reed, Carole Fay. "A History of the Grand Opera House in Peoria, Illinois." Master's thesis, Illinois State Normal University, 1963.

Reflections: A Pictorial History of Fremont, Nebraska—1870–1920. N.p., n.d.

Reps, John W. *Cities of the American West: A History of Frontier Urban Planning*. Princeton: Princeton University Press, 1979.

Resch, Tyler. *Deed of Gift: The Putnam Hospital Story*. Burlington, VT: Paradigm Press, 1991.

Reynolds, Moira Davison. *Uncle Tom's Cabin and Mid-Nineteenth Century United States*. Jefferson, NC: McFarland, 1995.

Rhoads, Jane G. *Kansas Opera Houses: Actors and Community Events 1855–1925.* Newton: Mennonite Press, 2008.

Richardson, Gary A. *American Drama from the Colonial Period through World War I: A Critical History.* New York: Twayne, 1998.

Richardson, Joanna. *Sarah Bernhardt and Her World.* New York: G.P. Putnam's, 1977.

Rieser, Andrew C. *The Chautauqua Movement: Protestants, Progressives, and the Culture of Modern Liberalism.* New York: Columbia University Press, 2003.

Roberts, Gwilym R. *New Lives in the Valley, Slate Quarries and Quarry Villages in North Wales, New York, and Vermont, 1850–1920.* Somersworth, NH: New Hampshire Printers, 2000.

Ronning, Kari. "Cather and the Theater in Red Cloud." Compilation from University of Nebraska research sent to author in 2003.

Ross, Alex. "Why So Serious? How the Classical Concert Took Shape." *New Yorker*, September 8, 2008, 79–81.

Rote-Rosen, Morris. *Granville Sentinel.* Columns, 1920s, 1930s, and 1940s.

Rusk, Ralph Leslie. *The Literature of the Middle Western Frontier.* Vol. 1. New York: Columbia University Press, 1926.

Ryan, Pat M. "Hallo's Opera House: Pioneer Theatre of Lincoln Nebraska." *Nebraska History* 45 (1964): 323–30.

Ryzik, Melena. "Mapping the Cultural Buzz: How Cool Is That?" *New York Times*, April 7, 2009, C1.

Salem (New York) *Review & Press.* 1897, 1884.

Sander, Kathleen Waters. *Mary Elizabeth Garrett: Society and Philanthropy in the Gilded Age.* Baltimore: Johns Hopkins University Press, 2008.

Sanford, Mollie Dorsey. *Mollie: The Journal of Mollie Dorsey Sanford in Nebraska and Colorado Territories, 1857–1866.* Rev. ed. Lincoln: University of Nebraska, 2003

Schanke, Robert A. "Fremont's Love Opera House." *Nebraska History* 55 (1974): 220–253.

Schilke, Parl. *Dickens and Popular Entertainment.* London: Allen & Unwin, 1985.

Schlesinger, Arthur M. *The Rise of Modern America: 1865–1951.* New York: Macmillan, 1951.

———. *The Rise of the City 1878–1898.* New York: Macmillan, 1933.

Schmidt, Barbara. "Archangels Unaware: The Story of Thomas Bethune also Known as Thomas Wiggins also Known as Blind Tom (1849–1908)." www.twainquotes.com.

Schoberlin, Melvin. *From Candles to Footlights.* Denver: Old West, 1941.

Scholes, Percy A. *The Puritans and Music in England and New England: A Contribution to the Cultural History of Two Nations.* New York: Russell & Russell, 1962.

Scott, Berkeley, and Jeanine Scott. *Images of America: Bourbon County: 1860–1940.* Charleston: Arcadia, 2001.

"See Troy First." *Troy* (New York) *Herald*, 1926, n.d.

Seller, Maxine Schwartz, ed. *Ethnic Theatre in the United States.* Westport, CT: Greenwood Press, 1983.

Senecal, Carol. "Opera Houses in Whitehall, NY." Unpublished paper, 2008.

Sharvey, Beth Conway. *The Little Theatre on the Square: Four Decades of a Small-Town Equity Theatre*. Carbondale and Edwardsville: Southern Illinois University Press, 2000.

Shiffler, Harrold C. "Religious Opposition to the Philadelphia Stage." *Educational Theatre Journal* 14, no. 3 (October 1962): 215–223.

Shipton, Clifford K. *Sibley's Harvard Graduates*. Vol. 15, 1761–1763. Boston: Massachusetts Historical Society, 1970, 15:485.

"Showboats Brought Entertainment to River Towns in the Early 1900s." Unidentified Louisville newspaper in Filson Historical Society Library archives.

Shrock, Joel. *The Gilded Age*. Westport, CT: Greenwood Press, 2004.

Siry, Joseph M. *The Chicago Auditorium Building: Adler and Sullivan's Architecture and the City*. Chicago: University of Chicago Press, 2002.

Skinner, Cornelia Otis. *Madame Sarah*. Boston: Houghton Mifflin, 1967.

Slote, Bernice. *The Kingdom of Art: Willa Cather's First Principles and Critical Statements 1893–1896*. Lincoln: University of Nebraska Press, 1967.

Small Towns Institute in the Humanities. *Aurora and Hamilton County, Nebraska*. Lincoln: University of Nebraska Press, 1979.

Smith, Alexander McCall. "And the Band Played Badly." *New York Times*, March 9, 2008.

Smith, Duane A. *Rocky Mountain West: Colorado, Wyoming, and Montana—1859–1915*. Albuquerque: University of New Mexico Press, 1992.

Smith, Eric Ledell. *African American Theater Buildings: An Illustrated Historical Directory, 1900–1955*. Jefferson, NC: McFarland, 2003.

Smith, Frank W. *The Stephens/Braden Brothers' Opera House in Watseka, Illinois*. Rev. ed. Watseka, IL: 1981.

Smith, Sol. *Theatrical Management in the West and South for Thirty Years*. New ed. 1868; reprint, New York: Benjamin Blom, 1968.

Solberg, Winton U. *Redeem the Time*. Cambridge, MA: Harvard University Press, 1977.

Spearman, Frank H. "The Great American Desert." *Harper's New Monthly Magazine* 77, July 1888.

Sper. Felix. *From Native Roots: A Panorama of Our Regional Drama*. Caldwell: Caxton Printers, 1948.

Sprague, Marshall. *Colorado: A Bicentennial History*. New York: W. W. Norton, 1976; copublished with American Association for State and Local History, Nashville.

Sprague, Terry. "The Beginnings of American Music Are Represented in Royall Tyler Play." *The Reformer*, July 30, 1976.

Springer, Marlene and Haskell Springer. *Plains Woman: The Diary of Martha Farnsworth 1882–1922*. Bloomington: Indiana University Press, 1986.

Stevenson, Louise L. *The Victorian Homefront: American Thought and Culture—1860–1880*. New York: Twayne, 1991.

Stewart, Julie J. *Historic Theatres and Opera Houses: Illinois Renovation and Restoration Projects*. Springfield: Illinois Historic Preservation Agency, 1998.

Stokes, I. N. Phelps. *The Iconography of Manhattan Island—1498–1909*. New York: Robert H. Dodd, 1915.

Stonington Centennial Committee. *Stonington-Past and Present*. Stonington: Centennial Committee of Stonington, Maine, 1977.

Street, Douglas O. "Band's Opera House, The Cultural Hub of Crete, 1877–1900." *Nebraska History* 60 (1979): 57–76.

Sweeney, William. "Old Paris (Kentucky) Grand Opera House," in Biddle research notes 3 from *Kentuckian-Citizen*, April 25, 1958.

Tarbell, Ida M. *The Nationalizing of Business 1878–1898*. New York: Macmillan, 1936.

"The First Eva." *Troy Record*, June 17, 1907.

"The Theatre in Charlottesville: The Town Hall, The Levy Opera House and Jefferson Auditorium." *Magazine of Albemarle County History* 31: (1973): 11–20.

The Times Argus, Barre-Montpelier. September 19, 1993.

Thom, Paul. *A Philosophy of the Performing Arts*. Philadelphia: Temple University Press, 1993.

Thornton, Dave. "Tales of Old Cambridge." *The Eagle*. May/June 1991.

———. *Tales of Old Cambridge: The Rocky Road of the Catholics of Cambridge*. Cambridge: Historical Perspectives, n.d.

Toll, Robert C. *Blacking Up: The Minstrel Show in Nineteenth-Century America*. New York: Oxford University Press, 1974.

Tomalin, Claire. *Charles Dickens: A Life*. New York: Penguin Press, 2011.

Tomsich, John. *A Genteel Endeavour: American Culture and Politics in the Gilded Age*. Palo Alto, CA: Stanford University Press, 1971.

Town Hall-Levy Opera House Foundation, Inc. *Let the Town Hall Levy House Live Again in Charlottesville: A Plan for Adaptive Restoration*. Charlottesville: Town Hall-Levy Opera, n.d.

House Foundation, Inc. n.d.

Trachtenberg. Alan. *The Incorporation of America: Culture and Society in the Gilded Age*. New York: Hill & Wang, 1982.

Trollope, Frances. *Domestic Manners of the Americans*. New York: Alfred A. Knopf, 1949.

Troy (NY) *Daily News*. September/October/November 1852.

Trustees of Public Reservations. *First Annual Report—1891*. Boston: George H. Ellis, 1892.

Turner, Frederick Jackson. *The Frontier in American History*. New York: Holt, Rinehart and Winston, 1965.

Twain, Mark. *Mark Twain's Autobiography*. Vol. 2. New York: P. F. Collier and Son, 1925.

Tyler, Ilene R., and Norman Tyler. "Historic Theatres as Tools of Economic Revitalization." *inLeague*, Spring 2004.

Tyler, Ricky W. "Social and Recreational Entertainments in Olathe, McPherson and Garden City, Kansas from the Introduction of the Railroad to the Building of the First Opera House: A Narrative History." Master's thesis, 1995. Later published by Michigan State University.

Uminowicz, Glenn. "Recreation in a Christian America: Ocean Grove and Asbury Park, New Jersey—1869–1914." In *Hard at Play: Leisure in America 1840–1940*, ed. Kathryn Grover. Amherst: University of Massachusetts Press, 1992.

United States Department of Commerce, Bureau of the Census. Decennial Censuses. Washington, DC: Government Printing Office.

United States Department of the Interior. *Report on the Population of the United States 1890*. Vol. 1. Washington, DC: Government Printing Office, 1895.

United States Special Commissioner of the Revenue. *Report of the Special Commissioner of the Revenue 1869*. January 1869.

Vale, Marcia. *The Gentleman's Recreation: Accomplishments and Pastimes of the English Gentleman—1580–1680*. Cambridge: D. S. Brewer, 1977.

Van Rensselaer, Marianna G. "The Metropolitan Opera-House." *American Architect and Building News* 15 (February 16, 1884): 86–89.

Vitz, Robert C. *The Queen and the Arts: Cultural Life in Nineteenth Century Cincinnati*. Kent: Kent State University Press, 1989.

Wagner, Sally Roesch, ed. *Daughters of Dakota*. Vol. 2, *Stories from the Attic*. Yankton: Daughter of Dakota, 1992.

Waller, Gregory A. *Main Street Amusements: Movies and Commercial Entertainment in a Southern City, 1896–1930*. Washington, DC: Smithsonian Institution Press, 1995.

Warring, Dennis G. *Manufacturing the Muse: Estey Organs and Consumer Culture in Victorian America*. Middletown: Wesleyan University Press, 2002.

Watson, Margaret G. *Silver Theater: Amusement of the Mining Frontier in Early Nevada—1850–1864*. Glendale: Arthur Clark, 1964.

West, Elliott. *The Saloon on the Rocky Mountain Mining Frontier*. Lincoln: University of Nebraska Press, 1979.

Whipple, Annette. Oral history, June 10, 1980, Crawford, Nebraska.

The Whitehall Chronicle. July 10, 1880.

Wicker, Cyrus French. "A Vermont Sketchbook. Uncle Tom's Cabin and the Underground Railroad in Vermont." *Vermont History* 22, no. 3 (July 1954).

Wharton, Edith. *The Age of Innocence*. New York: Alfred A. Knopf, 1993.

Wickman, Don. "Who Burned Down the Opera House?" *Rutland Daily Herald*, January 1, 2004, 1, 3.

Wilde, Oscar. "Impressions of America 1882." www.catbirdpress.com/firstchaps/usapdf.

Wilder, David H. "The Old Opera House: A Study in Architectural Surgery." Paper for Williams College Art Course 261, 1972.

Williamstown House of Local History and Williamstown 250th Anniversary Committee. *Williamstown: The First 250 Years—1753–2003*. Williamstown: n.p., 2005.

Wilmer, S. E. *Theater, Society and the Nation: Staging American Identities*. Cambridge: Cambridge University Press, 2002.

Wilmeth, Don B., and Tice L. Miller, eds. *Cambridge Guide to American Theatre*. Cambridge and New York: Cambridge University Press, 1993.

Winans, Robert B. "Minstrel Show Music 1843–53." In *Musical Theatre in America*, ed. Glenn Loney. Westport, CT: Greenwood, 1984.

Winthrop, Robert C. *Life and Letters of John Winthrop*. 2 vols. Boston: Ticknor and Fields, 1864–1867.

Wood, Walter C. "Bennington Opera House." Unpublished paper, n.d.

Woodress, James. *Willa Cather: A Literary Life*. Lincoln: University of Nebraska Press, 1989.

Woodruff, Paul. *The Necessity of Theater: The Art of Watching and Being Watched*. New York: Oxford University Press, 2008.

Woollcott, Alexander. *Mrs. Fiske, her views on actors, acting, and the problems of producton*. New York: Century, 1917.

Wyatt, Robert Lee, III. *The History of the Haverstock Tent Show:"The Show with a Million Friends."* Carbondale: Southern Illinois University Press, 1997.

Zeitlin, Richard H. *Germans in Wisconsin*. Rev. and expanded ed. Madison: State Historical Society of Wisconsin, 2000.

Zivanovic, Judith K., ed. "Opera Houses of the Midwest: An Introduction." Mid-Western Theatre Conference, 1988.

Index

Illustrations are indicated by "f" following page numbers.